Register, Genre, and Style

This book describes the most important kinds of texts in English and introduces the methodological techniques used to analyze them. Three analytical approaches are introduced and compared, describing a wide range of texts from the perspectives of register, genre, and style.

The primary focus of the book is on the analysis of registers. Part 1 introduces an analytical framework for studying registers, genre conventions, and styles. Part 2 provides detailed descriptions of particular text varieties in English, including spoken interpersonal varieties (conversation, university office hours, service encounters), written varieties (newspapers, academic prose, fiction), and emerging electronic varieties (e-mail, internet forums, text messages). Finally, Part 3 introduces advanced analytical approaches using corpora and discusses theoretical concerns, such as the place of register studies in linguistics and practical applications of register analysis. Each chapter ends with three types of activities: reflection and review activities, analysis activities, and larger project ideas.

DOUGLAS BIBER is Regents' Professor of Applied Linguistics at Northern Arizona University. He has worked in Kenya and Somalia, and has been a visiting professor at several universities, including the University of Uppsala, University of Helsinki, University of Zurich, the Freiburg Institute of Advanced Studies, and the Norwegian Academy of Arts and Sciences. His previous books include *Variation across Speech and Writing*, *Dimensions of Register Variation*, *Corpus Linguistics*, *The Longman Grammar of Spoken and Written English*, and *Discourse on the Move*.

SUSAN CONRAD is Professor of Applied Linguistics at Portland State University. She has worked in Southern Africa and Korea, and conducted workshops on discourse analysis and corpus linguistics in Europe, South America, and Thailand. Her previous books include *Corpus Linguistics*, *The Longman Grammar of Spoken and Written English*, and *The Student Grammar of Spoken and Written English*.

Register, Genre, and Style

Register, Genre, and Style

DOUGLAS BIBER

Northern Arizona University

SUSAN CONRAD

Portland State University

CAMBRIDGE
UNIVERSITY PRESS

CAMBRIDGE UNIVERSITY PRESS
Cambridge, New York, Melbourne, Madrid, Cape Town, Singapore, São Paulo, Delhi, Dubai, Tokyo

Cambridge University Press
The Edinburgh Building, Cambridge CB2 8RU, UK

Published in the United States of America by Cambridge University Press, New York

www.cambridge.org
Information on this title: www.cambridge.org/9780521860604

First published 2009

Printed in the United Kingdom at the University Press, Cambridge

A catalogue record for this publication is available from the British Library

Library of Congress Cataloguing in Publication data
Biber, Douglas.
Register, genre, and style / Douglas Biber, Susan Conrad.
  p.   cm. – (Cambridge textbooks in linguistics)
Includes bibliographical references and index.
ISBN 978-0-521-86060-4
1. Register (Linguistics)   2. Sociolinguistics.   3. English language – Social aspects.
I. Conrad, Susan.   II. Title.
P302.815.B536   2009
306.44 – dc22   2009024642

ISBN 978-0-521-86060-4 Hardback
ISBN 978-0-521-67789-9 Paperback

Contents

Acknowledgements

This book evolved over a considerable period of time, influenced by our experiences in several courses that we taught about registers and genres. Most importantly, the book has been shaped by the many helpful comments and suggestions from students in two courses at Northern Arizona University: ENG 422 in the Spring of 2008, and ENG 618 in the Fall of 2008. Students in both courses used pilot versions of the book and worked through the chapter activities, and in the process they identified several ways in which the book's content and presentation could be improved. In addition, we would like to thank the anonymous reviewer for Cambridge University Press who provided detailed criticisms and suggestions on an earlier draft of the book; those comments proved to be very helpful in shaping the content of the present book.

Acknowledgements

1   Registers, genres, and styles: fundamental varieties of language

1.1   Text varieties in your daily life

Before you begin this book, take a minute to think about all the different kinds of texts that you encounter over the course of a normal day. In the morning, maybe you have a conversation with a roommate. As you have breakfast, you might listen to a radio announcer or read the morning newspaper. Then you might make a telephone call to a friend or family member. As you get ready for a class, you might proofread a paper that is due that day or look over the reading you did for homework. When you attend the class, you probably talk with friends, listen to a lecture, and write notes. And that's just the first few hours of your day!

For most people, conversation is the most common type of spoken language that they produce. But people typically listen to many different kinds of spoken language: television shows, commercials, radio or television news reports, classroom lectures, political speeches, sermons, and so on. Written language also plays a very important role in daily life for many people. Students usually produce many kinds of writing: notes during class sessions, written assignments, term papers, and possibly numerous text messages and/or e-mail messages. But similar to spoken language, most people read more than they write. In fact, many people read even more different kinds of texts than they listen to: newspaper articles, editorials, novels, e-mail messages, blogs, text messages, letters and ads in the mail, magazine articles, ads in magazines, textbooks, research articles, course syllabi, and other written assignments or handouts.

This book investigates the language used in these different kinds of texts (both spoken and written). You will see how almost any kind of text has its own characteristic *linguistic features*. For example, it would not be surprising to end a conversation with the following utterance:

> ok, see ya later.

But it would be almost inconceivable that this sentence would end a textbook. Rather, language like the following is much more typical:

> Processes of producing and understanding discourse are matters of human feeling and human interaction. An understanding of these processes in

language will contribute to a rational as well as ethical and humane basis for understanding what it means to be human.   [the concluding two sentences from Tannen 2005.]

How are these two examples different linguistically? And why do those differences exist? These questions are central to the analysis of text varieties – *registers*, *genres*, and *styles* – the focus of the present book.

We use the terms *register*, *genre*, and *style* to refer to three different perspectives on text varieties. The register perspective combines an analysis of linguistic characteristics that are common in a text variety with analysis of the situation of use of the variety. The underlying assumption of the register perspective is that core linguistic features like pronouns and verbs are functional, and, as a result, particular features are commonly used in association with the communicative purposes and situational context of texts. The genre perspective is similar to the register perspective in that it includes description of the purposes and situational context of a text variety, but its linguistic analysis contrasts with the register perspective by focusing on the conventional structures used to construct a complete text within the variety, for example, the conventional way in which a letter begins and ends. The style perspective is similar to the register perspective in its linguistic focus, analyzing the use of core linguistic features that are distributed throughout text samples from a variety. The key difference from the register perspective is that the use of these features is not functionally motivated by the situational context; rather, style features reflect aesthetic preferences, associated with particular authors or historical periods.

The present book focuses mostly on the register perspective because this perspective is important for the description of all text varieties. That is, any text sample of any type can be analyzed from a register perspective. Because the other two perspectives are more specialized, we provide a less thorough treatment of their characteristics. However, we include discussion of those perspectives at several places in the book, when they are especially useful for understanding the text variety being described. For example, the style perspective is especially useful for discussing fictional prose. The genre perspective is especially useful for discussing academic research articles.

We return to a much fuller introduction of the three perspectives in Section 1.4 below. However, we first take up several more basic issues relating to the study of text varieties and their general role in language and society.

1.1.1   Why is it important to analyze text varieties?

As a native speaker of a language, you acquired many text varieties without explicitly studying them. For example, nobody explained formal rules for having conversations, or how the rules change when you converse with your closest friend rather than your mother or when you "converse" via text message rather than spoken language. However, many other varieties are usually learned with explicit instruction. For example, if you are training for a job as a preacher, you will probably explicitly learn about sermons. If you are training for a job as a journalist, you will practice writing the language of newspaper articles.

One of the most important goals of formal schooling is teaching text varieties that might not be acquired outside of school. Even before going to school, most children are exposed to written stories and learn how narratives are different from normal conversation. Early in school, children learn to read books of many different types, including fictional stories, historical accounts of past events, and descriptions of natural phenomena. These varieties rely on different linguistic structures and patterns, and students must learn how to recognize and interpret those differences. At the same time, students must learn how to produce some of these different varieties, for example writing a narrative essay on what they did during summer vacation versus a persuasive essay on whether the school cafeteria should sell candy. The amount of explicit instruction in different text varieties varies across teachers, schools, and countries, but even at a young age, students must somehow learn to control and interpret the language of different varieties, or they will not succeed at school.

Textual tasks become more and more demanding as a student progresses through school. A university education requires the ability to read and understand academic prose, a variety that is extremely different from face-to-face conversation. Further, students must learn how to produce written texts from many different specific sub-varieties within academic prose, including persuasive essays in freshman composition, lab reports in science courses, and summary/synthesis prose responses on final exams. One of the main goals of a university education is to learn the specialized register of a particular profession, whether electrical engineering, chemistry, sociology, finance, or English education. Success requires learning the particular language patterns that are expected for particular situations and communicative purposes.

The task of learning register/genre differences is even more challenging for a non-native speaker of a language. For example, thousands of students speak languages other than English but choose to attend a university where the primary language of education is English (e.g., in the US, UK, Australia, New Zealand, Hong Kong, Singapore, India, etc.). Traditionally, these students were taught general vocabulary and grammatical rules of English in preparation for advanced study. However, in recent years, many applied linguists have come to realize that this is not enough to ensure students' success. Students also need knowledge of register/genre differences to succeed in their university educations. This awareness has given rise to the general field of *English for Academic Purposes (EAP)*, which focuses on teaching the English-language skills that are especially helpful for the registers/genres used in universities. Similarly, the subfield of *English for Specific Purposes (ESP)* focuses on description of the language used in registers and genres from a particular profession or academic discipline (such as biochemistry or physical therapy), with the ultimate goal of developing instructional materials that will help students learn the particular language patterns that are typical for the different situations and different kinds of texts in those fields. But even proficiency with very specific registers/genres is not enough for students and professionals; some non-native speakers are criticized for sounding too much "like a book" when they speak. Thus, proficiency with spoken registers for conversations and meetings is also important.

Register, genre, and style differences are fundamentally important for any student with a primary interest in language. For example, any student majoring in English, or in the study of another language like Japanese or Spanish, must understand the text varieties in that language. If you are training to become a teacher (e.g. for secondary education or for TESL), you will shortly be faced with the task of teaching your own students how to use the words and structures that are appropriate to different spoken and written tasks – different registers and genres. Other students of language are more interested in the study of literature or the creative writing of new literature, issues relating to the style perspective, since the literary effects that distinguish one novel (or poem) from the next are realized as linguistic differences. While many literary scholars and creative writers become highly proficient without formal training in linguistic analysis, the tools provided in the present book provide an additional perspective for those tasks.

Overall, then, text varieties and the differences among them constantly affect people's daily lives. Proficiency with these varieties affects not only success as a student, but also as a practitioner of any profession, from engineering to creative writing to teaching. Receptive mastery of different text varieties increases access to information, while productive mastery increases the ability to participate in varying communities. And if you cannot analyze a variety that is new to you, you cannot help yourself or others learn to master it. This book provides the foundational knowledge that you will need to effectively analyze, understand, and teach awareness of differences among text varieties.

1.2   Texts, varieties, registers, and dialects

Variability is inherent in human language: people use different linguistic forms on different occasions, and different speakers of a language will say the same thing in different ways. Most of this *linguistic variation* is highly systematic. Speakers of a language make choices in pronunciation, morphology, word choice, and grammar depending on a number of non-linguistic factors. These factors include the speaker's purpose in communication, the relationship between speaker and hearer, the production circumstances, and the social characteristics of the speaker.

At the highest level, linguistic variation is realized as different languages (e.g., Korean, French, Swahili). At the lowest level, linguistic variation is realized as the differences between one speaker compared to another speaker, or as the differences between two texts produced by the same speaker.

In the present book, we use the term *text* to refer to natural language used for communication, whether it is realized in speech or writing. Thus, a research paper is a text, as is a novel or a newspaper article. In speech, a sermon and a face-to-face conversation are both texts.

The notion of text is somewhat fluid as we use it here. First of all, we sometimes distinguish between a **complete text** and a *text excerpt*. A complete text is an instance of extended discourse that has a clear start and finish, such as a research article or a sermon. However, many of the "texts" that we discuss in the book are actually text excerpts: segments of discourse extracted from a larger complete text. Thus, we might discuss a text excerpt of two–three paragraphs from a novel, or several turns of interaction from a conversation.

Further, the notion of complete text is in itself somewhat fluid. First, texts can be considered at different levels of generality. Thus, a chapter in a book might be considered a complete text, but the entire book might also be considered as a complete text. Similarly in spoken language, a joke told during a sermon might be considered as a complete text, but the entire sermon can also be treated as a complete text. Beyond that, the boundaries of complete texts are not always explicit or clear-cut. This is especially the case in speech. For example, suppose you are having a conversation with your friend Trisha, and then her friend Ami walks up and joins the conversation. A little later, you need to leave, but Trisha and Ami continue to talk. How many conversations have there been? And where are the boundaries of each? For example, did the conversation between Trisha and Ami begin when Ami arrived, or when you left?

In the following chapters we use the notion of *complete text* in cases where it is relatively clear-cut, such as for a complete research article that has a distinct beginning and ending. In other cases, we use the more general term *text* as a cover term for any extended segment of discourse from speech or writing.

Texts can be described according to their contexts, considering the characteristics of the people who produced the texts, and the characteristics of the situations and communicative purposes associated with the texts. The general term **variety** is used for a category of texts that share some social or situational characteristic. For example, a *national variety of English* refers to the texts produced by the speakers of English who reside in a specific country (e.g., British English, Australian English, Indian English, etc.).

Much of the research in sociolinguistics has focused on varieties that are associated with different groups of speakers (e.g. people who live in different geographic regions, different socio-economic classes, ethnic groups, women versus men, etc.). These socially defined varieties are referred to as *dialects*.

However, the present book deals instead with text varieties that occur in particular situations of use – registers, genres, and styles. Our primary focus in the book is the notion of register and the process of register analysis, introduced in the following section. However, we return to a fuller discussion of social varieties (dialects) and other perspectives on text varieties in later sections.

Figure 1.1 *Components in a register analysis*

1.3   Registers and register analysis: an overview

As noted above, we focus primarily on the register perspective in this book, because it can be used to describe any text excerpt from any variety. However, the methodological techniques used for register analyses are also applicable to the genre and style perspectives. In the present section, we provide an overview of register analysis, establishing the foundation that will be used throughout the book. Then, in Section 1.4, we provide a much fuller introduction to the genre and style perspectives in comparison to the register perspective.

1.3.1   Register analysis: situation, linguistic features, functions

In general terms, a *register* is a variety associated with a particular situation of use (including particular communicative purposes). The description of a register covers three major components: the situational context, the linguistic features, and the functional relationships between the first two components (Figure 1.1).

Registers are described for their typical lexical and grammatical characteristics: their *linguistic features*. But registers are also described for their *situational contexts*, for example whether they are produced in speech or writing, whether they are interactive, and what their primary communicative purposes are. One of the central arguments of the book is that linguistic features are always *functional* when considered from a register perspective. That is, linguistic features tend to occur in a register because they are particularly well suited to the purposes and situational context of the register. Thus, the third component of any register description is the functional analysis.

Registers can be identified and described based on analysis of either complete texts or a collection of text excerpts. This is because the linguistic component of a register analysis requires identification of the *pervasive* linguistic features in the variety: linguistic characteristics that might occur in any variety but are much more common in the target register. It is these pervasive linguistic features that are clearly functional, as exemplified below.

Situational varieties can also be described by analyzing language features that characterize complete texts, referred to as the genre perspective in the present book. Genre features are not pervasive; rather, they might occur only one time in a complete text, often at the beginning or ending boundary. They are also often conventional rather than functional. Section 1.4 below provides a fuller discussion of the similarities and differences between the genre and register perspectives on situational varieties.

For a simple example of the register analysis process, briefly consider face-to-face conversation. First of all, it is important to note the situational characteristics of conversation that distinguish it from other registers. Face-to-face conversation requires direct interaction between at least two people who are together in the same place at the same time. Both participants must speak (or the conversation would become a monologue). Furthermore, while many specific topics and purposes are possible, it is generally appropriate for participants to discuss events, thoughts, and opinions related to their personal lives or something in the immediate context.

The second step is to describe the typical (pervasive) linguistic features of conversation. This step requires consideration of multiple texts from the target register, to discover the linguistic features that are frequent across texts (and not characteristic of only a single text). Previous register studies have found three linguistic features (among many others) to be more common in conversation than in many other registers: first person pronouns (*I* and *we*), second person pronouns (*you*), and questions.

Finally, the third step of a register analysis is to interpret the relationship between situational characteristics and pervasive linguistic features in functional terms. To make these functions concrete, consider Text Sample 1.1, a typical passage of conversation.

Text Sample 1.1   Conversation (a group of friends is walking to a restaurant)

Judith: Yeah I just found out that Rebekah is going to the University of Chicago to get her PhD. I really want to go visit her. Maybe I'll come out and see her.

Eric: Oh is she?

Judith: Yeah.

Eric: Oh good.

Elias: Here, do you want one? [offering a candy]

Judith: What kind is it?

Elias: Cinnamon.

Judith: Oh.

Kate: Those are good.

Eric: They're good.

Elias: That's the joy of life.

Kate: Did you guys come through the plaza on your way?

Judith: No.

Kate: You have to go through it on your way home. It probably would be empty.

Elias: We drove through it tonight.

Judith: Yeah we'll do that.

Eric: I don't like the color lights on the tree though.

Kate: Did they put fake ones up in there one year?

Elias: No they're just all around on all the buildings.

Kate: Oh yeah.

Elias: I think it would be kind of dumb to put them on the ground.

[LSWE Corpus]

In this passage the specific topics switch abruptly, but – typical of conversation – the participants are discussing their own thoughts, attitudes, and actions with first person pronouns (*I just found out*, *I really want*, *I don't like*, *I think*), and they use second person pronouns to address each other (*Do you want...*, *Did you guys...*). Questions are used as part of the direct interaction with each other, often incorporating the use of first and second person pronouns. Thus, these linguistic features are especially frequent in conversation because they have a functional relation to the situational characteristics of both the physical context and the general communicative purposes of conversation.

Register characteristics become more salient if an analysis contrasts two different registers. For example, in contrast to the speakers in a conversation, the author of a front-page newspaper article is not addressing a specific person, and there is no direct interaction between a specific reader and the author. It is also not normally relevant for the author to describe her own personal feelings or other aspects of her personal life. As a result of these functional considerations, there are normally few first and second person pronouns and questions in front-page newspaper articles. These differences illustrate a key aspect of register analysis that we will return to repeatedly throughout the book: the characteristics of any individual register become much more apparent when it is compared to other registers.

1.3.2   More details about registers and register analysis

The last section introduced the notion of register as a variety associated with a particular situation of use (including particular communicative purposes). The description of a register has three major components: the situational/communicative description, the description of pervasive linguistic features, and the analysis of the functional associations between linguistic forms and situational contexts.

A few points deserve further development here:

1.3.2.1 The situational characteristics of registers are more basic than the linguistic features

Registers differ in both their situational and linguistic characteristics. However, the situational characteristics are more basic. All speakers use language in different contexts, under different circumstances, for different purposes. Those patterns of behavior cannot be derived from any linguistic phenomena. In contrast, the linguistic differences among registers can be derived from situational differences, because linguistic features are functional.

For example, imagine what it would be like if the linguistic considerations were primary. In that case, you might be sitting at your computer and suddenly feel like producing a text with lots of pronouns (*I* and *you*) and lots of questions, and only later realize that such a text must occur in a conversational context, so you would go around looking for someone to have a conversation with. Obviously this is not how communication works. Rather, you find yourself in a conversational situation, and because of that you start to produce language with the linguistic features that are appropriate for a conversation. Chapter 2 will introduce a framework for the situational analysis of registers, including the role of culture in defining them, but even this brief example illustrates how registers are determined by their situational characteristics.

1.3.2.2 Registers differ in their characteristic *distributions* of pervasive linguistic features, **not** the single occurrence of an individual feature

We will have much more to say about how to analyze the linguistic features of a register in Chapter 3, but it is important to note from the outset that very few registers can be identified by unique lexical or grammatical features. Instead, to carry out the linguistic analysis of a register, you must consider the extent to which linguistic features are used, in order to identify the linguistic features that are pervasive and especially common in the target register.

For example, it is not the case that conversation always uses pronouns and never any nouns, or that newspaper writing always uses nouns and never any pronouns. Instead both registers use both nouns and pronouns. However, conversation uses more pronouns and fewer nouns, while newspaper writing uses more nouns and fewer pronouns. In other words, the relative distribution of nouns and pronouns differs greatly between conversation and newspaper writing. The linguistic analysis of registers is based on such differences in the relative distribution of linguistic features, which are especially common and pervasive in some registers but comparatively rare in other registers.

1.3.2.3 Register analysis requires both situational and linguistic analysis, often applied cyclically

In a register analysis, both the situational components and the linguistic features are explicitly described. The functional interpretation, then, is based on comparison of the situational and linguistic analyses.

New register studies usually begin with at least some analysis of the situational characteristics. As Chapter 2 will explain in more detail, initial analysis of the situational characteristics can be important for selecting appropriate text samples to include in a study. However, often in a register analysis you will find that there are surprises resulting from the linguistic analysis: certain linguistic features will occur more frequently (or rarely) than you expected. These unexpected linguistic patterns will often require that you re-assess the situational characteristics of the register, especially with respect to less obvious characteristics like the communicative purpose. Thus, the process of register analysis is often iterative.

1.3.2.4   Register variation has a *functional* basis

The linguistic differences among registers are not arbitrary. For example, it is not sufficient to merely note that the language of conversation has many second person pronouns and questions because it is an accepted convention to use these features in conversation. Rather, register analyses always include description of the situational context and interpretation of *why* particular linguistic features commonly occur in that context. The functional associations between linguistic patterns and situational factors are at the heart of studying register variation, and are further discussed in Chapter 3.

1.3.2.5   Registers can be identified on different levels of specificity

A register can be extremely general, like textbooks. But what about textbooks in linguistics? Graduate-level textbooks in sociolinguistics? In fact, any of these can be identified as a register.

There is no one correct level on which to identify a register. Rather, it depends on the goals of your study. You may want to characterize the register of academic prose, a very general register. Or you may be interested in only research articles, a more specific register within academic prose. Or you might focus on medical research articles, or even only the methods sections of experimental medical research articles. All of these can be considered registers, differing in their level of generality. As a register category becomes more specific, it is possible to identify its situational and linguistic characteristics more precisely. Chapter 2 will have much more to say about general vs. specialized registers. At this point, it is simply important to realize that registers can be studied on many different levels of specificity.

1.3.2.6   Register analyses must be based on a representative sample of texts

Because a register analysis seeks to characterize a variety of language – not a particular text or an individual writer's style – it must be based on analysis of a sample of texts selected to represent the register as fully as possible. In many places in this book, we exemplify what is known about certain registers with single, short text passages; these texts have been carefully chosen to represent what previous research has shown to be typical in the register. At other places, we introduce some small case studies that show what you could do on your own, and we include many practice activities that ask you to work with a small number of short texts. Again, we have deliberately selected the texts in these activities to be representative of the more general patterns for the target registers (based on previous research studies).

In fact, many intriguing results can come from small register analyses. However, you should always remember that you cannot generalize to a register from an analysis with a small number of texts, unless you have supporting evidence from larger-scale studies. We will have much more to say about representativeness and small- vs. large-scale register analyses in Chapter 3.

1.3.3   Registers versus dialects

When asked to think about the different varieties of a language, like the different varieties of English, many people immediately think of dialects. For example, it is easy to notice that people from the southeast United States talk differently from people in Wales, and that the English used in Singapore is different from both.

Two main kinds of dialects are commonly distinguished in linguistics: *geographic dialects* are varieties associated with speakers living in a particular location, while *social dialects* are varieties associated with speakers belonging to a given demographic group (e.g., women versus men, or different social classes). Most recent dialect studies have used a comparative approach to study social dialects, describing the linguistic patterns of variation across social groups in major urban centers such as New York City, Norwich, Belfast, and Montreal.

When dialects are studied, analysts usually focus on linguistic features that are not associated with meaning differences. Phonological differences are often studied, such as pronouncing or omitting the "r" in *park*. Clearly, this phonological variation results in no meaning difference, though it does say a great deal about the region or social group that the speaker identifies with. Similarly, the grammatical and lexical features included in studies of dialect variation are selected so that they do not reflect meaning differences (e.g. the use of double negatives in African American Vernacular English vs. single negatives in mainstream upper middle class English, or the use of synonymous words like "soda" vs. "pop" vs. "soft drink"). Such linguistic differences are *not* functional. Rather, sociolinguists argue that these are arbitrary differences, where one linguistic form has come to be conventionally associated with a social group.

In this regard, the linguistic variables used in register studies are exactly the opposite from those used in dialect studies: register variables are functional, as opposed to dialect variables, which are by definition purely conventional. This difference is reflected in the way that linguistic variables are realized in the two subfields. Linguistic variables in dialect studies almost always consist of a choice between two linguistic variants. The variable score is a proportion, showing the relative preference for one or the other variant. In contrast, linguistic variables in register studies are the rate of occurrence for a linguistic feature, and a higher rate of occurrence is interpreted as reflecting a greater need for the functions associated with that feature. (The choice between two linguistic variants can also be included in a register analysis, but the preference for one or another variant is still normally interpreted in functional terms.)

It is, of course, possible to investigate the existence of functionally motivated linguistic variation across dialects. However, most sociolinguists exclude this possibility because of their theoretical/philosophical stance that all dialects are equivalent in their communicative potential. We return to this controversy in Chapter 9.

1.3.4   Comparing register variation and dialect variation

Although most sociolinguistic studies have traditionally focused on linguistic differences among dialects, the linguistic differences among registers are actually more extensive. When speakers switch between registers, they are doing different things with language – using language for different communicative purposes and producing language under different circumstances. The associated linguistic differences are functionally motivated, related to these differing purposes and situations, and thus the linguistic differences among registers are often dramatic. In contrast, dialect differences are largely conventional, expressing a person's identity within a social group. Regardless of any dialect differences, speakers using the same register are doing similar communicative tasks; therefore, in most basic respects the characteristic language features used in a given situation are similar across speakers from different dialects.

To illustrate, compare the language used in the following two conversations[1] – one between a working-class husband and wife in Hampshire, England (Text Sample 1.2), and the second between a middle-class husband and wife in Devon, England (Text Sample 1.3).

Text Sample 1.2   Working-class conversation (Hampshire, England)

Michael: Well I mean what's the alternative?
Wendy: Why?
Michael: What's the alternative? You know, I mean . . . she either . . . gets on with it or gets rid of them don't she?
Wendy: Well no –
Michael: It's simple!
Wendy: She can insulate the house
Michael: Well that don't stop it from . . . getting on her nerves, does it?
Wendy: Yeah, but it don't get on her nerves, that's the whole point! I mean she's obviously able to throw it off. I mean, she's in there Mick.

---

[1] These conversations are taken from the *British National Corpus*.

Michael: Mm.
Wendy: And when we hear it in here . . . she's got it worse in there cos she's in there
Michael: Yeah
Wendy: But I mean that yesterday afternoon – you'd have thought the bloody things
         were in here, wouldn't you?
Michael: Yes
Wendy: That was two of them but –
Michael: Yeah

                                                              [LSWE Corpus]

Text Sample 1.3   Middle-class conversation (Devon, England)

Pauline: See I was thinking this was gonna cost a lot – a lot of money to put the
         phones in, but it's not, because you just put one line in and then put different
         bits up the line, don't you?
Bob: No . . . no they come in, in separate lines
Pauline: But you cut it
Bob: You charge per – you'll charge per . . . in here, it's not just one line with four
         connections, they charge you per phone
Pauline: I was talking to Desmond about it and he reckons that once you've got your
         line you can muck about and put quite a few lines in there
Bob: No – no, doesn't work like that
Pauline: oh . . .
Bob: You can use the same – you can use the same number – alright?
Pauline: mm
Bob: eh, the same number on four lines, but if were want to go out . . . if four
         people were to phone in at the one time
Pauline: oh, of course, yeah
Bob: Do you see what I mean?
Pauline: I see what you mean
Bob: You've got to have four separate lines

                                                              [LSWE Corpus]

The speakers in these two conversations are from different social dialects and different geographic dialects. If you heard the conversations, the speakers would probably sound quite different. But there is only one obvious grammatical dialect marker that distinguishes the two: the use of *don't* with a third person singular subject in the working-class conversation (e.g., *that don't stop it; it don't get on her nerves*). Because dialect markers such as these are often highly stigmatized, a relatively rare occurrence of a few features can serve as an important indicator of dialect differences.

Overall, though, the most striking aspect of comparison between the two conversations is how similar they are. Situationally, the two conversations are very similar in their production circumstances, primary purposes, and interactiveness. Both conversations are spoken (rather than written), and they are produced in real time, with the words and grammatical organization being produced on the spot as the conversation unfolds. There is little time to plan ahead, and virtually no opportunity to edit afterwards. In addition, both conversations are personal and directly interactive. Conversational partners express their own personal attitudes, feelings, and concerns, and they interact with one another to build a shared discourse. These characteristics are tied to conversation as a register and are thus not affected by dialect differences.

The contextual characteristics shared by these two conversations have important linguistic correlates, and as a result the conversations are very similar linguistically. For example, since the speakers in both conversations are deciding what to say while they are speaking, both conversations have generally short sentences, with many utterances not being structurally complete sentences at all (assuming the traditional concept of a grammatical sentence). These latter include simple responses (*why?*, *yeah*, *no*, *oh of course*) as well as utterances that build on the shared physical context to supply missing information (e.g., *[it] doesn't work like that*). Both conversations also have numerous contracted or reduced forms, such as *what's, it's, she's, that's, don't, you'd, you've, 'cos, gonna*. In addition, the participants in both conversations assume familiarity with other people and the physical context, so references to people, objects, and places are often not explicitly identified (e.g., *she either gets on with it or gets rid of them; put quite a few lines in there*). The interactive nature of conversation results in further linguistic similarities between these two texts. For example, both conversations have frequent references to *I* (the speaker) and *you* (the addressee). Similarly, there are frequent questions in both (e.g., *What's the alternative? Why? does it? wouldn't you? Do you see what I mean? don't you? alright?*); these constructions would not be appropriate in other registers without a specific addressee (*you*).

The extent of the similarities between these two conversations from different dialects can be further illustrated by comparing them to a sample from a written, informational register. Text Sample 1.4 is taken from a university textbook.

Text Sample 1.4   Systems analysis textbook

The Method for Information Systems Enquiry, known colloquially as MINSE by the research project team, specifically addresses the problem of structuring the approach to information studies. It uses systems thinking to develop ideas about what information is needed to achieve a defined purpose, ideas that are independent in the first instance of how this information appears in practice. In the process an information model is built up on a computer database which is then used as a framework to explore the situation and identify problems at a number of levels (Fig 11.1).

[T2K-SWAL Corpus]

The situational characteristics of the textbook are very different from those of the conversations. The textbook is written, carefully planned, revised, and edited.

The text is not interactive; it is addressed to a large audience of students and professionals, but the writer and audience are not directly involved with each other. The primary purpose of the text is to present information about systems analysis, as opposed to the (inter)personal purposes of conversational participants.

Due to the influence of these situational factors, the linguistic characteristics of the textbook are dramatically different from those of the conversational texts. The sentences of the textbook are all grammatically complete, and often they are quite long and complex. None of the reduced or interactive linguistic characteristics common in conversation occur in this text. However, textbooks do contain numerous linguistic characteristics rarely found in conversation. In Text Sample 1.4, these linguistic features include passive constructions (e.g., *known colloquially as*; *is built up*; *is then used*) and complex noun phrase constructions (e.g., *the problem of structuring the approach to information studies*; *a computer database which is then used as a framework to explore the situation and identify problems at a number of levels*).

The extensive linguistic differences between this textbook and the conversations reflect the fundamental importance of register, associated with contextual differences in production circumstances, purpose, interactiveness, and so on. These contextual factors operate in similar ways in all dialects. Thus, conversation is essentially the same, regardless of the dialect of the speakers. Similarly, academic writing is essentially the same, regardless of whether the writer uses a British or American dialect. There are of course differences in pronunciation and word choice associated with different dialects, and there are even occasional differences in grammar. But these differences are minor when compared to the major linguistic differences among different registers, associated with different situations of use.

1.4   Different perspectives on text varieties: register, genre, style

In Section 1.1, we briefly distinguished among the register, genre, and style perspectives on texts. In fact, the terms *register*, *genre*, and *style* have been used in many different ways by previous researchers. In Sections 1.4.2 and 1.4.3 below, we survey some of those uses. First, we further clarify how we use these terms in the present book.

1.4.1   Register, genre, and style perspectives in this book

As noted above, we regard genre, register, and style as different approaches or perspectives for analyzing text varieties, *not* as different kinds of texts or different varieties. In fact, the same texts can be analyzed from register, genre, and style perspectives.

Table 1.1 *Defining characteristics of registers, genres, and styles*

Defining characteristic	Register	Genre	Style
Textual focus	sample of text excerpts	complete texts	sample of text excerpts
Linguistic characteristics	any lexico-grammatical feature	specialized expressions, rhetorical organization, formatting	any lexico-grammatical feature
Distribution of linguistic characteristics	frequent and pervasive in texts from the variety	usually once-occurring in the text, in a particular place in the text	frequent and pervasive in texts from the variety
Interpretation	features serve important communicative functions in the register	features are conventionally associated with the genre: the expected format, but often not functional	features are not directly functional; they are preferred because they are aesthetically valued

As shown in Table 1.1, the three perspectives differ in four major ways, with respect to: (1) the "texts" considered for the analysis, (2) the linguistic characteristics considered for the analysis, (3) the distribution of those linguistic characteristics, and (4) the interpretation of linguistic differences.

In the genre perspective, the focus is on the linguistic characteristics that are used to structure complete texts, while in both the register perspective and the style perspective, the focus is on the pervasive linguistic characteristics of representative text excerpts from the variety. As summarized in Table 1.1, the register perspective characterizes the typical linguistic features of text varieties, and connects those features functionally to the situational context of the variety. Because the focus is on words and grammatical features that are frequent and pervasive, the analysis can be based on a sample of text excerpts rather than complete texts.

In contrast to the focus of the register perspective, the genre perspective usually focuses on language characteristics that occur only once in a text. These features serve a crucial role in how texts from a particular variety are constructed. For this reason, genre studies must be based on analysis of complete texts from the variety. These language features are conventionally associated with the genre: they conform to the culturally expected way of constructing texts belonging to the variety.

For example, a genre study of business letters would analyze the expected textual conventions for complete letters. These conventions include the expectations that the letter will begin with the date at the top, followed by the name and address of the recipient, followed by a salutation and title ("Dear Mr. Jones"), followed by the main body of the letter. The letter will then close with some kind of politeness expression (e.g., "Sincerely"), followed by the signature of the letter writer. These conventions are part of what defines a letter, and they can be identified only by considering complete letters.

The genre perspective often focuses on the rhetorical organization of texts from a variety, especially the rhetorical conventions of written varieties. For example, by convention a front-page newspaper story begins with a concise title and the name of the place where the story occurred. The prose text opens with one or two sentences that summarize the main event that has occurred and the significance of that event. The text then has multiple paragraphs, each describing some aspect of the story: how the event came about, the background of the main participants, direct and indirect quotations, how other participants became involved, consequences of the event, and so on. These paragraphs are usually very short and self-contained. All of these genre features are exemplified in Text Sample 1.5.

Text Sample 1.5   Newspaper article

Investigators Take Last Look at Subway Wreckage

PHILADELPHIA (AP)

   A subway car derailment that killed three people and injured 162 may have been triggered by a dragging motor that hit a track switch, federal investigators said Thursday.

   The altered switch may have sent the last three cars in the six-car train onto another set of tracks Wednesday, causing one car to be yanked into steel support beams, said John K. Lauber of the National Transportation Safety Board. Evidence indicated the motor dropped when a nut came loose, Lauber said, adding that investigators were told that subway motors had dropped from their supports three times in the last 15 years, most recently just a month ago.

   "That probably resulted in the pivoting of the motor under the car . . . and that probably was the initiation of the accident," he said.

   A 37-block section of west Philadelphia's 12.8-mile subway and elevated train line, a major commuter artery in the nation's fifth-largest city, remained closed Thursday as federal investigators made their final inspection of the wreckage.

   Extra buses were pressed into service to handle some of the 100,000 people who typically ride the line twice a day. [. . .]

                                                                                    [LSWE Corpus]

The register and genre perspectives differ in the extent to which they can be applied. Complete texts are required to identify the linguistic characteristics associated with the genre perspective. Text excerpts are not adequate for genre analysis, because they do not necessarily represent the linguistic conventions that define the genre (e.g., the conventional ways to begin or end a text).

In contrast, any text sample can be analyzed from a register perspective, considering the typical linguistic features associated with the situational context. These linguistic features occur throughout texts from a register, and so complete texts are not required to analyze register characteristics. For example, Text Samples 1.1–1.4 above are all excerpts that illustrate the use of pervasive register features (like contractions, pronouns, and questions in conversation).

Complete texts that are analyzed from a genre perspective can also be analyzed from a register perspective. For example, Text Sample 1.5, which illustrates the genre conventions for opening a newspaper story, also illustrates the linguistic characteristics that are typical of the register of newspaper reporting. These linguistic features include past tense verbs (e.g., *killed, injured, said, indicated*), passive voice verbs (e.g., *been triggered, were told, were pressed*), and reported speech (both direct quotes and indirect reported speech). These features are pervasive in newspaper stories, distributed throughout these texts, and thus they can be identified in either complete texts or text excerpts.

Finally, the *style* perspective is similar to the register perspective in that it considers the typical linguistic features associated with a collection of text samples from a variety. The two perspectives differ in their interpretation – that is, in the underlying reasons for the observed linguistic patterns. The systematic linguistic patterns associated with the register perspective exist because linguistic variation is functional; linguistic features are used frequently in a register when they are required by the situational characteristics of the register (as described in Section 1.3 above). In contrast, the linguistic patterns associated with styles are not functional. Rather, these are features associated with aesthetic preferences, influenced by the attitudes of the speaker/writer about language. That is, a speaker or author often has attitudes about what constitutes "good style" resulting in the manipulation of language for aesthetic purposes.

Styles are normally distinguished for the texts with*in* a register or genre. The most common application of this concept is to describe systematic variation within the register/genre of fiction. However, a similar notion of style has been used to study variation within the register of conversation, where each subculture can be described as having a distinctive communicative style or conversational style (see, e.g., Tannen 2005), meaning that they have different norms for how they usually structure a conversation (relating to different speech rates, different pause lengths between turns, whether overlapping speech is considered to be polite or not, etc.).

Particular fictional styles are often associated with individual authors. For example, authors like Virginia Woolf and Toni Morrison preferred a fictional style with extremely long complex sentences mixed in with very short, single-clause sentences. In contrast, an author like Ernest Hemingway preferred a style with consistently short simple sentences. But styles can also be associated with different groups of authors or different historical periods. For example, in Chapter 6 we discuss how fictional style in the eighteenth century was generally different from contemporary fictional style. The key point here is that these differences are not functional. For example, the situational context for novels written by all authors is essentially the same. Rather, these linguistic differences are stylistic, reflecting differing attitudes towards language, or attempts to achieve different aesthetic effects through the manipulation of language.

As noted above, the same texts or varieties can be considered from register, genre, and style perspectives. For example, a genre perspective on scientific research articles would describe the conventional rhetorical structure of complete articles – how they begin with a title, the author's name, and an abstract, followed by the introduction, methods section, results, discussion/conclusion, and then concluding with a bibliography. However, these same scientific research articles can be studied from a register perspective, identifying the core linguistic features that are pervasive in this kind of writing (e.g., long noun phrases, nominalizations, passive verbs), and explaining the preference for those linguistic features in functional terms by reference to the production circumstances of writing and the typical communicative purposes of research articles. And the same texts can be studied from a style perspective, identifying the linguistic features associated with a particular author or a particular historical period, in association with notions of "good" writing or prose that is aesthetically pleasing.

1.4.2 Genre and style in literary studies

If you have experience with literary studies, you are probably already familiar with the concept of *literary genre*: varieties of literature that employ different textual conventions. This use of the term *genre* is similar to our use in the present book because of the emphasis on textual conventions. For example, three major literary genres are poetry, drama, and fictional prose. Read through Text Samples 1.6–1.8 and make note of any textual conventions that distinguish among these genres.

Text Sample 1.6   Poetry

CREDO
Goals are funnels
with walls that narrow
and finally at the neck–
the achievement–
a guillotine.
Better than goals are dreams
that can never be attained,
only lived.
Or dreamed.

[Scott Baxter, 2004. *Imaginary Summits.*]

Text Sample 1.7   Drama

RUTH: I'm going down to the school with you.
BEATRICE: Oh, no you're not! You're going to keep company with that corpse in
                  there. If she wakes up and starts gagging just slip her a shot of whiskey.
                  <The taxi horn blows outside.>
                  Quick! Grab the plants, Matilda – I'll get the big thing.
RUTH: I want to go! I promised Chris Burns I'd meet him.
BEATRICE: Can't you understand English?
RUTH: I've got to go!
BEATRICE: Shut up!
RUTH: <Almost berserk.> I don't care. I'M GOING ANYWAY!
BEATRICE: <Shoving RUTH hard.> WHAT DID YOU SAY?
TILLIE: Mother!
[Paul Zindel, 1970. The Effect of Gamma Rays on Man in the Moon Marigolds.]

Text Sample 1.8   Fictional Prose

I was living that year in a house on Yucca Avenue in the Laurel Canyon district. It
was a small hillside house on a dead-end street with a long flight of redwood steps to
the front door and a grove of eucalyptus trees across the way. It was furnished, and it
belonged to a woman who had gone to Idaho to live with her widowed daughter for a
while.

[Raymond Chandler, 1988. *The Long Good-bye*.]

What do you notice about the differences among these three texts? The most
obvious is probably the physical layout on the page. By convention, fictional prose
is presented as paragraphs, with an indentation at the start of the paragraph, and
each line filling the entire page. Fictional prose also normally employs complete
sentences, and standard sentence punctuation.

Drama has different conventions: it portrays conversational dialogue, and so
has a format that first identifies who the speaker is, followed by the utterance
for that speaker. Drama is intended to be performed in speech, even though its
origin is in writing. As a result, a dramatic text also includes language that gives
instructions for the performance, identifying events that occur during a conversation (<the taxi horn blows outside>, <shoving RUTH hard>) or describing
the manner of speaking that an actor should adopt (<almost berserk>).

Poetry differs from both drama and prose in that the physical arrangement
of text on the page is part of the creative effect. Poetry can employ complete
sentences, but the arrangement of lines on the page is more important. Meaning
relationships in poetry are often constructed from the physical juxtaposition of
words and lines, rather than through the use of complete sentences (*and finally*

at the neck – the achievement – a guillotine. can never be attained, only lived. Or dreamed.).

There is extensive linguistic variation among the texts with*in* a literary genre, and this is where the style perspective becomes especially important, to describe the characteristic discourse associated with different authors or time periods reflecting different aesthetic preferences. Like registers, styles can be described in terms of the frequent and pervasive linguistic features used in different kinds of discourse. For example, eighteenth-century fictional style is characterized by extremely long sentences, while twentieth-century fiction generally uses much shorter sentences (see Chapter 6). Authors also differ in their characteristic styles, sometimes famously. For example, Defoe is well known for writing in a simple and plain style of fiction, in contrast to the more typical styles of discourse in the early eighteenth century. Johnson, writing in the second half of the eighteenth century, is known for a much more elaborated style of discourse. (See the discussion of author style in fiction in Chapters 5 and 6.)

Literary styles can be studied using the same analytical techniques as registers. However, the underlying causes of style variation are related to aesthetic preferences and attitudes about language, rather than a more direct functional influence from the communicative situation.

For the most part, our focus in the present book is on the analysis of everyday kinds of speaking and writing, rather than literature. However, in Chapter 5 we return to fictional prose, describing some of its special situational and linguistic characteristics. Then, in Chapter 6, we show how historical change in the literary styles of novels can be approached from a linguistic perspective.

1.4.3   Register, genre and style in previous research

The terms *register, genre,* and *style* have been central to previous investigations of discourse, but they have been used in many different ways. Our treatment in the present book builds on this previous research, but it does not attempt to reconcile all previous definitions of these terms. As you read other studies, it is important to be aware that there is no general consensus concerning the use of *register* and related terms such as *genre* and *style*.

Register and *genre* have both been used to refer to varieties associated with particular situations of use and particular communicative purposes. Many studies simply adopt one of these terms and disregard the other. For example, Biber (1988), Bhatia (2002), Samraj (2002a,b), Bunton (2002), Love (2002), and Swales (1990, 2004) exclusively use the term *genre* rather than *register.* In some of these studies (e.g., Swales 1990), the analysis focused primarily on the organizational structure of whole texts, while in others (e.g., Biber 1988) it focused on pervasive linguistic patterns. Other studies – e.g., Ure 1982, Ferguson 1983, Hymes 1984, Heath and Langman 1994, Bruthiaux 1994, 1996, Biber 1995, Conrad 2001, and Biber *et al.* 1999 – exclusively use the term *register.* Some textbooks in sociolinguistics (e.g., Wardaugh 1986; Trudgill 1974) have used the term *register* to refer only to occupational varieties, such as computer programmer talk or auto mechanic talk.

Some fields of research have used both the terms *register* and *genre* and made a theoretical distinction between them. Most notable is work in Systemic Functional Linguistics, a theoretical framework based on work by Halliday (1985), which is concerned with the interaction of form, function, and context in human communication. In this framework, genre and register are said to be on different "semiotic planes" (Martin 1985). Genre is viewed as a social process in which participants within a culture use language in predictable sequential structures to fulfill certain communicative purposes; Couture (1986) calls genres "conventional instances of organized text" (p. 80). Register, on the other hand, has been characterized as the "expression-plane" of genre (Martin 1985), and is more concerned with the typical linguistic choices within different genres. The choices are seen as resulting from contextual variables called field, tenor, and mode in Systemic Functional Linguistics, which roughly mean topics/actions of language, participants/relationships, and mode/organization. The distinction between *register* and *genre* made in this book clearly shares some characteristics with the use of the concepts in Systemic Functional Linguistics, especially with respect to the genre perspective emphasizing the conventional features of whole texts, while the register perspective emphasizes variation in the use of linguistic features (see also Ferguson 1994). Systemic Functional Linguistics, however, has an extensive theoretical framework associated with these concepts (see Halliday 1985, 1989; Martin 1985, 1993, 1997, 2001; Matthiessen 1993).

Finally, another perspective on the study of genres has an entirely different focus from the present book. Sometimes called the "New Rhetoric" approach (Hyland 2002a), this perspective is more concerned with the socio-cultural context of different message types and the work that genres do, rather than describing linguistic characteristics of texts. Ethnographic descriptions of a particular community and the use and learning of genres within it (e.g., Artemeva 2008) are more typical than linguistic descriptions. While such studies are interesting for what they tell us about how language use is situated in socio-cultural contexts, they are less relevant for our purposes in the present book (which focuses more narrowly on the linguistic analysis of texts).

The term *style* has perhaps been used for an even wider range of concepts than either of the other terms. In the 1960s, descriptive linguists used the term *style* to refer to general situational varieties, similar to our use of *register* in the present book (see Joos 1961; Crystal and Davy 1969). Quantitative sociolinguists in the Labovian tradition use the term *style* to refer to language used for different purposes during a sociolinguistic interview; sociolinguistic styles are interpreted as reflecting production circumstances that require differing amounts of attention to speech (e.g., reading word lists versus an interview; see Labov 1966, 1972). In the book conclusion (Section 9.4), we return to a fuller discussion of sociolinguistic style variation in comparison to register variation.

More commonly, style has been treated as a characteristic way of using language. This general perspective has most often been applied to literary language, often referred to as **stylistics**; style in this sense has been studied as a characteristic of particular genres, particular periods, particular authors, and even particular texts (see, e.g., Leech and Short 1981; Freeborn 1996; P. Simpson 2004). This usage can also carry an evaluative sense, as when writing handbooks discuss writing with style (which carries the implication that many people write without style.) Finally, as noted above, a similar notion of style has been used to study conversational interactions, where cultures can be described as having distinctive conversational styles (e.g., Tannen 2005).

A number of publications are available for learning more about researchers' and theorists' use of these terms. Useful places to start include the general overviews in Lee 2001 and Hyland 2002a (pp. 10–22), while Nunan 2008 provides an accessible introduction to the concepts of *genre* and *register* in Systemic Functional Linguistics.

1.5   Register/genre variation as a linguistic universal

All cultures use language for different communicative purposes in different situations. Register variation focuses on the pervasive patterns of linguistic variation across such situations, in association with the functions served by linguistic features; genre variation focuses on the conventional ways in which complete texts of different types are structured. Taken together, register/genre variation is a fundamental aspect of human language. All cultures and languages have an array of registers/genres, and all humans control a range of registers/genres.

The universal nature of register/genre variation has been noted by many previous scholars. For example:

> register variation, in which language structure varies in accordance with the occasions of use, is all-pervasive in human language   Ferguson 1983: 154

> no human being talks the same way all the time ... At the very least, a variety of registers and styles is used and encountered   Hymes 1984: 44

> each language community has its own system of registers ... corresponding to the range of activities in which its members normally engage Ure 1982: 5

Given the ubiquity of register/genre variation, an understanding of how linguistic features are used in patterned ways across text varieties is of central importance for both the description of particular languages and the development of cross-linguistic theories of language use. Hymes argues that the analysis of register/genre variation – "verbal repertoire" in his terms – should become the major focus of research within linguistics:

> [the] sociolinguistic perspective... has the possibility of taking the lead in transforming the study of language, through developing and consolidating the systematic study of verbal repertoire...
>
> The abilities of individuals and the composite abilities of communities cannot be understood except by making "verbal repertoire," not "language," the central scientific notion.   Hymes 1984: 44

Although all societies and languages have a number of registers/genres, they do not necessarily have equivalent sets. For example, some languages/societies have only spoken registers/genres; in such cases, there might be individual speakers who are capable of producing language in all registers/genres of the language. In contrast, modern literate societies incorporate a much larger set of spoken and written text varieties. As a result, no individual speaker/writer can control the full set of text varieties found in the culture. Previous studies have documented these differences, noting that historical change in the system of text varieties in a language is fundamentally important. For example:

> The register range of a language is one of the most immediate ways in which it responds to social change. The difference between developed and undeveloped languages (Ferguson, 1968) is fundamentally one of register range, and language contact, which contributes to language development... is mediated by particular registers... This issue is concerned with both the pressures that make for change and the way in which these changes are realized linguistically.   Ure 1982: 7

> [one of the two main tasks requiring attention within sociolinguistics at present is] the description and analysis of the organization and change of verbal repertoires in relation to the main processes of societal evolution of our time...   Hymes 1984: 44–45

Register/genre variation is universal because all cultures use language in different situations for different communicative purposes. We have noted in several places above that we regard the register perspective as the most important: because linguistic features are functional, they are used to greater and lesser extents in different situations, and thus any text sample of any type can be described from the register perspective. This functional association between linguistic forms and situations of use results in the systematic patterns of register variation. The primary goal of the present book is thus to introduce you to these linguistic patterns, and to equip you with the tools needed to carry out your own register analyses. In addition, we will continue to describe patterns of genre variation and style variation, especially when those perspectives provide useful insights on a particular text variety.

1.6   Overview of the book

The following chapters provide information on two levels: first, they provide you with the methodological tools that you will need to carry out analyses of text varieties, and second, they give descriptions of several of the most important registers, genres, and styles in English. As noted in the first section above, our primary focus is on the analysis of registers, because that perspective can be applied to any text sample. However, we also include descriptions of genres and styles throughout the book, providing broad coverage of the distinctive characterisics of text varieties from all three perspectives.

In Part I of the book – Chapters 2 and 3 – we introduce the analytical framework that is employed for studying registers, and explain its application for studying genre conventions and styles as well. As described in Section 1.3 above, register analyses have three main components: situational analysis, linguistic analysis, and functional analysis. We describe the first of these analytical components – the situation of use – in Chapter 2, while the linguistic and functional analyses are described further in Chapter 3.

In Part II of the book, we move on to a more detailed description of different kinds of registers, genres, and styles. Chapter 4 covers three spoken interpersonal registers: conversation, university office hours, and service encounters. Chapter 5 then focuses on general written registers – newspaper writing, academic prose, and fiction – showing how these text varieties can be studied from the perspectives of register, genre, and style. Most of the case studies in Chapters 4 and 5 are based on previous large-scale register studies, but they are illustrated with short texts and a small number of linguistic features, in order to show you the scale of work you can easily do on your own.

Chapter 6 then discusses how these same text varieties can be approached from a historical perspective, documenting the ways in which registers, genres, and literary styles evolve over time. The last chapter in this part of the book (Chapter 7) describes the characteristics of several emerging electronic registers – e-mail, internet forums, and text messages – exploring how their situational characteristics and linguistic features compare with more traditional registers.

Finally, Part III of the book deals with larger theoretical concerns and more advanced analytical approaches, introducing methods and issues that you may want to pursue in the future. Chapter 8 introduces an analytical approach – multidimensional analysis – that can be used to describe the general patterns of register variation in a language. And finally, Chapter 9 returns to more general issues concerning the study of registers, such as the relationship between register studies and other sub-disciplines of linguistics, the study of register variation in languages other than English, the general relationship between speech and writing (probably the most influential register distinction of them all), a theoretical comparison of the role of register and dialect variation in language and society, and the practical applications of register analysis.

Text samples throughout the book are taken from three major corpora: the T2K-SWAL corpus, LSWE Corpus, and ARCHER Corpus. The TOEFL 2000 Spoken and Written Academic Language Corpus (T2K-SWAL Corpus) resulted from a project sponsored by the Educational Testing Service (see Biber *et al.* 2002; Biber 2006). The T2K-SWAL Corpus is relatively large (2.7 million words) and represents a range of spoken and written university registers. The Longman Spoken and Written English Corpus (LSWE Corpus) was used for the analysis of the *Longman Grammar of Spoken and Written English* (*LGSWE*; Biber *et al.* 1999). The LSWE Corpus is relatively large (c. 20 million words) and represents four major spoken and written registers: conversation, fiction, newspaper prose, and academic prose (see Biber *et al.* 1999: Chapter 1). Finally, the ARCHER Corpus was designed for the study of historical register variation. This corpus is also relatively large (c. 1.7 million words) and represents a number of written and speech-based registers, including personal letters, fiction, newspaper reportage, academic prose, and drama.

Each chapter ends with activities. In the *Reflection and Review* activities, you will review concepts and reflect on information covered in the chapter, applying it to your own life and other real-world situations, and designing possible future studies. Many of these activities are suitable for small group work during class, while others are likely to be more effective if prepared as homework which can then be shared in class. *Analysis Practice* activities will give you focused practice with real data. These activities provide texts and counts from previous research, or they ask that you use data that is easily accessible (such as a paper you have previously written). You will analyze the texts/data to practice the kinds of analyses that were presented in the chapter. When these activities have been completed for homework, they are also useful for small group discussion/review during class. Finally, *Project Ideas* provide suggestions for larger-scale studies that focus on the types of texts or issues covered in the chapter. Some text samples are provided, but students are also asked to collect their own texts.

Chapters 2–8 contain all three types of activities, while Chapters 1 and 9, which introduce and summarize conceptual information, concentrate on *Reflection and Review*. All of the text samples used in the activities are compiled in a single appendix at the end of the book. It is also possible for instructors to design other activities to meet their own students' needs by using these text samples.

Rather than providing a literature review with each chapter of the book, we have included a major appendix at the end of the book. This appendix provides an annotated bibliography of many of the most important register studies and genre studies published over the past few decades. In the appendix, studies are grouped according to their research focus (e.g., studies of general written registers, studies of spoken registers, etc.), providing a valuable resource if you would like to pursue further research on a particular topic.

Chapter 1 activities

Reflection and review

1. Think carefully over your entire day yesterday and *all* the language varieties you encountered. List them in four columns: registers you produced (spoken or written), registers you heard or read, dialects you produced, and dialects you heard. How many registers are there in total? Did you produce or receive more different registers? How does the number of registers you encountered compare to the number of dialects that you encountered?

2. Think of a time when you were learning a new register (in your native language or a second language). How did you learn the situational characteristics that defined the register? How did you learn the linguistic features that were effective? Were you ever aware of choosing linguistic features that were different from other registers you know? Did you receive any explicit instruction about the register? Compare your experience with other students' experiences.

3. Pick two registers that you think people in your culture would know well. Interview five people (not linguists!) and ask them questions that will elicit the defining characteristics of those registers. For example, ask "What makes a talk a 'sermon' rather than an 'academic lecture'? And what makes them similar?"

   What are the characteristics that distinguish between the two registers and what are the similarities? How much consistency is there in the answers you receive from the five different people? Did the answers fit your expectations?

4. Choose a variety that you know well and outline a study that would cover register, genre, and style perspectives on that variety. Include the following:

   - text samples to be used for each of the perspectives
   - a brief summary of situational characteristics that you think are important for a register analysis of this variety
   - specific parts of the texts that you would focus on for the genre study (i.e., are there places where you expect the texts to conform to certain rhetorical organization, or where you expect certain textual conventions?)
   - a specific emphasis for the style perspective (do you want to focus on variation across certain famous individuals, or some measure of effective vs. non-effective text, or historical periods, or some other stylistic factor?)
   - your predictions of linguistic characteristics that you would find to be important in an analysis of (a) linguistic features of the register, (b) textual conventions found in the genre perspective, and (c) language features that you will find in the stylistic perspective. Base these predictions on your previous experience and observations of this variety. (In later chapters, you can actually carry out analyses to see how accurate your predications are.)

Possible varieties include research articles in applied or theoretical linguistics, novels, children's literature, book reviews, political speeches, newspaper editorials, or any other variety you have substantial experience with.

PART I

Analytical framework

2   Describing the situational characteristics of registers and genres

2.1   Introduction

In the last chapter, we defined a register as a language variety associated with both a particular situation of use and with pervasive linguistic features that serve important functions within that situation of use. In this chapter we focus on the "situation," that is, on how to describe characteristics related to the situation of use, or what we call *situational characteristics*. These characteristics include the physical context, such as the actual time and place, but also many other considerations. For example, the situational characteristics of face-to-face conversation include the fact that there are two or more participants producing language in the spoken mode and interacting directly with one another in a shared place and time. The situational characteristics of newspaper articles are very different, with a single author producing language in the written mode for a large number of readers scattered across different places and times.

An analysis of situational characteristics is important for the genre perspective as well as the register perspective, and most of the issues discussed in this chapter relate to both. In contrast, style variation is independent of the situational context, and thus we do not address that perspective in this chapter.

This chapter begins by discussing two issues related to the identification of registers and genres – first, how these text varieties can be described at different levels of generality, and second, cultural distinctions among registers/genres. We then develop a framework for analyzing situational characteristics, providing a template that you can use for your own register/genre analyses. Chapter 3 builds on this framework, describing the next steps in the process: the analysis of linguistic features, and the integration of the linguistic and situational analyses.

2.2   Issues in the identification of registers and genres

Before analyzing the situational characteristics of a text variety, you must of course identify the variety that you want to investigate. Two issues are especially important here: recognizing the level of generality of different registers and genres, and appreciating the role of culture in identifying registers and genres.

2.2.1   General and specialized registers and genres

In Chapter 1 we introduced the idea that registers can be more or less specialized. For example, conversation is a very general register, with relatively few specifying characteristics: two or more participants, interacting directly with one another in the spoken mode. Telephone conversation is more specified, because the participants must be communicating via an electronic channel and do not actually share the same physical place. Family dinner-table conversation is even more specified, with a particular setting, a particular set of participants, and particular topics that are typically discussed. Speeches (or public speaking) is another example of a very general spoken register, with many more specialized registers (such as sermons, political speeches, academic lectures, etc.).

It is similarly possible to distinguish among general and specialized registers within writing. For example, academic prose is a very general register, characterized as written language that has been carefully produced and edited, addressed to a large number of readers who are separated in time and space from the author, and with the primary communicative purpose of presenting information about some topic.

There are many more specialized written academic registers. The distinction between textbooks and academic research books involves the intended audience (students versus other professionals) and the more specific communicative purposes (e.g., introducing and surveying an academic field versus presenting the results of a new research project). Similar to academic research books, research articles in an academic journal are also written for other professionals but focused on the results of a specific study. There are also important register differences among academic disciplines. For example, a psychology research article is different from a chemistry research article, and both are different from history research articles.

In fact, in the research articles of some academic disciplines, even more specific subregisters can be identified. For example, chemistry research articles typically have four sections: Introduction, Methods, Results, Discussion. The Methods section is quite different from the Introduction or Discussion sections: the Methods section focuses specifically on a description of the procedures and materials used in a study, while the Introduction and Discussion sections present more general surveys of previous research and discuss the broader motivation and implications of the study. As you will see in Chapter 5, even specific communicative differences like these result in systematic register differences associated with different sets of linguistic features.

It is important to recognize that there is no single "right" level for a register analysis. Rather, situational characteristics and linguistic features can be analyzed for a general register or a very specific register. An investigation may even start with a general register and then shift to analyzing the more specific registers within it. There will be more variation among texts within a general register than a specific subregister, and so the linguistic analysis of a general register will need to be based on a larger sample of texts.

When analyzing the situation of a register, there will be more characteristics than can be definitively specified for very specific registers, while general registers will have more variability within certain categories. Thus, for the general register of "conversation," it is not possible to identify specific communicative purposes or specific characteristics of the participants. In contrast, it is possible to be more specific in the situational description of workplace conversations among colleagues, or dinner-table conversations among family members. However, as Chapters 4–9 show, linguistic differences are functionally associated with situational characteristics when registers are specified at any level of generality.

While register differences can be regarded as a continuum of variation, genre differences are more discrete. Further, genres are not as easily analyzed along a hierarchy of generality. For example, it makes sense to describe the genre of the scientific research article, identifying the linguistic conventions used to structure texts. However, it is not useful to try to describe a more general genre of academic writing, since there are not general conventions used to structure the different kinds of texts that could be included in that category. Similarly, a specific spoken variety, like sermons delivered in Lutheran churches, can be described from a genre perspective. But it is unlikely that sermons of all types would share general genre conventions, and the general textual category of public speaking could certainly not be described from a genre perspective.

At the same time, there are cases where a genre is embedded in a larger genre. For example, introductory sections in scientific research articles can be analyzed as a genre (see Chapter 5) with its own conventional structure. From this perspective, the entire introductory section would be regarded as a complete text. These texts represent the genre of "Introductions" because they conform to the expected conventional organization (first reviewing previous research; then identifying a "gap" in previous research; and finally stating how the present study fills that gap). At the same time, research article introductions are embedded in the larger genre of the scientific research article, which has its own conventional structure (e.g., being organized as Abstract, Introduction, Methods, Results, Discussion).

2.2.2   Culturally recognized register/genre distinctions

In many cases, general registers/genres have short, simple names, while more specialized text varieties have longer more complex names. For example, "conversation" includes many different specialized kinds of interaction, but those are often referred to with longer names, like "telephone conversation," "casual conversation among colleagues," and so on.

However, speakers do sometimes employ short, simple names for specialized text varieties. For example, a "syllabus" is a specialized variety used only in school contexts, to describe the content of a course and set out the student expectations and requirements. A "deed" is a legal document that grants rights to some property or privilege. The fact that these specialized text varieties have simple names indicates that they are widely recognized within English-speaking cultures as distinct varieties that serve important functions.

Genres generally have simple names in a culture, but this is not always the case for registers. That is, genres are governed by specific conventions, generally recognized by members of a culture, and so the genre itself is named within the culture. These same varieties can also be analyzed from a register perspective, and we would use the same name. However, it is not the case that all registers have simple names. For example, "casual conversation among colleagues" describes a text variety that occurs in a particular situation of use, and there are linguistic features functionally associated with that situation. Thus, this variety can be analyzed from a register perspective, even though it does not represent a well-defined genre.

Further, not all text varieties with a simple name can be regarded as genres. For example, sermons and lectures might be regarded as specialized subregisters of "speeches" or the general register of "public speaking." But we would need to consider specific types of sermons to be able to apply the genre perspective. (So, for example, it is unlikely that a sermon delivered by a Roman Catholic priest will have the same genre conventions as a sermon delivered by a Southern Baptist preacher.) Similarly, "conversation" describes a very general register, but many conversations are not clearly structured by genre conventions.

In some cases, a very specialized domain has multiple genres/registers that are familiar to experts in the field, but not generally familiar to the public. For example, the legal domain includes genres/registers such as a "affidavit," "deposition," and "pleading." The legal/government domain includes "treaties," "regulations," "laws," and "ordinances." In the religious domain, there are "prayers," "benedictions," and "eulogies." Here again, the use of a simple name indicates that these varieties are overtly recognized by members of the sub-culture as representing meaningful distinctions, even though they may not be known by others outside the sub-culture.

It is normal for a culture to make genre/register distinctions that are not recognized in other cultures. For example, Duranti (1981, 1994) describes the different kinds of speeches that occur during the course of a *fono* in Western Samoa. English speakers would probably recognize the *fono* as a kind of village council to discuss political and judiciary matters. However, there are many speeches given in a *fono*, and it is unlikely that an English speaker would perceive those to be different registers. For a speaker of Samoan, however, the speeches given during a *fono* fall into several distinct genre/register categories, including:

> *lāuga* "the main ceremonial speech"
> *tali* "replies"
> *talanoaga* "discussions"

In addition, there are several distinct genres within a *lāuga*, including the *folasaga* ("introduction") and *fa'afetai* ("thanksgiving").

A second example of the importance of culture in genre/register identification comes from Basso's (1990: 114ff.) description of oral story-telling among the Western Apache. Four different kinds of stories are distinguished:

godiyihgo nagoldi'e: creation stories told by medicine men and women, to enlighten and instruct about how the universe came to be the way it is;

'agodzaahi: historical moral story about events that took place a long time ago (before the arrival of Europeans), intended to emphasize the importance of proper behavior and the bad consequences of improper behavior;

nłt'eego nagoldi'e: stories about events that occurred within the past several decades, told to entertain listeners;

ch'idii ("gossip"): stories about recent events, about other members of the Western Apache community who are currently living in the community.

In this case, members of English-speaking cultures in the US and UK would recognize all of these as stories. They would probably be able to describe the major differences in the stories, but those differences are not especially important in many English-speaking cultures (except for "gossip," which is widely recognized as a distinctive type of story). As a result, where members of Western Apache culture regard these as four different genres/registers, most members of Anglo culture would recognize only one or two genres/registers (simply "stories," or "stories" versus "gossip").

Often members of a culture distinguish two different registers primarily by their communicative purposes, while the physical circumstances might appear to be nearly identical to the casual outside observer. For example, the registers of *tafsiir* and *waᶜd* in Arabic-speaking Islamic cultures might both be perceived as "sermons" by a casual outside observer. Both are monologic registers, performed by a sheikh as part of a religious ceremony in a mosque. But the two differ in their primary communicative purposes: the *tafsiir* is more informational and explanatory, presenting content from the Quran and Hadith and explaining its meaning. In contrast, the *waᶜd* is more persuasive and exhortatory, encouraging audience members to be devout and practice the precepts of the religion. Normally, these two registers occur in sequence: the sheikh would first quote a passage from the Quran or Hadith, then move on to *tafsiir*, explaining the content of the passage, and finally present *waᶜd*, a discussion of the practical implications of the passage and an encouragement to act in a certain way based on those implications. These same kinds of language are common in what an English speaker would recognize as a "sermon." However, in Arabic-speaking cultures, the two are recognized as distinct registers.

All three of the above examples illustrate how genre/register distinctions are culture-specific. Furthermore, even when two cultures have seemingly equivalent genres/registers, they can turn out to be different because they have distinctive communicative purposes. For example, both American English and Somali cultures have a genre/register used for personal written communication, sent by surface mail from one individual to another: the "personal letter" in American English, and the *warqad* in Somali. Until recently, such texts were relatively common in each of the two cultures. (More recently, letters have come to be replaced by e-mail messages in American English. *Warqad* are rare now in Somalia because of the collapse of the central government and the postal system.)

Although these two genres/registers are similar in many respects, they differ in their typical communicative purposes: personal letters in American English are usually written for general interpersonal communication, to maintain a relationship and inform the addressee about recent personal events in the author's life. In contrast, *warqad* in Somali are usually written because the writer needs something from the addressee. These differences have important linguistic consequences. *Warqad* contain many "directives": statements that tell the addressee what they should do, using grammatical features like imperatives and "optative" clauses (which express wishes). In contrast, personal letters in American English contain many questions, asking the addressee about their circumstances, and first-person "stance" constructions, telling about the personal circumstances of the writer.

In summary, different cultures have different ways of dividing up the range of activities that are performed using language. One culture might perceive relatively small differences in purpose to be manifestations of different registers and/or genres, while another culture could perceive the same range of communicative events to all represent a single genre/register. Further, the "same" genre/register in two cultures can actually be characterized by important differences in purpose or other situational characteristics. Therefore, the first step in conducting an analysis is to identify and describe the situational characteristics of the genre/register.

2.3   A framework for situational analysis

Effective register analyses are always comparative. It is virtually impossible to know what is distinctive about a particular register without comparing it to other registers. So, for example, Kuiper and Haggo (1984) describe the register characteristics of livestock auctions by comparison to the more general registers of oral poetry and conversation. Some studies do focus exclusively on a single register, such as Ferguson's (1983) description of sports announcer talk, or Bruthiaux's (1996) description of classified ads. In these cases, the researcher relies on their intuitions and previous experience with other registers to identify the distinctive characteristics of the target register. This is not a recommended practice, because intuitions about "normal" behavior are often not reliable. Thus, in the present book, the analysis of register characteristics (situational and linguistic) will generally focus on the comparison of two or more registers.

Particular situational characteristics will be more or less important, depending on the registers that are being compared. For example, conversation and e-mail messages are similar in many respects: both are produced by a person addressing another person, often dealing with personal/social topics, and both are typically interactive, where the second person responds to the first. One of the main differences between the two registers is the physical mode: speech versus electronically conveyed writing.

In contrast, a comparison of conversation and sermons would need to focus on different characteristics. Both registers share the spoken mode, but they differ in their interactivity: conversation is highly interactive, with two or more participants contributing to the discourse, while sermons are produced by one person and are therefore not interactive. Of course, communicative purpose and topic are also major factors in distinguishing among these two registers. Conversation can be about any topic, and participants often shift among several communicative purposes: revealing their own personal feelings and attitudes, describing past events, and sometimes trying to persuade listeners. Sermons are much more constrained for both topic and purpose: the topic is generally related to religion, scripture, and lifestyle, while the purpose is generally informative and/or persuasive.

In the following section, we introduce the methods for conducting a situational analysis, suggesting several sources of information that can be used for this purpose. Then, in Section 2.3.2, we introduce a comprehensive analytical framework, identifying the set of situational characteristics that are potentially useful for register analyses. As noted above, this framework can be applied to analyze the situational characteristics of any text variety, whether the ultimate goal is to apply the genre perspective or the register perspective.

2.3.1   Methods for describing the situational characteristics of a register

There are a number of sources of information that can help you describe the situational characteristics of a register. The importance of each of the sources below will differ depending on how involved you are with the cultural group that recognizes the register, and how much experience you have with the register yourself. Furthermore, some characteristics will be easy to analyze based on your own experience, while others will require more research. For example, it is no problem to tell from your own observation whether a register is spoken or written even if you have no previous experience with it, but determining the communicative purposes of a register may require more primary research.

2.3.1.1   Your experience and observation

If you are part of the cultural group that uses a register and have personal experience producing the register effectively, your own knowledge can be one major source of information that you use for the situational analysis.

However, even in this case, it will require some thinking and discussion with other members of the cultural group to be confident about your interpretation.

For example, since you have had many experiences engaging in conversation with friends, you could list the situational characteristics of that register without consulting any other sources. Having also read many textbooks, you could probably describe their situational characteristics, including some of the variability in their purposes (such as how entertaining versus purely informative they are).

However, observers or novices in a professional domain generally cannot fully describe the registers identified by practitioners in that domain. For example, academic professionals make many fine distinctions among the various kinds of published articles, including research articles, review articles, book reviews, and "commentaries." Academic professionals also distinguish among the various venues for a published article, including refereed research journals, non-refereed journals, newsletters, and a chapter in an edited book. To casual observers and novices, all these registers are simply "published articles." Thus, many analyses require additional information than what you can obtain from your own experience and observation.

2.3.1.2   Expert informants

When you do not have a great deal of experience with a register, asking expert informants about it can help you identify its situational characteristics. To continue with the academic example above, if you were describing academic article registers, interviewing your professors about the characteristics of the registers would be invaluable. Of course, individuals vary in their perceptions, so it is always helpful to speak with several informants.

The expert informant is even more important if you are describing registers used in a culture that is not your own native culture because it is unlikely that an outside observer will fully understand the cultural significance of communication events. It is natural to interpret such events relative to the register distinctions that you recognize from your own native culture. In this case, the expert native informant is essential to help you recognize the register distinctions found in the target culture.

2.3.1.3   Previous research

Previous research that has covered the kinds of registers that you are interested in is also a good potential source of information about situational characteristics. Studies from a rhetorical perspective can help you understand how a register is used within its cultural context. For example, if you were studying scientific research articles, published case studies of professional writers in science could help you understand the purposes and audiences of the register (e.g., such as the early studies done by Bazerman 1988, and Latour and Woolgar 1986).

2.3.1.4   Analysis of texts from the register

Many descriptions of a register – based on your experience, or others' expertise, or sometimes even published work – represent beliefs or perceptions, rather than the results of an empirical investigation. Such descriptions are not necessarily accurate. For example, it is often the case that there will be some situational characteristics that are not consciously recognized by users of a register. For this reason, it is always useful to obtain additional information about situational characteristics by looking at the texts themselves.

Texts can aid in determining situational characteristics in one of two ways. First, it can be useful to look at texts during your initial situational analysis, in order to identify their typical communicative purposes. For example, this was necessary for us as the authors of this book when we carried out the case study of text messages in Chapter 7. Neither of us used text messages or really understood why other people used them. So besides looking at some previous studies of text messages and asking texters themselves why they texted, we looked at a large collection of messages to analyze the types of purposes that were apparent in the texts themselves.

Second, situational analyses of texts can be useful *after* the linguistic features are analyzed. That is, when you have completed your linguistic analysis, you might discover unanticipated linguistic patterns and realize that those patterns must correspond to situational characteristics that you were unaware of previously. For example, as we will explain in Chapter 3, in a study of classroom teaching, a group of researchers (including the authors of this book) were unable to predict some situational characteristics that became obvious after the linguistic features had been studied. Even though the researchers had all been producing classroom discourse for years, a fuller, explicit understanding of the situational characteristics came only when the linguistic features were connected to their functions. Thus, the process of doing a register analysis often includes refining the analysis of the situational characteristics after the linguistic analysis.

Despite the sometimes cyclic nature of the linguistic and situational analyses, the normal way to start a register analysis is by identifying and describing the situational characteristics that define the registers. The next section presents an analytical framework for this task.

2.3.2   The framework for analyzing situational characteristics

Since text varieties can be compared with respect to so many different situational characteristics, it is useful to have a general framework to apply in any analysis (for either the register or genre perspective). Some characteristics will not be relevant for some comparisons, but applying the framework can help you think through the full set of situational characteristics that need to be considered.

Table 2.1 lists the major situational characteristics that are relevant for describing and comparing registers and genres. These characteristics were compiled from a survey of previous theoretical frameworks that have been developed for

Table 2.1 *Situational characteristics of registers and genres*

I. Participants
    A. Addressor(s) (i.e. speaker or author)
        1. single / plural / institutional / unidentified
        2. social characteristics: age, education, profession, etc.
    B. Addressees
        1. single / plural / un-enumerated
        2. self / other
    C. Are there on-lookers?
II. Relations among participants
    A. Interactiveness
    B. Social roles: relative status or power
    C. Personal relationship: e.g., friends, colleagues, strangers
    D. Shared knowledge: personal and specialist
III. Channel
    A. Mode: speech / writing / signing
    B. Specific Medium:
        Permanent: taped / transcribed / printed / handwritten / e-mail / etc.
        Transient speech: face-to-face / telephone / radio / TV / etc.
IV. Production circumstances: real time / planned / scripted / revised and edited
V. Setting
    A. Is the time and place of communication shared by participants?
    B. Place of communication
        1. Private / public
        2. Specific setting
    C. Time: contemporary, historical time period
VI. Communicative purposes
    A. General purposes: narrate / report, describe, exposit / inform / explain, persuade, how-to / procedural, entertain, edify, reveal self
    B. Specific purposes: e.g., summarize information from numerous sources, describe methods, present new research findings, teach moral through personal story
    C. Factuality: factual, opinion, speculative, imaginative
    D. Expression of stance: epistemic, attitudinal, no overt stance
VII. Topic
    A. General topical "domain": e.g., domestic, daily activities, business / workplace, science, education / academic, government / legal / politics, religion, sports, art / entertainment, etc.
    B. Specific topic
    C. Social status of person being referred to

the study of register (e.g., Biber 1988, 1994; Crystal and Davy 1969; Halliday 1978; Hymes 1974; Basso 1974). In the following sections, we describe each of those characteristics in turn.

2.3.2.1   Participants

We begin with the participants: the person producing the text, and the person to whom the text is addressed. Every text is produced by someone: the ***addressor***. Most spoken registers are produced by individuals who are readily identifiable. However, the addressor can be less apparent in written registers. For example, the present book has been produced by two co-authors, and in fact any sentence in this book might have been written/revised/edited by both of us. Other written texts are not attributed to any individual. Some of these texts have an "institutional" addressor: they can be attributed to some institution, but there is no indication of who actually wrote the text. For example, newspaper editorials present the official point of view of a newspaper, but no author is identified. Similarly, a university catalog presents an official description of services and requirements with no indication of who produced the text. At the far extreme, there are anonymous written texts that are not even attributed to an institution, such as certain kinds of signs or advertisements.

The social characteristics of the addressor(s) have a major influence on the language produced in the text. For example, characteristics like the speaker's age, sex, level of education, occupation, and social class can all be important determinants of linguistic variation. Such characteristics are described under the rubric of social dialect variation (see Chapter 1). Although we will have little to say about social dialect variation in the present book, these characteristics of the speaker should be considered as part of the larger situational context for a register.

In addition to the addressor, communication requires an ***addressee***: the intended listener or reader. In many cases, the addressee can be an individual, as in a face-to-face conversation with a friend. Personal letters and e-mail messages are also often addressed to an individual. However, most of these texts can also be addressed to multiple individuals. For example, a dinner-table conversation can involve a group of individuals all discussing the same topic; everyone except the speaker can be the addressee of an utterance. University classroom teaching is addressed to a larger group of listeners, while a major conference lecture might be addressed to a group of several thousand listeners. In these cases, although the group of addressees may be very large, it is possible to identify who they are. There are some registers, however, that have an un-enumerated set of addressees. For example, it is not possible to specify (except in a very general sense) the set of individuals who listen to a radio broadcast or watch a television show. Published written registers provide even clearer examples of registers with an un-enumerated set of addressees. For example, a novel can exist physically for decades or even centuries, and there is no obvious way to identify who the set of readers will be over that time.

Finally, the situational context for some registers includes a group of *on-lookers*. These are participants who observe but are not the direct addressees of the register. For example, actors in a dramatic play are conversing, addressing one another on the stage, but that entire conversational interaction is observed by the audience of on-lookers. Similarly, participants in a debate or during court-room testimony directly address one another, but they are also aware of the audience of on-lookers. In fact, the role of the on-lookers might have more practical importance than the addressee. For example, during court testimony, a witness is directly addressing an examining attorney, but the major purpose of communication is to persuade a group of on-lookers: the jury. In cases like these, the distinction between addressee and on-looker is somewhat fuzzy. The most important point for register analysis is that you recognize the influence of both.

2.3.2.2   Relations among participants

Once you have identified the participants, the next step is to describe how they relate to one another. The most important consideration here is *inter-activeness*: to what extent do the participants directly interact with one another? At one extreme, there are registers like conversation, where all participants are present and able to directly respond to one another. At the opposite extreme are registers like university catalogs: since it is very difficult to even identify the exact authors of this text, it is virtually impossible to have a dialogue with them.

Most registers are intermediate in their degree of interactiveness. For example, participants in an e-mail interchange directly respond to one another, but that interaction can be spread over days and weeks. A university class session will normally be interactive, but not equally for all participants; rather, the instructor will typically produce most of the language and control the extent to which students can participate. A newspaper article is even less interactive, because the author is not easily accessible to address a response to. However, readers can write a "letter to the editor," allowing for a limited kind of interaction.

In addition to the extent of interactiveness, it is important to consider the *social roles* and *personal relationships* among participants. In many cases, participants can be socially equal, as in the case of two classmates having a conversation. But in other cases, there can be important social differences among participants. For example, power differences can influence language choices; even in a casual conversation, if you are talking to your teacher or boss you probably produce different language than when you talk to your best friend. Participants can also have different degrees of *shared background knowledge*. For example, imagine how you would describe your activities this past weekend when talking to your roommate (who knows most of your friends and the places where you like to go), in comparison to how you would describe those activities to a stranger. Speakers can also share "specialist background knowledge." Imagine discussing a linguistic analysis with one of your classmates, contrasted with how you would describe the same analysis to your parents. Written texts can also differ depending on specialist shared knowledge; for example, an academic research journal has articles addressed to other specialists in the field, while introductory textbooks are addressed to novices in the field.

2.3.2.3   Channel

One of the most obvious differences among registers is the physical *channel* or *mode*: speech versus writing. It turns out that the difference between speech and writing is intertwined with other situational characteristics. For example, registers produced in the spoken mode almost always have a specific addressor, and typically have specific addressees; in contrast, written registers can have an institutional addressor and un-enumerated addressees. Spoken registers are often interactive; written registers are rarely interactive. Spoken and written registers also differ in their typical production circumstances and even their typical communicative purposes (see below). For all these reasons, the distinction between spoken and written registers is one of the most important situational parameters for the linguistic description of registers (as we show in following chapters).

Of course, not all registers are spoken or written. There are other specialized modes of communication. Signing in particular is a fully developed mode of communication, while there are also much more restricted modes like drum talk or smoke signals. However, in the present book we restrict ourselves to the description of spoken and written registers.

It is also possible to distinguish among *specific mediums of communication* within speech or writing, such as telephone or radio for speech, and hand-writing, electronic (e.g., e-mail), and printed for writing. These more specific means of expressing language can also have an influence on the linguistic forms that speakers employ (see, e.g., the discussion of electronic registers in Chapter 7).

2.3.2.4   Production circumstances

As noted above, the choice of the spoken or written mode directly influences the production circumstances. Consider a normal conversation: The speaker is producing language at the same time that he is thinking about what he wants to say. The speaker usually does not have time to carefully plan what he will say next; if he takes too long thinking, his conversational partner might begin to talk, or the conversation might end in miscommunication. And if he says something unintended, he must completely start over again; a speaker cannot edit or erase language once it has been spoken.

Written registers typically differ in all of these respects: The writer has as much time as needed to plan exactly what she wants to write, and if she writes something unintended, she can revise/edit/delete/add language until she ends up with language that conveys exactly the intended meaning. Thus, the final written text that a reader sees may bear little resemblance to the initial words that the author wrote, and readers usually have no indication of the extent to which the author has revised the original text. (Spoken language can also be edited to some extent, as in the case of a taped radio interview. But in this case, the editing is restricted to removing unwanted language; it is not possible to change what had been said.)

The addressee similarly has different circumstances for comprehension in the spoken versus written mode. In speech, a listener has no choice but to hear and understand language at the same time that the speaker produces it; there is no opportunity to control the speed or sequence of information (apart from telling the speaker to slow down!). In contrast, a reader has complete control over the text. The reader can carefully read one word at a time, or she can quickly skim a text. She can even jump around in a written text, for example reading the conclusion before the introduction. (Of course, particular readers of a written text will engage in very different comprehension processes, depending on their prior background knowledge and purposes for reading.)

2.3.2.5   Setting

The setting refers to the physical context of the communication – the *time* and *place*. An important consideration here is whether the time and place are *shared*. In many spoken registers, the participants share the physical context and so they can directly refer to it (e.g., with words like *yesterday* or *here*). Such situation-dependent reference is not appropriate in most written registers, where the participants do not share the same time or place. However, some written texts do assume that the reader has knowledge of the time (and sometimes place) of production. For example, newspaper stories may mention a day of the week (e.g. *Monday* or even *yesterday*), showing that the paper is meant to be read the day it was produced. Personal e-mail messages and text messages generally assume even greater knowledge of the time and place of production.

In addition, there are general characteristics of the setting that can be important. For example, is the *place of communication* private (e.g., conversation, personal letters) or public (e.g., classroom teaching, textbooks)? Both private and public communication can occur in almost any particular setting; for example, it is possible to have both a private workplace conversation with a friend as well as a public workplace conversation with a customer. Written texts may have a specific setting by being published as part of a larger document, such as a chapter within a book. Furthermore, the *time of the communication* can be relatively contemporary or a historical time period.

2.3.2.6   Communicative purpose

All of the situational characteristics considered above have been tangible aspects of the context: who is participating, where they are, what physical mode of communication is being used, and what the production circumstances are. However, it is equally important to consider the "why" of communication: the communicative purpose. Communicative purpose can be described on several different levels. It is usually possible to identify the *general purposes* of a register, such as narrating or reporting past events, describing some state of affairs, explaining or interpreting information, arguing or persuading, providing procedural information about how to perform certain activities, entertaining the addressee, and revealing personal feelings or attitudes.

Many registers combine several communicative purposes. For example, textbooks usually combine descriptive and explanatory purposes. Textbooks in engineering disciplines will also include procedural information, while textbooks in the humanities will often include persuasive discussion and some narratives.

Further, it is possible to switch purpose in the middle of a communicative event. For example, you might be having a conversation with a friend where you are discussing political candidates, describing specific policies that a candidate endorses, and trying to persuade your friend that a particular candidate is the most qualified. In this case, you would be describing the current state of affairs, but also revealing your own attitudes, and also trying to persuade the listener about the correctness of your point of view. But then it would be very easy to switch purposes, for example telling a story about the last time that you went to vote, and how long you had to wait in line, and how someone else in line was behaving. This switch in purpose can be regarded as a shift in subregister, from one kind of conversation to another. We will show in the following chapters that it is possible to identify linguistic characteristics that hold for conversation generally, regardless of the particular purposes, but also that it is possible to identify linguistic characteristics for particular kinds of conversation, associated with particular communicative purposes.

Such shifts in communicative purpose can occur in writing as well as speech. In some cases, this shift is overtly marked in the text and allows the analyst to identify distinct *specific purposes* that distinguish between very specific subregisters. For example, as noted in Section 2.2.1 above, a typical scientific research article will be composed of four distinct sections that are explicitly labeled: Introduction, Methods, Results, Discussion. These sections can be regarded as subregisters, differing mostly in their communicative purpose. Introductions describe the current state of knowledge in the field, and might include some narration of past events or some explanation of concepts or previous research findings. Then the Methods section will switch to a procedural communicative purpose, describing how the study was conducted. Results sections are usually descriptive, stating what was found in the study, while the Discussion section is usually more interpretive, explanatory, and persuasive. All of these article sections have the same physical context: the same author, same readers, same production circumstances, and so on. But there are important linguistic differences across article sections, associated with the shifts in communicative purpose.

Another parameter relating to purpose is *factuality*: Does the addressor intend to convey factual information, personal opinion, speculation, or fiction/fantasy. These are not discrete differences, since speakers often mix fact and fantasy. Further, it might be argued that no personal account can be truly "factual." But this parameter is important for distinguishing among the primary intents of registers, such as a novel (fiction) versus a biography (factual), or an editorial (opinion) versus a newspaper article (factual).

A final parameter concerns the *expression of stance*. This parameter includes expressions both of personal attitudes and of epistemic stance (i.e., the extent to which information is certain or generalizable, or explanations of the source of the information). For example, within a newspaper there are different types of articles associated with different expressions of stance. A typical report of a news event has little or no overt expression of stance; it simply states what happens. It may still convey a certain ideology, but overt markers of stance are generally limited to statements of the source, such as *according to analysts...* Reports from a science section, on the other hand, are more concerned with expressing epistemic stance, especially the extent to which information is certain or generalizable. You would not be surprised to see expressions such as *it is possible that...* or *the findings suggest...* or *in general...*, all of which are linguistic markers of epistemic stance. Science reporting in a newspaper reflects the concern in the scientific community about the extent to which claims are verifiable or can be generalized. Finally, in restaurant and entertainment reviews, personal attitudes are important; in fact, the point of communication is to convey personal evaluations with overt comments such as *the flavor was **wonderful*** or ***unfortunately**, the one thing lacking was...*

2.3.2.7   Topic

Finally, topic is an open-ended category that can be described at many different levels. It is possible to distinguish among very *general topical domains*, such as science, religion, politics, and sports, but any text will have its own *specific topics*. Topic is the most important situational factor influencing vocabulary choice; the words used in a text are to a large extent determined by the topic of the text. This is true both at the level of general topical domains (e.g., science writing versus business news) and very specific topical domains (e.g., research writing on biogenetics).

In languages like Japanese, there is a special aspect of topic that directly influences linguistic choice: the social status of any person that is being talked about. In this case, specific honorific particles must be used that indicate social status.

In general, though, topical differences are not influential for determining grammatical differences. Rather, the pervasive grammatical characteristics of a register are mostly determined by the physical situational context and the communicative purposes. There are some grammatical differences that might at first seem to be related to topic. For example, passive verbs are much more common in science and engineering textbooks than in humanities textbooks. However, these differences are influenced mostly by the differing communicative purposes of these disciplines rather than simply by differences in topic. (These differences are discussed in Chapter 5.)

2.4   Applying the situational analytical framework in a register study

In Chapter 1, we presented the three major components of a register analysis: (1) describing the situational characteristics of the register; (2) analyzing the typical linguistic characteristics of the register; and (3) identifying the functional forces that help to explain why those linguistic features tend to be associated with those situational characteristics. Starting a register analysis with a thorough description of the situational characteristics can help you in several ways. For example, if you are studying a register used by a cultural group that you are not very familiar with, the situational analysis will ensure that you are not inadvertently mixing registers that the cultural group distinguishes. Similarly, if you are studying a very general register, it can ensure that you do not overlook subregisters within it. Even with registers that you know well, working through the characteristics in Table 2.1 will ensure that you do not disregard important situational characteristics that might be crucial in interpreting the linguistic patterns.

Usually, reports or academic papers that describe a register analysis (including the case studies in later chapters of this book) do not discuss all the situational characteristics of every register studied. They might only present the major characteristics that distinguish among registers, or they might focus on those characteristics that proved to be important in interpreting the linguistic features. Nevertheless, it is important to consider all situational characteristics during the analytical process and not jump to conclusions about which are the most influential. You may also find for very specific registers that you study that there are other, more specific situational characteristics that are important in differentiating the registers.

Chapter 2 activities

Reflection and review

1. Consider the following speech situations. They are all spoken and directly interactive, with minimal time for speakers to plan what they say, but these situations differ with respect to other characteristics. Identify the most important differences in the communicative purposes, social relationship between participants, and other aspects of the situational context:

    a. talking with your instructor after class, asking for an explanation of a difficult concept;

    b. talking with your advisor during office hours, planning your courses for next semester;

    c. talking with a fellow student, deciding when to get together to study, as you leave class to go to different appointments;

    d. talking with your best friend about what you did last weekend;

    e. talking with five friends at a restaurant about what to order;

    f. talking on the telephone with your mother about her recent vacation.

2. Think about another culture or sub-culture that you know well besides your home culture (or, if you choose, look at an ethnographic study that describes another culture). Describe one to three registers or genres that are different from registers/genres in your home culture. What are the situational characteristics that distinguish these registers/genres from others?

    Alternatively, identify examples of the "same" register/genre in two languages, and then identify any situational differences between the two.

Analysis Practice

3. "Cookbooks" and "restaurant reviews in magazines" deal with similar general topics but are quite different in many of their other situational characteristics. Complete the table of situational characteristics (Table 2.1) as completely as you can for the registers, noting the similarities and differences between the two registers. Use any sources of information that you need in order to complete the table. Compare your answers with another student and resolve any disagreements.

4. Newspapers are a very general register. Identify the range of more specialized registers within newspapers, and describe the situational characteristics that distinguish among them. Look at several newspapers (paper or online) to make sure you do not miss the different types of articles in them. Compare your answers with another student.

5. Make a list of all the e-mail messages or text messages that you receive over the next week. Describe the important situational characteristics of each one, including: demographic characteristics of the sender, the social relationship between you and the sender, whether you are the sole recipient of the message or not, the primary communicative purposes of the message, and whether you consider the message to be carefully revised and edited or not. Then, at the end of the week, try to develop a taxonomy of subregisters, based on the types of messages that you have received.

Project Ideas

6. Do an internet search for a keyword that relates to your favorite social activity, such as "running," "tennis," or "movies." Pick twenty different sites that are identified by the search, representing at least five different registers. Compare and contrast the important situational characteristics of each one, including the following: the author, the "sender" (if different from the author), the intended reader (including

whether general or specialist), the primary communicative purposes, and any other distinguishing characteristics. Based on your description, develop a preliminary taxonomy of the kinds of registers found on the Web.

7. Choose a professional field that is of interest to you. It could be a field that you have worked in or are planning to enter, or that students of yours will be in, or that your spouse is in, and so on. Using any sources of information that you need (your own experience, interviews with expert informants, previous research, sample texts) compile a complete list of all the registers that professionals in that field need to be competent with (receiving or producing). Briefly describe the distinguishing characteristics of each register.

3   Analyzing linguistic features and their functions

3.1   Introduction

Linguistic description is central to the analysis of text varieties from the three perspectives used in this book. For the register and style perspectives, the focus is on identification of the pervasive lexico-grammatical features that are especially prevalent in the variety. The key difference between the two perspectives is in the interpretation of observed differences: associated functionally with the situational context in the case of register analysis, or associated with aesthetic effects achieved by particular authors/speakers in the case of style analysis. The genre perspective differs from these other two in the focus of the linguistic analysis itself, describing the conventional devices or rhetorical organizations used to structure complete texts from a variety.

Because it is the most widely applicable, we focus here mostly on the methods for carrying out a register analysis. Previous chapters have introduced the three major steps of register analysis: first, describing the situational characteristics of the register, including distinctive aspects of the context and communicative purpose; second, identifying the distinctive linguistic characteristics of the register; and third, showing how the situational and linguistic descriptions are related to one another by interpreting the functions that the linguistic features serve. In Chapter 2 we introduced a framework for describing the situational characteristics. In this chapter, we introduce the methods for carrying out the second and third steps, the linguistic and functional analyses.

One major analytical problem discussed in the chapter is deciding on the linguistic features to analyze. First, however, the chapter begins with issues that are even more fundamental: the need for a comparative approach, quantitative analysis, and representative samples. With that background, the chapter then provides specific information about how to conduct quantitative analyses, how to choose the linguistic features to analyze, and how to undertake a functional interpretation that integrates the linguistic and situational information.

Later in the chapter, then, we describe the linguistic analysis of texts from the genre and style perspectives. While situational analyses from register and genre perspectives cover the same basic parameters, linguistic analyses focus on quite different considerations in the genre perspective (see Sections 3.2.2 and 3.6). In contrast, the situational analysis is less relevant in the style perspective, because writers and speakers are deliberately manipulating linguistic form for aesthetic effects, regardless of the actual situational context. In this case, the linguistic analysis is similar to the register perspective, but an analysis of aesthetic effect rather than direct communicative functions is undertaken (see Section 3.7 below).

3.2   Fundamental issues for the linguistic analysis of registers

In general, the goal of the linguistic analysis is to identify the language features that are typical or characteristic of the target register. A basic concern, therefore, is how to determine whether a linguistic feature is "typical" in a given register.

To begin this discussion, consider Text Sample 3.1 from a geology textbook. Take a minute to read through the text and list any linguistic features (lexical or grammatical) that you suspect might be typical of the textbook register.

Text Sample 3.1 Geology textbook

The rocks of the Jura are fossiliferous limestones. They are famous for fossils of extinct sea creatures called ammonites that lived in coiled shells resembling the modern coiled nautilus. In the early nineteenth century, when European geologists started to arrange fossils in the sequence in which they had lived, fossils in the Jura were selected as the types characterizing certain ammonites, and rocks containing ammonites were selected as the examples of Jurassic sedimentary rocks, named after the Jura hills.

[T2K-SWAL Corpus]

Probably the most noticeable characteristic of this text is the numerous long words; many of these are technical terms that you might not understand if you aren't a geology major (e.g., *fossiliferous*, *ammonites*, *Jurassic*, *sedimentary*). Beyond that, you might have noticed that this short passage has only three sentences, and that the third sentence is very long (fifty words), and so long sentences might be a second linguistic characteristic of textbooks.

But how do you know whether these features are "typical" for this register or not? Having read a lot of textbooks and other types of writing, you can probably make guesses based on your experience. But can you be sure other analysts would agree with you? Have you simply neglected to notice other more characteristic features? And what if you study a register that you are not very familiar with?

Determining what is typical in a register is associated with three major methodological considerations in a register analysis:

1. the need for a comparative approach;
2. the need for quantitative analysis;
3. the need for a representative sample.

In the following subsections, we discuss these considerations.

3.2.1   The need for a comparative approach

If you noticed the long technical words in the Text Sample 3.1 and suspected that such vocabulary is typical of textbooks, you were using your general prior experience with all registers as a basis of comparison. That is, you knew that you had rarely (if ever) seen these words before, and so you were able to identify them as rare words with technical meanings. Given that there were several such words in this short paragraph, it was reasonable to hypothesize that the use of technical long words is a general linguistic characteristic of textbooks.

But what about other linguistic features? For example, how do you know if a fifty-word sentence is "long"? Based on your prior experience with popular registers like newspapers and novels, this sentence probably seems to be long. But perceptions of this type can be quite personal, and another analyst might come to a different conclusion. This problem becomes even more acute when you consider other more basic linguistic characteristics. For example, is there anything distinctive about the use of nouns or pronouns in Text Sample 3.1? Is this use typical of textbooks? How do you know? That is, how can you offer evidence to support such conclusions?

An empirical **comparative** approach is crucial for providing an adequate basis for answering questions of this type. That is, to identify the distinctive characteristics of the target register, it is necessary to empirically compare the language in one register to the language in other registers. So, for example, compare the language of Text Sample 3.1 to Text Sample 3.2 from a novel, with the main character "K" starting a train trip:

Text Sample 3.2 Fiction

They pulled away from the siding and began to move through the back yards of Worcester, where women hung out washing and children stood on fences to wave, the train gradually picking up speed. K watched the telegraph wires rise and fall, rise and fall.

They passed mile after mile of bare and neglected vineyards circled over by crows; then the engine began to labour as they entered the mountains. K shivered.

He could smell his own sweat through the musty odour of his clothes.

They came to a halt; a guard unlocked the doors; and the moment they stepped out the reason for stopping became clear. The train could go no further: the track ahead was covered in a mountain of rocks and red clay that had come pouring down the slope, tearing a wide gash in the hillside. Someone made a remark, and there was a burst of laughter.

[from J. M. Coetzee, *The Life and Times of Michael K* (Penguin, 1988)]

First of all, this comparison supports the perception that the words in the textbook sample are long and technical. In contrast, the longest words in the novel (e.g. *gradually*, *mountains*) are not technical vocabulary, and there are many other short, simple words (e.g. *fences, wave, rise, fall*). Furthermore, while the fiction sample has sentences of over thirty words, none of the sentences come near the textbook's fifty-word sentence length.

The two passages are also very different in their use of nouns and pronouns. The textbook passage uses the pronoun *they* twice – once referring to *the rocks of the Jura* and once to *fossils*. However, the nouns *rocks* and *fossils* are themselves used repeatedly. In the fiction passage, in contrast, the pronoun *they* is used repeatedly to refer (somewhat vaguely) to the train passengers, and *he* and the possessive determiner *his* refer back to K. In larger studies of textbooks and fiction, these differences are seen on a wide scale: textbooks have fewer pronouns and more repetition of nouns, while fiction has more use of pronouns.

Most people do not notice common language features such as nouns and pronouns; they are pervasive features that are so common that speakers normally do not even notice their existence. However, linguistic differences of this type are central to register analysis. Such features can occur to some extent in all registers, but they are especially frequent, and therefore "typical," in particular registers. To identify register features of this type, it is necessary to employ a comparative approach that incorporates quantitative techniques (covered in 3.3 below).

3.2.2   Register features, register markers, genre markers, style features

The linguistic analysis of a register is based on **register features**: words or grammatical characteristics that are (1) pervasive – distributed throughout a text from the register, and (2) frequent – occurring more commonly in the target register than in most comparison registers. It is important to note that these linguistic features are not restricted to the target register. For example, passive voice verbs (e.g., *was based on*) are register features of academic writing: they are found to some extent in every register, but they are much more common in academic writing than in most other registers.

In addition, a few registers have distinctive linguistic constructions that do not occur in other registers. These are called **register markers**. For example, the expressions "the count is three and two" (or "it's three and two") and "sliding into second" are distinctive to broadcasts of baseball games. The first describes the pitching situation, and the second describes a player trying to get to second base especially quickly. Because the expressions are so fixed, anyone who knows baseball will immediately recognize the register from these expressions. (See Ferguson 1983, described on page 290 below.) Sports broadcasts of other kinds will use different formulae. For example, broadcasts of American football games will include expressions like "it's third and four" – which means it is the third down with four yards to go for a first down. Although it is similar to baseball, it will never be said as "the count," nor will the first number ever be a cardinal number rather than an ordinal number (you will never hear "it's three and four" in a football game broadcast). Thus, even within sports broadcasts, the formulae that function as register markers are distinctive.

Similar to register features, register markers are common and pervasive in the target register. The difference between the two is that register markers are not normally found in other registers. In fact, if a speaker uses a register marker in another situation, they are usually invoking the associated register. For example, if your friend suddenly says "the count is 'o' and two" in the middle of a conversation, she is somehow invoking a baseball game setting, maybe figuratively saying that you have already made two mistakes and can only make one more before you are "out."

Genre markers should be distinguished from both register features and register markers. Genre markers are the distinctive expressions and devices that are used to structure a text from a particular genre. Genre markers are not pervasive; rather, they normally occur only one time in a text. As such, they are also not frequent. But they are distinctive, normally being formulaic and occurring in only a particular location of a text from a particular genre (often at the beginning or end). For example, business letters normally begin with a genre marker like *Dear Sir*. Religious speech events are often highly structured as genres. For example, a Christian prayer begins with a genre marker like *Heavenly Father*, and ends with the genre marker *Amen*. Legal trials are also highly structured as genres, with fixed genre markers being used at the beginning and end of different sub-genres (e.g., *All rise, Have you reached a verdict?, We find the defendant . . .*).

Other kinds of texts are less rigidly structured but still often have genre markers. For example, an e-mail message can begin with various genre markers, depending on the relationship between the sender and receiver (e.g., *Dear Dr. Conrad* or *Hi Susan*). Similarly, there are several genre markers that could be used to end an e-mail message – e.g., *Best wishes, Sincerely, Talk to you later*. (Since the purposes and other contextual factors of e-mail messages and letters are closely related, these genre markers may be shared by the two genres.) Classroom teaching sessions are also less strictly structured as genres, but they can begin with a genre marker like *Ok, let's get started* and end with a genre marker like *Ok, see you on Wednesday*.

Finally, **style features** are similar to register features in being pervasive – distributed throughout texts that represent the style, and frequent – occurring more commonly in the style than in most comparison styles. As described in Chapter 1, the main difference between the two is that register features are functional, while style features are preferred for aesthetic reasons (see 3.7 below).

The key differences among register features, register markers, genre markers, and style features parallel the differences among the register, genre, and style analytical perspectives described in Chapter 1. Table 3.1 summarizes the differences.

Table 3.1 *Defining characteristics of register features, register markers, genre markers, and style features*

Type of linguistic characteristic	Analyzed in complete texts or text samples?	Distribution of the characteristic	Frequency of characteristic in a particular variety compared to other varieties	Use of the characteristic in other varieties	Characteristic functional or arbitrary / conventional?
register feature	text samples (or complete texts if short)	pervasive	more frequent	occurs in other varieties, but less commonly	functional
register marker	text samples (or complete texts if short)	pervasive	more frequent	does not occur in other varieties	formulaic and arbitrary / conventional (usually not functional)
genre marker	complete texts	often occurs only once, at a particular location in the text	often occurs only once, so not very common	usually does not occur in other varieties (may occur in closely related genres)	formulaic and arbitrary / conventional (usually not functional)
style feature	text samples (or complete texts if short)	pervasive	more frequent	occurs in other varieties, but less commonly	preferred for aesthetic value (usually not functional)

3.2.3 The need for quantitative analysis

If all registers had register markers, identification of registers would be an easy task; you would simply look for those distinctive markers. Unfortunately, register markers are rare. Most registers cannot be identified by the occurrence of a distinctive register marker. Instead, analysts must rely on *register features*: features that are pervasive and frequent in a register.

Analysis of register features requires consideration of the extent to which a linguistic structure is used. Register features can be structures at any linguistic level: words, vocabulary distributions, grammatical classes, syntactic constructions, and so on. The key point about register features is that the focus is on the **extent** to which the structure is used. That is, the linguistic feature in question might occur to some extent in most (maybe all) registers, but it will be notably frequent in only some registers and comparatively rare in other registers. This distributional difference is what makes the word or grammatical structure a register feature.

As noted in Section 3.2.1, determining whether a feature is frequent or rare requires a comparative approach: An analyst cannot legitimately claim that a feature is frequent in a register until she has observed the less frequent use of that same feature in other registers. But this also requires a quantitative approach: An analyst cannot legitimately claim that a feature is more frequent in one register than another unless he has counted the occurrences of the feature in each register. Since most people notice unusual characteristics more than common ones, simply relying on what you notice in a register is not a reliable way to identify register features.

An additional advantage of using the comparative, quantitative approach is that it enables the investigation of linguistic features that might otherwise go unnoticed, as exemplified with nouns and pronouns in Section 3.2.1. As a further example with these word classes, compare Text Samples 3.3 and 3.4. (Text Sample 3.3 repeats the geology textbook excerpt from Text Sample 3.1, and Text Sample 3.4 is part of a graduate-level rhetoric class.) Nouns are underscored and *pronouns in bold italics*.

Text Sample 3.3 Geology textbook

The rocks of the Jura are fossiliferous limestones. *They* are famous for fossils of extinct sea creatures called ammonites that lived in coiled shells resembling the modern coiled nautilus. In the early nineteenth century, when European geologists started to arrange fossils in the sequence in which *they* had lived, fossils in the Jura were selected as the types characterizing certain ammonites, and rocks containing ammonites were selected as the examples of Jurassic sedimentary rocks, named after the Jura hills.

[T2K-SWAL Corpus]

Text Sample 3.4 Graduate-level rhetoric class

Instructor: Alright the um, the other two <u>things</u> that *I* would like to do today, as *I* mentioned, are talk about some <u>themes</u> that have emerged in the <u>class</u> – uh and *I* do want *you* to write a final <u>essay</u> um and *we* can negotiate *that* entirely, but basically what *I* want *you* to do is to connect up some <u>strands</u> – *You* connect up <u>readings</u> and other <u>things</u> that *we*'ve discussed with those <u>strands</u> – um, and *I* thought that *we* might just talk a little <u>bit</u> today about potential <u>things</u> that *you* found useful, or found interesting in what *we*'ve been doing. um and *I*'ve got some <u>possibilities</u> but *I*'d rather have *you* <u>guys</u> uh start us off with *these* – uh, relevant to *that* maybe, um also <u>projects</u> that *you* are working on and *I* would like to get a quick <u>read</u> before *we* leave so the <u>others</u> here will have a <u>feel</u> for where *you*'re headed. Cos *we* do have two new <u>projects</u> going.

[T2K-SWAL Corpus]

Few readers immediately think of the use of nouns as a register feature, because all texts use nouns to some extent. As these passages illustrate, however, there is a noteworthy difference in the distribution of nouns and pronouns in these two registers. Nouns are much more common than pronouns in the textbook passage (23 nouns versus only 2 pronouns). In contrast, pronouns are more common than nouns in the class teaching text (17 nouns versus 24 pronouns). This difference is even stronger than it seems, because the classroom teaching excerpt is much longer than the textbook excerpt; thus, there is less opportunity to use nouns in the shorter passage. We return to this topic in Section 3.3 below, which explains how to compute actual rates of occurrence for such distributions.

3.2.4   The need for a representative sample

Finally, to identify the "typical" linguistic characteristics of a register, it is necessary to have a representative sample of texts. To understand this issue, consider one extreme example of *not* having a representative sample: Imagine the results that you would get if you set out to analyze the register of fiction writing, but the only novel you had was *Watership Down*, a story which revolves around a group of rabbits. When you considered the vocabulary, you would find that *rabbit* and *rabbits* were very common, as well as a place in the story called the *Great Burrow*. But it would of course not be fair to generalize and say that fiction writing has a high frequency of the word *rabbit* and the phrase *great burrow*. And while grammatical features generally vary less across texts than vocabulary does, the point of this example applies for all register analyses: you cannot generalize to a whole register from one (or a small number) of texts.

A representative sample of texts will capture the range of linguistic variation that exists in the register, with a majority of the texts having the linguistic characteristics that are typical of the register. Several considerations are important. Diversity in writers/speakers is necessary so that the style of a single individual does not unduly affect the results (unless you are studying the literary style of an individual author). If you are analyzing a register that has more specialized sub-registers within it, texts from all the subregisters must be included. For example, if you were trying to characterize the language used in newspapers, you would need not only news reports, but also editorials, sports page articles, reviews, and so on. If a register is short (such as e-mail messages), you can include whole texts, but for registers with long texts (such as novels), it is acceptable to take samples from the whole texts. All samples must be long enough to provide reliable counts of features. In addition, if there are sections of longer texts that have different communicative purposes (such as research article sections), you must include samples from each of the sections.

Exactly how many different text samples are enough? And exactly how long do text samples need to be? Unfortunately, there are no clear-cut answers to those questions. Some linguistic features are extremely common and pervasive in texts, like nouns, verbs, or pronouns. For those features, you can compute reliable counts from a few texts that are relatively short (e.g., even 100-word text samples). Other features, like relative clauses, are less common; to reliably capture the distribution of those features in a register, you would need longer texts and a larger sample of texts. (See Biber 1990, 1993 for fuller discussion of these issues.)

Compiling a representative sample of texts from a register can be a difficult task. Analyzing numerous linguistic features in a large number of texts is an even more daunting task. In fact, a comprehensive register analysis is unfeasible without computer assistance. Many of the larger studies that you read about in this book have used the tools of *corpus linguistics* to study registers. This methodological approach involves using a principled collection of texts that are stored on a computer (the corpus) and using computer-assisted techniques for the analysis. Section 3.8 below provides a fuller introduction to this approach.

Given the importance of a representative sample for describing a register, you may wonder if there is any point in doing an analysis with a small number of texts. Our answer is yes, and in fact, you will be asked to do several small case studies throughout this book. In the last section of this chapter, we will have more to say about small-scale and large-scale register analyses as they are used in this book. The most important point to always remember, however, is not to overgeneralize from analyses that are based on few texts.

3.3   Conducting quantitative analyses

In essence, quantitative register analysis requires simply that the analyst count how many times a linguistic feature occurs in a text. However, the major difficulty has nothing to do with numbers. Rather, the difficult part is the prerequisite to counting: categorizing all the linguistic features consistently. That is, before counting, it is essential to consistently and accurately identify every occurrence of the linguistic feature in question.

3.3.1   Classifying linguistic features in a principled and consistent way

Principled, consistent classifying of language features can be a surprisingly difficult task. Most people learn grammar from textbooks that have easy, clear-cut examples. But natural texts, from different registers, almost always contain linguistic forms that do not fit tidily into the textbook categories. In such cases, the register analyst should note the construction, make a principled decision about how to categorize forms of this type, and then systematically apply that decision to all similar cases.

This is an important point. Register analysts sometimes spend countless hours agonizing over decisions about how to classify a construction until they find the "correct" answer, but then experience a new round of doubts when they encounter a slightly different occurrence of the linguistic construction. In many of these cases, there is no single "correct" analysis. Rather, you should simply decide on a reasonable analysis that you can justify, and then apply that analysis systematically to all other relevant cases. If the feature has been discussed in previous studies, you can refer to the decisions made in those studies as evidence for your analysis. However, the main considerations are that you document your analytical decisions, give reasonable justifications for them, and then consistently apply them to all texts that you analyze.

The two short text excerpts in Samples 3.3 and 3.4 above provide several interesting examples of cases where principled, consistent decisions must be made. One of these involves the analysis of words that occur before a head noun, functioning as a noun modifier, as in _big dog_. Some traditional grammar books classify all of these words as "adjective." The text samples above provide several clear examples of adjectives pre-modifying a head noun, as in:

> fossiliferous limestones, extinct creatures, a little bit

There are two main reasons why these words should be analyzed as adjectives:

1. they can occur before nouns and they can also occur after the verb _BE_ (e.g., _the rock is fossiliferous, they are extinct, it was little_)
2. they are "gradable" in meaning and can be modified by an adverb (e.g., _highly fossiliferous, completely extinct, very little_)

Other structures in these texts are similar in having a word pre-modifying a head noun, but that word does not behave like a normal adjective, for example _sea creatures_. These forms do not pass either of the two tests for "adjectives": they cannot occur after the verb _BE_ (e.g., *_the view was sea_), and they cannot be modified by a gradable adverb (e.g., *_very sea_). Instead, these words can occur as the head of a noun phrase, and they can be modified by adjectives, as in:

> the deep blue sea

Based on these factors, we would count *sea* as a noun, and make a distinction between adjectives modifying a head noun (<u>*extinct*</u> *creatures*) and nouns modifying a head noun (<u>*sea*</u> *creature*). Thus, in Sample 3.3, the words *sea* and *Jura* are underlined as <u>nouns</u>, even though they occur as pre-modifiers of a head noun.

A second example is the words *read* and *feel* in the phrases *get a quick <u>read</u>* and *have a <u>feel</u> for* . . . (at the end of Text Sample 3.4). Your initial reaction might be to think of words like *read* and *feel* as verbs, but many words in English can function as either a verb or as the head of a noun phrase (e.g., *need, desire, hope, use, work, play, run, walk, catch*). When they are the head of a noun phrase, these words can take a determiner (*a* or *the*) and be modified by adjectives but not adverbs; thus, we classify them as nouns rather than verbs in that grammatical context.

Working with transcribed speech often involves other complex methodological decisions. For example, suppose you had planned to compare sentence length in Text Samples 3.3 and 3.4. Punctuation has been added by the transcriber in Text Sample 3.4. The speaker used intonation and pauses, together with hesitation markers like *um* and *uh*, to break up the text into smaller units, so the transcriber added dashes, commas, and periods to reflect these pauses and falling tones. But it is not clear which of these correspond to "sentences" in a written text. For example, the first "–" in the excerpt might be interpreted as separating two sentences:

> themes that have emerged in the class – uh and I do want . . .

In contrast, other uses of "–" occur when the speaker is adding on a clarification phrase and clearly not beginning a new "sentence":

> but I'd rather have you guys uh start us off with these – uh, relevant to that maybe . . .

Similarly, a period is sometimes used to separate structures that would not be regarded as complete sentences in writing:

> . . . so the others here will have a feel for where you're headed. Cos we do have two new projects going.

In fact, the notion of "sentence" is quite controversial in speech. You would probably be unable to find a meaningful basis for comparing sentence length between these spoken and written texts. Faced with this methodological problem, you could instead change your focus from sentences (which are based on punctuation) to clauses (based on grammatical structure). You can make principled, justifiable, and consistent decisions for identifying clauses, and still explain important contrasts between the texts. For example, there is a notable difference in the way that clauses are connected in the two texts, as will be discussed in Section 3.5.

You might think that controversies about classifying linguistic features are unusual. In fact, you will be required to make operational decisions of this

Table 3.2 *Counts of nouns and pronouns in Text Samples 3.3 and 3.4*

	No. of nouns	No. of pronouns
Text Sample 3.3: textbook	23	2
Text Sample 3.4: lecture	17	24

type nearly every time you undertake a quantitative linguistic analysis of a text.

Two general points are especially helpful to keep in mind as you begin to conduct register analyses. First, there is no escaping grammatical analysis, even for a task as simple as counting the number of nouns in a text. For this reason, many register analysts find it useful to have a comprehensive reference grammar to aid their analysis. Second, there is sometimes no single, "correct" grammatical analysis. You need to consider the alternatives and decide on an analysis which seems the most appropriate and has the strongest justification in your eyes. The most important considerations are that you make an explicit decision, that you can justify that decision, and that you then apply that decision consistently to all relevant cases.

3.3.2   Computing rates of occurrence (frequency counts)

The main point of this section (3.3) is to introduce the methods for quantitative analysis, but we have not even mentioned the actual counts yet. This is because numeric counts are useless if they are not based on careful linguistic analysis. The quantitative approach forces the analyst to be explicit and comprehensive about the linguistic methods. When writing up the results of a register study, this requirement should always result in a separate "methods" section or appendix, which provides details of the linguistic analysis and how problematic cases were treated.

But we are now ready to move on to the counts themselves. Let us return to the distribution of nouns and pronouns in Text Samples 3.3 and 3.4. The frequency counts are shown in Table 3.2.

A quick look at these results suggests that nouns are more frequent in the textbook than in the lecture, although the difference does not seem to be large. In contrast, there is a large difference for pronouns, which are much more frequent in the lecture than the textbook.

However, there is a methodological problem with these counts, because the two texts are different in length. The textbook passage is much shorter than the lecture (79 words in the textbook passage versus 157 words in the lecture passage). As a result, a linguistic feature has more opportunity to occur in the lecture passage; there might be higher counts in the lecture passage just because it is longer.

Table 3.3 *Normed rates of occurrence for nouns and pronouns in Text Samples 3.3 and 3.4*

	nouns per 100 words	pronouns per 100 words
Text Sample 3.3: textbook	29.1	2.5
Text Sample 3.4: lecture	10.8	15.3

To compensate for this problem, it is important to compute "normed" rates of occurrence – that is, the rate at which a feature occurs in a fixed amount of text. There is a simple formula for such conversions:

Normed rate = (raw count / total word count) * the fixed amount of text

For example, the raw counts above can be converted to rates per 100 words of text. In the case of nouns in the textbook passage, the formula would work as follows:

Normed rate for nouns in the textbook, per 100 words of text:
(23 nouns / 79 words total) * 100 words = 29.1 nouns per 100 words

This same procedure can be followed to "normalize" the counts for all features:

Normed rate for nouns in the lecture, per 100 words of text:
(17 nouns / 157 words total) * 100 words = 10.8 nouns per 100 words

Normed rate for pronouns in the textbook, per 100 words of text:
(2 pronouns / 79 words total) * 100 words = 2.5 pronouns per 100 words

Normed rate for pronouns in the lecture, per 100 words of text:
(24 pronouns / 157 words total) * 100 words = 15.3 pronouns per 100 words

Basing quantitative comparisons on normed rates of occurrence allows consideration of the actual extent to which a feature is used, and these can often reveal patterns that are quite different from what an analyst might have believed if the analysis had been based on raw counts. For example, compare the patterns in Table 3.3 to the raw counts in Table 3.2. We earlier observed that nouns were almost equally common in the two passages, but it is apparent from the normed frequencies that nouns are considerably more common in the textbook passage than in the lecture – in fact, almost three times as common. In contrast, the apparent difference between the two texts in the use of pronouns has been reduced somewhat, although the normed frequencies still show a dramatic difference for this feature.

You might have noticed that we have so far glossed over yet another methodological decision: what to count as a "word" in determining the total word count of a text. This is especially an issue when comparing spoken and written texts. For example, should contractions (e.g., *we've*, *I'm*, *that's*) be counted as one word or two? Should filled pauses (*um*, *uh*) be counted as words or excluded from the total word count? In the present case, we decided to use orthographic words, and so treated contracted forms as a single word rather than two words. We decided to exclude filled pauses from the total word count since these forms have no lexical content or grammatical function. But similar to the discussion in the last section, the most important consideration for such decisions is that you are able to justify them, and that you apply them consistently across all texts in the analysis.

3.4   Deciding on the linguistic features to investigate

There is no easy way to decide ahead of time which linguistic features to investigate for a register analysis, because almost any linguistic feature can have functional associations and so be useful for distinguishing among some registers. What we offer in this section is a list of features that you might consider.

Consulting a corpus-based reference grammar is useful for deciding which features to study (as with the analysis of linguistic features). We are (for obvious reasons) most familiar with the *Longman Grammar of Spoken and Written English* (*LGSWE*; Biber *et al.* 1999). Like a traditional grammar, the *LGSWE* provides a full description of the grammatical categories and structures in English. However, the *LGSWE* also provides information about the use of grammatical features in four different registers (conversation, fiction, newspaper writing, and academic prose), based on empirical analyses. Understanding how grammatical features are used in these four general registers can help you decide which linguistic features to focus on in your studies of other registers. In addition, there have been numerous research studies that explore the use of different linguistic features in different registers (see Appendix A).

One approach would be to focus your register analysis on a particular aspect of language use and compare that aspect across registers. For example, you might focus on referring expressions, and count all the linguistic features that can be used to refer to entities (nouns, personal pronouns, demonstrative pronouns, etc.). You can then see how different registers use the linguistic resources that are available for referring to things.

Another more common approach is to include several different kinds of language features. The appendix at the end of this chapter, provides a list of linguistic characteristics that have been shown to be useful register features in previous studies. This is by no means an exhaustive list, but it should give you some ideas for features to consider in your own register analyses.

How many features you analyze will depend on practical considerations and the focus of your study. If you are counting features by hand, you will not be able to include as many as if you have computer programs to assist you with the counting. Furthermore, if you are counting by hand, it is extremely time-consuming to count a feature that occurs very frequently, or a large number of features in a large number of texts. When our students do small-scale register analyses we generally ask them to count ten to fifteen features in a few texts. In comparison, you will read in later chapters about corpus-based analyses that used over 100 linguistic features in the analysis of hundreds of texts.

3.5   Functional interpretations

The final step in a register analysis – the functional interpretation – moves from description to an account of **why** these patterns exist. The descriptive facts on both sides – situational and linguistic – will already be clearly documented. On the one side, you will have described distinctive situational characteristics of the target register in comparison to other registers. And on the other side, you will have described distinctive linguistic characteristics. The task now is to match the two up, explaining why particular linguistic characteristics are associated with situational characteristics. This step is interpretive; you must explain why these linguistic features are especially common in this situational context, illustrating your interpretations with convincing examples.

To take a specific example, consider again the textbook and classroom teaching texts discussed earlier in this chapter. From a situational perspective, these two registers differ in several key respects, which are summarized in Table 3.4.

Table 3.5 provides a quantitative comparison for several linguistic features for these two text samples. (Of course, it would not be appropriate to generalize to the registers from these single texts. However, we have selected these particular texts because they illustrate the linguistic patterns found in previous large-scale analyses of these registers.)

By relating the information in Tables 3.4 and 3.5, it is possible to begin to formulate functional explanations for the linguistic differences. For example, pronouns have several specific functions, but they all generally refer to something that the listener is already familiar with. In many cases, pronouns refer to things that are present in the communication situation: oneself, the listener, other people or objects. Such people and objects exist in the situational context for classroom teaching, but not for a textbook (or at least, the author and reader would not be seeing the same objects). Although the pronouns *you*, *I*, and *we* can be used in textbooks to refer to the author and the reader, the higher frequency in the classroom reflects the use of these pronouns in referring to interactions in the classroom, for example:

> **I** thought that **we** might just talk a little bit today about potential things that **you** found useful, or found interesting in what **we**'ve been doing . . . .

In other cases, speakers in classroom teaching use pronouns because they assume that the listeners will know what they are referring to, comforted by the fact that

Table 3.4 *Key situational differences between textbooks and classroom teaching*

	Textbook	Classroom teaching
Participants	• an author addressing an un-enumerated number of readers	• an instructor addressing relatively few students
Relations among participants	• no interaction • author has more knowledge • all participants have some specialist knowledge • no personal relations	• interaction is possible • instructor has more knowledge • all participants have some specialist knowledge • instructor knows students
Channel	• written	• spoken
Production circumstances	• text has been carefully planned, revised and edited	• text has been planned but it cannot be revised or edited
Setting	• unknown	• speakers and addressees are physically together in a classroom
Communicative purposes	• convey information • explain concepts or methods	• convey information • explain concepts or methods • convey personal attitudes • directive – tell students what they should do

Table 3.5 *Normed rates of occurrence (per 100 words) for selected linguistic features in Text Samples 3.3 and 3.4*

Linguistic feature	Text 3.3: textbook	Text 3.4: lecture
pronouns	2.5	15.3
nouns	29.1	10.8
mental / desire verbs (e.g., *feel, want, believe*)	0.0	4.5
clause-initial *and/but*	1.3	4.5
finite relative clauses	2.5	3.2
nonfinite relative clauses	6.3	0.0

listeners can always ask for clarification. For example, the instructor's use of *that* in the discussion of the final essay in Text Sample 3.4 may not be entirely clear:

> – uh and I do want you to write a final essay um and we can negotiate **that** entirely, but basically what I want you to do is to connect up some strands . . .

Is the essay itself negotiable? Or how to connect strands? Or which strands to connect? If this is not clear for students, they can ask. In contrast, there is no opportunity to ask for clarification when reading a textbook, so authors use more full noun phrases, in an attempt to be unambiguously clear.

We noted above that classroom teachers have several purposes: informational (explaining concepts), personal (conveying their own opinions and attitudes), and directive (telling students what they should do). This characteristic is reflected in the frequent use of mental and desire verbs in classroom teaching. These verbs are typically used together with first or second person pronouns, expressing the instructor's personal attitudes and desires, for example:

> . . . the other two things that **I would like** to do today . . .
> . . . what **I want** you to do is . . .
> . . . **I thought** that we might just talk a little bit today about . . .

These personal desires serve as directives (e.g., "what I want you to do") and as organizers for the content of the day (e.g., to introduce topics). But because the interaction takes place in a face-to-face, interactive setting, the forms that the instructor uses incorporates communicating his personal attitudes. Because textbooks are more exclusively focused on conveying information, these constructions rarely occur.

As noted in Chapter 2, conveying personal stance was actually a situational characteristic of classroom teaching that we and our fellow researchers in a large study did **not** fully appreciate when we first did the situational analysis. Initially, we identified "conveying information" as the major communicative purpose of classroom teaching, with "conveying personal attitudes" as a much less important, secondary purpose. We subsequently carried out a linguistic analysis of a large corpus of classroom teaching, including hundreds of texts. While doing this linguistic analysis, we discovered that teachers make extensive use of lexical and grammatical devices to express their own "stance": personal attitudes, opinions, and assessments of certainty. In fact, these devices were used to essentially the same extent as in face-to-face conversation. In this case, the linguistic analysis forced us to reconsider our situational analysis, recognizing that the expression of personal stance is equally important to informational content for classroom instructors, and is in fact often intertwined with conveying content or giving instructions.

This important methodological point was mentioned in Chapter 2, but it is worth reemphasizing. It is normal to revise your situational analysis during the process of carrying out the linguistic analysis. Careful reading of texts from the register (required for the linguistic analysis), and discovering surprising linguistic patterns, can cause you to reevaluate your situational analysis. For speakers and writers, the situational context is primary – defining the register; but for the register analyst, the situational description does not necessarily need to be considered final before undertaking the linguistic description.

Returning to the functional interpretations of Table 3.5, it is also important to note that there are several features that relate to the different way in which clauses are constructed and connected in the two texts. Clauses are relatively short in classroom teaching, and they have a looser syntactic structure. One measure of this is the high frequency of clause-initial *and/but*, often co-occurring with fillers such as *uh* and *um*, for example:

> **uh and** I do want you to write a final essay / **um and** we can negotiate that entirely, / **but** basically what I want you to do is . . .

In contrast, the textbook has only one clause connector, the coordinator *and* connecting two clauses:

> fossils in the Jura were selected as the types characterizing certain ammonites, **and** rocks containing ammonites were selected . . .

The textbook has one extremely long sentence, rather than a series of short clauses, and uses the logical progression of ideas rather than coordinators to connect clauses and sentences.

These linguistic differences can be related to the differing production circumstances of these two registers. Classroom teaching is produced in real time, so the instructor does not have time to construct complex structures, instead connecting ideas and clauses with simple forms. In many cases, as in the example above, it makes more sense to describe the classroom discourse as a string of utterances, joined with the connectors. In contrast, textbook writers have extensive time to construct long, complicated sentences.

The opportunity for careful production in writing also results in other more complex structures, such as complex noun phrases. The frequent use of past and present participial clauses is one reflection of this factor. These clauses are used to pack more information into noun phrases with fewer words than in finite relative clauses, as in:

> sea creatures <u>called ammonites</u>
> coiled shells <u>resembling the modern coiled nautilus</u>
> the types <u>characterizing certain ammonites</u>
> rocks <u>containing ammonites</u>
> examples of Jurassic sedimentary rocks, <u>named after the Jura hills</u>

These are complex syntactic constructions, difficult to produce in real-time situations, but well suited to the focused informational purposes of textbooks. Thus, these features are much more common in textbooks than classroom teaching.

For many students, making functional interpretations is the most difficult part of a register analysis. There is no trick to knowing the best interpretations for the registers you are studying, although the more knowledge you have from previous studies, the easier it usually is to interpret functions in new texts. Chapters 4–6 will provide numerous examples of relationships between linguistic forms and functions. Table 3.6 lists several specific situational characteristics

Table 3.6 *Specific situational characteristics that are associated functionally with particular linguistic features*

Situational characteristics	Selected linguistic features associated functionally with the situational characteristic
Interactivity	questions, 1st and 2nd person pronouns
Personal stance	possibility adverbs, personal pronoun + mental or desire verbs (e.g. *I think that...*)
Referring to the time and place of communication	*here, there, yesterday, last week,* demonstrative pronouns
Referring to shared personal knowledge	pronouns, first names of friends, vague references (e.g., *thing*)
Referring to shared expert/professional knowledge	technical words and phrases, references to published research studies
General communicative purpose	
Narrative	past tense verbs, place and time adverbs, 3rd person pronouns
Description	adjectives, adverbs, stative verbs (e.g., *be, seem, appear, look*)
Directive	imperatives, obligation modals (e.g. *should, have to*), desire verbs with *you* (e.g. *I want you to...*)
Procedural ("how to")	ordinal numerals (e.g. *first, second*), imperatives
Explanatory / expository	nouns, relative clauses, attributive adjectives
Presentation of information	
Elaborating information	adverbial clauses, relative clauses
Condensing information	noun-noun sequences, prepositional phrases (instead of subordinate clauses), past and present participial clauses (instead of full relative clauses)
Marking logical relations	linking adverbials (e.g. *for example, however, thus*), finite adverbial clauses (e.g. *because, if, although*)
Production circumstances	
Real time	vague nouns (e.g., *thing*), hedges (e.g., *sort of*), pronouns, contractions, ellipsis, repairs, incomplete utterances
Careful production and revision	complex noun phrases, complete sentences

that are associated functionally with particular linguistic features. These functional associations have been described in several previous research studies (see the annotated bibliography in Appendix A). This information, along with any background you have from other functional analyses you have read, should provide you with a starting point for undertaking the functional interpretations. Most importantly, however, consider your own data. Interpret the function of the linguistic features in the texts that you are studying, and relate them to the situational characteristics that you found to be important in the registers, providing illustrative examples to support your interpretation.

In sum, we have shown in this section how the functional interpretation can proceed in large part inductively: Once the situational and linguistic analyses are completed, the functional analysis involves mostly matching up characteristics of the two. It is also important to realize that several linguistic features will usually have a common functional interpretation. Similarly, several different situational characteristics can be associated with a single linguistic characteristic. Do not expect a one-to-one correspondence between one linguistic feature and one situational characteristic.

Finally, concerning the final written report of a register analysis, there is an additional useful point to keep in mind. It is unlikely that you will discuss *all* of the situational characteristics and linguistic features that you analyzed. Space constraints, as well as the attention span of your audience, may dictate that you drop discussion of some points that are less interesting. As with all writing, we suggest that you cover the largest and most important points first, and then cover more peripheral points as appropriate for your context.

3.6   Textual conventions: the genre perspective

As described in Chapter 1 and Section 3.2.2, the genre perspective on textual variation differs from the register perspective by its focus on complete texts and the textual conventions that are expected in the texts of a given genre. While register features are frequent and pervasive in texts, textual conventions associated with the genre perspective are not pervasive. In fact, they often occur only once in a text, and thus it is necessary to consider complete texts to identify their existence.

Although the register and genre perspectives analyze different types of language features, it is often useful to add an analysis of genre features when undertaking a register analysis, in order to describe the text variety more fully. Chapter 1 presented the example of business letters, which usually begin with a series of textual conventions: the date, name and address of the recipient, and then an opening salutation (*Dear xx*). These letters also end with a politeness expression (e.g., *sincerely* or *best wishes*) followed by the name and signature of the writer. These features are not pervasive linguistic features – that is, they are not register features. However, they are clear signals of the type of text and they frame the main body of the letter. For a thorough analysis of business letters, then, it makes no sense to ignore these language features. Rather, business letters are a well-defined genre, with distinctive conventional genre markers, and it is also a text variety that can be described from a register perspective. Neither perspective is "correct." Rather, a complete analysis should cover both, while still clearly differentiating between language characteristics that are genre markers and those that are register features.

Usually the genre perspective is more easily applied to written varieties than spoken varieties, with textual conventions often clearly identifiable at the beginning and end of written texts. Newspaper articles, for example, begin with textual conventions: a headline in large print, sometimes followed by a sub-heading in smaller print, and then a by-line (optional) and the location of the reporter on the following line. In some cases, textual conventions are found internally in a text from a genre, as well as at the beginning and ends. For example, Chapter 5 discusses how scientific research articles are among the most conventionalized kind of text, with conventional textual components that occur in a fixed order (e.g., title and author, abstract, introduction, methods, results, discussion, bibliography).

Some spoken varieties can also be approached from a genre perspective. For example, specific types of prayers and sermons can be analyzed as complete texts, and within a particular religious tradition they often have fixed conventions for the beginnings and endings. Television news broadcasts also often have particular conventions that are used at the beginning and end, and also to structure the transitions from one story to the next. Even telephone conversations have some generic conventions. For example, phone calls to a friend (in English) generally begin with a self-introduction from the caller (*hi, this is Sally*) and end with some kind of leave taking (*ok, bye* or *ok, talk to you later*).

However, many varieties are less easily described from a genre perspective. Even among some written texts, the role of textual conventions may not be particularly important for distinguishing between varieties. For instance, almost all English-language books share the conventions of beginning with a title page and table of contents, and almost all academic books conclude with an index and bibliography. But beyond that, there are not many distinctive textual conventions that distinguish among the different types of books (fictional, popular non-fictional, academic, etc.).

Many spoken varieties are even less easily described with respect to textual conventions. Everyday conversation is probably the most extreme example. Stereotypically, speakers think of conversations as beginning with conventional greetings (*Hi Sam, How are you doing?*) and ending with a leave-taking (*see you later*). But surprisingly, many everyday conversations do not employ even these minimal conventions. This is especially the case for conversations that we have with people that we see several times a day. In fact, it is often difficult to determine where a conversation begins or ends, especially when participants enter and leave at different times. Conversation is fluid in this way, consisting of interactions with multiple participants, making it very difficult to even determine what constitutes a complete text.

In your own analyses of texts, you will need to decide if including some analysis of genre markers is useful, depending on whether the variety can be described from a genre perspective and if you have access to complete texts. If included, genre markers are typically identified in one of two ways. Simply by looking at several complete texts, you are likely to see consistent textual conventions. If you are already familiar with the variety, you may already have expectations about where they will occur and the form they will take (though you should always check your expectations against real texts). The other way that genre markers may become apparent is when you are analyzing linguistic features for a register analysis. As with the example of "dear" in letters, you may find that a language feature is not pervasive throughout the texts, but rather occurs at a particular point in all of the texts. In your analysis you would then identify that language feature as a genre marker, rather than a register feature.

After you identify genre markers, you must also consider whether they are purely conventional or functional. Some text conventions serve important functions. For example, headlines in newspaper stories facilitate reading comprehension, especially for readers who skim the stories in a newspaper. Other textual conventions are arbitrary – purely conventional – representing the generally accepted way of structuring a text from a particular genre, but not serving particular functions. However, many genre markers incorporate both function and convention. For example, parenthetical references in academic texts are functional, providing support for an author's claim and telling readers where to find that support, but the exact form of the references – whether based on the American Psychological Association or Modern Language Association or another system – is purely conventional.[1]

3.7   Pervasive linguistic features that are not directly functional: the style perspective

Finally, the style perspective incorporates the same kind of linguistic analysis as the register perspective: a relatively comprehensive analysis of core lexical and grammatical features (see Appendix to this chapter), employing quantitative techniques to describe the extent to which a feature is used. However, the basis of comparison is different from the register and genre perspectives.

---

[1] The sub-discipline of "contrastive rhetoric" focuses on the differing ways in which the "same" genre is realized in different languages/cultures (see Connor, Nagelhout, and Rozycki, 2008). For example, many cultures have genres like letters, newspaper stories, and academic articles, which appear to be comparable from a casual inspection. However, closer analysis shows that these texts have different genre conventions in different cultures, such as different rhetorical organizations or different conventions used for openings and closings.

That is, the style perspective is usually used to compare texts with**in** a single genre/register, such as comparing novels written by different authors or written in different historical periods. In this case, linguistic differences are not associated functionally with the situational context, because all of these texts are produced in similar situations. Rather, the interpretation of linguistic differences has to do with the literary or aesthetic effects created by the different styles.

For example, there are several major stylistic parameters that distinguish among the different types of novels. An author can choose to narrate a story from the first person perspective of one of the characters, or from a third person perspective (usually a person who is not a character in the story but able to observe every-thing that occurs). Sometimes a story is told mostly through prose description of events and places; in other cases, a story is told mostly through the dialogue of the main characters. Sometimes a third person narrator actually tells us what characters are thinking and feeling; in other cases, a third person narrator can only observe physical actions and events, like any normal person would be able to do. Choices like these have important implications for the typical linguistic features used in a text, and those features in turn have an important influence on the aesthetic effect that the text has on readers. We discuss such patterns in much more detail in Chapters 5 and 6. With respect to methodological consid-erations, though, the important point is that the linguistic analyses undertaken from the style perspective are essentially the same, but the interpretations involve literary/aesthetic considerations rather than direct functional associations to the situational context.

3.8   Embedded registers and genres

In most cases, it is safe to think of the relationship between situation and linguistic form as one-directional: register is determined by the situation, and speakers use language forms that functionally match the requirements of that situation. However, writers and speakers can also embed one register within another or create a register by deliberately violating the expectations of a situation. For example, the register of conversation is often embedded within newspaper reporting or novels, because authors quote people's speech.

Genres can also be embedded in a text from a different genre. For example, a novel can contain a letter. A conversation can contain a joke or a personal narrative. As noted in Section 2.2.1 above, methods sections are embedded in a scientific research article. To analyze cases like these, it is necessary to consider the embedded unit as a separate but complete text embedded in a larger text. Thus, these embedded texts – a letter, joke, personal narrative, or methods section – are complete and have well-defined genre markers, such as conventional beginnings or endings, or a conventional rhetorical organization. At the same time, the larger text can often be analyzed as an instance of a different genre, with its own conventional genre markers.

A different kind of embedding occurs with register shifts, usually in conversation, when a speaker switches to a different linguistic register, in a sense creating a new situation by evoking the situational characteristics of the adopted register. This is usually done for humorous effect. In this case, the linguistic form is primary. That is, the linguistic form is deliberately chosen because it is associated with a particular situational context other than the actual context of the interaction. In this way, the language evokes some aspect of that other situational context.

For example, in the following interaction between two students, Adam switches to the linguistic register of classroom teaching, imitating the language used by his instructor during a lecture:

> Roger: You know it was like I was going yeah hey that's really too much, you know.
> Adam: Yeah – [switching to a deeper tone of voice] in a sense it doesn't change the facts of the matter, which is the point you're getting at, which is quite correct. On the other hand, if I think I'm prepped in some deterministic mechanism, I have in effect degraded the notion of aliveness.
> Roger: Yeah, what's that supposed to mean?

In these cases, the physical situation remains the same, but the speaker (or writer) switches to language that has been borrowed from some other situation and linguistic register. Such cases can provide interesting register analyses in themselves, to describe the communicative effects of these embedded or created registers.

3.9   A short introduction to corpus linguistics

We have noted several times in this chapter how register analyses are often conducted using the methodologies of "corpus linguistics." There are several introductory textbooks that introduce this subfield of linguistics (e.g., Biber, Conrad, and Reppen, 1998; McEnery, Xiao, and Tono 2006). You will find these introductions very useful if you choose to pursue more advanced register studies.

According to Biber, Conrad, and Reppen (1998: 4), the essential characteristics of corpus-based analysis are:

- it is empirical, analyzing the actual patterns of use in natural texts;
- it utilizes a large and principled collection of natural texts, known as a "corpus," as the basis for analysis;

- it makes extensive use of computers for analysis, using both automatic and interactive techniques;
- it depends on both quantitative and qualitative analytical techniques.

Several of the advantages of the corpus-based approach come from the use of computers. Computers make it possible to identify and analyze complex patterns of language use, based on consideration of a much larger collection of texts than could be dealt with by hand. Furthermore, computers provide consistent, reliable analyses – they do not change their mind or become tired during a register analysis. Taken together, these characteristics result in a scope and reliability of analysis not otherwise possible.

However, it is important to emphasize that the quantitative and computational aspects of corpus analysis do not lessen the need for functional interpretations in register studies. Rather, corpus-based analyses must go beyond simple counts of linguistic features. It is essential to include qualitative, functional interpretations of the quantitative patterns discovered in a corpus-based register analysis. In this regard, all register studies follow the same major methodological steps, whether they are corpus-based or not.

3.10   Small-scale versus large-scale register analyses

The analytical steps described in Chapters 2 and 3 are at the heart of all register analyses. The same basic analytical steps are required no matter how large or small a study is: describing situational characteristics, counting linguistic features, interpreting the functional associations between the two, and comparing two or more registers to identify what makes them distinctive.

A small-scale study is based on analysis of relatively few texts from a register, and the linguistic analyses are typically carried out without the aid of computers. Most of the activities at the end of each chapter are designed as small-scale studies. These are investigations that you will be able to complete using only the analytical techniques presented in this book.

In contrast, a large-scale, comprehensive register analysis uses the techniques of corpus linguistics. The analysis will be conducted with a principled corpus of texts designed to represent the registers, with a large number of different texts and lengthy samples that reliably capture both diversity and similarities among texts in the registers (see Section 3.3.2). Often, a large number of linguistic features will be included in the analysis, and in most cases more than two registers will be compared.

In addition, large-scale register analyses often describe the patterns of linguistic variation using statistical techniques. For example, the description of typical linguistic features will focus on the ***central tendencies*** of each register (usually reporting mean scores). A comprehensive analysis will also compare the diversity of features within the registers, describing how tightly texts within the register conform to the central tendency. This aspect of the discussion will most likely present *standard deviations* (a measure of how tightly clustered or loosely scattered scores are around the mean). Comparisons of the distribution of features in two or more registers may report statistics which show that the differences are unlikely to be due to chance. Although we do not cover the use of statistical analysis for register studies in the present book, you will want to develop proficiency in these techniques if you choose to pursue large-scale register studies later on.

Both small-scale and large-scale register analyses are useful. In the following chapters of this book, you will be exposed to register analysis of both types. You will read some small-scale case studies, following the procedures for the register analysis step by step (for example, in the case studies of electronic registers in Chapter 7). But you will also read about the findings from several large-scale register studies (e.g., in Chapter 8).

In many places in this book, we describe the characteristics of a register while referring to a single text or a small number of texts. In these cases, we have chosen example texts that are typical for the register based on the findings of previous large-scale register analyses. Similarly, we have chosen the particular texts for the chapter activities so that they are representative of their registers, again based on our knowledge of previous large-scale analyses of these registers.

However, you should be cautious about generalizations from small-scale analyses, including the chapter activities. When you base a register description on a small number of texts and short samples, it is important to remember that the results are preliminary. Additional research, based on a larger, more representative corpus of texts from the register, will provide greater confidence in the extent to which a linguistic description is generally accurate.

Chapter 3 activities

Reflection and review

1. Think of at least one register marker and one genre marker that have not been named in this book. Tell the markers to at least two other people, to check if they accurately identify the varieties you expect.

2. Table 3.7 presents raw counts for three linguistic features in two texts. Convert the raw counts to normed counts (per 1,000 words) and make an equivalent table for the

Table 3.7 *Raw counts of features in two registers*

	Register 1 conversation sample	Register 2 academic prose sample
Total words in sample	5580	8750
Nouns	1060	2538
Pronouns	837	184
Adjectives	123	744

normed counts (including a title). Compare with another student; your answers should be the same.

3. In Section 3.3.1 we discuss the importance of principled linguistic analysis as the basis for quantitative register descriptions. One of the examples used in that section was the analysis of nouns in Text Samples 3.3 and 3.4.

   Look at these two text samples again and try to document the grammatical decisions that we made for analyzing "pronouns." What principles were followed? What justifications can you offer for the decisions? Write out your explanation as you would for a methods sections in a study.

4. Pretend you have been given a grant to design a large, principled corpus to study register variation in the writing of university students. Outline an initial design for the corpus, seeking to capture subregisters and variation in situational characteristics. Then outline how you will gather information to finalize your design. (That is, what other information do you need and how could you get that information in order to make sure you have designed a representative corpus?)

Analysis practice

[Note: All activity texts are contained in Appendix B]
5. Using activity texts 5 and 15 (a newspaper report and a personal letter), calculate the raw count for pronouns in each sample. What principles will you follow in identifying the pronouns? Specifically, do you need to modify the defining criteria used for activity no. 3 above? Write out your explanation as you would for a methods section in a study.

6. Figures 3.1 and 3.2 display counts for five features from a large corpus-based study of newspapers and fiction writing (Biber *et al.* 1999). Propose a functional interpretation of these findings, explaining how the linguistic differences correspond to situational characteristics. Use the newspaper and contemporary fiction activity texts in Appendix B, or other typical texts from these registers that you have on hand, to study how these features are functioning and to get examples to illustrate your interpretations.

Project ideas

7. Find two texts that are written or spoken by the same person but represent different registers/genres. For example, you can use a popular science text and a professional research article written by Stephen J. Gould, or a speech and an autobiographical essay by Barak Obama. Follow all the steps of a complete register/genre analysis. First, analyze the situational characteristics of the text variety. For the register perspective, make principled counts of eight to ten linguistic features in the texts (with documentation of the principles that you followed). Interpret your findings in functional terms, discussing aspects of the register's situational differences that account for the linguistic differences that you find. For the genre perspective, identify distinctive genre markers in the different texts and discuss the extent to which those markers represent the normal conventions of the respective genres.

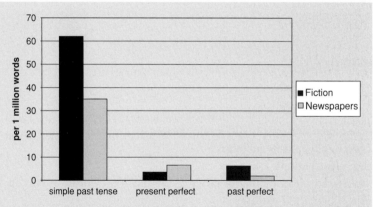

Figure 3.1 *Frequency of verb tense and verb aspect features in newspapers and fiction (normed per million words). (Based on findings in Biber* et al. *1999: chapter 6)*

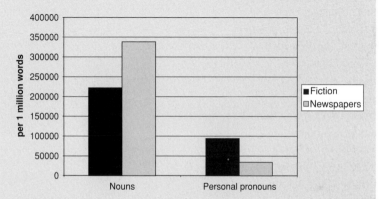

Figure 3.2 *Frequency of nouns and personal pronouns in newspapers versus fiction (normed per million words). (Based on findings in Biber* et al. *1999: chapter 4)*

8. Carry out a small-scale register comparison of newspaper reports and novels, based on analysis of activity texts 1–6 (three contemporary novel samples and three newspaper reports). Include the five features given in activity 6, plus seven to ten additional features that you count in the samples. Follow all the steps for a complete register analysis, including analyzing situational characteristics, making principled counts (with documentation of your decisions), and making functional interpretations. Remember to make counts for each text, norm them to a rate per 100 words of text, and then compute average scores for each of the registers.

The following features are some possibilities for inclusion in your analysis: average paragraph length, progressive aspect verbs, adjectives, nouns as nominal pre-modifiers, relative clauses, prepositional phrases as adverbials versus noun modifiers, passive verb phrases (finite versus nonfinite).

Appendix to Chapter 3
Linguistic features that might be investigated in
a register analysis

1. Vocabulary features
   - the use of a specific multi-functional word (e.g., *have, make*)
   - lists of the common words in different registers
   - specialized words (e.g., legal terms)
   - vocabulary distributions
     - type/token ratio (the number of different words / total words, usually in the first 100 or 1000 words)
     - average word length
     - number of once-occurring words
2. Content word classes
   - nouns (e.g., *salary, institution*)
   - verbs (e.g., *emerge, eat*)
   - adjectives (e.g., *external, clear*)
   - adverbs (e.g., *quickly, fast*)
3. Function word classes
   - determiners
     - articles (*a, the*)
     - demonstratives (*this, that, these, those*)
   - pronouns (see 6 below)
   - pro-verb *do*
   - modal verbs (e.g., *might, could, can, will*)
   - prepositions (see 8 below)
   - coordinators (e.g., *and, or, but*)
   - discourse markers (e.g., *well, ok, alright*)
   - vocatives and attention-getters (e.g., *hey, Karen, honey*)
   - expletives (e.g., *damn*)
4. Derived words
   - nominalizations (e.g., *realization, development*)
   - derived verbs (e.g., *dislike, simplify, itemize*)
   - derived adjectives (e.g., *functional, attractive*)
   - derived adverbs (e.g., *repeatedly, happily*)
   - "conversion" (e.g., *walk → a walk*)
5. Verb features
   - verb valencies (intransitive, ditransitive, etc.)
   - copular verbs (e.g., *be, become, get* – as in *"I got tired."*)
   - phrasal verbs (e.g., *look out, turn off*)
   - tense (present, past)

- aspect
  - simple (e.g., *he walks*)
  - progressive (e.g., *he is walking*)
  - perfect (e.g., *he has walked*)
- voice
  - active (e.g., *She used a computer.*)
  - passive
    - agentless passive (e.g., *A computer was used for the analysis.*)
    - *by*-passive (e.g., *A computer was used by the research team for the analysis.*)
- modal verb classes
  - possibility (*can, could, might, may*)
  - necessity (*must, should*)
  - predictive (*will, would, shall*)
  - semi-modal verbs (e.g., *have to, ought to*)
- semantic classes of verbs
  - activity (e.g., *play, meet, put, show, leave*)
  - communication (e.g., *say, tell, report, claim*)
  - mental (e.g., *think, guess, expect*)
  - desire (e.g., *want, wish, need*)
- action verbs with inanimate subjects (e.g., *the study demonstrates*)

6. Pronoun features
- person
  - 1st: *I, we, me, us*
  - 2nd: *you*
  - 3rd: *he, she, they, him, her, them*
- pronoun *it*
- demonstrative pronouns (*this, that, these, those*)
- indefinite pronouns (e.g., *anybody, nothing*)

7. Reduced forms and dispreferred structures
- contractions (e.g., *I'm, they'll, can't*)
- complementizer *that* deletion (e.g., *I think [0] he went*)
- relative pronoun deletion (e.g., *The dog [0] I saw at the park.*)
- other kinds of ellipsis and incomplete sentences (e.g., *[0] want more?*)
- stranded prepositions (e.g., *the place I was thinking of*)

8. Prepositional phrases
- *of*-phrases versus other prepositions (e.g., *of, to, for, with*)
- functioning as adverbial (e.g., *They stayed in town after the storm*)
- functioning as noun modifier (e.g., *The Post Office in town is new.*)

9. Coordination
- independent clause coordination (e.g., *It was my birthday and I was excited.*)
- phrasal coordination (e.g., *The paper is interesting and innovative.*)

10. Main clause type
   - declarative
   - interrogative (questions)
     - *yes-no* questions (e.g., *Did you shut the door?*)
     - *WH*-Questions (e.g., *Who shut the door?*)
     - tag questions (e.g., *You shut the door, didn't you?*)
   - imperative (e.g., *Shut the door.*)
   - average clause (or "sentence") length
11. Noun phrases
   - semantic category of noun
     - animate noun (e.g., *teacher, child, person*)
     - cognitive noun (e.g., *fact, knowledge*)
     - concrete noun (e.g., *rain, dirt, house*)
     - group/institution noun (e.g., *committee, congress*)
     - process nouns (e.g., *application, meeting*)
   - determiner / article use:
     - definite articles
     - indefinite articles
     - "zero" articles
     - demonstrative determiners
   - nominal pre-modifiers
     - attributive adjectives (e.g., *big house*)
     - participles (e.g., *flashing lights*)
     - nouns (e.g., *airport security measures*)
   - nominal post-modifiers
     - restrictive versus non-restrictive relative clauses
     - *that* relative clauses (e.g., *people that we know*)
     - WH relative clauses (e.g., *the guy who started the fire*)
     - past participial clause (e.g., *the results summarized below*)
     - present participial clause (e.g., *a society consisting of educated people*)
     - *to* relative clauses (e.g., *the person to see*)
     - prepositional phrases (e.g., *a school for disabled children*)
     - appositive noun phrases (e.g., *Mark Olive, appeals attorney for Tafero*)
     - multiple post-modifiers
   - gender reference (*chairperson* vs. *chairman*)
     - dual gender reference (*he or she*)
   - noun complement clauses
     - *that*-clauses (e.g., *the fact that. . .*)
     - *to*-clauses (e.g., *the proposal to. . .*)
     - *of + ing*-clause (e.g., *risk of failing. . .*)
     - *of + WH*-clause (e.g., *the problem of how to. . .*)

12. Adverbials
- major type
  - circumstance (e.g., *quickly, in the afternoon*)
  - stance (e.g., *possibly, unfortunately*)
  - linking (e.g., *however, so*)
- syntactic realization
  - single adverb (e.g., *obviously*)
  - prepositional phrase (e.g., *in the park*)
  - finite clause (e.g., *because he couldn't come*)
  - non-finite clause (e.g., *to begin the story*)
- syntactic position
  - initial, medial, final
- circumstance adverbial types
  - place (e.g., *over there, to the store*)
  - time (e.g., *then, after dinner*)
  - manner (e.g., *quickly*)
  - extent/degree (e.g., *just, only*)
  - etc.
- stance adverbial types
  - doubt (e.g., *maybe, possibly*)
  - certainty (e.g., *obviously, of course, certainly*)
  - source of knowledge (e.g., *according to. . .*)
  - attitudes (e.g., *surprisingly, importantly*)
- adverbial clause types
  - temporal (e.g., *After she went back to work. . .*)
  - causative (e.g., *Because he could not be sure. . .*)
  - conditional (e.g., *If they made it back. . .*)
  - concession (e.g., *Although they tried all night. . .*)
  - purpose (e.g., *They stopped working to have a little rest.*)
13. Complement clauses
- major type
  - *that*-clause (e.g., *I think that he already went*)
  - *to*-clause (e.g., *I want to go*)
  - *WH*-clause (e.g., *I don't know why he did that*)
  - *ing*-clause (e.g., *She doesn't like reading those articles*)
- syntactic role
  - controlled by a verb
    - mental verbs (e.g., *I think it's Monday.*)
    - communication verbs (e.g., *Bob said it's Monday.*)
    - desire verbs (e.g., *I want you to finish it by Monday.*)
    - etc.
  - controlled by an adjective (e.g., *I was surprised that you could finish it.*)
  - controlled by a noun (e.g., *The fact that you could finish it. . .*)

14. Word order choices
    - extraposition (e.g., *It is amazing that...*)
    - raising (e.g., *They are hard to get*; *Andy seems to know everything*)
    - particle placement (e.g., *You should look that word up*)
    - indirect object placement (e.g., g*ive the book to Sam* versus *give Sam the book*)
    - by-passive vs active (e.g., *Sally was shocked by the news* versus *The news shocked Sally*)
    - clefts and focus devices (e.g., *It was in April of that year that Seattle had finally awakened to the possibility...*)
15. Special features of conversation
    - backchannels and simple responses (*ok, mhm*)
    - coordination tags (e.g., *and stuff, and things like that*)
    - general vague words (e.g., *thing, stuff*)
    - pauses (silence) and fillers
    - repetitions
    - greetings, attention getters

PART II

Detailed descriptions of registers, genres, and styles

4   Interpersonal spoken registers

4.1   Introduction

Spoken registers differ from written registers in several fundamental ways. The most obvious, of course, is that they are produced in the spoken mode. This difference also entails less opportunity for planning what you are going to say, and no possibility of editing or revision. A speaker can say something again in speech, but he cannot erase the original utterance.

In addition, there are differences in the typical communicative functions of many spoken registers when compared to written registers. Many previous studies in linguistics have focused on the *ideational* function of language: how speakers use language to communicate ideas and information. Language is intimately connected to ideational functions: it is nearly impossible to communicate a new idea without using language. Ideational functions are also important for the description of registers. For example, in Chapter 5 we show how many written registers have the primary purpose of communicating new information.

However, in everyday speech, speakers are often more concerned about conveying their own feelings and attitudes than describing or explaining factual information. In addition, spoken registers are usually interactive; most of the time when we talk, we are using language to communicate with a specific person – the *interlocutor* – who responds directly to us. In this case, we use language to support and develop the relationship with our interlocutor. These uses of language – the *interpersonal functions* – are fundamentally important in most spoken registers.

In most spoken registers, the speaker is talking to someone, even if the speaker is talking to himself, and it is normal for the addressee to be able to talk back, even in the case of a lecture given to a large audience. Most spoken registers can therefore be regarded to some extent as interpersonal. However, there are important differences among spoken registers in their specific circumstances and communicative purposes. In the present chapter, we describe three of those registers: everyday face-to-face conversation, university office hour meetings between a student and faculty member, and service encounters. Although all three of these registers are directly interactive, they differ in their situational contexts and thus have important linguistic differences as well.

4.2   Conversation

Conversation is the most basic register of human language. Most of us spend much more time participating in conversations than any other use of language. Conversation is acquired naturally; all children learn how to participate in conversations, and all cultures and languages have a conversational register. In contrast, relatively few adults ever learn how to produce written registers like newspaper editorials or legal opinions. In fact, many adults never write extended prose of any type, and some cultures / languages have no written registers at all.

Other spoken registers are also much less basic than conversation. Although adult speakers of English readily recognize spoken registers like radio news reporting, sports broadcasts, political speeches, and classroom teaching, few speakers are actually required to produce the language of those registers. But conversation, at the other extreme, is universal and can be regarded as the basic register of human communication: all native speakers understand and regularly participate in conversations.

Conversation is a general register category, and it is possible to distinguish among specific subregisters such as telephone conversations or workplace conversations. One basic characteristic of all conversation is that it takes place in the spoken mode. As a result, conversational participants can utilize paralinguistic devices to communicate, including loudness, pitch, and length. For example, say the following sentence out loud, placing special emphasis on the word *really*:

He was **REALLY** smart.

Now say the sentence again, paying attention to the speech characteristics that indicate the emphasis on the word *really*. All three paralinguistic devices can be used to indicate emphasis: pronouncing a word more loudly, taking longer to say the word, and using an exaggerated pitch or tone. In writing, the author can use typographic devices to indicate emphasis, such as bold face, underscoring, or capital letters. As we will see in Chapter 7, one interesting aspect of interpersonal written registers (like e-mail messages) is the extent to which they rely on these extra typographical devices, in comparison to informational written registers (like newspaper articles). In contrast, all spoken registers employ loudness, pitch, and length as part of their communicative repertoire.

Paralinguistic features are one aspect of conversation that can be analyzed. In addition, conversation can be described from a traditional register perspective, for its distinctive situational characteristics and linguistic features. These are described in the following two sections.

4.2.1   Situational characteristics of conversation

Imagine a group of college friends who have gotten together at a restaurant. They are almost certainly talking to one another: having a conversation.

But what are they talking about? Have they planned their speech ahead of time? What communicative goals are they achieving through their conversation?

Following is an excerpt of a conversation from a situation of this type. Read through it with the above questions in mind.

Text Sample 4.1 Conversation among friends in a restaurant

Ayesha: This bread is awesome. You know what the honey thing is?
Nadia: What were you just saying – the bread's good.
Ayesha: Oh I was saying you know Tuscan bread would never go down here. No one would ever like it. Probably 'cause it's got no salt in it.
Nadia: Yeah and 'cause it's warm.
Ayesha: But I am – I'm totally stuck on it. Hi Lise.
Nadia: There's different kinds of bread.
Lise: Oh god, the bread is awesome.
Ayesha: <laugh>
Lise: So are you going to go home today, or –
Ayesha: Yeah I have to.
Lise: Why?
Nadia: Go tomorrow Ayesha.
Lise: God I hate you for that.
Ayesha: Well I guess you keep – oh we're ordering it now?
Marcus: I don't know, but do you want anything to drink?
Ayesha: No, that's good enough.

[LSWE Corpus]

Several important situational characteristics that distinguish conversation as a register are apparent in even this short extract. First, conversations involve two or more *participants*, who *directly interact* with each other, taking turns as they build the discourse. In terms of the setting, these participants share the *same temporal context* and they usually share the *same physical space* (apart from special cases, like with a telephone conversation). In the conversation among friends, because they share the setting, it is clear to the participants what Ayesha means by *that* in "that's good enough," even though an analyst cannot tell without seeing a video.

As a face-to-face spoken register, conversations are *produced in real time*. Participants have very little time to think ahead about what they want to say. Rather, they are producing language immediately in response to what their interlocutor has just said. If they don't like the way that something comes out, they are still stuck with the utterance: there is no way to revise or retract language that has already been produced. They can repair the utterance by saying it again, trying to restate the idea. But the original utterance still exists as part of the conversation. Thus in the above example, there are utterances where a speaker needs to start over again (e.g., *But I am – I'm totally stuck on it*).

Typical of many conversations, it is difficult to identify a single topic in the above interaction. Participants talk about the bread, going home, and ordering something to drink in quick succession. Probably none of these topics were deliberately identified ahead of time. Rather, these are topics that arise naturally with the situation. Notice also that participants are not really concerned with explaining concepts or conveying specific information. Rather, they are much more concerned with their own personal feelings, attitudes, desires, likes, and dislikes: what we refer to as the expression of personal *stance*.

In the following section, we shift our focus to the linguistic characteristics of conversation, showing how the typical language features used in conversation can be directly linked to the typical communicative purposes and situational contexts of this register.

4.2.2   Linguistic characteristics of conversation

The language of conversation is highly distinctive compared to the language of books. In fact, native speakers have no problem identifying the conversational register of many utterances taken completely out of context. For example, consider the following utterances from the conversation above:

> But I am – I'm totally stuck on it.
> Yeah I have to.
> I hate you for that.

It is hard to imagine an informational written text (such as a textbook or business report) where sentences like these would ever be used. Similarly, it is hard to imagine a classroom lecture or a television news broadcast that would use forms like these. Some written registers, such as novels or newspaper articles, contain direct quotes, and thus they might use these sentences. But in general, these are clearly linguistic forms that belong to interpersonal interactions rather than to other kinds of registers (spoken or written).

What is it that makes the linguistic style of conversation so distinctive? Part of the answer relates to conversation being interactive. The different participants *take turns* making contributions to a conversation. These turns are often organized as *adjacency pairs*: a conversational structure that involves two adjacent turns. To take a simple example, a question is often followed by a response, as in:

> Lise: So are you going to go home today, or –
> Ayesha: Yeah I have to.

Greetings are also normally structured with adjacency pairs, as in this example from another conversation:

> Joseph: Hi Joe, how are you? It's good to see you again. How have you been?
> Jack: Oh man pretty busy. How about you?
> Joseph: Oh hanging in there.

In this example, Joseph initiates an adjacency pair with a greeting and an inquiry about Jack (*How are you?*). Jack responds to the greeting/inquiry (*Oh man pretty busy*) and then initiates his own adjacency pair (*How about you?*). Joseph completes the second adjacency pair with his response (*Oh hanging in there*). The sub-discipline of Conversation Analysis focuses on the exchange structure of conversations and how participants work together to create coherent interactions.

Other typical linguistic forms of conversation occur as a consequence of the physical circumstances: the spoken mode, real-time production, and the shared setting. For example, consider Text Sample 4.2, a conversation between Brian and Ram (while they are riding together in a car):

Text Sample 4.2 Conversation among friends riding in a car

Brian: On the original Star Trek didn't they have, didn't they have little machines where they got their food? I, I was under the impression that it never was very clear how it worked but they –

Ram: Yeah this is, this is more expansive. It, it uh,

Brian: It could make not only only but

Ram: It substantiates the answers or the scenario better by uh, by envisioning the actual technology that could conceivably do it and it gets rid of or it alleviates more of the problems that they aspired to by uh, uh, by having a more extensive scenario. It's not just, it's not just that the robots build the cars, but the robots build all the cars that you could conceive of at, at no cost basically. And everyone uh, and everyone has control over, over it.

Brian: That means there's no costs because there's no scarcity.

[LSWE Corpus]

First of all, notice that there are many repetitions in this interaction (e.g., *I, I; only only*). In several cases, repetitions occur together with filled pauses (e.g., *it, it uh*; *by uh, uh, by*). These repetitions usually occur when the speaker is having trouble figuring out what to say. In most cases, repetitions result in **self-repairs**, where the speaker starts over and then successfully completes the utterance on his own. For example:

> didn't they have, didn't they have little machines ...
> I, I was under the impression ...

These repairs, repetitions, and filled pauses are all linguistic features associated with the real-time production of speech.

In some cases, when a speaker is having trouble encoding a thought, the other speaker takes over to complete the thought, illustrating the **co-constructed** nature of conversation. For example:

> Ram: It, it uh
> Brian: It could make not only only but
> Ram: It substantiates the answers ...

In fact, conversation can be described as being co-constructed in its entirety, because the participants work together to create the total discourse of a conversation. This phenomenon is possible because of the shared setting and some shared background, as well as being associated with the production circumstances and interactive nature of conversation.

Another feature related to the real-time production circumstances of conversation is that speakers often take shortcuts with their language, reflected by frequent contractions and other structural reductions. Read through the following conversation and see how many phonological and structural reductions you can spot:

Text Sample 4.3 Conversation among friends discussing moving

Margaret: You and Nancy took it out, didn't you? I often wondered how you ever got that out of the house.

Susan: We rented a dolly and we took the legs off and stood it up just, I mean, the guy at this music store told us just how to do it and I went to a music store and said how do you move a grand piano?

Margaret: Yeah, but going down the steps and everything.

Susan: We didn't, we backed the truck up with a ramp

Peter: We're trying to figure out how to move a two thousand pound pool table, next week. My dad's pool table.

Margaret: Oh yeah.

Susan: Won't you come back? <laugh>

Margaret: Can't help you there. Whatcha gonna do?

Peter: My dad bought it from the old Pontchartrain Hotel

[LSWE Corpus]

Contractions are reductions in pronunciation where two or more words are pronounced as a single word. Without a phonetic transcription, the analyst can identify only the reduced forms that have standard orthographic representations: *didn't, we're, won't, can't, watcha, gonna*. In addition, the above excerpt illustrates how speakers often omit structural elements. In most cases, it is easy to understand what the omitted elements are, so there is no loss of meaning. Several examples occur in the conversation above; we have repeated these below with the omitted elements added in [square brackets]:

> [I] can't help you
> [you were] going down the steps
> [It is] my dad's pool table
> we didn't [go down the steps]

The production of language is much slower in writing, and authors have extensive opportunity to revise and edit the text. As a result, a writer does not experience the same pressures to produce contracted and reduced forms. In addition, there are stylistic expectations for most written texts that strongly disfavor the use of contracted and elided forms. For these reasons, reduced forms are rarely found in most written registers.

Finally, Text Sample 4.4 illustrates other linguistic features that are typical of conversation: "attention getters" (*hey*), vocatives (*Tom*), and minimal responses (*hmm?*, *okay*).

Text Sample 4.4 Conversation among friends

Jack: Hey Tom
Tom: Hmm?
Jack: I'm gonna run to Burger King real quick.
Tom: Okay

[LSWE Corpus]

These features are common in conversation because there are multiple participants, who directly address and respond to one another.

Linguistic features like the ones described above are especially salient: readers notice these features in a conversational transcript because they are dramatically different from the linguistic forms that they normally encounter in a written text. However, these linguistic features are not unique to conversation. For example, the instructor in a classroom lecture will likely use repetitions, filled pauses, and self repairs, reflecting the challenges of real-time production of language in that situation. The language of classroom teaching can also be co-constructed, with the teacher and students engaging in interactions and even completing the thoughts of one another. Similarly, some of these conversational features can be found in interpersonal written registers (such as e-mail messages or chat rooms; see Chapter 7).

As discussed in Chapter 3, linguistic descriptions of a register usually do not identify absolute differences among registers. Rather, registers are distinctive in that they rely on selected linguistic features to a greater or lesser extent than other registers. Thus, the conversational features described above are especially common in this register.

In fact, there are many other less salient linguistic features that are at least as common and important in determining the linguistic nature of conversation. These features are less noticeable because they are core grammatical devices that could potentially be found in any text. However, because of the typical purposes and situational circumstances of conversation, it turns out that these features are much more common in conversation than in most other registers.

For example, second person pronouns refer directly to the addressee. Since most written texts are addressed to a general audience rather than a specific addressee, authors do not usually refer to *you* very often. In contrast, speakers are usually interacting face-to-face with a specific person in conversation, and thus we make very frequent reference to *you*.

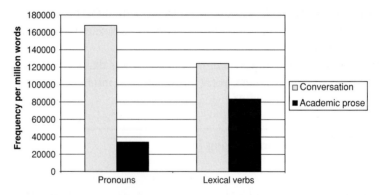

Figure 4.1 *Comparison of pronouns and lexical verbs in conversation versus academic prose (based on* LGSWE, *Figs. 2.6, 2.9, 5.8)*

Similarly, speakers use frequent *yes-no* questions and WH questions in conversation. Questions are devices that request specific information or at least a response, and thus they make sense only when there is a specific addressee who can give that response. In written texts, there are sometimes ***rhetorical questions***. However, these devices are rare and have a very specialized function: to raise an issue with no expectation of a response given to the author from the reader. In contrast, direct questions are relatively frequent in conversation, where addressees typically respond with the requested information. For the same reasons, imperatives are relatively common in conversation but rare in most written registers.

4.2.3   Quantitative linguistic differences between conversation and other registers

As described in Chapters 1 and 3, corpus-based analysis is an important methodological approach used to describe the linguistic differences among registers. Corpus-based analysis is especially useful for quantitative analyses, to identify linguistic patterns that are generally true for a register. By studying the language used in hundreds of texts from the same register, it is possible to measure the extent to which linguistic features are common or rare.

For example, Figure 4.1 compares the patterns of use for lexical verbs and pronouns in conversation versus academic prose, based on analysis of the Longman Spoken and Written English Corpus. (The findings are taken from the *LGSWE* [Biber *et al.* 1999]).

Figure 4.1 documents a pattern that is not especially surprising: that verbs and pronouns are much more common in conversation than in academic writing. However, in many other cases, the findings from quantitative corpus-based analyses are surprising, contradicting prior expectations. Even discourse analysts tend to notice distinctive register characteristics that occur almost exclusively in one register: features like repetitions and self repairs in conversation, which are described above. Without quantitative analyses, analysts often fail to notice core grammatical features, even when the use of such features is much more common in one register than others.

For example, attention is often given to the use of semi-modals in conversation: forms like *going to* (*gonna*), *have to* (*hafta*), *got to* (*gotta*), and *better*. These forms are almost never used in formal written registers, and so they are especially salient when reading a conversational transcript. For example, Text Sample 4.5 contains several semi-modals:

Text Sample 4.5 Conversation between a couple waiting for another couple to arrive to meet for breakfast

[very long pause]

Peter: Oh brother.

Gayle: They might not even have left there yet . . . the hotel.

Peter: Yeah they were just getting organized.

Gayle: Yeah.

Peter: Were Bob and Dorothy up already?

Gayle: Oh yeah they were up. I think we **better** wait. You know we go out to breakfast every Sunday after church. <laugh> And they'll never, they'll never stay there. I mean they always, Bob's always **gotta** go home for some reason. He's **got to** have his bacon and egg muffin. We took him to breakfast on Sunday, all he did was complain. <laugh> Of course he gets mad cause he can't smoke cause we always take non-smoking.

Peter: Oh well.

Gayle: See they've got a brand new van and we didn't know what we were **gonna** be doing, you know, if Karen did go into labor. And they wouldn't take their van cause Bob wanted to smoke and uh, Ed said he said he'd stop but he can't smoke in the van. I mean it's all carpeted and everything and you know you can't get that smoke out.

Peter: Yeah I know.

Gayle: And Dorothy said Bob's getting terrible with, with the smoking. Uh, he's really getting defiant about it because there are so many restaurants where you can't smoke and he just gets really mad and won't go to them.

Peter: That's kind of sad.

Gayle: Yeah well Dorothy told me, she says I always said if he ever quit drinking I wouldn't complain about anything else but she said the smoking bit is really getting to me.

[LSWE Corpus]

Figure 4.2 shows the frequencies of semi-modals in a corpus of conversation, in comparison to their use in three written registers: about 6,000 per million words in conversation, versus less than 1,000 per million words in academic prose. These results probably do not surprise you.

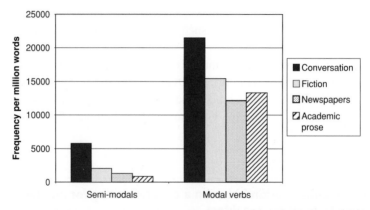

Figure 4.2 *Comparison of semi-modals and modal verbs in conversation versus three written registers (based on* LGSWE, *Fig. 6.9)*

But more surprisingly, Figure 4.2 shows that the core modal verbs (e.g., *can, might, will, would*) are also much more common in conversation than in most written registers. Did you notice modal verbs in Text Sample 4.5? In fact, there are many of them:

> they **might** not even have left
> he **can't** smoke
> they **wouldn't** take their van
> he **can't** smoke in the van
> you **can't** get that smoke out
> restaurants where you **can't** smoke
> and **won't** go to them
> I **wouldn't** complain

It would be easy to overlook the importance of modal verbs as a characteristic of conversation. They tend to blend into the text, because modal verbs are also found frequently in written registers. However, quantitative corpus analysis shows that modals are an important characteristic of conversation: they are actually more common than semi-modals, and they are more common in conversation than in most written registers. (Most of the modal verbs in the conversation in Text Sample 4.5 occur with negative verb phrases. However, corpus research shows that this is not generally true of conversation. Rather, this association here reflects the particular topic of this conversation.)

Many of the grammatical features typical of conversation reflect the dense use of short, simple clauses. The frequent use of lexical verbs, adverbs, and pronouns in conversation (see Figure 4.1 above) is a direct consequence of the reliance on short clauses: Each clause requires a verb and a grammatical subject (often a pronoun), and these clauses are often modified by adverbs. As a result, the conversational style of discourse, which relies on many short clauses, is characterized by the frequent use of verbs, adverbs, and pronouns.

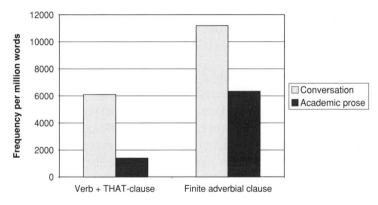

Figure 4.3 *Comparison of selected dependent clause types in conversation versus academic prose (based on* LGSWE, *Fig. 9.6, 10.20)*

Text Samples 4.1–4.5 above all illustrate this predominant conversational style. (In contrast, we show in Chapter 5 how informational writing tends to rely on long main clauses, often with only a single main verb but many different noun phrases and prepositional phrases.)

Given these characteristics of conversation, you might assume that this register utilizes only the simplest syntactic constructions. However, this is far from the case. In fact, conversation commonly relies on dependent clauses, and some kinds of dependent clause are actually much more common in conversation than in informational writing. It turns out that many of the short clauses found in conversation are embedded in higher-level clauses. The main verbs in the following examples (taken from Text Sample 4.5 above) are marked in **bold**:

> Of course he **gets** mad [cause he can't **smoke**]
> I **think** [we better **wait**]
> Dorothy **said** [Bob's **getting** terrible with the smoking]

In some cases, there are multiple levels of embedding, as in:

> Dorothy **told** me – she **says**⎡I always **said** ⎡if he ever **quit** [**drinking**]⎤
> [I wouldn't **complain** about anything else]⎤

Figure 4.3 shows that two types of dependent clause are especially common in conversation: *that* complement clauses controlled by a verb (e.g., *I think [(that) we better wait]*), and finite adverbial clauses (especially *because*-clauses and *if*-clauses). WH complement clauses controlled by a verb are also very common in conversation (e.g., *we didn't know [what we were gonna be doing]*). (In contrast, informational writing relies mostly on non-finite dependent clauses and post-nominal modifiers like relative clauses; see Chapters 5 and 6.)

These dependent clause types are often used to express "stance" in conversation: the controlling verb expresses the personal attitude, while the complement clause contains the new information. For example:

> I **think** [that the kids will learn to like that].
> I **hope** [that uh Kathleen faxed that order].
> I **know** [what you're talking about].

Almost any conversation will illustrate the use of these complement clause types and finite adverbial clauses. It is interesting that these features do not stand out reading through conversational transcripts. Thus, many observers never notice these distinctive linguistic characteristics of conversation, reinforcing the general belief that conversation is syntactically simple. For linguistic features like these, quantitative analysis can help to uncover important characteristics of a register that otherwise would go unnoticed.

Our goals in the preceding sections have been to identify several of the most important situational and linguistic characteristics of conversation. However, conversational interactions can occur in different contexts for different purposes. You will have the chance to explore some of those differences in the chapter activities. In the following section, we turn our attention to a special kind of spoken interpersonal register: university office hours.

4.3   University office hours

There are many interpersonal spoken registers that are closely related to conversation and might even be regarded as more specialized subregisters of conversation. Each of these shares many situational characteristics with conversation, but occurs in particular situations and has its own special characteristics. The interaction between a student and an instructor or faculty advisor during office hours is one of these specialized varieties.

Like everyday conversations, office-hour interactions involve participants in a direct face-to-face situation, sharing the same place and time, with each taking turns to communicate. Because of these similarities, these interactions employ most of the same core linguistic features of conversation that were described in Section 2 above. Activity 1 at the end of the chapter asks you to identify several of these linguistic features in the following office hour, including an adjacency pair, repetition, contraction, semi-modal and modal, and various types of clauses.

Text Sample 4.6 Office hour – an advising session about a student's graduation requirements

Advisor: all right so say again what's the problem
Student: well I planned on getting out in December
Advisor: are you going to go to summer school?
Student: yes
Advisor: mhm

Student: and – but Management 435, which I need, is not offered this summer or in the fall

Advisor: you're sure?

Student: I'm – well it's not in the books

Advisor: yeah well then it's not in if if they should happen to offer it then you would pick it up at the time

Student: well my question is is it – I don't know if it's being offered right now but if it is I wanna know why I'm not in it

Advisor: we'll substitute something for Management 435

Student: we can do that

Advisor: I can do it

Student: OK

Advisor: yeah

Student: OK um what I have here for this – BA 340 and 396 I plan on taking it in the fall or in the summer instead of in the fall

Advisor: no no wait a minute I can't follow that

Student: well here

Advisor: just tell me, summer 99, what do you have?

Student: well I have I have it written down here

Advisor: OK

Student: this is first session

Advisor: mhm so 301

Student: 301

Advisor: and 363 – oh one and 360

Student: and three it's it's CIS 360 which I know I I need both of

Advisor: all right and then?

Student: and then also BA 490 and uh

Advisor: History 380

Student: yes

Advisor: OK by the time that second summer session rolls around, will you be all done with these courses above BA 490?

Student: all these are done – let's see – that's done – uh 301 I'm taking this summer

Advisor: OK I I I see that

Student: and 360, yes so everything above 490

Advisor: all right you're done with that OK um

Student: so really I have – I want to take four this summer and then four in the fall is how it's working out

Advisor: all right now here's what you should do if you want me to go over your graduation papers you gotta do it this semester because if you wait until the summer or the fall

Student: uh huh

Advisor: then you'll have to go through somebody else and it'll just take longer

Student: yeah so I can do that then – and what do I do?

Advisor: go down to Rosemary's office and get the papers

[T2K-SWAL Corpus]

At the same time, there are important differences between office-hours and everyday conversations. Even to a casual observer of the setting, office hour interactions seem different from normal conversations. They always occur in a particular location – the "office" – with the participants seated at a table or desk. Often, there are written documents on the table, and the participants frequently use those documents in the interaction. These might be a textbook, a student paper, a university catalog, registration forms, or records on a computer.

There are other differences from normal conversation that are not as obvious just from looking at the setting. First, the instructor/advisor has more authority and expertise than the student, and this difference is made stronger because the interaction occurs in the advisor's office. However, the student is the person who initiates the interaction, by coming to the office (unless the meeting has been called by the instructor). The student usually needs assistance of some kind, and beyond that the student will usually have highly specific communicative goals, such as registering for classes, discussing progress on a thesis, or asking for clarification about course content. The instructor/advisor has more general communicative goals during office hours, namely to address the academic needs and concerns of any student who happens to show up. In both cases, participants usually expect topics to be far more restricted than in typical conversation. (Of course, even without changing the physical setting, participants can change from the specialized office-hour register to general conversation as part of the same meeting; in some university cultures this is not uncommon as faculty try to build more personal rapport with students.)

The situational differences between office-hours and casual conversations correspond to several important linguistic differences. Look again at Text Sample 4.6 above and see if you can notice any linguistic features that are used to a greater extent than in the everyday conversations discussed in Section 4.2. Look especially at how the participants respond to one another, and how they begin new turns.

One linguistic feature that is especially prevalent in office hours is discourse markers: *ok*, *well*, *all right*, *so*. Almost half of all turns in Text Sample 4.6 use a discourse marker near the beginning of the utterance, and some turns use two discourse markers. Although these forms do not have precise meanings, they serve to structure the overall discourse. They are especially important in office-hour interactions because the two participants are solving problems together – in Text Sample 4.6, trying to figure out what courses the student needs to take to graduate. Discourse markers have two main functions in these interactions: (1) to show that the speaker has understood the previous utterance (and, if necessary, mark the connection to the forthcoming response), and (2) to initiate a new idea.

The discourse marker *ok* serves both of these functions. *Ok* is often used as a simple response, indicating that the speaker has understood and accepted the preceding utterance, as in:

> Advisor: I can do it
> Student: **OK**

In other cases, *ok* marks a transition to the next step in the discussion, initiating a new sub-topic, as in:

> Student: **OK** um what I have here for this . . .
> Advisor: **OK** by the time that second summer session rolls around . . .

The discourse marker *all right* is less common than *ok*, but it is similar in being used to initiate a new topic, as in the opening of the text sample:

> Advisor: **all right so** say again what's the problem

In contrast, the discourse marker *well* almost always marks a response to some previous utterance, rather than initiating a new sub-topic. Beginning a response with *well* often indicates that the information in the utterance is somehow counter to the expectations raised by the preceding utterance. For example, when the advisor asks whether the student is sure, she responds **well** *it's not in the books* – that is, she is not absolutely sure, but there is no indication that she is wrong.

One direct reflection of the specific communicative purpose of this office-hour interaction is that it is focused on written documents. It would be much easier to notice this aspect of the interaction if we could actually see the physical setting. But there are direct linguistic consequences of this focus, in that the participants often refer directly to the written documents with ***deictics***. In this case, the student and advisor are working together on a program of study, repeatedly pointing to information on the page as they plan the student's future coursework:

> OK um what I have **here**
> well **here**
> well I have I have it written down **here**
> will you be all done with **these courses above** BA 490?
> **all these** are done
> OK I I I see **that**
> all right you're done with **that**

The problem-solving nature of office hours is also reflected in the high frequency of adverbial clauses, especially conditional clauses. For example:

> Advisor: **if** they should happen to offer it then you would pick it up at the time
> Student: **if** it is, I wanna know why I'm not in it
> Advisor: **if** you want me to go over your graduation papers you gotta do it this semester **because if** you wait until the summer or the fall then you'll have to go through somebody else

We noted in the last section that adverbial clauses were considerably more common in conversation than in academic writing. However, Figure 4.4 shows that finite adverbial clauses are even more frequent in office hours, with over

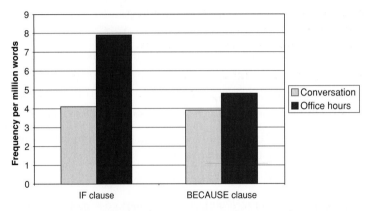

Figure 4.4 *Comparison of* if-*clauses and* because-*clauses in everyday conversation versus office hours (based on* LGSWE, *Fig. 10.20, and Biber 2006, Fig. 4.12)*

twice as many conditional clauses as in everyday conversation (and slightly more causative clauses as well). These clauses are more common because of the more focused communicative purposes of office hours: to solve problems together, considering the outcomes of different possibilities.

In addition to its problem-solving focus, office hours are distinctive in that the two participants have different communicative goals from one another: the student has certain problems or needs that must be resolved, and the advisor proposes solutions and ultimately tells the student what to do. Because students often overtly identify their needs, the main verbs *want* and *need* are especially common in office hours; for example:

> Student: and – but Management 435, which **I need**, is not offered this summer **I wanna** know why I'm not in it and three it's it's CIS 360 which I know I **I need I want** to take four this summer

Advisors commonly use these same verbs, but with the pronoun *you* referring to "the student." Thus, these utterances function as indirect directives, telling the student what to do:

> Advisor: yeah all right what **I want you to** do is to come back um on Thursday OK so that's what **you need to** work on –

There are actually several different linguistic devices that advisors use to give directives. Even conditional clauses serve this function. Thus, almost 50% of all conditional clauses in office hours begin with "if **you** ... ," often proposing a course of action for the student, as in these examples from different office hours:

> ...**if you** do that you'll have no problem graduating...
> ...**if you** go over to-to registrar, they will, get you going.
> ...**if you** haven't thought about that I-I'd recommend it

In the case of most conditionals, the directive force of the utterance is quite indirect. But other grammatical forms have more explicit directive meanings. For example, advisors commonly use the modal verbs *should* and *have to* as directives:

> here's what you **should** do
> then you'll **have to** go through somebody else

Less commonly, advisors also use imperatives as explicit directives:

> go down to Rosemary's office and get the papers

In summary, we have seen in this section how spoken interactions can vary depending on their specific communicative purposes. Because office hours share many situational characteristics with conversation, they are structured like casual everyday conversations (with turns, adjacency pairs, repetitions, greetings and leave-takings, etc.), and they use many of the same core linguistic features as everyday conversation (e.g., first and second person pronouns, frequent verbs, questions, etc.). But office hours have much more specific communicative purposes than typical everyday conversations, focused on problem-solving and addressing specific needs or concerns of the student. These communicative purposes have important linguistic consequences, so that the language of office hours is different from everyday conversation in several important ways.

Analyzing the differences and similarities among these registers also helps to explain why the specialized register of office hours is often challenging for students new to American universities. Students who are non-native speakers of English may have difficulty recognizing when they are being given a directive; as the analysis has shown, there are many forms of directives in office hours and some of them are quite indirect, so difficulty in interpretation is not surprising. Furthermore, discourse markers may cause difficulty for students. Using them to structure conversation is also a complex skill, and students who learned English as a foreign language are often unaware of their functions, but they are used commonly in office hours. Even students who are familiar with American culture but are new at a university often feel unsure about how much like a conversation an office-hour interaction can be: Is it ok to introduce an interesting topic if it is tangential to class/advising, or do office-hour interactions have to stick to a clear purpose? Is it ok to comment on something in the advisor's office because it's in the shared context? How directly should they express their needs or desires? Of course, there is individual variation in all of these factors, but even from a general register perspective, it is easy to understand why office hours can be a confusing new register for novices, since the situational and linguistic characteristics are both similar to and different from conversation.

4.4   Service encounters

Service encounters – interactions between an employee and a customer – are an even more specialized kind of spoken interaction. The most common type of service encounter is at the "check-out" of a business, when an employee determines the cost of the goods that the customer wants to buy and the customer pays. But there are many other kinds of service encounters. For example, a customer might ask about the location of a product in the grocery store, or the availability of a new book in the book store. Placing an order in a restaurant can be regarded as a service encounter, as well as requesting information at the library reference desk.

These interactions are all conversational in that they involve two participants interacting with one another in a face-to-face situation. Beyond that, though, there are few similarities to everyday conversation. In a normal service encounter, the customer does not know the employee, and the two have no interest in talking about their own personal lives. Rather, the focus is on accomplishing a business transaction or obtaining specific information.

One specific linguistic consequence of this goal-oriented focus is a very high use of questions with *can I ... ?*, produced by customers requesting the service. The following examples are all produced by students in service encounters at a university:

> **[at the registrar's office]**
> Student: Hey. I need to pay for my registration and dorm. **Can** I pay
>   for both here?
>
> **[at the front desk of an office]**
> Student: Hi **can** I get an application?
> Service provider: Sure.
> Student: Thank you.
>
> **[at the front office for a dormitory]**
> Student: Hi, **can** I get toilet paper?
> Service provider: Yeah
> Student: **Can** I just take these?
> Service provider: Yeah go for it
> Student: Thank you
> Service provider: You're welcome

The use of *can I* expresses the customer's need in an indirect, polite manner. More direct expressions of customer needs are also found in service encounters, but they are less common, and they may be perceived as somewhat impolite by some people; for example:

[at the copy shop]

Clerk:	Hey there.
Customer:	Hi.
Clerk:	How's it going?
Customer:	OK. **I want these, uh, copied**, just as they are.
Clerk:	Mhm.
Customer:	[2 syllables unclear] and the holes punched and the whole bit.
Clerk:	OK. How many copies?
Customer:	Tabs, you don't have to worry about the tabs – I'll worry about the tabs. Wait **you need to mark** where the tabs go though.

One of the most striking characteristics of service encounters is how repetitive they are, especially for the service provider, who works in the same location all day and thus responds to the same kinds of requests repeatedly. This characteristic often results in highly formulaic discourse. In many cases, the same utterances are repeated from one service encounter to the next, as with the other common use of *can I* in service encounters, when the clerk prompts the customer to state what is needed:

Can I help you?
Can I help who's next?
What **can I** do for you?

Since an expression such as *Can I help you?* occurs only once in a service encounter and predictably at the beginning of the interaction (often right after a greeting) it can be considered a genre marker. In fact, service encounters have such a conventionalized structure that it is possible to consider them from a genre perspective. There are slight variations depending on particular circumstances, but in their most basic form, most service encounters include the following elements:

A. Greeting exchange
   [Optional: request by Server, asking what the customer wants]
B. Customer statement of need – Server response
   [Optional: possible server statements of need, with customer response]
C. Closings

For example, this basic structure is followed in the following exchange (Text Sample 4.7) from a university business office (where students pay bills, such as tuition). Greetings are exchanged in lines 1–2. The customer follows the greetings by immediately stating his needs (in line 2, *I need to pay*). There is then a sequence of the clerk stating needs (waiting for the debit charge to go through, asking for a signature) as well as some discussion when the charge is not approved (which is not a part of the basic generic form). The interaction ends with closings.

Text Sample 4.7 Service encounter – paying a bill at the university

Clerk: hello.
Student: hi. I need to pay this
Clerk: OK. [types on keyboard] seven oh eight [. . .] OK it's going to take just a minute for that to go through
Clerk: alright
[printer sounds]
Clerk: OK it declined on that
Student: it declined? oh well then use this
Clerk: OK . . . OK try that
[printer sounds]
Student: it's probably too big a withdrawal
Clerk: well yeah and uh bank cards sometimes they have a limit of like five hundred or whatever so
Student: yeah
[printer sounds]
Clerk: OK go ahead and sign that for me
[printer sounds]
Clerk: there you go
Student: thanks
Clerk: have a good day
Student: you too

[T2K-SWAL Corpus]

Several genre makers are illustrated in this example. *Hello* and *hi* are typical greetings (also used in conversation). *There you go* is a typical genre marker for a pre-closing in a service encounter, used at the juncture when the clerk gives the customer a receipt and/or the merchandise that has been purchased right before the final closing. Along with *thanks, have a good day* is a typical closing in American service encounters.

The analysis of service encounters illustrates how the investigation of some interpersonal spoken registers can include a genre perspective. However, for many other spoken interactions, including conversation, routinized openings and closings are often the only feature that can be analyzed from a genre perspective.

In other ways, the structuring of the interaction and the corresponding linguistic features may be too varied for a genre approach.

4.5 Conclusion

Not all spoken registers are interpersonal. However, even less directly interactive spoken registers are influenced to some extent by the presence of specific interlocutors. Activity 6 gives you the opportunity to explore one spoken register of this type – classroom teaching – analyzing the extent to which its linguistic characteristics are similar to conversation.

In Chapters 5 and 6, we describe registers with the opposite situational and linguistic characteristics: informational written registers. But there are also intermediate registers, such as personal letters or e-mail messages. Although these registers are written, they are also interpersonal, and their linguistic characteristics reflect these hybrid situational characteristics. Interestingly, many new "e-registers," like blogs and text-messaging, are hybrid in this sense. We discuss registers of that type in Chapter 7.

Throughout the remainder of the book, we keep returning to the characteristics of conversation as a baseline for describing the distinctive characteristics of other registers. As the following chapters show, some of these registers differ from conversation in just about every conceivable way, while other registers are more similar, both situationally and linguistically.

Chapter 4 activities

Reflection and review

1. Read through Text Sample 4.6 in this chapter, the office hour, and identify one or more examples of each of these conversational linguistic features:

a. adjacency pair   f. modal verb and semi-modal verb
b. repetition   g. *that*-complement clause with *that* omitted
c. self repair   h. sentence relative clause
d. contraction   i. *WH*-complement clause
e. question   j. finite adverbial clause

2. Using the information from the analysis of service encounters in Section 4.4, outline a lesson that you would give to tourists coming to the US who have an intermediate level of English and want to engage in service encounters in English successfully. What genre information would they need? Are there specific genre markers and register features that you would prepare them for? How would you use this information to prepare the tourists (how would you give the tourists practice)?

You can also incorporate your own experience as you outline the lesson. For example, if you have a lot of experience with service encounters in another country, you can use your experience for helpful contrasts.

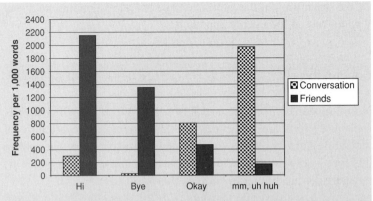

Figure 4.5 *The use of common greetings, leave-takings, and minimal responses: face-to-face conversation versus* Friends *(adapted from Quaglio 2004, Figs. 6.14 and 7.6)*

Analysis practice

3. One defining characteristic of a "good" TV sitcom is that the dialogue feels natural, almost like we had just videotaped normal people having a conversation. However, there are some systematic linguistic differences between TV dialogue and natural face-to-face conversation, associated with the more specialized circumstances and purposes typical in a sitcom.

Think about the situational characteristics of TV sitcoms: What are the typical settings? Who are the participants? What kinds of actions and events are normally portrayed? What are the participants doing with language?

One study of TV sitcom language is Quaglio 2004, who studied the TV sitcom *Friends* in comparison to a corpus of face-to-face conversation. Figure 4.5 identifies a few of the major differences that Quaglio uncovered, for the use of greetings/leave-takings, and for the use of minimal responses. Describe the linguistic patterns in Figure 4.5, and provide a functional explanation of why these differences exist.

4. There are many different subregisters within conversation, associated with different participants, their relationships with one another, and their communicative goals. Activity Texts 7–9 present excerpts from three different kinds of conversation: a family riding together in the car (on the way to school), two friends talking at a café, and two colleagues talking at work. Describe the situational differences among these three contexts of communication. Also identify the topic of conversation, including whether the focus is on past events, future plans, the on-going situation, and so on.

Then compare the linguistic characteristics of these conversations, identifying distinctive linguistic characteristics of each one (e.g., incomplete utterances, length of utterances, minimal responses, word choice and use of specialized vocabulary, verb tense and aspect, use of nouns and pronouns, complex syntax, etc.). Use quantitative analysis to support your linguistic descriptions. Finally, interpret the linguistic patterns by reference to the situational characteristics.

5. Over the next week, pay attention to the language used during your service
encounters in at least two different locations. Possibilities include the checkout at a
grocery store, checking out a book at the library, or settling your bill at a restaurant.
Especially pay attention to any utterances that seem to be fixed expressions (write the
utterances down as soon as you can after you leave the service encounter). Are any of
these utterances register markers? genre markers? Provide justification for your
analysis. Also compare the use of these fixed expressions to determine which ones
are used across service encounters versus the ones that are more specialized for a
particular type of service encounter.

6. Is classroom teaching a spoken interpersonal register? Use Activity Text 10, a
classroom teaching excerpt, for a practice analysis to answer this question.

 The sample is from American university-level classroom teaching (a first-year
English composition class). The extract is entirely monologic – only the instructor is
talking. However, it illustrates many of the situational and linguistic characteristics of
interpersonal registers. Compare and contrast this text from classroom teaching to the
typical characteristics of face-to-face conversation (described in this chapter and
Activity Texts 7–9), describing both situational and linguistic characteristics.

Project ideas

7. Do your own investigation similar to the one in activity 3 above, comparing TV
dialog to real conversation. Use an internet search engine to locate a website with
transcripts from a sitcom. (There are many such sites. You can search for a specific
show, such as "Sex and the City transcripts" or find a general site by searching for
"TV show transcripts.") Download 3–4 transcripts from one show, and carry out your
own linguistic analysis to identify typical linguistic characteristics. (If you are using
corpus analysis techniques, the project should be based on a larger sample of
transcripts.) Determine whether the patterns shown in Figure 4.5 hold for this sitcom,
and also try to identify other salient linguistic features in these interactions. Offer
functional explanations for any observed patterns.

8. Carry out your own investigation of interpersonal spoken registers using corpora
that are currently available on-line. Two major corpora are readily accessible and
have on-line research tools:

- The British National Corpus (BNC): A 100-million word corpus of
  British English spoken and written registers, which includes a
  five-million word sub-corpus of conversation. Online research tools have
  been designed by Mark Davies at Brigham Young University:
  corpus.byu.edu/bnc
- The Corpus of Contemporary American English (COCA): A corpus of
  more than 360 million words of speech and writing, compiled by Mark
  Davies at Brigham Young University. The speech component contains
  approximately 76 million words of unscripted conversation from TV and
  radio programs (such as *All Things Considered, Good Morning America,
  60 Minutes*, etc.). While this is not the same as spontaneous casual

conversation, it is another type of conversation you may wish to study and the only large corpus of American speech with on-line research tools: www.americancorpus.org

Carry out a register analysis of two or three spoken registers that are available in these corpora. Be sure to compute normed rates of occurrence, since the sub-corpora for different registers will not be the same size. Interpret any observed differences in the use of linguistic features.

9. Expand your analysis from activity 6 above to base it on a more representative sample of university classroom teaching texts, taken from The Michigan Corpus of Academic Spoken English (MICASE): quod.lib.umich.edu/m/micase/ Compare your findings to those reported in Biber 2006a.

   Then, use your findings to critique the presentation of information in two or three ESL textbooks that teach academic lecture listening skills. How do the text examples in the ESL textbooks compare to the actual language of classroom teaching? And does the discussion in the textbooks focus on the linguistic features that are especially prevalent in actual classroom teaching? As a teacher, what sort of supplemental materials or practice would you give students?

5 Written registers, genres, and styles

5.1 Introduction

In this chapter we turn our attention to three commonly encountered general written registers – newspaper writing, academic prose, and fiction. A fundamental difference between the spoken registers in the last chapter and written registers concerns time for planning and revising. Of course, you can choose to write a quick note, or you can even write a quick academic paper (perhaps with disappointing results when you get the grade!). Unlike speech, however, writing allows you to sit and think about what you want to say, look over what you have written, and revise it. As we shall see, these characteristics have important consequences for the language of written registers generally. But writers can also choose to use their planning and revising time to create very different kinds of texts, and this chapter also illustrates some of the variation that exists among different written registers.

One major situational characteristic shared by many written registers is a primary focus on communicating information rather than on developing a personal relationship. Of course, there are few uncontestable "facts," and so most communication – in writing or speech – reflects some ideological perspective. Further, it is possible in writing to be interpersonal, and registers like personal letters or e-mail messages can be focused more on sharing personal feelings and attitudes than conveying information. But for many general written registers – exemplified in this chapter by newspapers and academic prose – readers and writers usually do not expect to share any personal connections with the author. In fact, you may never even know the name of a person who wrote a newspaper article if there is no by-line, and even if you do see a by-line, it is unlikely that you know that person. Similarly, that writer does not know you. The focus is on communicating information about the story, rather than revealing personal details about the author or attempting to learn about the personal lives of readers.

In this chapter we also use newspaper writing and academic prose to further illustrate the idea that it is possible to identify registers with varying levels of specificity. We first discuss these two general registers in contrast to conversation, and in relation to each other. We go on to discuss variation among subregisters within each of these registers – first comparing editorials with news reporting, and then comparing academic research articles with textbooks. Finally, we investigate register differences on an even more specific level by looking at how the sections within research articles differ in terms of their purposes and corresponding linguistic features.

The final analysis in the chapter focuses on a very different kind of register by examining fiction. Unlike the other written registers described in the chapter, the primary goal of fiction is not to convey information, but rather to tell a story, with the underlying goals of entertaining or providing social commentary in an entertaining way. Fiction is further distinguished from almost all other registers by including imaginary worlds and authors' stylistic choices, which actually have more influence on the linguistic characteristics than the real-world situational characteristics do. The investigation of fiction thus incorporates analysis of style into the register analysis.

Throughout the chapter, the analyses illustrate how the register perspective facilitates understanding the challenges that writers and readers face. Informational written registers are among the most important registers to master for gaining access to information and for success in school; understanding their complexity is especially helpful for teachers and students. The analysis of fiction, on the other hand, illustrates the linguistic sophistication of creative texts, increasing your appreciation of the ways in which language can be manipulated for stylistic purposes.

5.2   Situational characteristics of newspaper writing and academic prose

When you begin investigating a register, certain situational characteristics are likely to strike you as obviously important. However, as discussed in Chapter 2, it is useful to think through as many situational characteristics as possible as you begin your analysis. To illustrate this process, Table 5.1 summarizes the major situational characteristics of newspaper writing and academic prose, illustrating the use of the Appendix to Chapter 2 for an initial situational analysis.

When the situational characteristics of registers are laid out comprehensively, certain similarities and differences usually become clear. Here, one notable similarity for newspaper writing and academic prose is that a number of the characteristics cannot be specified. That is, since these are *general* written registers, many situational characteristics vary among the subregisters within the more general category.

For example, consider the different communicative purposes among subregisters within a newspaper. An editorial is meant to express an opinion overtly and persuade readers to that opinion. However, a straight news report is expected not to state an overt opinion but rather to report the event with as little bias as possible.

Table 5.1 *Situational characteristics of newspaper writing and academic prose*

Situational characteristic	Newspaper writing	Academic prose
I. Participants		
A. Addressor		
1. Single / plural / institutional / unidentified	may be single, plural, institutional or unidentified	usually singular or plural, sometimes institutional
2. Social characteristics	often adult journalist but varies with subregister (e.g., any reader can writer a letter to the editor)	often adult trained professional but varies with subregister (e.g., can be student)
B. Addressee		
1. Single / plural / un-enumerated	group (very general)	group (more specialized than for newspaper – e.g., other professionals in the academic field, students, etc.)
2. Self / other	other	other
C. On-lookers?	N/A	N/A
II. Relationships among participants		
A. Interactiveness	no direct interaction	no direct interaction
B. Social roles	varies	varies
C. Personal relationship	none	none
D. Shared knowledge	varies. Some knowledge of the city of the newspaper and current events expected.	varies
III. Channel		
A. Mode	writing	writing
B. Specific medium	printed and/or on-line	printed, some on-line
IV. Production and Comprehension Circumstances		
A. Production	time for planning, revising, editing (often includes tight deadlines). Often have strict space constraints.	time for planning, revising, editing. Space constraints vary.
B. Comprehension	varies depending on reader – careful reading or skimming; opportunity for re-reading	often careful reading but may be skimmed quickly; opportunity for re-reading

(cont.)

Table 5.1 (cont.)

Situational characteristic	Newspaper writing	Academic prose
V. Setting		
A. Time and place shared by participants?	no physically shared time or place but expected to be read on same day as produced	no shared time or place
B. Place of communication		
1. Private / public	public (available for others to view)	public (available for others to view)
2. Specific setting	usually associated with a specific city; may be read more widely; certain articles may be produced by a wire service with no specific setting	no specific setting
C. Time period	contemporary (in this study)	contemporary (in this study)
VI. Communicative purposes		
A. General purposes	informational – report events; some articles do analysis	informational – inform and explain/interpret
B. Specific purposes	vary within a reporting and informing purpose (e.g., news reports report daily events, human interest stories may seek to entertain, editorials seek to persuade)	vary within an informative, explanatory purpose (e.g., research article presents new findings, textbook explains information for novices)
C. Factuality	factual reports separated from opinion pieces	factual with interpretation
D. Expressing stance	varies, not expected to be overt (except in editorials)	varies, not usually expected to be overt
VII. Topic		
A. General topic area	current newsworthy events in many areas; varies with different sections of paper	varies
C. Specific topic	varies	varies

Similarly, although both research articles and textbooks are academic prose, they have different specific purposes and embody different sets of relationships between writer and reader. Research articles published in academic journals must present new findings and convince readers of the trustworthiness of the research and the significance of the findings relative to what is already known about the topic; the readers are expected to already have expert background in the research area and so they are relatively equal in status to the writer. A textbook, on the other hand, is meant to explain concepts to readers who are new to the field. The author has considerably more background in the field and more authority than the readers.

In addition, some situational characteristics vary by the individual situation. For example, one reader might skim a newspaper article or academic article very quickly, while another reader will read the same article in detail. Writers and editors know that both types of readers exist. Linguistic features may relate to meeting the needs of both such readers.

Of course, there are other situational characteristics that can be specified for these two general registers, and Table 5.1 shows that the registers are similar with respect to several of those. For example, both newspaper and academic prose conform to the prototypical production and comprehension circumstances of writing. The authors have time to plan, revise, and edit. Even a newspaper reporter working under a tight deadline has much more time for planning and revising than a participant in a conversation. Readers also have the opportunity to re-read what has been written as many times as they care to.

A second situational similarity between these two general registers is that there is no direct connection between the reader and writer. They have no personal relationship, no direct interaction, and do not share the same setting (except to the extent that most newspapers are read in the same city where they are produced and usually on the same day).

A third important similarity concerns the communicative purposes of the registers. Both have a generally informational purpose (as opposed to, for example, mystery novels, whose purpose is to entertain). The content is generally factual, not imaginative, and the overt expression of stance is generally not expected (except, as noted above, in editorials).

At the same time, these two general registers also have some clear situational differences. One concerns their specific communicative purposes. Newspaper news reports recount events, describing what happened, rather than offering interpretations. The distinction between news reports and analysis/interpretation articles is made very clear, usually with a label on the "news analysis" piece. Editorials, which are overtly opinionated, are given their own special section in the newspaper. On the other hand, all academic writing is expected to go further than just narrating events. It needs to explain and interpret the information that is presented – whether it is in a textbook or a research article.

The two registers also differ in their topic areas. Although both have variation in specific topics, newspapers are always focused on current newsworthy events.

Even a historical event will be connected to its present-day anniversary, survivors, or continuing impact. For academic writing, it is impossible to specify a topical focus. Different disciplines – history, biology, medicine, mathematics, etc. – all have different foci, and the attention paid to current relevance depends on the more specific register (a research article must make its current significance clear, but a textbook explaining historical developments might not).

5.3   Linguistic features in newspaper writing and academic prose

In this section, we survey the linguistic features typically used in newspaper writing and academic prose, connecting them to the situational characteristics discussed in the previous section. We begin by contrasting both of these general written registers with conversation, the prototypical spoken register (described in Chapter 4), and then move on to comparing the two written registers to each other.

5.3.1   Writing vs. conversation

Table 5.2 provides an overview of fifteen linguistic features that are typical of newspaper writing and/or academic prose. In a study of your own, you would have frequency counts from a small collection of texts in each register. The description here is based on large-scale corpus analyses of these two registers. Many more features could, of course, be included in a study; we use these fifteen to exemplify a range of different kinds of linguistic features.

A quick glance at Table 5.2 shows that nominal features are one of the most obvious ways in which these two written registers differ from conversation. All of the features having to do with noun phrases – nouns, premodifiers of nouns (i.e., other nouns and attributive adjectives), post-modifiers of nouns (e.g., prepositional phrases and past participle clauses) – are much more common in the written registers. In contrast, personal pronouns and most verb phrase features (e.g., present tense and modal verbs) are more common in conversation than the written registers.

Text Samples 5.1 and 5.2 illustrate the complex kinds of noun phrases common in informational writing. Text Sample 5.1 is from a textbook about foodservice and 5.2 is from a newspaper article about beer.

Text 5.1 Academic prose – textbook about foodservice

What people expect

Diners walking into a commercial facility for the first time bring with them a number of expectations. They expect good, safe food, clean surroundings, and pleasant service. Together these elements make up a pleasant dining experience.

It is a challenge to managers of commercial and noncommercial establishments to direct a number of activities at once, including employee training and management; and the purchasing, preparation, and service of food. Foodservice managers generally expect to meet the diners' expectations. Managers *assume* that they are going to provide good, safe food in clean surroundings with friendly service. This assumption, especially regarding safe food and clean surroundings, should be based not only on a foundation of goodwill and good intentions, but on a sound understanding of sanitary policies and procedures.

[Educational Foundation of the National Restaurant Foundation, *Applied Foodservice Sanitation* (4th edn.; Dubuque, IA: Kendall/Hunt Publishing Company, 1995), 3–4]

Text 5.2 Newspaper – story about harvesting hops

A peak beer experience

It's hop harvest – time to revel in the fleeing season of fresh-hop beer

The 20-foot-tall vines are mostly harvested now, hacked down and denuded during several weeks of 'round-the-clock bustle [. . .]

Most hops are dried and pressed after pickling so they can be baled for use through the year. Some are frozen; some are processed into dry pellets; some are distilled into essential oils. So fresh-from-the-vine hops are a fleeting thing available only during the hop harvest, and brewers are taking full advantage with a round of beers and parties to celebrate dear old *Humulus lupulin*.

It seems a curious object of veneration, this sticky, weedlike cousin of cannabis that grows inches a day during high summer. Its cones are used for nearly nothing but the preservation of beer and giving it varying degrees of bitterness, tasks for which they are uncannily perfect – far better than the witches' brews of herbs and spices that brewers used in the centuries before hops became the standard. Without hops in the mix, beer would be a sweet grainy gruel where bad bugs would thrive.

[A peak beer experience. *The Oregonian*, September 25, 2007, p. FD1&7.]

The sentences are long in these text excerpts, often containing only one finite verb but many nouns, resulting in a much higher frequency of nouns than verbs. The first sentence in the textbook, for instance, has one main verb (*bring*) and five nouns (*diners, facility, time, number, expectations*), in a total of seventeen words. Although the newspaper article starts with a higher frequency of verbs, the first sentence of the third paragraph has one verb in the main clause (*seems*) and one verb in the relative clause (*grows*), but seven nouns (*object, veneration, cousin, cannabis, inches, day, summer*).

Further, nouns tend to be modified by adjectives and prepositional phrases in these texts, so that the referents are very specific. For instance, the textbook refers to not just any "managers" but *managers **of commercial and noncommercial establishments***. The text encourages not just any "understanding" but *a **sound** understanding **of sanitary policies and procedures***. The newspaper article refers to ***fresh-from-the-vine*** hops, *a **curious** object

Table 5.2 *Distribution of selected linguistic features in two general written registers (based on Biber 1988, Biber et al. 1999, Conrad 1996, Conrad 2001)*

Linguistic feature	Newspapers	Academic prose	Conversation
1. Nominal Features			
Nouns	very common, even more common than in academic prose	very common	less common
Nominalizations	common	extremely common, especially -tion	rare
Prepositional phrases after nouns	common	extremely common	less common
Attributive adjectives	common	extremely common	less common
Nouns as premodifiers of nouns	extremely common	common	rare
Personal pronouns	slightly more than in academic prose, still uncommon	rare	extremely common
2. Verb characteristics			
Present tense	less common than in academic prose; slightly more common than past tense	more common than in news; far more common than past tense	very common
Past tense	much more frequent than in academic prose; slightly more common than in conversation	rare	uncommon

Modals	uncommon; slightly less common than in academic prose; *will* and *would* most common	uncommon; slightly more common than in news *can* and *may* most common	more common than in news or academic prose (about 15% of all finite verb phrases)
Passives	about 15% of all finite verbs	more common than in news; about 25% of all finite verbs	rare
3. Circumstance adverbials of time and place	Time adverbials by far most common; place also common	Time and place adverbials rare	Time and place adverbials both common
4. Linking adverbials	rare	very common	*so* and *then* are very common
5. Other features Sentence structure	standard syntax	standard syntax	many fractured clauses, incomplete utterances, etc.
Questions	rare	rare	very common
Type-token ratio	higher than academic prose	higher than conversation	lowest

of veneration, *this* **sticky, weedlike** *cousin* **of cannabis** . . . In contrast, Chapter 4 showed how conversational participants make frequent use of pronouns and other kinds of vague expressions, relying on the physical context to identify the specific reference.

It is easy to see how these features relate to the differences in purpose, production/comprehension circumstances, and physical settings of informational writing versus conversation. Newspapers and academic prose have a general purpose of informing, and there is plenty of time for planning, revising, and editing the language. Informing readers about a specific topic requires precise noun phrases. The time allowed for production of the text enables writers to formulate the more dense noun phrases, and they know readers will have time to process them. Furthermore, these specific noun phrases are useful for identifying the precise concepts that will be covered in the textbook – e.g., *employee training and management*; *the purchasing, preparation, and service of food*; *sanitary policies and procedures.* In the newspaper article, the noun phrases name a variety of objects that are associated with the general topic (hops): *dry pellets, essential oils, hop harvest, brewers, cones,* etc. Conversation, on the other hand, is produced and processed in real time, by people who are face-to-face, sharing personal information and developing a personal relationship. Shorter noun phrases result from both the communicative focus – on *you* and *I* – and the fact that the participants are together in the same place and time.

Several other linguistic features are tied to the communicative purpose and production circumstances of the written versus spoken registers. These written registers have a high "type-token ratio": a measure of how many different words are used in a text. This characteristic reflects the precision of noun phrases with their variety of modifiers, the need to be precise about the reference of noun phrases, and the variety of topics raised. The complete, well-formed syntax of the written texts also results from the time for production and editing.

In sum, there are major linguistic differences between conversation and informational writing, associated with the major situational differences between these general registers. At the same time, there are interesting linguistic differences between the two informational written registers as well. These are discussed in the following section.

5.3.2   Comparison of newspaper writing and academic prose

Although newspaper writing and academic prose appear quite similar to each other when compared to conversation, there are also intriguing linguistic differences between them, and these differences relate to their differences in situational characteristics. Two of the differences between newspapers and academic prose are their specific purposes and topics. We noted in Section 5.2 that newspapers focus more on current newsworthy events and have more emphasis on simple reporting, while academic prose is always expected to analyze and explain, not just report. Certain linguistic features clearly relate to these differences, most notably present versus past tense verbs, types of circumstance adverbials, and linking adverbials (see Table 5.2).

Academic prose uses far more present tense verbs than past tense verbs, while in newspapers the frequency of the two tenses is about the same. With respect to circumstance adverbials, newspapers have more time adverbials than other adverbials, but also use place and process adverbials commonly. In academic prose, neither place nor time adverbials are common.

The focus on reporting current events in newspapers clearly corresponds to these verb tense and adverbial choices. For example, newspapers commonly use past tense verbs to narrate what recently happened. Text Sample 5.3, from a front-page story about a man's encounters with a rattlesnake, illustrates the use of past tense to narrate a sequence of events. The sequence is further clarified through the use of time adverbials, such as *in early August, three weeks afterward,* and *a short time later.* Since readers are expected to be reading the article the same day that the paper was published (a Wednesday), even a time adverbial such as *Tuesday* is useful for understanding the events. Finally, the physical setting of the events is made clear with place adverbials such as *off the highway near Maupin.*

Text Sample 5.3 Newspaper article

In early August, snake collector Matt Wilkinson of Southeast Portland grabbed a 20-inch rattler off the highway near Maupin.

Three weeks afterward, in a show of daring for an ex-girlfriend, Wilkinson stuck the snake in his mouth.

A short time later, he was near death with a tongue swollen to the point it blocked his throat when emergency room and trauma surgeons at OHSU Hospital saved his life.

The 23-year-old became a celebrity of sorts Tuesday when broadcast and cable news all over the country learned about his story. On the phone, still out of sorts with sore muscles and nerves from the venom, he sounded circumspect.

[*The Oregonian*, Wednesday September 19, 2007, p. D1.]

In the retelling of the events in Text Sample 5.3, it is also easy to see why no linking adverbials are used. The sequence of events makes it possible for the reader to infer the cause-effect relationships. Readers are expected to understand on their own that the man was bitten by the snake when he put it in his mouth, and that the bite is what caused his throat and tongue to swell. Making the relationships even more explicit with linking adverbials such as *consequently, therefore,* or *as a result* is unnecessary.

Present tense verbs are also common in newspaper articles because they describe current events. For example, Text Sample 5.4 discusses a plan for a bird protection program. Every main verb in the opening paragraphs is in the present tense (*has come up with, lays, like, are, wander, relies,* etc.) In this case, the news report explains facts about the birds, and also describes a current plan, but gives background information in the past tense (e.g. *the plover was listed as threatened*).

Text Sample 5.4 Newspaper – news report about a bird protection program

Education is big part of plover protection

Recovery | Private and government groups will warn beach visitors that nests may be underfoot

By Patrick O'Neill

The Oregonian

The federal government has come up with a way to protect a tiny beach-dwelling bird that lays its eggs in areas where people like to play Frisbee.

At less than 2 ounces, western snowy plovers are no match for the increasing number of humans who wander through their nesting grounds without ever realizing the nests are there.

The plan, released Monday by the U.S. Fish and Wildlife Service, relies heavily on cooperative efforts between private organizations and government agencies to help the birds. Because the plover shares the beach with people, the plan uses a large public education component.

[...]

Laura Todd, field supervisor for the Newport office of the Fish and Wildlife Service, said the number of plovers has grown from about 50 along the Oregon and Washington coasts in the early 1990s to about 104 plovers in Oregon and 60 in Washington in 2005. The plover was listed as threatened in 1993 under the federal Endangered Species Act.

[*The Oregonian*, Tuesday September 25, 2007, p. B1]

Academic prose is similar to the newspaper article in sample 5.4 in that the communicative focus is usually on facts that have continuing relevance. Text Sample 5.5 illustrates this pattern in an introduction section of a research article that concerns the same bird species as in the newspaper article. All the information is in the present tense (*is widely believed*, *include*, etc.), informing readers of the most current knowledge about the breeding of the birds.

Text Sample 5.5 Academic prose – research article about breeding of birds

Long-distance breeding dispersal of snowy plovers in western North America

Lynne E. Stenzel, Jane C. Warriner, John S. Warriner, Katherine S. Wilson, Frances C. Bidstrup and Gary W. Page

Introduction

Breeding site tenacity is widely believed to be characteristic of most species of birds
that depend on relatively stable resources. Potential advantages include intimate familiarity with the food resources and habitat characteristics of a site, the latter possibly
beneficial for birds seeking refuge from predators or defending sites in intraspe-
cific conflicts (Hinde 1956; Harvey, Greenwood & Perrins 1979; Greenwood 1980;
Horn 1983). Recognized benefits of dispersal, even in stable environments, include
increased gene flow, increased access to potential mates, and reduced competition
with relatives or conspecific (Hamilton & May 1977; Greenwood 1980). Dispersal
theoretically has been shown to be of additional benefit in temporally variable habi-
tats (Roff 1975), as exemplified in the extreme by the movements of nomadic species
(Andersson 1980). Sex bias with respect to breeding dispersal is a well recognized
phenemenon (reviewed in Greenwood 1980, 1983). [. . .]

[*Journal of Animal Ecology* 63, 1994: 887–902]

Text Sample 5.1 from the foodservice textbook is also written in the present
tense, since the authors discuss food sanitation generally, not a specific case of it
(as might be reported in a newspaper article).

The discussion of general (sometimes abstract) patterns and concepts in academic prose is also connected with another linguistic difference from newspapers: academic prose tends to have a higher frequency of nominalizations. In the
research article introduction, concepts such as *breeding site tenacity, familiarity*,
and *benefits of dispersal* are discussed. If these ideas were expressed without
nominalizations (that is, with verbs or adjectives), the focus of the discourse
would change. Consider this rewriting of the opening sentences of the research
article:

> Most species of birds that depend on relatively stable resources are tenacious
> about breeding sites. They may have an advantage when they are familiar
> with food resources . . . When the birds disperse, they benefit from increased
> gene flow . . .

In these rephrased sentences, the birds themselves, as grammatical subjects,
become the topic of the discourse, and the introduction is no longer about general concepts. Similarly, the foodservice textbook in Text Sample 5.1 discusses
management, expectations, and *intentions*. The focus of the entire book is about
foodservice sanitation – a general concept rather than a specific action.

Since academic prose is expected to develop arguments rather than to simply
report events, linking adverbials are more common. Data in an academic text
is not just reported; rather, an interpretation must be made, and a conclusion
reached. Text Sample 5.6, for instance, is a passage from another research article
about animal breeding, in this case about a mouse (Peromyscus Californicus). In
this excerpt from the discussion section, the author is comparing his results to
previous studies.

Text Sample 5.6 Academic prose – research article discussion section

[linking adverbials in **bold**]

... **However**, their field data from nine females indicate an average of 1.8 litters per season (McCabe and Blanchard 1950; p. 118). Number of litters per breeding season does not appear to vary considerably among Peromyscus, but **rather** the days between litters correlates positively with length of breeding season (Millar 1989). The primary breeding season in this study was around 8 months long (Fig. 1a and b) and average interbirth interval within a season was 60.3 days. **In contrast**, interbirth intervals for other Peromyscus species range from 25 to 30 days ... Data from P. Californicus **thus** agree with the general trend ... There was, **however**, considerable variation in interbirth intervals ...

[D. O. Ribble, Lifetime reproductive success and its correlates in the monogamous rodent, Peromyscus Californicus. *Journal of Animal Ecology* 61 (1992): 457–468, p. 466]

The author repeatedly marks the connections he is making, whether contrast (*however*, *rather*, *in contrast*) or summing up the significance of the review (*thus*).

Another difference between the two written registers is the devices used to identify sources of information, an aspect of epistemic stance. Research articles all have references with names and dates in parentheses – e.g., *(McCabe and Blanchard 1950)* and *(Millar 1989)* in Text Sample 5.6. Newspaper articles, on the other hand, give attribution to sources less precisely. Some articles (e.g., Sample 5.4 above) name a specific individual: "Laura Todd, field supervisor for the Newport office of the Fish and Wildlife Service, said ..." But more commonly, newspaper articles rely on less precise attribution, using the phrase *according to*. Information in newspaper articles can be attributed to a variety of sources, including other documents, organizations, or unnamed people:

according to court documents
according to a government report
according to a source close to the case
according to diplomatic sources
according to the Criminal Justice Institute
according to the army

[all from AP wire stories]

Finally, the dense use of passive verbs in academic prose is interesting because it has been so stigmatized, with some critics claiming that it is used merely to sound objective and to distance the practice of science from human agents (compare *No significant differences were found* to *We found no significant differences*). While it is conventional to use passives to report research findings in many fields, there are also functional factors that affect the choice of passive. Even a brief analysis of some functions that passives serve will show that general advice to students such as "avoid passive voice" is misguided.

In many cases where passives are used, the subject of an active voice verb would just be a vague group of researchers, perhaps *The members of our research team who did the statistical analysis found no significant differences*. In these cases, the passive voice expression (*no significant differences were found*) is more economical and equally informative.

Even more importantly, passive voice allows concepts and objects (rather than people) to be the grammatical subject of the sentence, making the discourse topic clear. This is not just important for research articles; consider the advice from the foodservice textbook (Text Sample 5.7):

Text Sample 5.7 Foodservice textbook

Meats, poultry, and finfish *should be checked* for color, texture, and temperature on delivery. Live molluscan shellfish and crustacea *must be delivered* alive or properly packed fresh or frozen. Produce must be fresh and wholesome. Milk, eggs and other dairy products *must be checked* for temperature and freshness. (p. 114)

In this paragraph, each sentence begins with the object that is being discussed, while disregarding irrelevant information about the people doing the actions. Using active voice would require rewriting sentences such as:

> Whoever receives a delivery should check meats, poultry and finfish for color, texture and temperature. When someone delivers molluscan shellfish and crustacea, they must be alive . . .

In cases like these, rephrasing the sentences with active voice would make it difficult for readers to skim quickly and see the main points by looking at the subject of each sentence. An academic writer's preference for passive thus often corresponds to clearly structuring dense, informational prose.

Passives occur in newspapers less frequently but with similar functions. In many cases, the agent is obvious, irrelevant, or simply not known. In the following examples, it is well known that "the police" is the human agent who arrests a suspect (a), while in (b) it is simply not known who stole the truck:

> a. The suspect *was arrested* after . . .
> b. The truck *was stolen* Monday and still was missing Wednesday.
>   [AP stories]

In both of these examples, identifying the agent would obscure the main point of the discourse – the suspect and the truck.

However, there are other newspaper articles where agents and their acts are the point of the story, and so active voice is preferred. For example, the report concerning the snake bite in Text Sample 5.3 and the story of the plan to protect the breeding birds in sample 5.4 have no passives. Thus, newspapers overall have a lower frequency of passive voice than academic prose does.

5.4   Variation within the general registers

We noted in Section 5.2 that there are several subregisters within each of these two general written registers. For example, newspapers have articles identified as "news analysis," sports reports, editorials, letters to the editor, and movie and restaurant reviews. These subregisters differ in their particular communicative purposes, and so we would predict that there will be corresponding linguistic differences. In the following sections, we provide two examples of the linguistic variation among subregisters: news reports versus newspaper editorials (within the general register of newspapers), and research articles versus textbooks (within the general register of academic prose).

5.4.1   News reports and newspaper editorials

In basic news reportage, it is expected that the writer will not overtly state opinions about an issue. Editorials, however, have the specific purpose of stating an opinion and arguing for it. Consider the excerpts from editorials in Text Sample 5.8:

Text Sample 5.8 Editorials

A. . . . something needs to be done. Here's one suggestion.
Gov. Ted Kulongoski should pick up the phone today and offer DHS director Bruce Goldberg a simple reminder . . . [*The Oregonian*, October 1, 2007, p. E4]

B. If any good can come from the incident in which U.S. security contractors are alleged to have killed at least eight Iraqi civilians, it's that it focuses attention on a largely unseen facet of the war. While debate in this country has focused on diplomatic initiatives and the role of the military, the largest component of the U.S. presence in Iraq is a privately employed army of cooks, technicians and gun-carrying security guards who, in some cases, operate with minimal insight . . .
If the United States is truly interested in cultivating what President Bush calls "a free nation that can govern itself, sustain itself and defend itself" in Iraq, it can start by making its contractors accountable. It can take steps to ensure that contractors operate under the same rules of engagement as military forces.
And it can help root out contractors who undo diplomacy by firing their weapons too freely. [*The Oregonian*, September 19, 2007, p. D6]

C. Beginning soon, though, the bureau's 9-1-1 operators will put callers who don't have true emergencies on hold while screening the next call. In the long term, this change could be lifesaving. In the short term, it may mean that 9-1-1 operators don't sound as polite as usual.
The operators shouldn't use it as an excuse to amp up the rudeness, though. This is still Oregon. There's still room for a little politeness, even when a house is on fire. [*The Oregonian*, September 19, 2007, p. D6]

In all of these editorials, opinions are clearly stated, evaluating what happened and recommending what should happen. Specific linguistic features are used for these functions. For example, there are frequent modals in editorials compared to typical newspaper reportage. Many of these are directive, telling people the best behavior to follow. The modal *should* is common, as illustrated in editorials A and C above:

> Gov. Ted Kulongoski *should* pick up the phone . . .

> The operators *shouldn't* use it as an excuse to amp up the rudeness . . .

Other modals are used to identify preferred actions, as in this example with *can*:

> . . . it *can* start by making its contractors accountable. It *can* take steps to ensure . . .

Since many editorials describe future events or possible future consequences, modals are also used for a predictive function:

> Beginning soon, though, the bureau's 9-1-1 operators *will* put callers who don't have true emergencies on hold . . .

> . . . it *may* mean that 9-1-1 operators don't sound as polite as usual.

Editorials also tend to have a high concentration of conditionals to discuss hypotheticals (often in conjunction with modals), predicting events if particular actions are or are not followed:

> *If* the FCC were to reimpose the Fairness Doctrine, talk radio *would* no longer be part of the GOP base.   [© 2007 Los Angeles Times – reprinted *The Oregonian*, October 8, 2007, p. C4. Behind all the talk about talk.]

In contrast to the overt opinions of editorials, consider the news report in Text Sample 5.9 (about the same events as in Text Sample 5.8-B):

Text Sample 5.9 Newspaper report

Employees of Blackwater USA have engaged in nearly 200 shootings in Iraq since 2005, in the majority of cases firing their weapons from moving vehicles without stopping to count the dead or assist the wounded, according to a new report from Congress.

 In at least two cases, Blackwater paid victims' family members who complained, and they sought to cover up other episodes, the congressional report said.

[The Oregonian, October 2, 2007, p. A1]

The news report simply narrates the event. There are no opinions overtly expressed, no suggestions for next steps, no discussion of hypothetical situations or possibilities for the future. Correspondingly, modals and conditionals are absent.

Editorials and news reports are included in the same publication and read by the same audience. However, they have distinct communicative purposes. Even examining just two linguistic features – modals and conditionals – it is easy to see how different subregisters within a single general register have systematic linguistic differences associated with their different purposes.

5.4.2   Research articles vs. textbooks

While newspapers include different subregisters as part of the same publication, academic prose encompasses many different kinds of publications. Research articles and textbooks are two of these.

The comparison of these two more specific academic subregisters has interesting implications in a university educational context. Many university classes ask students to read textbooks, and these are likely to be the register students are most familiar with, having used them throughout their school years. However, in many cases, even in low-level university classes, students are asked to write original research papers, using the register features of research articles. As they advance, they are asked to read more research articles as well. Many students find the move from textbooks to articles to be challenging, for production and comprehension – and the register perspective helps to explain why.

The most obvious situational differences between research articles and textbooks concern their participants and communicative purposes. Research articles are usually written by professionals who are experts in a specific field, and they are written for other experienced professionals. In contrast, textbooks are written by experts for novices in the field. Although both of these registers have a general purpose of conveying information, their specific purposes vary. Research articles must contribute new knowledge to the field and convince other experts that this knowledge has scientific merit; in contrast, textbooks generally seek to inform students of knowledge that is already established in a field of study. Even from these situational characteristics, it is immediately easy to see why research articles are often difficult for students to read: they are not the intended audience, and they are probably unskilled in recognizing established knowledge vs. new knowledge, and in evaluating scientific merit. When they write an article, students are also in an awkward position. They are faced with producing a new register, but they must also adapt that register for their school context (since they are students writing for instructors, not experts writing for other experts).

Several linguistic features correspond to the situational differences between textbooks and professional research articles. Text Samples 5.10 and 5.11 illustrate the typical linguistic characteristics of the two registers. Both texts are from the discipline of biology, and both discuss the same general topic: the response of organisms to their environment. However, Text Sample 5.10 reports findings from a new research study (from an academic research article), while 5.11 reports more general information for the non-expert reader (from a textbook), summarizing the results from several previous research studies.

Text Sample 5.10 Research article – biology

There were marked differences in root growth into regrowth cores among the three communities, both in the distribution of roots through the cores and in the response to elevated CO2. In the Scirpus community, root growth was evenly distributed throughout the 15-cm profile, with no significant differences in root biomass among the 5-cm sampling intervals within a treatment (Fig. 1). Exposure to elevated CO2 has a pronounced effect on root regrowth . . .

                 P. S. Curtis, L. M. Balduman, B. G. Drake and D. F. Wigham, Elevated atmospheric CO_2 effects on belowground processes in C3 and C4 estuarine marsh communities, *Ecology* 71 (1990): 2001–2006.

Text Sample 5.11 Textbook – biology

Migration, thus, is not an easy out; but for many bird species there is no alternative. Physical or behavioral adaptations to particular feeding strategies alone may dictate fall flight. The herons, for example, with their stilt-legged manner of fishing for a living in shallow water, have no way of coping with even a thin, temporary cover of ice. They have, in effect, become too specialized. The fly-catchers, as well, once their insect prey have metamorphosed and become sedentary for the winter, must move southward to find food on the wing. And so, too, must the soaring birds of prey . . .

                 P. J. Marchand, *Life in the cold: an introduction to winter ecology*, 2nd edn. Hanover, NH: University Press of New England, 1991: 4.

One important linguistic difference between research articles and textbooks is the use of complex noun phrases. We noted the preponderance of complex noun phrases when we discussed the general register of academic prose. However, research articles and textbooks differ in their reliance on these structures. In the research article above, a specific research topic is discussed – root growth into regrowth cores – and complex noun phrases are used to facilitate precise identification of the referents. Thus, many noun modifiers are used, including attributive adjectives, nouns premodifying nouns, and prepositional phrases – *marked differences in root growth into regrowth cores among the three communities*; *no significant differences in root biomass among the 5-cm sampling intervals within a treatment*.

In the textbook passage, the description is more general, with fewer complex noun phrases. The passage discusses a more general concept – reasons for migration – and uses several examples to illustrate the concept – herons, fly-catchers and birds of prey. There are some simple statements with simple noun phrases, such as the opening "Migration, thus, is not an easy out." More description is given for many of the referents, rather than just naming them. For example, herons are described in a sentence that has no complex noun phrases: "They have, in effect, become too specialized." The greater emphasis on explanation and exemplification of a concept thus corresponds to a lower density of complex noun phrases.

Oddly enough, the complex noun phrases can be both a help and a hindrance to students. On the one hand, the complex noun phrases contain more information and more precise, technical information, and are therefore more difficult to understand or produce. On the other hand, the noun phrases in a research article cover a very limited technical topic. Especially for second language speakers, the restricted vocabulary and topic might make an article easier than a textbook, which will have a great diversity of referents and more idiomatic language (such as "an easy out").

Another interesting linguistic difference between the two academic registers concerns the use of passives. Textbooks tend to use passive voice less often than research articles. The passage in Text Sample 5.12 from a history textbook illustrates the common use of active voice:

Text Sample 5.12 Textbook – history

They [English colonial planters] *hoped* to reproduce Spanish successes by dispatching to America men who would similarly *exploit* the native peoples for their own and their nation's benefit. In the 1580s a group that *included* Sir Humphrey Gilbert and his younger half-brother Sir Walter Raleigh *promoted* a scheme to establish outposts that could trade with the Indians and *provide* bases for attacks on New Spain. Approving the idea, Queen Elizabeth I *authorized* Raleigh and Gilbert to colonize North America. Gilbert *failed* to plant a colony in Newfoundland, dying in the attempt, and Raleigh was only briefly more successful.

M. Norton, D. Katzman, P. Escott, H. Chudacoff, T. Paterson and W. Tuttle, *A people and a nation*. I. *To 1877*, 3rd edn. Boston: Houghton Mifflin, 1990: 20.

The greater use of active voice in textbooks results in more passages with an action-oriented narrative. In contrast, research articles often use passive voice to focus on objects rather than people, for example:

> The dimensions of the wild bison resource on the Southern Plains, and the Great Plains in general, *have been much overstated* in popular literature. (Flores 1991: 469)

> Runaway ads *were published* in a milieu that took seeing and describing seriously. (Prude 1991: 127)

> Most often, however, early maps *are not read* as documents, but *reduced* to decorations. (Nobles 1993: 11)

Overall, then, there is less action in research articles, with more emphasis on the significance and interpretation of events or documents. This different emphasis is required as researchers argue the importance of their research (a crucial function for student researchers to learn), while the more action-oriented textbooks are likely to be more engaging for student readers.

5.5   More specific subregisters: research article sections

So far we have covered distinct subregisters within the general register of academic prose. However, even subregisters can have even more specialized registers within them.

One group of specific subregisters that has been described in previous research is the sections of scientific research articles: Introduction, Methods, Results, and Discussion. These sections have become an entrenched convention in traditional scientific disciplines. Each section has a different communicative purpose:

Introduction – Describes what is known so far about this area of research and what additional information this study will add.
Methods – Reports the data, techniques, and procedures used in the study.
Results – Reports the findings of the analysis.
Discussion – Interprets the results and argues what their significance is, referring back to what was previously known about this area of research.

Each of the four sections contributes to an article's overall purpose of contributing new information to the field and convincing readers that this new information is significant and trustworthy. But since each section has a different specific purpose, each section also has its own characteristic linguistic features.

For example, consider the distribution of verb tense in Introduction and Methods sections. Text Sample 5.5 (above) came from the introduction section of a research article about the breeding of snowy plovers. If you look back, you will see that this text passage is written exclusively in the present tense – *Breeding site tenacity **is** widely believed . . . potential advantages **include** . . .*, and so on. Present tense fits the function of telling the current state of knowledge.

That linguistic pattern can be contrasted with the methods section from the same article:

Text Sample 5.13 Academic prose – research article about breeding of birds – methods section

Materials and methods

We uniquely *color-banded* adult and fledgling snowy plovers, and closely *monitored* their presence, nests and broods at the Monterey Bay focal study area from 1984 to

> 1989 and at the Point Reyes focal study area from 1986 to 1989. To qualify as a breeder in either focal area, plovers *had to be found* with a clutch of eggs or a brood during the study period. We also *included* in this study observations of qualifying breeders occurring prior to these periods or extending into 1990. Before 1984, some areas . . . *were checked* only infrequently. At Salmon Creek, plovers *were regularly monitored* only in 1989 and 1990. At both focal study areas, field methods *were similar* to those of Warriner *et al.* (1986) . . .
>
> [Lynne E. Stenzel, Jane C. Warriner, John S. Warriner, Katherine S. Wilson, Frances C. Bidstrup and Gary W. Page, Long-distance breeding dispersal of snowy plovers in western North America, *Journal of Animal Ecology* 63 (1994): 887–902]

In contrast to the introduction section, the methods section narrates specific past events, and so all verbs are in the past tense. Corpus research studies have shown that the difference in verb tense illustrated here is typical of introduction and methods sections generally, with the introduction describing what is currently known about a topic (with frequent present tense verbs) and the methods section describing what was done to conduct a particular study (with frequent past tense verbs). Although this correspondence between form and function may seem obvious to you here, many students learning to write research articles have difficulty recognizing and using these register features appropriately.

The distribution of passive voice verbs provides a second example of the linguistic differences across sub-sections of articles. In general, passives are much more frequent in methods sections than in the other sections. As Text Sample 5.13 illustrates, the focus in the methods section is on the research procedures, not the actors who carried out those procedures. That is, it makes no difference if it was an individual or the entire research group who performed an action. The important point is to understand how the experiment was conducted. As a result, passive voice is the norm in this section.

Most people are surprised to learn that passive voice is also much more common in discussion sections than in the introduction or results section. Discussion sections make statements that summarize the evidence in the study and argue for its scientific significance. These summaries are often written in passive voice, for example:

> [From a research article about differential survival in male and female wild horses]
> The tendency for sex ratios of adults to be skewed towards females, therefore, *can be attributed to* differential survival.

> [From a research article about competition between two insects]
> Competition for space between these two study insects *was* readily *documented* for two reasons . . .

As noted in Section 5.3.2 for academic prose generally, the use of passive voice here allows an abstract concept (in this case, the findings of the studies) to be the topic of the discourse.

5.6   Research articles from a genre perspective

Since research articles have a conventionalized structure, it is possible to analyze them from a genre perspective as well as a register perspective. In fact, traditional (experimental) research articles are one of the clearest examples of a variety that is structured according to textual conventions. Nearly all experimental research articles have the same overall organization: beginning with an abstract followed by the four major sections described above (Introduction, Methods, Results, Discussion). Each of these components of the text has its own typical communicative goals. All five components are expected to occur in the text, and always in the same order. Several studies included in Appendix A cover research articles from a genre perspective.

Despite their conventional organization, however, research articles have few genre markers (as defined in Chapter 3). The labels of each section (Introduction, Methods, etc.) can be considered genre markers, since they occur at predictable points in the article structure and are used once (as single words, they may be used as part of other sentences in the article). Beyond that, the language used in the different sections needs to be described from a register perspective. As discussed in Section 5.5, certain features are used with greater frequency in different sections in order to meet the communicative purposes of the section. Characterizing the language therefore requires the quantitative, comparative approach of register analysis.

There is another, more specialized way in which research articles have been analyzed from a genre perspective: with respect to the conventional sequence of *rhetorical moves* found within a section from a research article. For example, Swales (1981, 1990) analyzed research article introductions as consisting of three major rhetorical moves:

Move 1 – Establish a territory (by claiming centrality of the issue, making topic generalizations, and reviewing previous research).
Move 2 – Establish a niche (by giving counter claims, or indicating a gap, or raising questions, or explaining how the study continues a tradition).
Move 3 – Occupy the niche (by outlining the purpose of the study, and [optionally] announcing the research findings and indicating the structure of the article).

In this case, even the introduction of a research article can be regarded as a well-defined genre, with a conventional structure for how the "text" should begin and end. We explore this perspective on genre analysis further in the chapter activities.

5.7   Variation in fiction due to style

Many people simply read fiction for enjoyment, while literary scholars often analyze fiction for characteristics like character and plot development. However, fictional texts can also be analyzed linguistically, just like any other texts. A linguistic analysis makes it especially clear just how complex fiction is and how adept authors are at manipulating language for different purposes and effects, even if they are not consciously aware of their linguistic expertise. Fiction also provides another perspective on how a general register can vary. As explained below, in this general register a great deal of linguistic variation comes not from specialized subregisters, but from deliberate choices by authors depending on how they want to convey a story. Therefore, analysis of fiction must cover characteristics of the imaginary world and choices of style: choices whose functions are associated more with aesthetic preferences than the real-world situational context of the register.

From a situational perspective, fiction is one of the most complicated registers. Like newspaper reports and academic prose, fiction is produced by an author who has extensive opportunity for planning, revision, and editing of the text. Fiction is further similar to newspaper reports in that it is written for a large, general audience, who has little personal knowledge about the author and also does not share a high level of professional/specialist knowledge with the author. There is normally no interaction between author and reader, and readers normally do not know the time and place where the text was written.

However, these external situational characteristics have almost no influence on the linguistic characteristics of a fictional text.[1] It is almost irrelevant whether the author interacts with the reader, whether they know one another, and so on. This is because the relevant situational context for a fictional text is the fictional world that the author creates in the text itself. Thus, fictional characters interact with one another in that fictional world, even though the author of the text never interacts with the reader. Further, fictional characters often reveal their own personal thoughts and attitudes, even though the author herself never directly describes her own personal attitudes. The determining factors for the language used in a fictional text are the ways in which the fictional world is constructed, rather than the "real-world" situation of the text.

One of the most important factors that influences fictional style is the perspective that the author chooses for narrating a story: Is the story told from a first person perspective, as if the author were one of the main characters? Or is the story told from a third person perspective, as if the author were an outside observer of the events? This distinction obviously has immediate linguistic consequences.

---

[1] The one exception here is the production circumstances: authors need extensive time to plan, revise, and edit a fictional narrative.

For example, the Sherlock Holmes stories are told from the first person point of view of Dr. Watson, as if Watson (rather than Arthur Conan Doyle) were the author.

Text Sample 5.14 Fiction: Arthur Conan Doyle, *The Hound of The Baskervilles*, 1902

An instant afterwards he [i.e. Sherlock Holmes] gave a little cry of satisfaction, and, following the direction of his eager eyes, I saw that a hansom cab with a man inside which had halted on the other side of the street was now walking slowly onwards again.

"There's our man, Watson! Come along! We'll have a good look at him, if we can do no more."

At that instant I was aware of a bushy black beard and a pair of piercing eyes turned upon us through the side window of the cab.

First person fiction obviously has frequent occurrences of the pronoun *I*, like any first person narrative, where someone is narrating events that they personally experienced (e.g., in a personal letter or a conversation). In addition, first person fiction usually reports the sensual perceptions, thoughts, and attitudes of the narrator, as in *I saw* and *I was aware of* in Text Sample 5.14. As described in Chapter 4, this results in frequent complement clause constructions (*that*-clauses and *to*-clauses), where the verb or adjective in the main clause expresses a "personal stance" about the information in the complement clause:

That-clauses:
I could not *doubt* **that some grave and deep reason lay behind it** . . .
I was suddenly *aware* **that I was not the only witness of their interview**.
It *seemed to me* **that she was straining away from him** . . .
It *seemed to me* **that Stapleton was abusing Sir Henry**

To-clauses:
I was *surprised* **to observe that by the gate there stood two soldierly men**
But I was *eager* **to get back to my charge**.
I was *astounded* **to see Miss Stapleton sitting upon a rock** . . .
I was deeply *ashamed* **to have witnessed so intimate a scene** . . .

In contrast, a third person narrative is told from the point of view of an external observer. In this case, the book's narrator can be a normal observer, who can observe only the physical phenomena that any of us could observe, or a super-human observer, who is aware of the inner thoughts and feelings of characters. In the former case, the description of events is relatively "objective," in some ways similar linguistically to the prose in a newspaper report with frequent third person pronouns, past tense, communication verbs, and so on. The passage in Text Sample 5.15 from Upton Sinclair's *The Jungle* illustrates this style of prose. Here the narrator describes the pain and emotion evident on a character's face, but cannot directly detect her actual internal thoughts and feelings:

Text Sample 5.15 Fiction: Upton Sinclair, *The Jungle*, 1906

She stood in the doorway, shepherded by Cousin Marija, breathless from pushing through the crowd, and in her happiness painful to look upon. There was a light of wonder in her eyes and her lids trembled, and her otherwise wan little face was flushed. She wore a muslin dress, conspicuously white, and a stiff little veil coming to her shoulders. There were five pink paper roses twisted in the veil, and eleven bright green rose leaves. There were new white cotton gloves upon her hands, and as she stood staring about her she twisted them together feverishly. It was almost too much for her – you could see the pain of too great emotion in her face, and all the tremor of her form.

In contrast, an omniscient third person narrator is able to describe the inner thoughts and feelings of characters, as in the excerpt from *Lord of the Flies* in Text Sample 5.16:

Text Sample 5.16 Fiction: William Golding, *Lord of the Flies*, 1954

Piggy and the parody were so funny that the hunters began to laugh. Jack felt encouraged. He went on scrambling and the laughter rose to a gale of hysteria. Unwillingly Ralph felt his lips twitch, he was angry with himself for giving way.

The fictional world described by an omniscient external narrator includes numerous stance expressions, because the narrator is privy to the inner attitudes and feelings of characters. One linguistic reflection of this characteristic is frequent mental verbs controlling complement clauses, similar to the style expected in a first person narrative. Examples from *Lord of the Flies* include:

> Ralph . . . *decided* **that the shadows on his body were really green**.
> He . . . *decided* **that a toothbrush would come in handy too**.
> . . . for a moment they *felt* **that the boat was moving steadily astern**.
> Startled, Ralph *realized* **that the boys were falling still**
> He *noticed* **that he still held the knife aloft**

A second major parameter of variation among fictional stories is the extent to which the author decides to report the dialogue of characters. For example, in *The Hound of The Baskervilles*, much of the story is portrayed through the dialogue of characters rather than through narrative prose. In this case, Watson is the first person narrator, but much of the story is presented as dialogue with

Sherlock Holmes. The reader observes Holmes solving a mystery, understanding what happened by listening to Holmes talk about the various possibilities (Text Sample 5.17):

Text Sample 5.17 Fiction: Arthur Conan Doyle, *The Hound of The Baskervilles*, 1902

[Holmes said] "I think we have drawn as much as we can from this curious letter; and now, Sir Henry, has anything else of interest happened to you since you have been in London?"

"Why, no, Mr Holmes. I think not."

"You have not observed anyone follow or watch you?"

"I seem to have walked right into the thick of a dime novel," said our visitor. "Why in thunder should anyone follow or watch me?"

"We are coming to that. You have nothing else to report to us before we go into this matter?"

"Well, it depends upon what you think worth reporting."

"I think anything out of the ordinary routine of life well worth reporting."

Sir Henry smiled. "I don't know much of British life yet, for I have spent nearly all my time in the States and in Canada. But I hope that to lose one of your boots is not part of the ordinary routine of life over here."

"You have lost one of your boots?"

"My dear sir," cried Dr Mortimer, "it is only mislaid. You will find it when you return to the hotel. What is the use of troubling Mr Holmes with trifles of this kind?"

"Well, he asked me for anything outside the ordinary routine."

"Exactly," said Holmes, "however foolish the incident may seem. You have lost one of your boots, you say?"

This style of fiction thus employs many of the grammatical features that are common in face-to-face conversation, such as second person pronouns (in addition to first person pronouns), present tense verbs, questions, contractions, and ellipsis. (We show in Chapter 6 how authors' representations of fictional dialogue have changed historically over the past three centuries to become increasingly similar to actual face-to-face conversation.)

Other fictional styles incorporate little dialogue. For example, a first person narrative can simply report past events and places as observed by the main character, but omit reports of conversational interactions. This style of fiction is in some ways similar linguistically to other kinds of reflective first person writing, like diaries. There is a high frequency of first and third person pronouns (but not second person pronouns), past tense verbs (but not present tense verbs), adverbials of time, markers of personal stance, and so on. Text Sample 5.18 provides an example of this style from a mystery book, with the typical features highlighted:

Text Sample 5.18 Fiction: Sue Grafton, *'C' Is for Corpse*, 1986

I met Bobby Callahan *on Monday of that week. By Thursday, he was* dead. *He was* convinced someone *was* trying to kill *him* and it *turned* out to be true, but none of us *figured* it out in time to save *him*. *I*'ve never worked for a dead man before and I hope I won't have to do it again. This report is for *him*, for whatever it's worth.

[...]

It *was August* and I'*d* been working out at Santa Teresa Fitness, trying to remedy the residual effects of a broken left arm. The days *were* hot, *filled* with relentless sunshine and clear skies. I *was feeling cranky and bored*, doing push-downs and curls and wrist rolls. *I'd just* worked two cases back-to-back and *I'd* sustained more damage than a fractured humerus. I *was feeling emotionally battered* and *I needed* a rest.

The same distinction in dialogue use is found in third person narratives. For example, the prose in *Mr. Sammler's Planet* (Text Sample 5.19) focuses mostly on the inner thoughts and feelings of the main character, together with a narration of past events as perceived by that character. There is very little dialogue reported in this style of fiction, and thus few features typical of face-to-face conversation.

Text Sample 5.19 Fiction: Saul Bellow, *Mr. Sammler's Planet*, 1970

But *now he wondered* whether *he had* not drawn too close, whether *he had* also been seen seeing. *He wore* smoked glasses, *at all times* protecting *his* vision, but *he* couldn't be taken for a blind man. *He did*n't have the white cane, only a furled umbrella, British-style. Moreover, *he did*n't have the look of blindness. The pickpocket *himself wore* dark shades. *He was* a powerful Negro in a camels-hair coat, *dressed* with extraordinary elegance, as if by Mr. Fish of the West End, or Turnbull and Asser of Jermyn Street. (Mr. Sammler *knew* his London.) The Negro's perfect circles of gentian violet banded with lovely gold *turned* toward Sammler, but the face *showed* the effrontery of a big animal. Sammler *was* not timid, but *he had* had as much trouble in life as *he wanted*. A good deal of this, waiting for assimilation, would never be accommodated. *He suspected* the criminal was aware that a tall old white man (passing as blind?) *had* observed, *had* seen the minutest details of *his* crimes.

In contrast, a novel like *The Lord of the Flies* (Text Sample 5.20) integrates the full spectrum of information: narration of events, description of the personal feelings of characters, as well as extensive dialogue with characters talking to one another. For example:

Text Sample 5.20 Fiction: William Golding, *Lord of the Flies*, 1954

The fair boy began to pick his way as casually as possible towards the water. He tried to be offhand and not too obviously uninterested, but the fat boy hurried after him.

"Aren't there any grown-ups at all?"

"I don't think so."

The fair boy said this solemnly; but then the delight of a realized ambition overcame him. In the middle of the scar he stood on his head and grinned at the reversed fat boy.

"No grown-ups!"

The fat boy thought for a moment.

"That pilot."

The fair boy allowed his feet to come down and sat on the steamy earth.

"He must have flown off after he dropped us. He couldn't land here. Not in a plane with wheels."

"We was attacked!"

"He'll be back all right."

The fat boy shook his head.

As this text sample illustrates, this style relies on both conversational features and narrative features. For example, there are frequent present tense verbs, modal verbs, contractions, ellipsis, and questions – typical of conversation – as well as frequent past tense verbs and third person pronouns, typical of prose narration.

An alternative style to all those described above is to narrate the story as though it is being told orally or in a personal letter to a specific addressee. Consider the example from *Slaughterhouse Five* in Text Sample 5.21:

Text Sample 5.21 Fiction: Kurt Vonnegat, *Slaughterhouse Five*, 1969

I would hate to tell you what this lousy little book cost me in money and anxiety and time. When I got home from the Second World War twenty-three years ago, I thought it would be easy for me to write about the destruction of Dresden, since all I would have to do would be to report what I had seen. And I thought, too, that it would be a masterpiece or at least make me a lot of money, since the subject was so big.

In this case, there is little direct reported dialogue, but there are numerous linguistic features of conversation, because the story is written as if it were an oral telling of the personal events, feelings, and attitudes of the narrator. First person pronouns are common, since the story is told from the perspective of a first person narrator. The addressee is directly addressed as "you," as if the narrator were actually sitting in our living room telling us the story. And the narrator tells us his own personal feelings and attitudes, using frequent modal verbs, complement clause constructions, stance adverbials, and so on. However, the entire passage is written in past tense, because the focus is on the report of past events.

A final parameter of variation among fictional novels is whether the story is told as a narration of past events, or as a description of events as they occur at the time of the telling. The more common style is to narrate past events, as in all of the text excerpts given above. However, in a few cases, the story is written as if the narrator is describing the events in real time, as they are occurring. This style of discourse results in frequent features like present tense verbs and time adverbials, describing events that are actually in progress, as illustrated in this sample from *The Middleman*:

Text Sample 5.22 Fiction: Bharati Mukherjee, *The Middleman*, 1988

All day I *sit* by the lime green swimming pool, sun-screened so I *won't* turn black, going through my routine of isometrics while Ransome's indios *hack* away the virgin forests. Their hate *is* intoxicating. They *hate* gringos – from which my darkness *exempts* me – even more than Gutierrez. They *hate* in order to keep up their intensity.

I *hear* a litany of presidents' names, Hollywood names, Detroit names – Carter, chop, Reagan, slash, Buick, thump – *bounce* off the vines as machetes *clear* the jungle greenness.

We spoke a form of Spanish in my old Baghdad home. I always *understand* more than I *let* on.

Meanwhile, Ransome *rubs* Cutter over his face and neck. They'*re* supposed to go deep-sea fishing today, though it *looks* to me as if he'*s* dressed for the jungle. A wetted-down towel *is* tucked firmly under the back of his baseball cap. He'*s* a Braves man.

This stylistic choice helps to create a greater sense of immediacy and involvement than in typical past tense narratives.

In summary, fiction is one of the most complex varieties to analyze from a register perspective, because the author must create a fictional world and can choose to describe that world from many different possible perspectives. In the present section, we have been able to describe only a few of the many variations possible in fictional prose: the choice of first vs. third person perspective; the choice of a normal or omniscient third person narrator; the extent to which the author reports dialogue, narration of events, description of people and places, or the inner thoughts and attitudes of characters; and the choice of narrating in past or present tense. These choices are all stylistic choices. That is, their use is not associated with the real-life situational context of the writer and reader, but with the authors' preferences for how they want to tell their stories. The linguistic features do have functions, as illustrated in the text samples, but the variation concerns style, rather than register.

5.8   Conclusion

In this chapter, we explored three general written registers and illustrated the analysis of those registers with increasing specificity. On a general level, two informational written registers – newspaper writing and academic prose – were shown to share certain situational characteristics and linguistic features that set them apart from conversation. At the same time, the two general registers differ from each other with respect to their specific topics and communicative purpose, and these situational differences are reflected in linguistic differences for verb tense, voice, time and place adverbials, and modals.

On a more specific level, we described patterned variation corresponding to the specific subregisters within these general registers. For example, editorials differ from news reports, and research articles differ from textbooks. And even more specific subregisters, such as the sections within research articles, can be distinguished by their linguistic patterns of use.

Finally, the analysis of fiction illustrated how linguistic variation can be influenced by style choices rather than the normal factors that determine register differences. In the next chapter, we show how register, genre, and style perspectives can all be applied to the study of how a written variety has changed historically.

Chapter 5 activities

Reflection and review

1. Read through Activity Text 11, the university student research paper, and identify the *first* instance of each of these linguistic features:

   a. attributive adjective
   b. nominalization
   c. prepositional phrase modifying a noun
   d. noun phrase that includes two prepositional phrases as modifiers
   e. passive voice (as a main verb)
   f. past tense verb
   g. present tense verb

2. The popular impression of prototypical speaking is that it focuses largely on interpersonal concerns and is unplanned. In contrast, prototypical writing is concerned with conveying information and contains carefully planned and revised language. Can you think of registers (besides those already mentioned in this book) that vary from these prototypes? Can you think of registers other than face-to-face conversation, newspaper writing, and academic prose that fit these prototypes?

Table 5.3 *Selected linguistic features in academic prose and a student research paper (normed per 1,000 words) (academic prose counts based on findings reported in the* Longman Grammar of Spoken and Written English; *preposition count based on Biber 1988: Appendix III)*

Linguistic feature	Academic prose	Student research paper
Nouns	290	253
Prepositions	140	120
Attributive adjectives	71	50
Personal pronouns	21	66
Present tense verbs	61	67
Past tense verbs	18	42
% of finite verbs that are passive	25	10
Linking adverbials	7	10

3. Choose another general written register – for example, magazine writing, letters, drama, comic books, children's books, or some other register of your choice. Fill in a table outlining all the situational characteristics of that register. Which characteristics can you specify the least because of variation among more specialized registers within the general register?

Analysis practice

4. Table 5.3 displays the quantitative findings for a comparison of the student research paper excerpt (Activity Text 11) and academic prose. Using the activity text to see how the features are used, write a short summary of the findings. How is the student paper similar to and different from academic prose generally? Propose functional interpretations to account for the differences (tying them to the specific situational characteristics of the paper). Are there some differences that you think are just the student's personal style or a sign of less experience with academic writing?

5. Analyze the use of three to five linguistic features in three pages of this book. Is your analysis consistent with the findings of previous studies of academic prose and textbooks as described in this chapter? Why or why not?

6. As described in Section 5.6, Swales' (1990) genre analysis of introductions of research articles has Move 2 described as follows:

> Move 2 – Establish a niche (by giving counter claims, or indicating a gap, or raising questions, or explaining how the study continues a tradition).

Although there are not "genre markers" that always identify this move, this specific rhetorical function is likely to correspond to differences in the use of linguistic features.

Consider the following "Move 2" statements from biology research articles. Identify any linguistic features that appear to be associated with "establishing the niche" – that is, with giving counter claims or indicating a gap or raising questions. Why are these features useful for this rhetorical function?

> Records of long-distance within a breeding season are rare . . . The paucity of long-distance records is undoubtedly in part due to a lack of opportunity . . .   [Lynne E. Stenzel *et al.*, Long-distance breeding dispersal of snowy plovers in western North America, *Journal of Animal Ecology* 63 (1994): 888]

> No study to date has measured the variance in lifetime reproductive success in a monogamous mammal.   [D. O. Ribble, Lifetime reproductive success and its correlates in the monogamous rodent, Peromyscus Californicus. *Journal of Animal Ecology* 61 (1992): 458]

> Perhaps because of this lack of baseline information, little attention has also been given to the climatic controls of tree growth in tropical moist or wet forests.   [D. A. Clark and D. B. Clark, Climate-introduced annual variation in canopy tree growth in a Costa Rican tropical rain forest. *Journal of Ecology* 82 (1994): 866]

> . . . we still do not have a sense of how reproductive investment is regulated among shoots within individual plants, and how similar the two morphs are in this respect.   [L. F. Delph, factors affecting intraplant variation in flowering and fruiting in the gynodioecious species of Aebe subalpina. *Journal of Ecology* 81 (1993): 288]

> The microhabitat of these two species has not previously been described quantitatively, nor have root distribution and shoot morphology been related to physiological responses.   [P. S. Nobel, M. E. Loik, and R. W. Meyer, Microhabitat and diel tissue acidity changes for two sympatric cactus species differing in growth habit. *Journal of Ecology* 79 (1991): 168]

Project ideas

7. Choose another specific subregister from newspapers (other than news reports or editorials), and compare the use of linguistic features in that subregister to those described in this chapter. Gather several sample texts from at least two newspapers, analyze ten to twelve linguistic features, and interpret your findings with reference to the situational characteristics of the subregister.

8. Compare a popular-science article (from a newspaper or popular magazine) to an article on the same topic from an academic research journal. Compare the use of eight to ten linguistic features, including verb tense and voice. How do the differences and similarities in the use of the linguistic features correspond to the situational characteristics?

9. Analyze three of your own academic papers and compare your use of linguistic features with the findings for academic prose generally. Interpret differences, making clear which are due to the particular subregister that you employed, and which are more likely to be stylistic differences or differences having to do with your experience writing academic prose.

Alternatively, if you write short stories, analyze three of your stories. Compare the style features of your stories to those discussed in Section 5.7.

6 Historical evolution of registers, genres, and styles

6.1 Introduction

The preceding chapters have approached the analysis of registers from a synchronic perspective, considering the situational and linguistic characteristics of present-day varieties. These same techniques can be applied to registers from earlier historical periods. In many cases, these analyses show that a register has changed over time in some of its typical linguistic characteristics. Such changes reflect changes in the situational context of the register, like a shift in communicative purpose, a shift in the audience targeted by the register, or even changing attitudes about good style. In some cases, these changes can be so extreme that it is reasonable to ask whether the earlier variety actually represents the same register as the modern variety.

In the present chapter, we consider case studies illustrating these various kinds of change. We begin with a discussion of the fictional novel, showing how it has been recognizable as the same general register over the past four centuries. At the same time, there are some notable linguistic changes that distinguish typical novels in the eighteenth century from their modern-day equivalents.

Our second case study considers changes in scientific research articles. In contrast to the first case study, the linguistic and communicative changes documented in the second study are so extensive that they might be regarded as a shift to a new register – despite the fact that the study is based on research articles published in a single academic journal (*The Philosophical Transactions of the Royal Society of London*).

Finally, we take up the topic of how historical change in the use of particular linguistic features is mediated by register factors. We first show how grammatical change in noun phrase complexity is mediated by register differences, so that registers have evolved over time to become more sharply distinguished from one another. We then consider the expression of stance, again showing how the relations among registers has changed historically.

The linguistic patterns that are discussed in this chapter come from studies of the ARCHER corpus, a large corpus (1,037 texts and c. 1.7 million words) designed for the study of historical register variation (Biber and Finegan 1989a, 1997). Texts in the ARCHER corpus are sampled systematically over the last three and a half centuries to represent as wide a range of register variation as possible. Among the written registers, the corpus includes personal styles of communication (journals/diaries and personal letters), prose fiction, popular exposition represented by news reportage, and specialist expository registers, represented by legal opinions, medical prose, and scientific prose. The corpus similarly includes several different kinds of speech-based registers: dialogue in drama and dialogue in fiction as reflections of casual face-to-face conversation, and sermons as a reflection of planned monologue styles. The present chapter focuses mostly on historical change in fiction and scientific research articles (Sections 6.2 and 6.3), but we also include descriptions of medical research articles, newspaper reportage, drama, and personal letters (in Section 6.4), and even historical change in advertisements (in Activity 11).

6.2   Historical change I: the fictional novel

In other courses you might have studied English literature from earlier historical periods, such as plays by Shakespeare or novels by Defoe. From a genre perspective, these varieties are defined by many of the same textual conventions as their modern-day equivalents. However, from a register and style perspective, these texts have undergone extensive change in their typical linguistic features over the centuries. In the present section, we describe some of the major linguistic changes that have occurred in novels over the past three centuries, and then discuss the larger situational context that accounts for those changes.

6.2.1   A genre perspective on the historical novel

For the most part, novels from the last three centuries are all recognizable as belonging to the same general genre, with the same major textual conventions and components. As noted in Chapter 1, for literary genres the notion of *textual convention* is somewhat different than what we have discussed in previous chapters for non-literary genres. That is, there are generally no formulaic beginnings or closings in literary genres, but there are expected conventions for constructing a text from a particular genre. For example, the expected textual conventions for novels include the existence of protagonists and antagonists, some kind of story conflict, a climax, a resolution of the conflict, and discourse that shifts across several major communicative goals (e.g., narration, dialogue, descriptions of the inner thoughts of the main characters, background descriptions).

The following passages from *Amelia* (Text Sample 6.1), written by Henry Fielding in 1751, illustrate several of these textual components. The passage begins with a sequence of narrative events (A) involving Booth, one of the main characters. This narrative then transitions into an extended dialogue (B) between

Booth and a bailiff. A little later in the chapter, there is a paragraph devoted to Booth's frame of mind and his inner thoughts (C), while the following paragraph includes a description (D) of the apartment where Booth was waiting. Although written over 250 years ago, these passages are readily recognizable as taken from a novel, employing the same major textual conventions as modern-day novels.

Text Sample 6.1 Henry Fielding, *Amelia* (Chapter 1 of the 8th Book), 1751

[A]

When Amelia went out in the morning, she left her children to the care of her husband. In this amiable office he had been engaged near an hour; and was at that very time lying along on the floor, and his little things crawling and playing about him, when a most violent knock was heard at the door; and immediately a footman running up stairs, acquainted him, that his lady was taken violently ill, and carried into Mrs. Chenevix's toy-shop.

Booth no sooner heard this account, which was delivered with great appearance of haste and earnestness, than he leapt suddenly from the floor; and leaving his children roaring at the news of their mother's illness, in strict charge with his maid, he ran as fast as his legs could carry him to the place; or towards the place rather: for, before he arrived at the shop, a gentleman stopt him full butt, crying,

[B]

"captain, whither so fast?" – Booth answered eagerly, "whoever you are, friend, don't ask me any questions now." – "You must pardon me, captain," answered the gentleman; "but I have a little business with your honour – In short, captain, I have a small warrant here in my pocket against your honour, at the suit of one Dr. Harrison." "You are a bailiff then," says Booth. "I am an officer, sir," answered the other. – "Well, sir, it is in vain to contend," cries Booth; "but let me beg you will permit me only to step to Mrs. Chenevix's – I will attend you, upon my honour, wherever you please; but my wife lies violently ill there."

[. . .]

[C]

Notwithstanding the pleasantry which Booth endeavoured to preserve, he in reality envied every labourer whom he saw pass by him in his way. The charms of liberty against his will rushed on his mind; and he could not avoid suggesting to himself, how much more happy was the poorest wretch who without control could repair to his homely habitation, and to his family; compared to him, who was thus violently, and yet lawfully torn away from the company of his wife and children. And their condition, especially that of his Amelia, gave his heart many a severe and bitter pang.

[D]

At length he arrived at the bailiff's mansion, and was ushered into a room; in which were several persons. Booth desired to be alone, upon which the bailiff waited on him up stairs, into an apartment, the windows of which were well fortified with iron bars; but the walls had not the least outwork raised before them; they were, indeed, what is generally called naked, the bricks having been only covered with a thin plaister, which in many places was mouldered away.

There is one textual convention used in many eighteenth-century novels that is notably different from modern novels: the author's relation to the reader. In most modern-day novels, the author is hidden. As described in Chapter 5, many modern-day novels are written as a first-person account by one of the main characters. Other modern novels are written from the point of view of an omniscient third person narrator, but there is no hint of who that person is. However, many eighteenth-century novels differ from both of these modern conventions: they are written from the perspective of a third person narrator, but the author explicitly identifies him/herself as the narrator. As a result the author directly refers to "the reader" and to him/herself (often as *we*). Fielding is typical in this regard. Thus, a little later in the same chapter as Text Sample 6.1 above, we find the following passage:

Text Sample 6.1 (cont.) *Amelia*

The serjeant, however, *as the reader hath seen*, brought himself the first account of the arrest. Indeed, the other messenger did not arrive till a full hour afterwards. [. . .]

Here the reader may be apt to conclude, that the bailiff, instead of being a friend, was really an enemy to poor Booth; but in fact, he was not so. His desire was no more than to accumulate bail bonds: for the bailiff was reckoned an honest and good sort of man in his way, and had no more malice against the bodies in his custody, than a butcher hath to those in his; and as the latter when he takes his knife in hand, hath no idea but of the joints into which he is to cut the carcase; so the former when he handles his writ, hath no other design but to cut out the body into as many bail bonds as possible. As to the life of the animal, or the liberty of the man, they are thoughts which never obtrude themselves on either.

CHAPTER 2. Containing an account of Mr. Booth's fellow sufferers

BEFORE we return to Amelia, we must detain our reader a little longer with Mr. Booth, in the custody of Mr. Bondum the bailiff, who now informed his prisoner, that he was welcome to the liberty of the house with the other gentlemen.

When they were directly addressing the reader, authors in the eighteenth and nineteenth century also felt free to provide overt social commentary. In the present passage, Fielding discusses how butchers and bailiffs are similar in that they are both just doing their job, with no regard for the harm they might be causing to others. In modern-day novels, authors almost never directly address the reader, and any social commentary is expressed through the words and action of characters rather than as an overt statement outside of the narrative.

In sum, novels in English have continued to employ many of the same textual conventions over the past three centuries. Of course, in other respects, some modern novels have evolved to employ literary devices and styles not found in earlier novels (such as the present tense narration of events as they are occurring, or the blurring of the distinction between speech and thought). For the most part, though, even the earliest novels are recognizable as belonging to the same general genre as modern-day novels.

6.2.2 Style characteristics of particular eighteenth- and twentieth-century novels

From a style perspective, eighteenth-century novels are also similar to modern novels in many of their typical lexical and grammatical characteristics. It is somewhat difficult to specify what a "typical" modern novel is, because there is considerable experimentation with a wide range of linguistic styles. But the following excerpts illustrate a range of these styles, with passages from three well-known contemporary authors: Kurt Vonnegut, Toni Morrison, and Robert Ludlum. Vonnegut (Text Sample 6.2) employs a very colloquial style, with the story narrated in the first person, almost as if the narrator is telling us the story in person. In contrast, Morrison (Text Sample 6.3) employs an omniscient third person narrator who is privy to the innermost thoughts of the main characters. Ludlum (Text Sample 6.4) also uses third person narration, but with a story line that is much more focused on action than character development.

Text Sample 6.2 Kurt Vonnegut, *Slaughterhouse-Five*, 1969

I have this disease late at night sometimes, involving alcohol and the telephone. I get drunk, and I drive my wife away with a breath like mustard gas and roses. And then, speaking gravely and elegantly into the telephone, I ask the telephone operators to connect me with this friend or that one, from whom I have not heard in years.
[. . .]
  And I let the dog out, or I let him in, and we talk some. I let him know I like him, and he lets me know he likes me. He doesn't mind the smell of mustard gas and roses.
  "You're all right, Sandy," I'll say to the dog. "You know that, Sandy? You're O.K."
  Sometimes I'll turn on the radio and listen to a talk program from Boston or New York. I can't stand recorded music if I've been drinking a good deal.
  Sooner or later I go to bed, and my wife asks me what time it is. She always had to know the time. Sometimes I don't know, and I say, "Search me."
  I think about my education sometimes. I went to the University of Chicago for a while after the Second World War. I was a student in the Department of Anthropology. At that time, they were teaching that there was absolutely no difference between anybody. They may be teaching that still.
  Another thing they taught was that nobody was ridiculous or bad or disgusting. Shortly before my father died, he said to me, "You know – you never wrote a story with a villain in it."
  I told him that was one of the things I learned in college after the war.
  While I was studying to be an anthropologist, I was also working as a police reporter for the famous Chicago City News Bureau for twenty-eight dollars a week. One time they switched me from the night shift to the day shift, so I worked sixteen hours

straight. We were supported by all the newspapers in town, and the AP and the UP and all that. And we would cover the courts and the police stations and the Fire Department and the Coast Guard out on Lake Michigan and all that.

Text Sample 6.3 Toni Morrison, *Beloved*, 1988

"We could move," she suggested once to her mother-in-law.

"What'd be the point?" asked Baby Suggs. "Not a house in the country ain't packed to its rafters with some dead Negro's grief. We lucky this ghost is a baby. My husband's spirit was to come back in here? or yours? Don't talk to me. You lucky. You got three left.

Three pulling at your skirts and just one raising hell from the other side. Be thankful, why don't you? I had eight. Every one of them gone away from me. Four taken, four chased, and all, I expect, worrying somebody's house into evil." Baby Suggs rubbed her eye-brows. "My first-born. All I can remember of her is how she loved the burned bottom of bread. Can you beat that? Eight children and that's all I remember."

"That's all you let yourself remember," Sethe had told her, but she was down to one herself – one alive, that is – the boys chased off by the dead one, and her memory of Buglar was fading fast. Howard at least had a head shape nobody could forget. As for the rest, she worked hard to remember as close to nothing as was safe. Unfortunately her brain was devious. She might be hurrying across a field, running practically, to get to the pump quickly and rinse the chamomile sap from her legs. Nothing else would be in her mind. The picture of the men coming to nurse her was as lifeless as the nerves in her back where the skin buckled like a washboard. Nor was there the faintest scent of ink or the cherry gum and oak bark from which it was made. Nothing. Just the breeze cooling her face as she rushed toward water. And then sopping the chamomile away with pump water and rags, her mind fixed on getting every last bit of sap off – on her carelessness in taking a shortcut across the field just to save a half mile, and not noticing how high the weeds had grown until the itching was all the way to her knees. Then something. The plash of water, the sight of her shoes and stockings awry on the path where she had flung them; or Here Boy lapping in the puddle near her feet, and suddenly there was Sweet Home rolling, rolling, rolling out before her eyes, and although there was not a leaf on that farm that did not make her want to scream, it rolled itself out before her in shameless beauty. It never looked as terrible as it was and it made her wonder if hell was a pretty place too. Fire and brimstone all right, but hidden in lacy groves. Boys hanging from the most beautiful sycamores in the world. It shamed her – remembering the wonderful soughing trees rather than the boys. Try as she might to make it otherwise, the sycamores beat out the children every time and she could not forgive her memory for that.

Text Sample 6.4 Robert Ludlum, *The Icarus Agenda*, 1989

Kendrick felt a third presence but, turning in the chair, saw no one else on the deck of the pleasure yacht. Then he raised his eyes to the aft railing of the bridge. A figure stepped back into the shadows but not quickly enough. It was the excessively tall, deeply tanned contributor from Bollinger's library, and from what could be seen of his face, it was contorted in hatred.

"Are all of the Vice President's guests on board?" he asked, seeing that the Mafioso had followed his gaze.

"What guests?"

"You're cute, Luigi."

"There's a captain and one crew. I've never seen either of them before."

"Where are we going?"

"On a cruise."

The boat slowed down as the beam of a powerful searchlight shot out from the bridge. The Mafia soldier unstrapped himself and got up; he walked across the deck and down into the lower cabin. Evan could hear him on an intercom, but with the wind and the slapping waves was unable to make out the words. Moments later the man returned; in his hand was a gun, a standard issue Colt .45 automatic.

Linguistically, there are some interesting differences among these three twentieth-century authors. Vonnegut blurs the line between narration and speech, using oral linguistic features in the narrative story. For example, the passage above uses several features that are typical of conversation:

- the copular verb *get*:
  *I **get** drunk*
- simple clauses connected by coordinators:
  ***And** I let the dog out, **or** I let him in, **and** we talk some.*
- sentence-initial *and*:
  ***And** then, speaking gravely . . . ; **And** I let the dog out . . . ,*
- "coordination tags":
  *And we would cover the courts and the police stations and the Fire Department and the Coast Guard out on Lake Michigan **and all that**.*

Morrison, in contrast, employs a wide range of sentence styles within a single passage of prose. Her dialogue is colloquial and portrays many of the characteristics of African-American Vernacular English; for example:

- *ain't*:
  *Not a house in the country **ain't** packed to its rafters with some dead Negro's grief.*
- omission of the copula *be*:
  We [0] lucky this ghost is a baby. . . . You [0] lucky.

Morrison's narrative prose sections often describe a thought process rather than a sequence of actions. These passages employ many short, single-clause sentences, often with little or no modification of any kind; for example:

> Unfortunately her brain was devious. [. . .] Nothing else would be in her mind.

In fact, many sentences in the Morrison novel are phrases without a main verb:

> Just the breeze cooling her face as she rushed toward water.

Some of these sentences consist of just one or two words (e.g., *Nothing. Then something.*). But these sentences are sometimes in immediate proximity to long, complex sentences with multiple clauses. For example:

> Then something. The plash of water, the sight of her shoes and stockings awry on the path where she had flung them; or Here Boy lapping in the puddle near her feet, and suddenly there was Sweet Home rolling, rolling, rolling out before her eyes, and although there was not a leaf on that farm that did not make her want to scream, it rolled itself out before her in shameless beauty.

Finally, the narrative sections in the Ludlum novel often consist of short clauses with activity verbs; for example:

> he raised his eyes . . . A figure stepped back . . . The boat slowed down . . . The Mafia soldier unstrapped himself and got up; he walked across the deck . . .

However, novels from all historical periods generally share the same primary communicative purpose of narrating a story, and as a result, most novels have frequent "narrative" linguistic features, including: past tense verbs, third person pronouns, proper nouns, adverbials of time and place, reporting verbs (e.g., *say, tell, ask, suggest, answer*), and direct and indirect reported speech. These features are found in both modern novels as well as eighteenth-century novels. Thus compare the following two passages from *Amelia* and *The Icarus Agenda*, with the linguistic features used for narration and dialogue underlined:

Text Sample 6.5 Comparison of eighteenth- and twentieth-century passages

[with "narrative" linguistic features underlined]

Amelia
When Amelia went out in the morning, she left her children to the care of her husband. In this amiable office he had been engaged near an hour; and was at that very time lying along on the floor, and his little things crawling and playing about him, when a most violent knock was heard at the door . . .
    For, before he arrived at the shop, a gentleman stopt him full butt, crying, "captain, whither so fast?" –Booth answered eagerly, "whoever you are, friend, don't ask me any questions now." – "You must pardon me, captain," answered the gentleman . . .

The Icarus Agenda
Kendrick felt a third presence but, turning in the chair, saw no one else on the deck of the pleasure yacht. Then he raised his eyes to the aft railing of the bridge. A figure stepped back into the shadows but not quickly enough. It was the excessively tall,

---

deeply tanned contributor from Bollinger's library, and from what could be seen of
his face, it was contorted in hatred.

"Are all of the Vice President's guests on board?" he asked, seeing that the Mafioso
had followed his gaze . . .

Thus, despite their stylistic differences, these texts are realizations of the general fictional register, having the same general narrative purposes, and many
of the same linguistic features used commonly in association with those
purposes.

6.2.3   General stylistic differences between eighteenth-century and modern novels

The preceding chapters have made a distinction between *register* and
style. Register features are pervasive linguistic features that are functional; that
is, they are frequent because they conform to the situational context and communicative purposes of the texts in the register. Style features are similarly pervasive
linguistic features, but they are not directly functional. Rather, they reflect attitudes about language, and aesthetic or artistic preferences. Thus, texts from the
same register, sharing the same situational context and the same communicative
purposes, can differ in their linguistic *styles*.

Fictional novels provide one of the clearest illustrations of the difference
between *register* and *style*. From a register perspective, most novels employ
"narrative" linguistic features (e.g., past tense verbs, perfect aspect, third person
pronouns, time adverbials) which have a direct functional association with the
communicative purpose of telling a story of events which have occurred in the
past. At the same time, there is considerable stylistic variation among novels,
as described in Chapter 5 and in Section 6.2.2, with different authors preferring
particular linguistic features for aesthetic or attitudinal reasons.

It is also possible to compare the typical linguistic style of different historical periods. That is, certain linguistic features have been preferred in different
historical periods, not because the communicative purposes of the register were
different, but because those features conformed to the prevailing attitudes about
"good" style.

The most obvious difference between eighteenth- and twentieth-century novels
has to do with spelling and word choice. This difference actually results from
linguistic changes to the English language rather than a change in preferred style.
For example, the Fielding passage (Text Sample 6.1 above) illustrates several
forms that are no longer used, such as *stopt* rather than "stopped"; *a footman
acquainted him that* . . . rather than "told" or "informed" him; and the question
whither so fast? rather than "where are you going so fast?"

However, there are also some more pervasive differences in the typical linguistic characteristics of novels from these two historical periods. These do not

Table 6.1 *Comparison of sentence lengths in narrative from four text samples*

Novel	Average length	Longest sentence	Shortest sentence
18th c.; Fielding	42	95	12
20th c.; Vonnegut	15	25	6
20th c.; Morrison	20	70	1
20th c.; Ludlum	18	25	11

reflect a change to the linguistic system, but rather a change in the way that authors exploit the resources offered by the linguistic system. Perhaps the most important change has been in the syntactic complexity typical of eighteenth-century versus modern novels. Sentence length is one measure of this difference; Table 6.1 compares the sentence lengths from the narrative portions of Text Samples 6.1–6.4.

The eighteenth-century novel by Fielding uses much longer sentences than is typical in modern novels. Fielding's longest sentence is 95 words, but this is by no means atypical: five other sentences in Text Sample 6.1 are longer than 60 words. Vonnegut represents the opposite extreme, with an average sentence length of only 15 words. This pattern reflects his colloquial style of narration, almost as if the narrator were telling an oral story. But the other two twentieth-century novels similarly use much shorter sentences than Fielding. Ludlum's average sentence length is 18, with relatively little variation in length. Morrison has a dramatically different style, with one sentence 70 words long, and other sentences only 1–2 words long. In fact, Morrison likes to alternate sentences with widely varying lengths. For example, the long prose paragraph in Sample 6.3 above is composed of sentences with the following lengths:

33 10 16 5 23 7 25 20 1 11 57 2 70 20 10 12 25

Because of this variation, Morrison maintains an average sentence length roughly the same as Ludlum and Vonnegut, in contrast to the much longer average sentence length employed by Fielding.

This difference in sentence length is not an idiosyncratic trait of these particular authors; it rather reflects a difference in the typical linguistic styles of fiction in the eighteenth versus twentieth centuries. It is thus possible to track the gradual evolution from one extreme to the other over the intervening decades. For example, Table 6.2 presents the average sentence lengths for several novels from these periods. While there is some variation at any given historical period, there is also a very steady progression from the extremely long sentences of Defoe to the short sentences of Vonnegut and Bellow.

Table 6.2 *Comparison of sentence lengths in narrative, across historical periods (based on samples of c. 500 words of narrative prose from each novel)*

Date	Author	Novel	Average sentence length
1720	Daniel Defoe	*Life and Adventures of Duncan Campbell*	144
1720	William Pitts	*The Jamaica Lady*	44
1736	Eliza Haywood	*Adventures of Eovaai*	74
1751	Henry Fielding	*Amelia*	42
1764	Horace Walpole	*The Castle of Otranto*	27
1778	Clara Reeve	*The Old English Baron*	40
1818	Jane Austen	*Persuasion*	28
1828	David Moir	*The Life of Mansie Wauch*	24
1850	Herman Melville	*White-Jacket*	27
1880	Edward Bellamy	*Dr. Heidenhoff's Process*	26
1897	Stephen Crane	*The Third Violet*	18
1923	P. G. Wodehouse	*The Inimitable Jeeves*	25
1969	Kurt Vonnegut	*Slaughterhouse-Five*	15
1970	Saul Bellow	*Mr. Sammler's Planet*	13
1977	P. D. James	*Death of an Expert Witness*	16
1988	Toni Morrison	*Beloved*	20
1989	Robert Ludlum	*The Icarus Agenda*	18

To a large extent, this difference reflects changing punctuation practices – especially a much more extensive use of colons and semi-colons in earlier historical periods. For example, sentences like the following are common in the 1720 novel by Defoe:

Text Sample 6.6 Daniel Defoe, *The Life and Adventures of Duncan Campbell*, 1720

One day, I remember, when he was about nine years of age, going early to the house where he and his mother lived, and it being before his mother was stirring, I went into little Duncan Campbell's room to divert myself with him, I found him sitting up in his bed with his eyes broad open, if it had not been for a lively beautiful colour which the little pretty fair silver-haired boy always had in his cheeks, as if he had been quite dead; he did not seem so much as to breathe; the eyelids of him were so fixed and immoveable, that the eyelashes did not so much as once shake, which the least motion imaginable must agitate; not to say that he was like a person in an ecstacy, he was at least in what we commonly call a brown study, to the highest degree, and for the largest space of time I ever knew.

In this passage, punctuation marks are used in a radically different way from modern practice. Semi-colons are commonly used where modern-day authors would likely use a sentence-end punctuation mark, and even simple commas are used to separate completely independent clauses that express different ideas (e.g., *I went into little Duncan Campbell's room to divert myself with him, I found him sitting up in his bed*); these would be treated as separate sentences in modern prose. The full-stop (.) functions almost like a paragraph marker rather than a sentence marker in eighteenth-century novels. The Fielding passage in Text Sample 6.1 is similar to this passage from Defoe in its liberal use of semi-colons to construct very long sentences.

However, the syntactic complexity of eighteenth-century novels extends well beyond punctuation practices. One of the most important differences from modern novels involves the syntactic complexity of noun phrases. In eighteenth-century novels, noun phrases tend to have many modifiers, especially relative clauses. In this prose style, authors embed descriptive details in noun phrases as noun modifiers, rather than using separate clauses. For example, the following passage repeats paragraphs C and D from Fielding's novel *Amelia* (Text Sample 6.1 above), with all relative clauses underlined.

> Notwithstanding the pleasantry which Booth endeavoured to preserve, he in reality envied every labourer whom he saw pass by him in his way. The charms of liberty against his will rushed on his mind; and he could not avoid suggesting to himself, how much more happy was the poorest wretch who without control could repair to his homely habitation, and to his family; compared to him, who was thus violently, and yet lawfully torn away from the company of his wife and children. And their condition, especially that of his Amelia, gave his heart many a severe and bitter pang.
>
> At length he arrived at the bailiff's mansion, and was ushered into a room; in which were several persons. Booth desired to be alone, upon which the bailiff waited on him up stairs, into an apartment, the windows of which were well fortified with iron bars; but the walls had not the least outwork raised before them; they were, indeed, what is generally called naked, the bricks having been only covered with a thin plaister, which in many places was mouldered away.

In contrast, modern novels rely to a much greater extent on separate clauses, while noun phrases tend to be much less complex. For example, the Vonnegut passage above (Text Sample 6.2) has only two noun phrases with relative clauses:

> I ask the telephone operators to connect me with this friend or that one, from whom I have not heard in years.

> I told him that was one of the things I learned in college after the war.

The Ludlum passage has no relative clauses and only one moderately complex noun phrase, which is modified by a following "appositive" noun phrase:

> in his hand was a gun, a standard issue Colt .45 automatic

Instead of complex noun modification, modern novels tend to employ simpler syntax with more verbs and simple clauses. Descriptive details are often given in adverbials rather than being embedded inside noun phrases. For example, the **verbs are in bold** and <u>adverbials are underlined</u> in the following sentences from the Ludlum passage:

> Kendrick **felt** a third presence but, **turning** <u>in the chair</u>, **saw** no one else <u>on the deck of the pleasure yacht</u>. <u>Then</u> he **raised** his eyes <u>to the aft railing of the bridge</u>. A figure **stepped** <u>back into the shadows but not quickly enough</u>. [...]
>   The boat **slowed** down <u>as the beam of a powerful searchlight</u> **shot** out <u>from the bridge</u>. The Mafia soldier **unstrapped** himself and **got up**; he **walked** <u>across the deck and down into the lower cabin</u>. Evan could **hear** him <u>on an intercom</u>, but <u>with the wind and the slapping waves</u> **was** unable to **make out** the words. <u>Moments later</u> the man **returned**; <u>in his hand</u> **was** a gun...

There are other differences in the typical linguistic styles of eighteenth-century versus modern novels. For example, the activities at the end of the chapter allow you to explore linguistic differences in how dialogue is portrayed in these historical periods.

In sum, the present section has illustrated historical variation and change within the confines of a single genre and register. That is, the general textual conventions and communicative purposes of the novel have remained largely the same over the past three centuries, and so it is possible to regard these texts from the eighteenth century as belonging to the same general genre as their modern-day counterparts. From a register perspective, novels from all periods are similar in their frequent use of grammatical devices associated with narration, reported speech, and direct portrayals of dialogue (e.g., past tense verbs, third person pronouns, reporting clauses). However, there have also been notable changes in the typical linguistic styles of novels from these periods. The following section discusses the social context of these linguistic changes.

6.2.4   Social contexts of eighteenth-century and modern novels ▬

The preceding sections have shown how eighteenth-century and modern novels can be regarded as realizations of the same general genre and register, while at the same time there have been systematic changes in the typical linguistic styles of novels from these different periods. For example, eighteenth-century novels used an elaborated linguistic style, with long sentences and complex noun phrases, while twentieth-century novels have changed so that they typically rely on a simpler style with more verbs, short clauses, and adverbials.

In Chapter 5, we described how an individual author can choose a linguistic style to achieve a particular literary or artistic effect. In contrast, the linguistic differences here correspond to general patterns for the authors of a period collectively adopting a style. The generalization is stronger for eighteenth-century authors, who as a group tended to use a more elaborated style than modern authors (who show more variability among themselves in their preferred styles).

One obvious question that we could ask at this point is whether these are simply stylistic differences, reflecting changes in aesthetic preferences, or whether these are to some extent register differences, reflecting changes in the extra-linguistic context? That is, are there social/situational differences between the periods that correspond to this shift in preferred literary style?

One major change that might have had an influence is the target audience. At the beginning of the eighteenth century, relatively few adults could read and write, mostly restricted to members of the upper class or aristocracy. But the eighteenth century was a time of dramatic social change, with literacy spreading to the middle class. Thus, by the end of the eighteenth century, over 50% of adults in England had basic literacy skills. With the rise of mass schooling in the nineteenth century, these literacy skills were extended to the majority of the population. Because of these demographic changes, novels came to be written for a much wider reading public in the nineteenth and twentieth centuries than in earlier periods.

However, a more important change has been the shift in attitudes about good style. These attitudes were already changing in the seventeenth century as a result of new methods for scientific inquiry (see Section 6.3 below). For example, Sprat wrote a *History of the Royal Society* in 1667, where he praised a "plain" prose style that presented information with "a primitive purity and shortness." In contrast, Sprat criticizes all "amplifications, digressions, and swellings of style," concluding that "eloquence ought to be banished out of all civil societies as a thing fatal to peace and good manners."

While these values came to be adopted by many scientific researchers in the late seventeenth and early eighteenth centuries, it took longer for literary authors to change their preferred styles. However, the late eighteenth century and early nineteenth century witnessed a wider philosophical interest in nature and a general preference for linguistic styles that were perceived to be "natural." This preference was acknowledged by many commentators. For example, in 1800, Wordsworth writes in his influential preface to *Lyrical Ballads* how he attempted to write with "a selection of language really used by men," which conveys feelings and ideas in "simple and unelaborated expressions," as opposed to the "arbitrary and capricious habits of expression" used by earlier authors. Similarly, Hazlitt writes in 1822 that "It is not pomp or pretension, but the adaptation of the expression to the idea that clenches a writer's meaning . . . I hate anything that occupies more space than it is worth."

The linguistic changes between eighteenth- and twentieth-century novels reflect these changing attitudes about language. Thus, there is a fairly steady progression towards simpler, more colloquial styles in novels across these periods. In this case, these texts all belong to the same general genre and register – the novel – shown by similarities at a basic level in their textual conventions, purposes, and associated linguistic features. But the typical linguistic styles of eighteenth- and twentieth-century novels have changed, associated with differences in attitudes about good style in the two periods.

In the following section, we take up an even more extensive example of historical change: the scientific research article, which has changed in its basic communicative goals as well as typical linguistic styles.

6.3   Historical change II: the scientific research article

Research writing in science is extensive: there are entire libraries filled with books and academic journals devoted to the sciences. However, the situation in the seventeenth and eighteenth centuries was quite different, when scientists had very few outlets where they could publish the results of their research. Probably the most influential scientific journal in English during these periods was the *Philosophical Transactions of the Royal Society of London* (*PTRS*). The Royal Society was founded in 1660 to promote "Physico-Mathematical Learning." From its outset, the Society focused on "Experimental Learning," following Francis Bacon in advocating the first-hand empirical study of nature, in opposition to earlier scholars who attempted to describe nature in more general, abstract terms by reference to Aristotelian philosophy.

To disseminate the results of these empirical studies, the Society began to publish the *Philosophical Transactions* (*PTRS*) in 1665. As mentioned above, this publication was probably the most influential record of scientific research during the seventeenth and eighteenth centuries. But more importantly for our purposes here, the *PTRS* has a continuous history of publication from 1665 to the present, and has continued to be an influential journal throughout that entire period.

These texts have all been published as research articles in the same academic journal. However, the textual conventions of these articles have changed considerably over the centuries, raising the question of whether they should be regarded as realizations of the same genre or not. Similarly, from a register perspective, the frequent linguistic features used in these research articles have changed dramatically, associated with shifts in communicative purpose and the target audience. The following sections describe these historical patterns from both genre and register perspectives, based on analyses of research articles in the ARCHER corpus (see also Atkinson 1992, 1996, 1999).

6.3.1   Historical change in research articles: a genre perspective

In addition to discovering new scientific information, the Royal Society in its early years had a rhetorical agenda of advocating the superiority of empirical research over general philosophical discussions. As a result, early articles in the *PTRS* usually gave an account of a concrete scientific event or a description of specific scientific phenomena that were observed first-hand by the researcher. Many articles are purely descriptive, characterizing natural phenomena observed in nature by the author. For example, see Text Sample 6.7.

Text Sample 6.7 J. Beal, ... *upon Frosts in some parts of Scotland*, 1675

But to return to our Vulgarities, which may chance to have the richest usefulness or pertinence to our inquiries. In the sharpest Frost, that I have known these many years, the ground having been also some daies cover'd with Snow, I saw a small stream (no bigger than might run from the mouth of an ordinary quart Bottle, as now we have them of green Glass,) sliding merrily, and smoaking all the way over the lawns: I could not discern, that any Snow had fallen within five or six foot no each side; if it did, none remained there, and so far the Grass at that time, about Christmas, was as green as any Leek, and the Frost (so far) apparently dissolved: Of this I then wrote to our Worthy friend Mr. Evelyn, not for any wonder, (for perhaps there are or may be thousands of such smoaking Streams in England,) but only representing, How such a Stream may warm a mansion, and cherish tender evergreens well sheltered from winds, and flowry Gardens, all the hard Winter, and do us better service in an extream hot Summer. I have been perplext in observing my self, an hundred times, the difference of Heat and Cold between two Villages, within a mile of each other, where we could discern no disparity of Hills or Rivers; only the Springs in the one were all shallower, in the other some were deeper. In a large Tract of Land the surface was of so hot a ferment, that at every step I trod up to my ankles. I caused it to be examined by the Spade, and found it, as far as I tried here and there, at a foot depth, as thick set with Pibble-stones as if a Causey had been pitcht there ...

[ARCHER Corpus]

In other early studies, the researcher carried out a kind of scientific experiment, deliberately manipulating natural phenomena. In these cases, the article describes the procedures in detail (Text Sample 6.8).

Text Sample 6.8 Cristiaan Hugyens and M. Papin, *Some Experiments made in the Air Pump upon Plants*, 1675

I took one day a small Recipient shaped like that, described formerly, and instead of an Iron wire, I passed into the little hole a sprig of a known Plant, which was Baulme, so as that the Top of the plant was within the Recipient, and the Roots without. Then I closed the rest of the hole with cement, that so I might keep it void a good while: But because I was not willing, that it should embarass the Engin, 'twas necessary to find a means of taking it away when exhausted. For that purpose I used the following method, which is very sure and very commodious, and which hath served me for many other Experiments hereafter to be related.

The method was this: I caused the edges of the side Orifice of my Recipient to be well ground, so as that being applyed, it every where touches the glass-plate, which had also been very smoothly ground to serve for a cover to the same; and I spread a piece of Lambskin wetted over the said plate, and having thus applyed it to the Engin, I put my Recipient over it: But in one place there was a Hail-shot of lead, which kept the Receiver from being exactly applied to its cover, that so the Air might more freely get out. And having afterwards whelmed another great Receiver over all, I caused the Pump to be plyed. All being well evacuated, I shook the Engin, so as that the little Receiver fell off from the Hail-shot, and stood every where close to the skin, expanded over the cover of the Glass-plate.

[ARCHER Corpus]

From a genre perspective, many of these articles adopted the textual conventions of a letter addressed to the publisher of the *PTRS*, beginning with the salutation "Sir" and ending with a formulaic closing (e.g., *Your humble Servant*). But these conventions had little influence on the main body of the text, which normally transitioned quickly into a description of scientific phenomena. For example, the passage in Text Sample 6.7 above begins as a letter, shown in Text Sample 6.9:

Text Sample 6.9 J. Beal,... *upon Frosts in some parts of Scotland*, 1675

Sir,

It may seem, by the curious Remarks sent to you from Scotland that we are yet to seek out the Causes and original Source, as well as the Principles and Nature, of Frosts. I wish, I were able to name all circumstances that may be causative of Frosts, Heats, Winds, and Tempests. I know by experience, that the scituation of the place is considerable for some of these; but after much diligence and troublesome researches, I cannot define the proximity or distance, not all the requisites, that ought to be concurrent for all the strange effects I have observ'd in them.

[ARCHER Corpus]

Similarly, the letter-article shown in Text Sample 6.10 begins with a salutation but immediately shifts to a discussion of a particular scientific issue:

Text Sample 6.10 Dr. Nettleton, Observations concerning the height of the barometer, 1725

SIR,

Being curious to learn by Observation, how far the Mercury will descend in the Tube at any given Elevation, for which there is sufficient Opportunity hereabouts, I proposed to take the Altitude of some of our highest Hills; but, when we attempted it, we found our Observation so disturbed by Refractions, that we cou'd come to no Certainty. Having measur'd one Hill of considerable height, in a clear Day, and observed the Mercury at the Bottom and at the Top, we found, according to that Estimation, that about 90 Feet, or upwards, were required to make the Mercury fall one Tenth of an Inch;...

[ARCHER Corpus]

These letter-articles are virtually identical in subject matter and linguistic style to other early articles in the *PTRS*, except that they begin with a salutation and they end with a formulaic closing.

Scientific articles followed these same textual conventions throughout most of the eighteenth century, but by the early nineteenth century, there was more variability in the accepted conventions. Several *PTRS* articles in the early nineteenth century continued to use the conventions of a letter to the editor, as in Sample 6.11:

Text Sample 6.11 Samuel Hunter Christie, On the magnetism developed in copper, 1825

Dear Sir,

[A] As you inform me that you are drawing up an account of your magnetical experiments, I send you a brief account of those which I have made: they may possibly bear upon some of the points which you have had under consideration; and in this case you will not be displeased at being able to compare independent results.

[B] After having made experiments with a thin copper disk suspended over a horseshoe magnet, similar to those I witnessed at Mr. BABBAGE'S, I made the following.

[C] A disk of drawing paper was suspended by the finest brass wire (no. 37) over the horse-shoe magnet, with a paper screen between. A rapid rotation of the magnet (20 or 30 times per second) caused no rotation in the paper, but it occasionally dipped on the sides, as if attracted by the screen, which might be the effect of electricity excited in the screen by the friction of the air beneath it.

A disk of glass was similarly suspended over the magnet: no effect produced by the rotation.

A disk of mica was similarly suspended: no effect.

The horse-shoe magnet was replaced by two bar magnets, each 7.5 inches long, and weighing 3 oz. 16 dwt. each, placed horizontally parallel to each other, and having their poles of the same name contiguous. These produced quick rotation in a heavy disk of copper 6 inches in diameter, and suspended by a wire, No. 20.

[ARCHER Corpus]

In this article, the author actually begins with a paragraph [A] written directly to the editor, addressing the editor directly as *you*. This is followed by a short paragraph [B] written in the first person, attributing the research reported in the following paragraphs of the article to the author (i.e., *I made the following*). However, beginning with paragraph [C], there is a dramatic transformation of style, with absolutely no references to the author. Instead, the focus has shifted to the objects being studied and the events that occurred. Linguistically, this shift is realized in two ways: (1) by the use of agentless passive clauses rather than active clauses:

A disk of drawing paper was suspended . . .
A disk of glass was similarly suspended . . .
The horse-shoe magnet was replaced . . .

(2) by the use of active voice clauses with inanimate rather than human subjects:

A rapid rotation . . . caused no rotation
it [i.e. the "paper"] occasionally dipped on the sides
These [i.e. the "two bar magnets"] produced quick rotation

Other articles from the early nineteenth century do not adopt the textual conventions of a letter, but they follow the same rhetorical progression of beginning as a first person narrative, and then shifting into an impersonal presentation of procedures and findings (as in Text Sample 6.12 below). The same two linguistic devices (agentless passives and inanimate subjects) are used for the impersonal presentation of information in these articles. Thus, in Text Sample 6.12, notice the abrupt shift between the first person account in paragraphs [A] and [B] – *I shall be able to prove* – to the inanimate subject of the first sentence in paragraph [C] – *This enquiry has . . .* Then, in paragraph [D], there is a further shift to passive voice: *The ova . . . which have been selected . . . are found . . .* In this paragraph, the author also uses impersonal *we* to refer to anyone who performs these procedures.

Text Sample 6.12 Everard Home, Observation on the changes the ovum of the frog undergoes during the formation of the tadpole, 1825

[A] In the year 1822, I laid before the Society a series of observations on the progress of the formation of the chick in the egg of the pullet, illustrated by drawings from the pencil of Mr. Bauer, showing that in the ova of hot-blooded animals the first parts formed are the brain and spinal marrow. I have now brought forward a similar series on the progress of organization in the ova of cold-blooded animals, illustrated in the same manner by microscopical drawings made by the same hand.

[B] By comparing together the first rudiments of organization in the ova of these very distinct classes of animals, I shall be able to prove that, in both, the same general principle is employed in the formation of the embryo.

[C] This enquiry has its interest considerably encreased, by the ova not being composed of similar parts.

[D] The ova of the frog, which have been selected for this investigation, are found to have no yelk. If we examine these ova in the ovaria in which they are formed, we find them to consist of small vesicles of a dark colour; when they enter the oviducts they enlarge in size, and acquire a gelatinous covering, which increases in quantity in their course along those tubes; but the ova can neither be said to have acquired their full size, nor to have received their proportion of jelly,

> till they arrive at a cavity close to the termination of each oviduct, formed by a very considerable enlargement of those tubes, corresponding, in many respects to the cloaca in which the pullet's egg is retained till the shell becomes hard.
>
> [ARCHER Corpus]

By the late twentieth century, two additional rhetorical changes have occurred in scientific research articles. First, the majority of the articles published in *PTRS* are no longer directly experimental or descriptive. Rather, most recent articles published in *PTRS* have theoretical concerns. This change reflects the high status of the *PTRS* as a general science journal, dealing with research issues that have fundamental theoretical importance. These theoretical articles have completely different genre conventions, which are outside the scope of the present description.

The second change, though, concerns the genre conventions and linguistic register characteristics of those research articles which are empirical and experimental: the direct descendent of the observational/experimental articles published in the *PTRS* from the seventeenth to the nineteenth century. From a genre perspective, the modern experimental science article follows rigid rhetorical conventions: an abstract, followed by the main body of the article with four major sections (Introduction, Methods, Results, Discussion/Conclusion), followed by a bibliography. Further, even the organization of these major sections has become highly conventualized, being organized as a sequence of rhetorical "moves." These textual conventions are described in detail in Chapter 5. The shift to these textual conventions occurred quite recently, being essentially a twentieth-century development. However, experimental research articles can now be regarded as one of the most highly conventualized genres in English.

6.3.2   Historical change in research articles: a register perspective

From a register perspective, there have also been major linguistic changes to the typical linguistic styles used in experimental science articles. Extending the trend begun in the nineteenth century, there are almost no first person references in modern articles; rather, agentless passives and inanimate subjects are common. However, these two linguistic strategies have become more specialized: inanimate subjects are commonly used in the Introductions and Discussion sections of research articles, while agentless passives are used extensively in Methods sections.

Introductions use relatively few passive voice clauses but extensive active voice clauses that have inanimate subjects; for example:

Text Sample 6.13 Genetic identification of Spotted Owls...,
***Conservation Biology*, 2004**

Introduction.

Hybridization between species can severely affect a species status and recovery (Rhymer & Simberloff 1996). Threatened species (and others) may be directly affected by hybridization and gene flow from invasive species, which can result in reduced fitness or lowered genetic variability (Gilbert *et al*. 1993, Gottelli *et al*. 1994, Wolf *et al*. 2001). In other cases, hybridization may provide increased polymorphisms that allow for rapid evolution to occur (Grant & Grant 1992; Rhymer *et al*. 1994). Species can also be influenced indirectly, because hybridization may affect the conservation status of threatened species and their legal protection (O'Brien & Mayr 1991a, 1991b; Jones *et al*. 1995; Allendorf *et al*. 2001; Schwartz *et al*. 2004; Haig & Allendorf 2005). The Northern Spotted Owl (*Strix occidentalis caurina*) is a threatened subspecies associated with rapidly declining, late-successional forests in western North America (Gutierrez *et al*. 1995). Listing of this subspecies under the U.S. Endangered Species Act (ESA) attracted considerable controversy because of concern that listing would lead to restrictions on timber harvest.

Similar to the pattern of use in nineteenth-century articles, the subject noun phrases of active voice clauses sometimes refer to the physical objects of the investigation (e.g., *The Northern Spotted Owl*). But it is more common in modern articles to use inanimate subject noun phrases that refer to an abstract concept, such as:

> *hybridization between species* can severely affect a species status
> *hybridization* may provide increased polymorphisms
> *listing of this subspecies* ... attracted considerable controversy
> *the legal status of hybrids under the ESA* is ambiguous
> *the ability to identify hybrids* is the first step
> *visual and vocal identification of hybrids* can be difficult

In contrast, the use of passive voice is especially prevalent in Methods sections. The excerpt in Text Sample 6.14 is typical, with all procedures for the study being described in the passive voice:

Text Sample 6.14 Extreme sensitivity of biological function to temperature in Antarctic marine species, *Functional Ecology*, 2004

[passive verbs shown in **bold**]

Methods.

Experimental animals **were collected** by scuba divers from 8 to 15 m depth in Hangar Cove, Rothera Point, Adelaide Island (67 34′20″ S, 68 07′ 50″ W). Specimens of L. elliptica and N. concinna **were held** for 24 h in aquaria at ambient temperature before **being used** in experiments. Constant low-light levels **were maintained**, to mimic Antarctic summer conditions. In studies at ambient temperature animals **were**

used immediately after the 24 h acclimation period. For elevated temperatures animals **were held** in jacketed water baths and temperatures **raised** at 0.1 °C h^{-1}, until required temperatures **were reached**. Video recordings **were made** to determine burrowing or turning rate and times to completion. Data **were collected** using a Panasonic Ag6124hb 24 h time-lapse video recorder, and subsequently **analysed** using a JVCBR-S610E video analysis machine. At each temperature for each species 18–26 animals **were evaluated**.

In Chapter 5, we identify many other register features that are typical of modern research articles. Most of these linguistic characteristics are recent innovations, representing a shift from the typical linguistic styles of earlier periods. For example, the dense use of article citations, referring to other publications on related topics, is a linguistic device that came into use only during the twentieth century.

The register of scientific writing has also changed dramatically in the kinds of nouns that it uses, and even the overall density of nouns. Science articles from earlier periods were mostly personal narratives of one kind or another. As a result, these texts were composed of numerous clauses with a high density of verbs. Thus, Text Sample 6.15 repeats the article beginning from Text Sample 6.10 above (from 1725), while Text Sample 6.16 repeats the procedural description from Text Sample 6.8 above (from 1675). The density of verbs in these samples is shown by use of **bold text**.

Text Sample 6.15 Dr. Nettleton, 1725

[with verbs in **bold**]

Being curious to **learn** by Observation, how far the Mercury **will descend** in the Tube at any given Elevation, for which there **is** sufficient Opportunity hereabouts, I **proposed** to **take** the Altitude of some of our highest Hills; but, when we **attempted** it, we **found** our Observation so **disturbed** by Refractions, that we **cou'd come** to no Certainty. **Having measur'd** one Hill of considerable height, in a clear Day, and **observed** the Mercury at the Bottom and at the Top, we **found**, according to that Estimation, that about 90 Feet, or upwards, **were required** to **make** the Mercury **fall** one Tenth of an Inch; . . .

[ARCHER Corpus]

Text Sample 6.16 Cristiaan Hugyens and M. Papin, 1675

[with verbs in **bold**]

The method **was** this: I **caused** the edges of the side Orifice of my Recipient to **be** well ground, so as that **being applyed**, it every where **touches** the glass-plate, which **had** also **been** very smoothly ground to **serve** for a cover to the same; and I **spread** a piece of Lambskin **wetted** over the said plate, and **having** thus **applyed** it to the Engin, I **put** my Recipient over it: But in one place there **was** a Hail-shot of lead, which **kept** the Receiver from **being** exactly **applied** to its cover, that so the Air **might** more freely

> **get out**. And **having** afterwards **whelmed** another great Receiver over all, I **caused** the Pump to **be plyed**. All **being** well **evacuated**, I **shook** the Engin, so as that the little Receiver **fell** off from the Hail-shot, and **stood** every where close to the skin, **expanded** over the cover of the Glass-plate.
>
> [ARCHER Corpus]

In contrast, modern research articles tend to use few verbs but numerous nouns and complex noun phrases. For example, Text Sample 6.13 above contains the following clauses having few verbs but complex noun phrases:

> [**Hybridization** between **species**] can severely affect [a **species status** and **recovery**]
>
> [Threatened **species** (and others)] may be directly affected [by **hybridization** and **gene flow** from invasive **species**]
>
> [**Hybridization**] may affect [the **conservation status** of threatened **species** and their legal **protection**]
>
> [The **Northern Spotted Owl** (*Strix occidentalis caurina*)] is [a threatened **subspecies** associated with rapidly declining, late-successional **forests** in western **North America**]

We can find similar examples in any modern experimental research article. The most striking examples of this linguistic pattern are clauses that have only the minimal verb *BE*, connecting extremely complex noun phrases or adjectival phrases; for example:

> [The **cranberry fruitworm**, Acrobasis vaccinii Riley], is [a major **pest** of Vaccinium spp. in the eastern **U.S.A.**]
>
> [The overwhelming **cause** of **HIV-1 infection** in **infants**] is [the **transmission** of **infection** from the **mother** during the **course** of **pregnancy** (in utero), **labor** (intrapartum) or through **breast milk** (postpartum)].
>
> Therefore, [**host selection**] is [a critical **decision moment** in the **Lepidoptera**], as [**offspring survival** and **development**] are [dependent on the **recognition** of a suitable **host** by the **adult female**]

One noteworthy characteristic of these examples is the frequent occurrence of nouns modifying other nouns, like *conservation status*, *cranberry fruitworm*, *host selection*, *decision moment*, and *offspring survival*. While these noun-noun sequences were grammatical in earlier historical periods, they were generally rare. (This important historical change is discussed further in Section 6.4 below.)

6.3.3   Genre/register change, or change to a new genre/register?

We have shown in the previous sections how the scientific research article has undergone substantial change over the past four centuries, both with respect to its textual conventions as well as in the characteristic linguistic features associated with science writing as a register. This case study raises a basic question: How can researchers distinguish between change within a genre/register versus change to become a different genre/register? This question is especially perplexing because such changes are gradual, with numerous intermediate stages, and considerable variation attested within any given historical period.

Unfortunately, there is not a definitive answer to this question. If we compare the two ends of this tradition – seventeenth-century and twentieth-century research articles – it would be easy to argue that there are at least two distinct genres and registers. The two have dramatically different textual conventions, different typical linguistic styles, and they differ in communicative purpose: earlier studies are personal narrative accounts of research, often written with the textual conventions of a personal letter, while recent articles focus on the research findings themselves and their theoretical relevance in relation to related research studies, written with a strict Introduction, Methods, Results, Discussion conventional format.

However, the opposite conclusion is also reasonable: that these texts have always been identified as "scientific research articles," over their entire 350-year history. From this perspective, science research articles have shifted in their specific purposes, and they have become much more narrowly defined in terms of textual conventions, but throughout they have maintained the basic communicative goal of conveying the results of scientific inquiry.

It is interesting that the historical evolution of research articles has followed a different linguistic progression from the pattern of change for fictional novels. That is, the last section showed how novels used elaborated and structurally complex sentence structures in earlier centuries, and how this linguistic style evolved steadily towards simpler, more colloquial linguistic styles in modern novels. In contrast, the present section has shown that research articles changed in the opposite direction: from prose styles that relied on simple clauses towards a greater use of complex noun-phrase structures in present-day articles. We take up such historical changes in the patterns of register variation in the following section.

6.4   Historical change in the patterns of register variation

At the end of the last section, we noted how fictional novels and science research articles have evolved to become more sharply distinguished from one another over the past three centuries. Such changes show that the patterns of register variation are not static; individual registers can take quite different evolutionary paths, and, as a result, the relations among registers can be quite different today from what they were centuries ago.

In the present section, we present two case studies illustrating the ways in which the patterns of register variation can change historically. In the first, we focus on complexity in the noun phrase, providing more details about the differences between fiction and research articles that we noted at the end of the last section. Then we consider historical change in the expression of "stance" – features which express the author's evaluation of certainty and other attitudes – comparing four written and speech-based registers.

6.4.1 Historical register change in the complexity of noun phrases

Although readers might not notice it, the structure of noun phrases has been one of the most dramatic areas of historical change in English over the past three centuries. Noun phrases can be elaborated through both "pre-modifiers" (which come **before** the head noun) and "post-modifiers" (which come **after** the head noun). There are two major kinds of pre-modifier in English:

Attributive adjectives: *a **special** project, an **internal** memo*
Nouns as premodifiers: *the **bus** strike, the **police** report*

There are several structural types of postnominal modifiers, but two of these are especially important:

Relative clause:
*the penny-pinching circumstances **that surrounded this international event***
Prepositional phrase:
*compensation **for emotional damage***
*this list **of requirements***

As described in Sections 6.2 and 6.3, informational written registers have steadily evolved to use more complex noun phrases over the last three centuries. Fiction, on the other hand, evolved to use less-elaborated clause structures over this same time period. However, apart from relative-clause constructions, fiction has remained relatively unchanged in its use of relatively simple noun phrases. Figures 6.1 and 6.2 document these patterns of change for medical research articles and fiction.

Figure 6.1 plots the patterns of change from the eighteenth to the twentieth century for noun pre-modifiers. In the eighteenth century, these two registers were very similar in their patterns of pre-modification: attributive adjectives were relatively common in both registers, while noun-noun sequences were comparatively rare in both registers. By the twentieth century, though, large register differences have developed: the use of both attributive adjectives and noun-noun sequences increased dramatically in medical research articles over this period, while fiction remained essentially the same (in the use of adjectives) or showed a modest increase (in the case of noun-noun sequences).

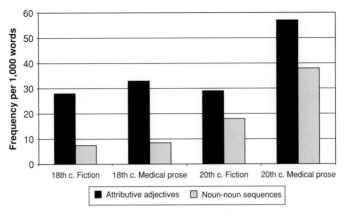

Figure 6.1 *Change in the use of noun pre-modifiers: fiction vs. medical research articles*

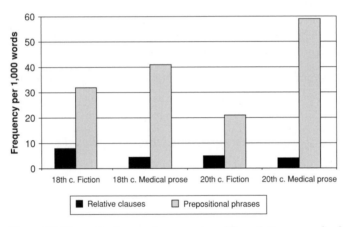

Figure 6.2 *Change in the use of noun post-modifiers: fiction vs. medical research articles*

The historical patterns for post-modification, shown in Figure 6.2, are equally striking. Again, the two registers were similar in their linguistic patterns in the eighteenth century: relative clauses were somewhat more common in fiction than medical articles, but only moderately common overall; prepositional phrases were considerably more common than relative clauses in both registers. In fiction, relative clauses decreased in use over the centuries, while the frequency of relative clauses remained essentially constant in medical articles. But extremely large register differences have developed in the use of prepositional phrases: a steadily decreasing use in fiction, but a large increase in use in medical research articles. Many of these prepositional phrases are *of*-phrases, especially in earlier historical periods. But the recent increase in research articles is mostly due to the use of other prepositional phrases (especially *in*, *with*, *for*, *to*), which are less commonly used in popular written registers. Text Sample 6.17 illustrates the dense use of these complex noun phrases in a recent research article:

Text Sample 6.17 Medical research article. N. Irvine, *et al.*, The results of coronary arteriography . . . *Scottish Medical Journal*, 1985

[noun-noun sequences underlined; *of* in **bold italics**; OTHER PREPOSITIONS in **BOLD CAPS**]

The case records *of* 50 consecutive male patients aged 40 years or under who were investigated by selective coronary arteriography **AFTER** myocardial infarction were reviewed . . . The features *of* myocardial infarction **ON** the ECG were less marked **IN** the group *of* patients **WITH** normal coronary arteriograms . . .

Cigarette smoking was very common **IN** the whole group, 86 per cent *of* patients being moderately heavy cigarette smokers. Five *of* the 14 patients **IN** the "non-occlusive" group were non-smokers and only two *of* the 36 patients **IN** the "occlusive" group were non-smokers (P <is less than> 0.01). The fasting serum cholesterol was significantly lower **IN** the "non-occlusive" group than **IN** the "occlusive" group. There was no significant difference **BETWEEN** the two groups regarding blood pressure, family history *of* ischaemic heart disease, obesity or alcohol consumption. There was, however, a high incidence *of* heavy alcohol consumption **AMONGST** patients who subsequently required coronary artery surgery . . .

The present study was carried out to investigate the pattern *of* coronary artery disease **IN** young men **IN** North East Scotland following myocardial infarction and to determine whether there is any relationship **BETWEEN** the clinical features *of* infarction, risk factors, post-infarction progress and the presence or absence *of* obstructive coronary artery disease.

You can contrast the noun phrases in Text Sample 6.17 with those in modern novels, such as Text Samples 6.2, 6.3, and 6.4 in Section 6.2 above. As described in the last section, one noteworthy characteristic of noun phrases in research writing is that they employ few verbs or clauses, even though they are extremely long and complex. The last noun phrase from the text sample above – with the head noun *relationship* – is typical:

> any [relationship] **BETWEEN** the clinical features *of* infarction, risk factors, post-infarction progress and the presence or absence *of* obstructive coronary artery disease

In sum, the present section has documented a marked increase in the extent of register variation across time: fiction and medical research writing were relatively similar in their patterns of noun-phrase modification during the eighteenth century, but they have evolved in opposite ways over the centuries. Thus, at present, there are large differences in the linguistic styles of noun-phrase complexity in these two registers.

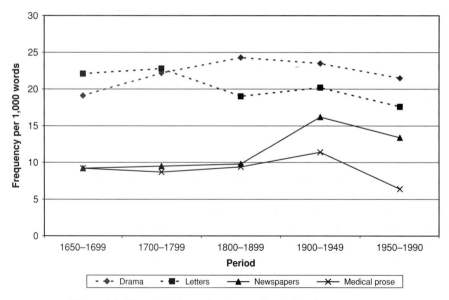

Figure 6.3 *Historical change in the use of modal verbs*

6.4.2   Historical register change in the linguistic expression of stance

Modern registers in English differ considerably in their use of grammatical devices used to express "stance": epistemic or attitudinal comments on propositional information. We have discussed these characteristics in several previous chapters. For example, spoken registers (including conversation and classroom teaching) use frequent stance devices from multiple grammatical categories (e.g., modal verbs, semi-modals, hedges, emphatics). At the other extreme, academic writing uses comparatively few stance expressions. The present section traces historical change in the use of stance devices, to determine if speech-based and written registers have always been so sharply distinguished in the use of these features. The description is based on comparison of four registers, again taken from the ARCHER Corpus: drama, personal letters, newspaper reportage, and medical research articles.

Modal verbs (e.g., *can*, *may*, *must*, *should*) are the stance feature used most widely across modern registers, expressing meanings related to possibility/permission/ability, logical necessity/obligation, and prediction/volition. In Chapter 4 (Figure 4.2), we discussed the use of modals in conversation, showing that they are considerably more common in conversation than in written registers like newspapers or academic prose. Figure 6.3 shows that interpersonal registers (drama and letters) were already sharply distinguished from informational written registers in the seventeenth and eighteenth centuries, with modals being common in the interpersonal registers but relatively rare in the informational registers. Text

Sample 6.18 illustrates the dense use of modal verbs in a seventeenth-century letter:

Text Sample 6.18 Personal letter from Valentine Greatrakes to Sir George Rawdon, 1665

[with modal verbs in **bold**]

Sir

I WAS at your lodgings before I left Dublin, but missed the happiness of meeting you there, and my occasions not giving me leave to stay longer, made me depart so abruptly. I went home by the way of the Queen's Country, which caused me to stay so long that your letter was at my house before me, so that I **could** not answer it last post. Sir, I thought fitting to send Dean Rust's letter unto you, which when you have perused, I **shall** desire you to return by the post to your servant, who resolves, by the first vessel, to sail for England: and therefore I **shall** desire you**'ll** take some speedy course for the payment of the £155 which I desire **may** be paid to Sir Thomas Stanley, a Parliament man, now in Dublin, to my use (which I design for the purchasing of the thirds which by the bill I am to lose) and that on receipt he **would** signify so much to me by a line or two; but you need not let him know to what end you pay it, for it's my desire, according to Dean Rust's advice, that nothing in your affair **might** be known. I know it **will** seem strange to all that know me, that I who never received pension or gratuity from any man hitherto, **should** propose any thing of a reward to myself now:
[...]
I **must** desire you to let me know the name of my Lord Conway's house, and nigh what market town it lie, and what course I **must** take from Bristol thither. I **must** beg your pardon for my prolixity,

subscribing myself (Sir)
Your humble servant,
VA. GREATRACKS.

[ARCHER Corpus]

There was a slight rise in the use of modal verbs in the early twentieth century, especially in newspaper reportage. But then modals decreased in all four of these registers in the period 1950–1990. Other studies have shown that this decrease is even more notable after 1990.

An obvious question is whether some other linguistic feature has increased in use to take the place of modal verbs. Semi-modal verbs (e.g., *have to*, *gotta*, *be going to*) are one likely possibility; semi-modals express many of the same meanings as core modal verbs, but they are especially common in the spoken interpersonal registers (see Chapter 4). Figure 6.4 shows that semi-modals have in fact increased in use over the past 100 years. However, this increase has been restricted primarily to drama and letters. Thus, the decline in modal use

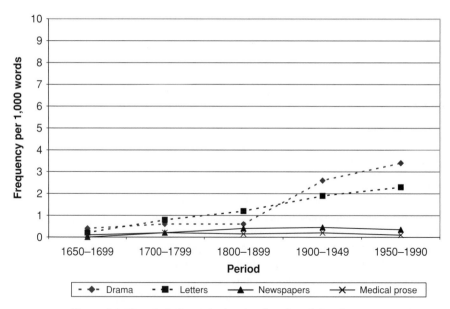

Figure 6.4 *Historical change in the use of semi-modal verbs*

for newspapers and academic prose is not offset by a corresponding increase in semi-modal use in those registers.

Figures 6.3 and 6.4 show different historical register patterns for modals versus semi-modals: For the use of modal verbs, interpersonal registers were already sharply distinguished from informational registers in the seventeenth and eighteenth centuries. More recently, modals have declined in all registers, but less so in drama. In contrast, semi-modals were extremely rare in all registers in the seventeenth and eighteenth centuries. Over the past 100 years, semi-modals have increased in frequency, but only in the interpersonal registers; they are still rare in the informational written registers.

There are other grammatical devices used in English to express stance, and so it is possible that the informational written registers might be changing to use some of these other devices more frequently. Stance adverbials are one of these other features, expressing meanings of certainty (e.g., *undoubtedly, obviously, certainly*), likelihood (e.g., *evidently, roughly*), or other attitudes (e.g., *surprisingly, hopefully*). As Figure 6.5 shows, stance adverbials have steadily increased in use across these periods. In the most recent period, this increase continued in drama and (to a lesser extent) personal letters. Following are some examples from 1950–1990 drama:

> You **never** can be **really** sure what's going on in their heads.

> So she **actually** talks of me as a drip, does she?

> No. **Matter of fact**...speaking as a professional politician...I **kind of** admire what he's doing.

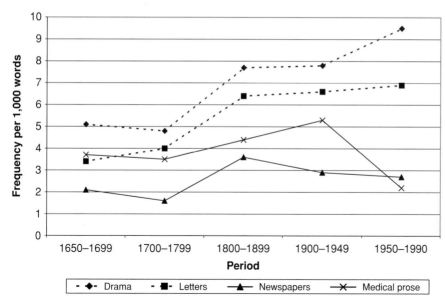

Figure 6.5 *Historical change in the use of stance adverbials*

WOOD: It's a **sort of** code, is it?
SIMON: **No doubt** it seems a rather squalid one, to you.
[...]
SIMON: I also realized that I couldn't **possibly** do her any harm.

In the nineteenth century, newspaper and medical prose participated in the increasing use of stance adverbials, in a similar way to drama and letters. However, Figure 6.5 shows that this increase was reversed in the twentieth century. Thus the present-day use of stance adverbials shows the same split as for other stance features, being common in the personal, colloquial registers (drama and letters) but relatively rare in the informational written registers (news and medical prose).

In sum, the case study presented here has shown increasing patterns of register diversification in the use of stance features. Only modal verbs have undergone a general decrease in use, while semi-modals and stance adverbials have generally increased in use across the historical periods in this study. Thus overall, the findings suggest that stance meanings are being expressed more commonly, with the most notable increases occurring in the present century. These developments indicate a general shift in cultural norms: speakers and writers are more willing to express their personal attitudes and evaluations in recent periods than in earlier historical periods.

More importantly for our purposes here, the findings show increasing register diversification in the marking of stance. First, the popular registers included in this study – drama and personal letters – are clearly leading the way in the increased use of stance markers. News reportage uses these stance devices to a lesser extent, while medical prose actually shows a decrease in the use of these devices across time. Overall, the patterns of change are similar to those for noun modification, in that there are much greater differences among registers in the modern periods than there were during the eighteenth century. However, in this case the personal registers show increased use of these linguistic features, while research articles (and newspaper reportage) have declined in the use of stance features.

Chapter 6 activities

Reflection and review

1. Choose a textual variety that has had a continuous history in English for the past three centuries (e.g., drama, personal letters, newspaper reports). Does that textual variety represent the "same" register and genre in the seventeenth and twentieth centuries? Why or why not?

2. Choose one of the twentieth-century fiction excerpts in Activity Texts 18–21 and rewrite it in eighteenth-century style. Identify and justify the linguistic features that you changed.

3. The chapter does not fully explain why, from the eighteenth to twentieth centuries, personal registers have generally increased in use of stance features while research articles and newspaper reportage have decreased. There is no way to know for certain, but what possible explanations can you think of? What social conditions or factors may have had an impact?

4. All the case studies in this chapter deal with English-language registers from British/North American culture. Choose another culture/language that you know and outline the plan for a historical study of one or more registers. What is the focus of your study, and why? What texts or corpus will you need? What registers/genres are likely to be especially interesting? Do you have any expectations for the findings?

Analysis practice

5. The language of drama is one of the best indications of what natural conversation might have been like in past historical periods. However, dramatic discourse is also influenced by the writer's ideals of what dialogue should be like, and by the needs to convey a story through the dialogue of actors.

Table 6.3 compares findings from a small study of two excerpts from plays – one from 1819 (Activity Text 12) and the other from 1975 (Activity Text 13). If these data are typical, what historical changes have occurred in this register? Based on the descriptions in Chapter 4, to what extent do you think the language in these plays is representative of natural conversation? Write a short summary, referring to the texts for your interpretations and examples.

6. Expand the analysis that was started for Activity 5. Use the two drama samples (Activity Texts 12 and 13) to compare between five and ten more features and expand your discussion of the changes (and consistencies) in the register. Remember to norm your counts.

Table 6.3 *Frequency of selected features in two plays from 1819 and 1975 (normed per 100 words)*

Linguistic feature	1819 sample *The Steward*	1975 sample *Otherwise Engaged*
Questions (based on use of "?" to signal rising intonation)	0.8	4.1
Contractions	1.3	6.8
Modals	3.8	0
Semi-modals	0	1.4
Length of sentences (based on use of end punctuation)	15 words/sentence	7 words/sentence

7. Personal letters have the possibility of being extremely colloquial or extremely literate. They deal with the personal concerns and feelings of the author, and they are directly interactive (although in a less immediate way than conversation). But they are also written, and so can be carefully planned, revised, and edited. The relative weighting of these factors is not necessarily constant across time periods (or even across authors). Consider two letters, Activity Texts 14 and 15 – one written by Lady Mary Wortley Montagu to her good friend Alexander Pope in 1716, and the other written by an anonymous woman to her best friend in 1989. Describe the characteristic linguistic features of each letter, and relate those to differences in the historical contexts of these texts.

8. Newspapers had a relatively small circulation in the early eighteenth century, but by the twentieth century they were read by a large, popular audience. At the same time, mass communication resulted in there being more newsworthy topics to report every day, resulting in the need for space economy in modern newspapers.

Compare the two newspaper stories presented in Activity Texts 22 and 23, one from 1744 and the other from 1990. Pay attention to the use of both "oral" and "literate" linguistic features, including direct and indirect quotes, contractions, stance features, verb tenses, and noun phrase structures like relative clauses, noun-noun sequences, and appositive noun phrases.

Project ideas

9. The general shift to more colloquial styles in fiction can be analyzed in greater detail, focusing on differences among subregisters. For example, a casual reading of novels suggests the following development: Authors in the eighteenth century used comparatively few contractions; authors in the nineteenth century used contractions in fictional dialogue but less often in narrative prose and description; authors in the twentieth century are more likely to use contractions in both dialogue, narration, and description (especially in first person narratives). Another change is the shift to presenting unattributed dialogue in twentieth-century novels (e.g., speech that is not framed by a speech-act verb and is not overtly attributed to a speaker), while dialogue in earlier centuries is normally attributed to a character in the novel.

Choose five of your favorite novels from the eighteenth, nineteenth, and twentieth centuries, and identify dialogue, narrative, and descriptive passages from each novel. Then analyze those passages to evaluate the above generalizations and to identify additional ways in which each subregister of fiction has changed historically.

10. Expand the analysis that was started for Activity 5, 6, 7, or 8: Collect additional texts representing the varieties from all historical periods, and analyze those texts to determine the extent to which these historical patterns are generalizable.

11. The register of magazine advertising has changed dramatically over the past few centuries. Collect eight to ten advertisements from your favorite magazine and do a register analysis of their communicative purposes and typical linguistic features. Then compare and contrast those characteristics with the ads in Activity Text 24, from the April 11, 1772 edition of *The Censor*.

7 Registers and genres in electronic communication

7.1 Introduction: new technology and new registers

E-mail. Instant message. Blog. Cell phone. Text message. It is hard to believe that in the early 1980s, these words meant nothing to most people, and even in the early 1990s, many people were only beginning to be aware of them. You may use a computer and cell phone almost every day, but a few decades ago the only people to use computers were computer programmers, and phones were always connected to walls. Then, as the technology became affordable and accessible, communication via electronic means increased tremendously. In 2007, it was estimated that over 1,240,000,000 people were using the internet (www.internetworldstats.com, 2007). Even by 2000 it was estimated that over 800 million people were using e-mail (Crystal 2001). In 2006, over 18 billion text messages per month were sent in the US and 3.5 billion per month in the UK (www.cellsigns.com, 2006; Mobile Data Association, 2007). With this fast growth and wide use, anyone interested in register variation will wonder how language is used in these new registers.

In the last chapter, we described historical register change and some case studies where registers evolved gradually over time. In the present chapter, we describe case studies of registers that emerged much more suddenly, becoming established in only a few years following the growth of computers, the internet, and cell-phone technology.

The three registers described here are similar in that they rely on electronic means for conveying a message, as opposed to speech or conventional printed writing. To limit the situational variation, we have chosen registers that include interaction between individuals, but there are other specific situational differences among them. We begin with the form of electronic communication which was the first to become widely used – e-mail. We compare it to conversation and academic prose, to contrast the newer electronic register with the more prototypical forms of speech and writing that were covered in Chapters 4 and 5. We then present investigations of two more recently developed electronic registers, e-forum postings and text messages, showing their similarities and differences with e-mail and other longer-established registers.

7.2   Individual e-mail messages

E-mail is a general register, distinctive by the fact that it is sent via computer, from one mail account to another. Like face-to-face conversation, e-mail messages can involve single or multiple recipients, and they can be motivated by many communicative purposes. These purposes include mass advertising, fraudulent attempts by an anonymous person to get money, general institutional information-sharing, and social communication among friends. In this section we limit our discussion to the register of individual e-mail messages: messages written to a specific person from another person. We include messages with both business and social topics and purposes.

Our register description of e-mail is based on a relatively small case study, similar to what you could do on your own. Situational characteristics were analyzed by reference to our own experiences as senders and recipients of e-mail, short interviews with several associates and friends about their use of e-mail, and an analysis of characteristics of e-mails stored on our e-mail accounts. The linguistic features of e-mails were investigated with a mini-corpus of e-mail messages received by one of the authors, as further described in Sections 7.2.2 and 7.2.3. Obviously, this small case study cannot be representative of all e-mails, and, among other limitations, our mini-corpus is clearly biased towards an academic setting, which Gains (1999) found to be more variable than commercial e-mails (see Appendix A). Nevertheless, the investigation provides provocative findings about e-mail as a register and may give you ideas to pursue in larger or more focused studies in the future.

7.2.1   Situational characteristics of personal e-mail messages

In their situational characteristics, personal e-mail messages have some distinct similarities with and differences from conversation. The most noticeable similarity is that both of these registers are interactive. A person communicates with another specific person in e-mails and conversation. The social roles of the participants can vary (as explored in Section 7.2.3), but no matter who the participants are, addressors expect the addressee of a message to respond (at least acknowledging receipt of the message). A sequence of e-mail messages can be analyzed as a series of turns, showing the interaction of participants, just as conversation has turns (as described in Chapter 4). For example, Text Sample 7.1 displays a sequence of three e-mail messages, beginning with a request for information, followed by a response, and then an acknowledgement:

Text sample 7.1 A sequence of three e-mail messages

Doug – Joe Silex in the Graduate College would like to know if Donna Smith has met her conditions of admission yet. Please advise and I will let Joe know.
   Thanks, – FL

It looks to me like this student is still provisional (GPA of around 2.8) – Doug

thanks! – F

Another important similarity between personal e-mail and conversation is that both typically convey personal feelings and attitudes in addition to specific information. For socially oriented e-mail messages, an expression of personal stance is usually considered very appropriate. For workplace messages, the amount of personal stance considered appropriate likely varies across workplace contexts. However, in the mini-corpus studied here, it was clear that users considered workplace e-mails an appropriate place to convey personal stance. The following examples come from different workplace-related messages:

> It **would be great** to have a lesson on these structures.
> I**'d be happy** to have your vote.
> **Hope** you have a **great** trip!
> Well, I find our grammar discussions **very interesting** and **would love** to talk about Tom's writing sample . . .

At the same time, individual e-mail messages have some important differences from conversation. Prime among these are the mode and medium. Conversation is spoken, while e-mail is written and then sent electronically. E-mail is therefore slower than conversation, since most people can produce more language in a given amount of time in speech than in writing. However, because it is written, e-mail has the potential to be more carefully planned, revised, and edited. If they choose to, writers can delete whole sentences, add explanatory comments, and re-write an e-mail message. However, few people report spending as much time revising their writing in an e-mail as in a printed paper. It is also possible to send an e-mail message without any planning or editing at all.

Since e-mail messages are sent by a software package, they automatically follow certain formatting conventions. E-mail recipients always see the sender's e-mail address, name, the day when the e-mail was sent, information about the path the e-mail took, and a topic line (if the sender filled it in). Some senders include a "signature," which gives their full name and position. When recipients use a "reply" function, the original message is often included with the reply. Finally, most mail programs make it easy to save copies of both outgoing and received messages, an advantage that some users noted for workplace interactions. Some of these features that come from the electronic medium are equivalent to conditions of face-to-face conversations – e.g., seeing the person who is addressing you.

Other features, such as the potential for saving messages, make e-mail more like prototypical written texts.

Another distinct difference between conversation and e-mail is the extent to which the addressor and addressee share time and space. In a normal face-to-face conversation, both space and time are directly shared. As a result, the speaker can refer to *right now* and *over there* with confidence that the listener will understand the reference. These "deictic" expressions make direct reference to the physical context where a text is produced.

In personal e-mail messages, time and space are shared to a lesser extent. In some cases, if both writer and reader are on-line at the same time, messages can be exchanged in rapid succession. In other cases, a sender of a message obviously expects the recipient to read the e-mail within a few hours, for example, asking the question "Do you know what room we're in for the meeting this afternoon?" In these cases, time is shared to a large extent. In other cases e-mails are exchanged over a period of days or weeks, so it is less likely that the reader will understand a reference to a specific time such as "this afternoon."

Physical space is rarely shared in e-mail messages, and so the writer cannot make direct reference to the physical environment without explanation. For example, the statement *That's really obnoxious* would make sense in a face-to-face conversation where participants were looking out the window at fifty-mile-an-hour winds blowing the trees. However, this same statement in an e-mail message would be uninterpretable, because the recipient would have no idea what the pronoun (*that*) referred to.

Interestingly, a number of the advantages that users noted with e-mail are associated with this lack of shared setting between participants. Thus, e-mail enables direct interaction with people in almost any part of the world. But some users also commented on the advantages of using e-mail to communicate with someone who is physically present (e.g., in the office next door), because it is less obtrusive than face-to-face or phone conversations. The recipient can read and attend to the message when convenient. The lack of shared time also means that recipients have the opportunity to complete requested tasks without keeping anyone waiting, an advantage noted for workplace interactions especially. Other users mentioned that e-mail saved time because they could eliminate the social niceties of person-to-person interaction that they felt were required in person or by phone.

Overall, it seems clear that users recognize the unique combination of situational characteristics in e-mail as a register. It is interactive, but less directly so than conversation. It is expected to be composed and processed fairly quickly, like most speech, but can be saved because it is written. It can refer to shared personal background information but is less obtrusive than communication in a completely shared setting. Interestingly, a few users noted that as soon as an issue needed discussion or became controversial, they switched to a phone or face-to-face conversation. In those cases, they saw the lack of direct interaction and lack of shared setting as a disadvantage.

7.2.2   Linguistic characteristics of personal e-mail messages

To investigate the linguistic characteristics of e-mail messages, we compiled a mini-corpus of messages sent to one of the authors. The corpus consists of 76 messages, with a total of 15,840 words.

A comprehensive linguistic analysis of e-mail messages would consider the full range of lexical and grammatical features. However, we focus here on just a few major characteristics that are related to the major situational characteristics discussed above: the interpersonal and interactive nature of e-mail (which is similar to conversation but not as directly and immediately interactive), and the production circumstances and lack of shared physical context (which makes e-mail more like prototypical written registers).

One interesting characteristic of e-mail concerns the structure of turns. We noted above that the interactive nature of e-mail is apparent, because sequences of messages are generally structured like turns in conversation. However, in conversation, participants often contribute minimal responses, which function simply to acknowledge hearing and paying attention to the speaker. For example, in Text Sample 7.2 (part of a conversation from Chapter 4), Gayle's first turn is a minimal response:

Text Sample 7.2 Conversation

Peter: Yeah they were just getting organized.
Gayle: **Yeah.**
Peter: Were Bob and Dorothy up already?

In sequences of e-mail messages, such minimal responses are rare. Instead, e-mail exchanges generally have more equivalent contributions from both interlocutors (the length of turns is further investigated in the next section). In the e-mail mini-corpus, sequences often ended with a short message expressing simply that the information had been received, usually with an expression of appreciation (as in the thanks message ending text sample 7.1 above). However, even this minimal response is often omitted. Some regular users of e-mail mentioned that they sometimes would not send a closing acknowledgement when they did not need to respond with information, because they did not want to clutter someone's inbox with extra e-mail. Thus, while minimal responses are a common, accepted part of face-to-face conversation, they are relatively rare in the newer electronic register, likely reflecting the fact that interaction in e-mail is not as direct and immediate as in conversation.

More specific linguistic features in e-mail messages also clearly reflect the situational characteristics. For example, Figure 7.1 compares the frequency of three basic grammatical features – lexical verbs, pronouns, and nouns – in e-mail messages, conversation, and academic prose. E-mail messages are similar

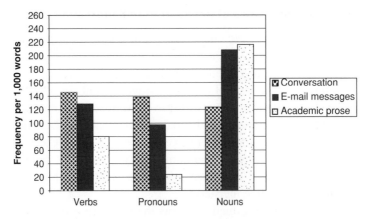

Figure 7.1 *The use of major word classes in e-mail messages, compared to conversation and academic prose*

to conversation in their frequency of lexical verbs. They are intermediate in the use of pronouns, using many more pronouns than academic prose, but not as many as in face-to-face conversation. Finally, they are very similar to academic prose in their overall use of nouns, which are much more common than in conversation.

The frequency of lexical verbs indicates that the e-mail messages incorporate frequent clauses, as conversational discourse does. Given their production circumstances, e-mail messages could be similar to the densely packed, informational prose of academic writing (with elaborated noun phrases, including numerous attributed adjectives, prepositional phrases and other noun modifiers – see Chapter 5). But e-mail messages are rarely focused on abstract concepts, or on explaining information and developing arguments as academic prose does. Rather, the focus is usually interpersonal or task-focused, resulting in a clausal style similar to conversation. For example, notice the relatively short clauses and numerous lexical verbs in the e-mail in Text Sample 7.3 in contrast to the textbook Sample in 7.4 (repeated from Chapter 5):

Text Sample 7.3 E-mail

[lexical verbs in **bold**]

Dr. Biber –

   I would **love** to **meet** with you in the afternoon on March 10. Anytime is fine. Just **name** the time and **describe** directions to your office. I **appreciate** all of your help in this. I have **emailed** Sandy Jackson to possibly **meet** about teaching placements and have been in contact with Andrea. **See** you in a few weeks!

– Dora

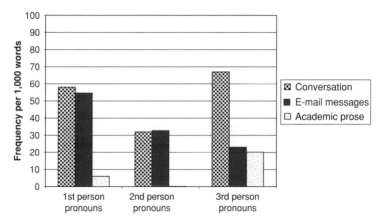

Figure 7.2 *The use of pronoun classes, comparing conversation to e-mail messages*

Text Sample 7.4 Textbook

[lexical verbs in **bold**]

It is a challenge to managers of commercial and noncommercial establishments to **direct** a number of activities at once, including employee training and management; and the purchasing, preparation, and service of food. Foodservice managers generally **expect** to **meet** the diners' expectations. Managers **assume** that they are going to **provide** good, safe food in clean surroundings with friendly service. This assumption, especially regarding safe food and clean surroundings, should be **based** not only on a foundation of goodwill and good intentions, but on a sound understanding of sanitary policies and procedures.

Fast production and a focus on activities rather than concepts both contribute to the high frequency of lexical verbs. This is strengthened by the use of imperatives in many e-mails (e.g., *please advise* in Text Sample 7.1, *name the time* and *describe directions* in 7.3), and by the ellipsis of subjects that are obvious from the context (e.g., *See you . . .* rather than *I will see you*).

However, the frequency of nouns and pronouns in e-mails is surprising given the above descriptions. Because e-mail messages are interactive, you might expect that pronouns would be used to the same extent as in conversation. Instead, we find more pronouns in conversation but more nouns in e-mail messages.

To explain these patterns, we need to undertake more detailed analyses. The first step is to consider the use of pronouns for each person separately: first, second, and third person.

Figure 7.2 shows that first person pronouns (*I, we*) and second person pronouns (*you*) are equally common in conversations and e-mail messages, indicating that these two registers are very similar in their overall interactivity. (In contrast, first person pronouns are much less common in academic prose, while second person pronouns are extremely rare in that register.) However, the pattern of use for third person pronouns is completely different: common in conversation, but relatively rare in both e-mail messages and academic prose. Instead, e-mail messages and academic prose tend to rely on full nouns for third person references.

Text Sample 7.5, a part of the conversation introduced in Chapter 4, illustrates the dense use of third person pronouns in conversation:

Text Sample 7.5 Conversation between friends in a restaurant

[third person pronouns marked in **bold**]

Ayesha: Oh I was saying you know Tuscan bread would never go down here. No one
    would ever like **it**. Probably 'cause **it**'s got no salt in **it**.
Nadia: Yeah and 'cause **it**'s warm.
Ayesha: But I am – I'm totally stuck on **it**.
[...]
Lise: So are you going to go home today, or –
Ayesha: Yeah I have to.
Lise: Why?
Nadia: Go tomorrow Ayesha.
Lise: God I hate you for **that**.
Ayesha: Well I guess you keep – oh we're ordering **it** now?
Marcus: I don't know, but do you want anything to drink?
Ayesha: No, **that**'s good enough.

Many of these third person pronouns are ***anaphoric*** – referring back to a noun phrase that has been previously mentioned. For example, the first four occurrences of the pronoun *it* in Text Sample 7.5 are all anaphoric, referring to *Tuscan bread*. However, many other third person pronouns in conversation are used to refer to the general situation, or to refer to some entity in the physical context. When Lise says *I hate you for **that***, she's referring to the general circumstances of Ayesha's going home. When Ayesha says *oh we're ordering **it** now*, she is referring to the meal or some part of it. When she says ***that**'s good enough*, Ayesha is apparently pointing to the drink that she already has (perhaps a glass of water).

These uses of third person pronouns are much less common in e-mail messages, because they would be difficult to understand when the addressee is not in the same physical space. Instead, messages like the e-mail below are common:

Text sample 7.6 E-mail from a researcher in Europe

[third person pronouns marked in ***bold italics***; nouns underlined]

Dear Professor Biber,
    <u>Things</u> are moving on for <u>IALCC2004</u>. The <u>Program Committee</u> met yesterday: we received 140 <u>submissions</u> and we have accepted around 90 <u>papers</u> for oral <u>presentation</u>. There will be also some <u>poster presentations</u>, but I do not know the <u>number</u> yet, because the "<u>call</u> for <u>posters</u>" is still open.

> I believe we have not talked about the proceedings yet. We plan to publish as usual two volumes of proceedings before the conference (Proceedings are usually distributed at the conference). *This* means that the delay is quite short for the editing work and we will have several people working on *it*. Of course, we would like to include the text of your talk in this book. Would it be possible for you to send us your text by the end of January? I am sorry I did not mention *that* to you earlier. I hope the delay will be ok for you.
>   <...>

Notice first of all that this message incorporates numerous first and second person pronouns, referring directly to the writer (*I*) and the addressee (*you*). However, the message uses comparatively few third person pronouns, and the ones that do occur are directly anaphoric, referring to the preceding proposition or a noun phrase in the preceding discourse. There are no third person pronouns in this message that have a vague reference to the general situation or that refer directly to some entity in the writer's physical context. In contrast, there are numerous full nouns, referring to many entities and concepts in an explicit manner. The use of pronouns and nouns thus corresponds to the situational characteristics of high interactivity coupled with the lack of shared physical context.

7.2.3   Variation in addressee and purpose in e-mail messages

As noted in preceding chapters, the linguistic features within a register vary depending on specific situational characteristics. For example, a conversation between two family members will be different from a conversation between two colleagues, and a conversation about a personal situation will be different from a conversation about business matters, even when they take place between the same two colleagues. Thus, the relationship between the participants and the primary communicative purpose (personal/social vs. professional/business) influence the register characteristics of conversation.

It is similarly possible to distinguish among different types of individual e-mail messages in the mini-corpus, and examine the linguistic variation among the types. To investigate e-mail subregisters, we classified all e-mail messages in our mini-corpus into three sub-categories: e-mails from friends and family on non-professional topics, e-mails from colleagues on professional topics, and e-mails from "strangers" on professional topics. Table 7.1 shows the breakdown of messages across these categories.

One obvious difference in these e-mail types is clear from Table 7.1: length. E-mail messages to friends and family on personal topics tend to be much shorter than e-mails on professional topics; professional e-mails to strangers tend to be the longest. This difference exists in part because e-mails to friends can assume much more background knowledge, and therefore require much less explanatory prose. At one extreme, there are e-mail exchanges like Text Sample 7.7, where people, places, and contexts require no explanation.

Table 7.1 *Composition of the mini-corpus of personal e-mail messages, classified according to addressee and purpose*

Category	No. of messages	Total words	Average length of message
Friends and family; personal topics	23	2,852	124 words
Colleagues; professional topics	32	7,360	230 words
Strangers; professional topics	21	5,628	268 words
Total:	76	15,840	

Text Sample 7.7 Two e-mails from friends planning a social get-together

Doug, climbing gym tomorrow night, 6-ish, Scott

ok – see you then – Doug

In contrast, professional e-mails to strangers tend to be much longer, because the writers need to introduce themselves (or remind the recipient of who they are), state the reason for writing, provide any necessary background, and frame the whole discussion in a polite manner. Even a quick reminder about a meeting generally has more context than the exchange between friends (see Text Sample 7.8).

Text Sample 7.8 E-mail from stranger confirming a meeting

Dr. Biber,
    Just wanted to e-mail and confirm that we were still on for meeting at 2:00 tomorrow. Hope to see you then. I don't know if I had CCd you, but I will be meeting with Dr. Bock at 1:30 and Dr. Edwards at 2:30, so it will be a whirlwind tour of the hallway!
    If there are any problems, please call me at (111) 241–1925, as I will not have access to e-mail until then. Thanks and I look forward to meeting with you.
Sincerely,
Donna Johansson

Not surprisingly, workplace e-mails between colleagues tend to fall between these two extremes. As exemplified in Text Sample 7.1, colleagues who interact regularly often write short messages that get directly to the point and assume a great deal of shared background (such as how a student meets conditions of admissions), yet they still require more explanation than friends making typical social arrangements.

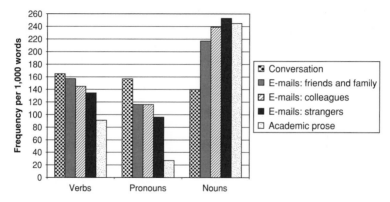

Figure 7.3 *The use of major word classes, comparing conversation to e-mail subregisters*

By this point, you have probably thought of other linguistic characteristics of individual e-mails. For example, e-mails between friends on social topics are relatively unconstrained by formal grammar and punctuation rules (similar to conversation), while e-mails from strangers tend to be more like standard written documents (more similar to academic prose).

Overall, there is a continuum of language variation among the e-mail message subregisters: e-mail messages to friends and family on personal topics tend to be more similar to conversation in their linguistic characteristics; at the other extreme, e-mail messages to strangers on professional topics tend to be more similar to formal (academic) writing. E-mail between colleagues on professional topics fall inbetween the two extremes. The differences in linguistic features among the e-mail categories are not discrete differences, but rather different tendencies in patterns of use that can be detected through quantitative analysis.

For example, Figure 7.3 repeats the information in Figure 7.1, but it distinguishes among the three e-mail types. Although the linguistic differences among the three types are small, they are entirely consistent: "friends and family" e-mails are closest to conversation; "professional stranger" e-mails are closest to academic prose. Figure 7.4 plots the register distributions for a selection of other linguistic features, showing the same consistent patterns, but with the differences among e-mail types being relatively large for some features. For example, activity verbs and time/place adverbs are much more common in the "friends and family" e-mails than in the other categories, reflecting the primary focus on everyday activities rather than conceptual discussions. In contrast, attributive adjectives and nominalizations are much more common in the professional e-mails, especially those written by "strangers," reflecting their informational focus (similar to academic prose). These figures show how linguistic variation is finely stratified across these situational parameters.

As noted above, the three e-mail types differ with respect to two major situational parameters: the relations between writer and receiver, and the primary

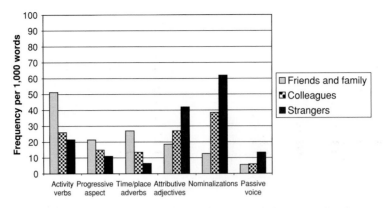

Figure 7.4 *The use of selected grammatical characteristics across e-mail subregisters depending on the relationship between addressor and addressee*

communicative purpose. Some of the earliest research in sociolinguistics studied the influence of role relations on linguistic variation. For example, Brown and Gilman (1960) describe how the choice of second person pronouns in Romance languages (e.g., *tu* versus *vous*) is influenced by the role relation between speaker and addressee. Brown and Ford (1961) describe how the choice of address terms in American English (e.g., first name versus title plus last name) is influenced by similar factors. In analyzing e-mails between people with different relationships, we are thus following in the tradition of much sociolinguistic research, but with consideration of less salient linguistic characteristics, such as verbs, nouns, and adverbs.

7.2.4   Genre markers in e-mail messages

Taking a genre perspective on e-mail messages, we can ask whether there are particular textual conventions used for opening and closing a message. It turns out that there are, but that there is also variation in the use of these conventions depending on the role relation between the sender and receiver.

Figure 7.5 shows the preferred textual conventions used for openings in e-mails of different types. E-mails to friends and family rarely identify the recipient in the salutation used to open the message. Many of these e-mails begin with a simple greeting (such as *hi*), while other e-mails launch directly into the message with no salutation at all (especially when they are not the first message in a sequence). Only about 30% of "friends/family" e-mails identify the recipient in the salutation, using one of two major patterns: *hi* + first name, or first name only. Text Sample 7.7 above illustrates these typical patterns; the first message begins with a "first name only" salutation, while the reply begins with no salutation at all.

At the other extreme, professional e-mail messages to strangers almost always identify the recipient in the salutation, usually using Title plus Last Name (e.g.,

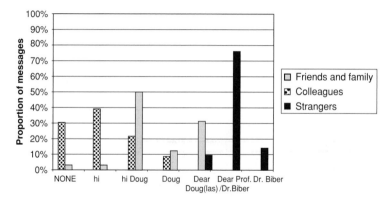

Figure 7.5 *Differences in e-mail salutations depending on the relationship between addressor and addressee*

Dr. Biber). These e-mails have an additional reflection of the formality and distance between writer and receiver: the use of the salutation *Dear*. Over 70% of the professional e-mails from strangers combine both characteristics, opening with Dear plus Title plus Last Name (see Text Sample 7.6 above). Overall, the messages to strangers on professional topics tend to use the genre markers of written letters more consistently than the other categories.

Figure 7.5 also shows that these salutation patterns reflect the fine patterns of stratification across these three e-mail types: professional e-mails written to colleagues are intermediate between the "friends/family" e-mails and "professional stranger" e-mails. Similar to "professional stranger" e-mails, the "professional colleague" e-mails usually identify the recipient by name. But these e-mails always use First Name rather than Title plus Last Name. In addition, these e-mails rarely begin with *Dear* (only about 30% of the time), instead usually beginning with Hi plus First Name, or a simple First Name salutation.

Figure 7.6 shows that the textual conventions for closings are also stratified across the three e-mail types, although the patterns of use are less distinctive than with salutations. A signature of First Name Only is the strongly preferred pattern for "friends/family" e-mails, sometimes introduced with an expression of personal affection (e.g., *love, hugs*). In contrast, there is a strong expectation of a formal leave-taking in "professional stranger" e-mails (e.g., *sincerely, best wishes*, etc.); these forms are almost never used in "friends/family" e-mails.

In sum, the descriptions in this section provide a further illustration of how register and genre can be studied at any level of specificity. Many of the register descriptions in this book have focused on major differences among text categories, for example, between conversation and academic prose. However, registers can be defined much more precisely, by focusing on specific situational parameters. In the present case, we have shown how there are systematic patterns of linguistic variation among sub-registers within the general category of e-mail message, depending on the role relation between sender and receiver, and depending on the

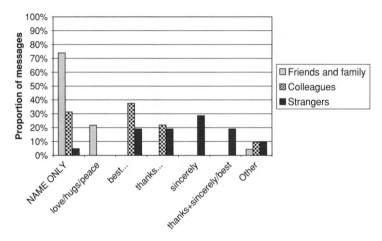

Figure 7.6 *Differences in e-mail signatures depending on the relationship between addressor and addressee*

primary communicative purpose of the message. Similarly, these same situational parameters are associated with different sub-genres, each employing different preferred textual conventions for opening and closing the message.

7.3   E-forum postings

In our second exploration of electronic registers, we consider the messages on an electronic forum. Forums are websites where users post messages about a certain topic. The "postings" (or "posts") are all available for public viewing, and any participant can respond. Forums are designed to be a place where people with a similar interest (usually called the "community") can discuss that interest. Forums serve many of the same purposes as a face-to-face club meeting, where participants share information and enthusiasm. However, they are an entirely new way of discussing something, made possible by computer technology. Their similarities to and differences from face-to-face conversations and e-mails make forums an interesting focus for a register analysis.

Forums do not have a "leader" as such, though there is usually an administrator who makes sure that discussions remain on topic and civil. Administrators have the power to deny access to anyone who does not follow the rules of the forum (such as being personally offensive or repeatedly posting off-topic messages). Most sites also have a status system, showing the ratings of participants in the forum. The ratings are usually based on judgments of helpfulness to other participants (as rated by the participants). The number of postings an individual has made is also usually listed.

The e-forum we use for our case study was set up to discuss issues related to the iPhone, Apple's handheld device with phone, music, video, e-mail, and other internet capabilities. The site is part of Apple's corporate website, hosted as part of their support services. The website has a "User Discussion" section, which is described as "a user-to-user support forum" where "you can participate in discussions about various products and topics, find solutions to help you resolve issues, ask questions, get tips and advice, and more" (Apple, 2007).

After a free registration process, anyone can post a message on the forum, either adding a comment to an already established "thread" (a particular topic), or starting a new thread. The forum has five status levels, depending on how often another user has rated a poster's answer as helpful. Occasionally, an employee of Apple contributes to the forum; the employees are identified with a specific symbol so that other participants know they work for the company. An employee serves as the administrator of the site.

Our case study is based on postings from the e-forum on September 30, 2007, the day after the iPhone went on sale in stores (although some people acted as testers for earlier versions). The release was much anticipated, and long lines formed waiting for stores to open. Once in possession of an iPhone, users had to activate it and learn how to use its various functions. We used all the postings from 28 different threads, for a total of 129 postings. Our analysis of situational characteristics is based on discussion with participants in other e-forum sites and the content of the postings used in the linguistic analysis.

7.3.1   Situational characteristics of e-forum postings

Postings to a forum are similar to e-mail in that they are written. Senders can take as long as they want for planning and revising their messages before they post them, and readers can re-read at their leisure – but users can also choose to read and write messages very quickly.

Beyond being written and sent in the form of electronic communication, the postings present some interesting differences from e-mail. First, information about each person and their place in the "community" is visible to all participants. When you get an e-mail, you see the sender's e-mail address, their name, the day when the e-mail was sent, information about the path the e-mail took to get to you, and the topic line. In the e-forum postings, beyond that information, there is also information about the number of postings the user has made to the forum, the country the user is in, when the user first registered, information about the equipment they are using, and the user's level rating (Figure 7.7). All of this information is clearly displayed in a "profile." Thus, even if you have never seen the user's name before, you get some sense of how involved they are in the community.

Another difference from e-mail is that the e-forum postings are a mixture of personal and group interactions, rather than being an interaction between individuals. An individual posts a message which can be answered by one or more other individuals, and can be read by everyone who looks at the website (whether or not they are registered for the forum). There typically is an exchange

username7 Re: iphone sending the same SMS again and again   ↩ Reply ✉ Email
            Posted: Nov 15, 2007 3:47 PM   ⬆in response to: lk

Posts:
1,381
From:
Florida
Registered:
Jul 3, 2007

Reset both phones (hold down the home and sleep/wake buttons at the same time until the Apple logo comes up)

iMac   Mac OS X (10.4.10)

Figure 7.7 *E-forum posting layout*

of turns as people seek resolution to a problem or share experience. However, at the first posting, no individual is addressed, and later, any individual may join the exchange. In this way, the e-forum is more like a multiple party conversation than it is like personal e-mail. Here, for example, is the beginning of a thread identified as "Topic: iPhone motion detection broken." The following exchange takes place in 18 minutes. The first two participants interact back and forth, and then a third participant enters to explain his observation.

Text Sample 7.9 Sequence of seven e-forum postings

Person 1
When i run safari or ipod features, the phone goes into landscape automatically and doesnt seem to respond to rotating the device. is there a setting somewhere i'm missing or is my motion detector not working? anyone else have this problem?

Person 2
hold the iPhone in a "vertical" nature and then turn it, it's how accelerometers work. if you have it flat, like it was sitting on a table, it won't work.

Person 1
hmm. i've tried every angle, including vertical as you describe. it's completely unresponsive. i think the accelerometer must be faulty in this case.

Person 2
ah, well, if you're holding it so the screen is perpendicular to the ground and it's not working, then yeah, i'd suggest bringing it in and having them check it out, cause it's certainly possible to have a bad one.

Person 3
I've noticed that when rotating the iphone to landscape mode, to view pictures, it won't always respond.
  It doesn't happen often, and most of the time it works fine, but I have noticed it. Maybe it's just a slow response?

Person 2
The biggest cause I've seen of this problem is people not quite understanding how accelerometers work.

The device needs to have the screen perpendicular (or close to it) to the ground in order to function properly. If you held it in your hand, flat like a pancake or something, it can't work. $< \ldots >$

Person 3
Well, don't I feel slightly lame. And all sorts of dumb.
But you're right on the money, there. Works every time.
Thanks for clearing that up!

The amount of shared time and space is another difference from e-mail. As noted above, many of the exchanges in an e-forum take place in a relatively rapid sequence. In contrast, it is not surprising for a personal e-mail to go unanswered for a day, or two (or several!). In the e-forum, responses usually come quickly and often the participants are on-line at the same time. However, postings can also be read days later (as other people seek to resolve a similar problem). For the particular day we studied, many participants clearly were on-line simultaneously as they tried out their new iPhones, but this will of course vary for different days and different e-forums.

The focus on a single topic is also a difference from e-mail. Topics are strictly predetermined in the e-forum, where all issues must clearly relate to the central topic, in this case the iPhone. Compliance is nearly uniform, and any aberrant postings are commented on. For example, in response to a posting that apologized for a previous off-topic posting, a participant responded:

Text Sample 7.10 E-forum posting

then why in the world would you post another one??
and what does this have to do with the iPhone??
please post in the appropriate forum

Since the administrator for the site can block individuals who do not follow the community's rules, there is strong motivation to conform.

Within the topic area, there are a number of purposes for communication. A prime purpose is resolving problems. One posting even explicitly noted the purposes of postings: "Forums by nature tend to contain mostly negative posts by people seeking resolution from the community . . ." By far the majority of the postings concern problems and suggested solutions. Others volunteered information that the participant thought might be helpful to others. Finally, as illustrated in the next section, some postings serve simply to share exciting events or emotions.

7.3.2   Linguistic features of e-forum postings

The mini-corpus of 129 postings had a total of 5,874 words. A first difference from e-mail is the average number of words per message, which is far higher for e-mail (see Table 7.2). This difference is probably no surprise.

Table 7.2 *Average length of e-mail messages and e-forum postings*

	average length (words per message)
E-mail	208
E-forum	46

Although there is variation in the length of the postings, very few are long. Rather, they tend to be extremely focused on a specific problem or answer and for the most part are sent back and forth quickly – much more quickly than e-mail.

Before examining specific linguistic features, it is useful to note that, in general, the e-forum postings follow the traditional rules for grammar and punctuation found in written texts. The most common non-standard modification (exemplified by Text Samples 7.9 and 7.10 above) is to use no or only occasional capitalization. There is also some ellipsis, particularly skipping subject pronouns, as in these examples from different postings:

> Worked for me too. [*It* subject deleted.]
> solved my own problem [*I* subject deleted.]
> Any ideas? [*Do you have* subject + verb deleted.]

Such ellipsis is more typical of conversation than writing, and corresponds to the quick interactive nature of these postings. Some writers also apparently feel the constraints of written language for expressing emotions and attitudes that are more easily expressed in paralinguistic features in speech, such as intonation, pitch and speed. Punctuation is occasionally used in non-standard ways to express these feelings, as exemplified in Text Samples 7.11–13:

Text Sample 7.11 E-forum posting

Mine restarts during the sync. every. time.
this is frustrating.

Text Sample 7.12 E-forum posting

I CALLED APPLE!
Everyone is going to receive an e-mail on july 4th w/ the EXACT date of your Iphone shipment! They are expecting it to be within that week if you ordered early online.
<...> I can't wait to see my phone!!!!

Text Sample 7.13 E-forum posting

Alright!
Another person that actually READs the manual! :)

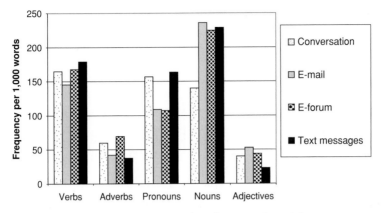

Figure 7.8 *Linguistic features in e-mails, e-forum postings and text messages*

Sample 7.12 uses periods to express the slowness of the iPhone restarting when it shouldn't. Sample 7.13 uses capitalization and repeated exclamation points to express excitement. Sample 7.14 uses an "emoticon" made of punctuation marks to show a smiley face, expressing positive emotion. Only a small minority of the messages use these techniques, however.

With respect to its use of major grammatical features, e-forum postings are generally similar to e-mails. Figure 7.8 shows that e-forum postings have a somewhat higher frequency of verbs, a much higher frequency of adverbs, slightly fewer nouns and adjectives, and almost the same frequency of pronouns.

Like e-mails and conversation, the e-forum postings have frequent short clauses. The postings are very focused on what is happening or what to do, resulting in an even higher use of verbs and adverbs than in e-mail. A large number of the postings ask for advice after they describe what the iPhone is doing or what they have tried. Verbs are required for all these functions, as in these excerpts (verbs in bold):

> ... whilst **charging** I **cannot get** the thing to **start, go** on, **reset**.. **HELP!**

> Yes, I **have** itunes 7.3 **installed**. I **can't get** it too **mount**. I **have restarted, reinstalled** 7.3 and **unplugged** it and **replugged** it a handfull of times . . . . any other ideas?

> when I **plug** in iphoto **opens**. Itunes **is** not **recognizing** the iphone.

The high frequency of adverbs relates in part to their usefulness in explaining problems as they are used in conjunction with verbs or in giving advice about how to use the phone properly, for example (adverbs in bold, verbs in italics):

> Descriptions of problems:
> When i *run* safari or ipod features, the phone *goes* into landscape **automatically**

> **still** *waiting* [for phone activation to work]

> Advice on proper use:

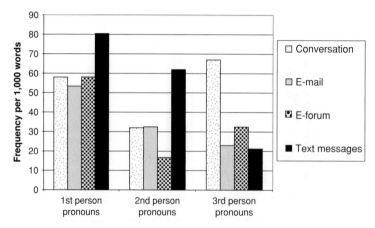

Figure 7.9 *Personal pronouns in e-mails, e-forum postings and text messages*

The iPhone *requires* both 10.4.10 and iTunes 7.3 to *function* **correctly**.

If you *use* a Mac with the iPhone it will *work* **perfectly**.

The iPhone Manual **specifically** *says* that the iPhone WILL *DISCHARGE* **COMPLETELY** if *left connected* to a sleeping/hibernating Mac

The use of adverbs also corresponds to expressions of emotion in this e-forum. Upon getting their new iPhone, many users expressed a high level of excitement (or disappointment). These comments are often intensified with an adverb (bold):

Totally agree !!! [in response to: "words do not describe this device – this will change everything, it's a new world"]

I want one **sooo** bad! But they are not in Australia!

. . . We're buying because it's **incredibly** functional.

. . . It's **absolutely** awesome.

I am **really** disappointed in Apple for this one.

Although Figure 7.8 shows that pronouns overall are equally common in e-mails and e-forum postings, Figure 7.9 shows that the breakdown across specific pronoun types is quite different: first person pronouns are common in both registers, but second person pronouns are much more common in e-mails than e-forum postings. In contrast, third person pronouns are more common in the e-forum. These differences reflect the fact that personal e-mails have an individual recipient, who is commonly addressed as *you*. In contrast, the e-forum postings are more often addressed to the general community. But the e-forum has a very restricted topical domain, in this case focused on a single object, and so third person pronouns are more common.

In terms of genre markers, the openings and closings of e-forum postings offer another interesting contrast to e-mail. Of the 129 postings, only 4 have some sort of salutation and only 11 have a closing signature. Of the four that have a salutation, three are direct responses to a previous question, using "hi" and the

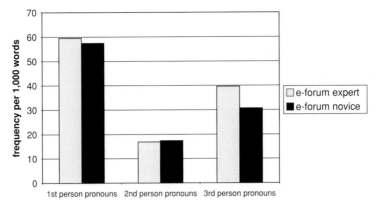

Figure 7.10 *Pronouns in expert vs. novice e-forum postings*

username of the person whose question is being addressed, for example, "Hi TBatey." The closing "signatures" consist of a first name or initials. Clearly, the norm of the community is to have no salutation or signatures. Interestingly, however, it is the regular users with some status in the community who are flouting the norms by using salutations and signatures, perhaps because they expect their names to be recognized by the community and thus give more credibility to their postings. Although the numbers are too small for any general conclusions, this is a finding you can compare with other on-line communities in the activities at the end of this chapter.

7.3.3   A closer look at the use of personal pronouns by users of different status

We noted in our study of e-mail messages that some linguistic differences corresponded to differences in the relationships between participants (family/friend vs. colleague vs. stranger). The e-forum postings provide an additional participant characteristic: status rating within the community. This rating is independent of job, education, age, or any other traditional characteristic. Rather, it is based solely on helpfulness ratings by other participants. Previous studies of other interactive registers have documented the linguistic correlates of social status, but e-forum postings are one of the first registers to actually quantify a measure of status in the community as part of its situational context.

To explore the linguistic features associated with these distinctions, we identified two major user groups in the e-forum postings: "experts" and "novices." The "experts" were the users rated "2" and above – that is, those with numerous postings that had been rated helpful by other participants. The novice group consisted of the users with no rating. Figure 7.10 compares the use of personal pronouns in these two groups. First and second person pronouns are used with similar frequencies by both groups (with first person pronouns being much more common than second person). However, third person pronouns are used more commonly by the expert group than the novice group.

Both groups relate their own experience with first person pronouns. They also refer to certain objects (the iPhone, accessories, associated objects) with the third person pronoun *it*:

Text Sample 7.14 Two e-forum postings

[first and third person pronouns in **bold**]

Novice community member:
   I spent all night gertting **it** activated, had to reset, replace, used all the troubleshooting advice . . . and now **i** can recieve calls – but not make **them** . . .

Expert community member:
   Yes indeed! last night **I** went to bed at almost 4am playing with **it**, today **I** woke up, for a second thought **it** had been a dream but no the iphone was there as beautiful as ever, **I** picked **it** up checked my e-mail, got up and came to work (**I** didn't want to put **it** in my pocket so **I** put **it** back in the box to bring **it** to work, lol) **i** have **it** on **my** desk and everybody comes in and takes long looks at **it**.

Second person pronouns are far less common in both groups, being used only occasionally for questions or giving advice to others with problems.

The greater use of third person pronouns by the expert group appears to be associated with offering more explanation of what other people have said or written. While many people offer their own experience, the expert group offers more information from other sources, as in these examples:

Text Sample 7.15 Two "expert" e-forum postings

[third person pronouns in **bold**]

   This is gonna upset you because **it** upset me greatly – the business center, the ONLY group in all of AT&T that can remove your "corporate liability" – is closed. i waited online for 1.5 hours before someone from the store called me, and **she** told me that **they** had closed. i called back, and indeed, **they** had closed.
   [Level 2 participant]

   There are posts from folks who were having issues porting other companies cell numbers and **they** were told to activate with a new number now and in the next few weeks, after the rush, ATT customer service can help **them** port an old number after the fact.
   [Level 3 participant]

Although this sample is too small for drawing strong conclusions, it may be that part of what makes a user an "expert" is sharing information beyond their own immediate situation, resulting in the greater use of third person pronouns. You will have the opportunity to investigate this possibility more in the activities for this chapter.

7.4   Text messages

Our third case study of a new electronic register focuses on text messages. Text messages (also sometimes called "short messaging services" or SMS) are written messages sent electronically to the recipient's cell phone. With technology developed in the 1990s, the first text messages were generally sent only from other cell phones, but it is now also possible to send them from computers. Although there is usually a limit on the number of characters a cell phone can receive, few messages come close to that limit (see, e.g., Thurlow 2003) and the length of messages seems more constrained by other factors (discussed below) than by the actual length the technology can handle.

To investigate this new e-register, we used a mini-corpus of 300 text messages.[1] The messages were collected in response to a request sent to a variety of internet lists and posted on social websites such as MySpace. Volunteers were asked to answer a short on-line survey about their text messaging use, and to contribute the messages that were stored on their phone, both sent and received. Along with providing each message in its exact form, the participants were asked to explain the context of the message. Although this convenience sample has numerous limitations – including the self-selection of the participants and the fact that some phones did not store outgoing messages – it resulted in a diverse sample of participants and messages. One hundred and thirty participants are included, with received messages from an even larger number of people. Participants from China, Estonia, Canada, and Denmark responded, but the vast bulk of the messages come from participants in the United States, with residents of twenty-four different states included. Participants ranged in age from eighteen to fifty-two and reported a huge variety in employment status, from unemployed to student to lawyer, teacher, bankteller, store manager, executive assistant, bartender, cashier, social worker, barista, medical illustrator, and many more. Only messages sent from individuals were used; messages sent from a company (for example, saying that a payment had been received) were excluded. Messages of any topic (personal or business) were included, but it turned out that only three messages were business-related.

For the authors of this book, describing the situational characteristics of text messages was a particular challenge, since we had little personal experience with them ourselves. We thus employed the methods described in Chapter 2, basing our situational description on participants' survey answers, previous published descriptions, interviewing "expert informants" who had extensive experience with text messaging, and examining the messages themselves.

---

[1] The messages are a subset of a text message corpus being compiled by Wynde Dyer. We are grateful to Wynde for giving us permission to use the corpus.

7.4.1   Situational characteristics of text messages

Text messages have some interesting situational differences from the other e-registers described in this chapter. In terms of participants and their relationships, the messages were sent from one individual to another, all of whom had some personal relationship; in this way, they are similar to e-mail but different from the e-forum, where an individual writes a message to the entire community. Many texters identified the privacy of texting as an advantage over talking on the phone, since speech can be overheard. Interestingly, however, some texters also noted that they feel ok showing a text message to a third person, while they feel that forwarding an e-mail without permission would violate privacy. The existence of onlookers may therefore be a little more common for texting than e-mail.

From the messages themselves and from texters' comments, it is clear that text messages are expected to be interactive, much more immediately so than e-mail. In fact, many text messages are the first part of an adjacency pair, most often a question and answer having to do with impending plans. Many of these exchanges take place very quickly (for written text), such as this exchange which took place over a period of just more than a minute:

Text Sample 7.16 Sequence of three text messages

A: Gym?
B: yeah be over in about a half
A: Ok see you when you get here!

Sometimes the messages do not necessarily require a message back, because the participants will shortly meet face-to-face, as when this friend sends a message to say when he will arrive:

Text Sample 7.17 Text message

Seconds away

A disadvantage of texting mentioned by some users is not knowing for sure if the message was received if they get no response. An apparent consequence of this is that minimal responses are often sent in response to a message. Complete messages that served as responses include:

> Cool
> K!
> Roger
> Ha ha :) [for acknowledging a funny message]

Overall, then, texting is a highly interactive form of communication, closer to conversation than e-mail in being more immediately and directly interactive.

Shared background knowledge is also high in this register. This is clear from the casual mention of people and locations which would be unknown to most other readers, as in these two messages:

> Meet me between smith and cramer asap

> I got you and Taylor tix to Rise Against in pit section.

Even messages that might appear transparent to outsiders turn out to have more specific meaning, understood because of the shared backgrounds of participants. For example, the recipient of this message knew that it was a reminder to get a special kind of milk for the baby on the way home:

> get some milk please

Other messages can be completely mysterious without the shared context:

> over on min.

The recipient of the message knew that his friend, with whom he shares a phone plan, was telling him that he had checked their use against their free allotment of minutes, and they had gone over. Finally, even business-related messages, which are between people with less shared background than friends, tend to be very contextualized, for example:

> what can we do to bring the numbers down for a one day shoot?

Understanding this message requires knowing what photography "shoot" is being referred to and that "the numbers" refers to a cost estimate that was previously sent.

Much of the interaction in text messages makes it clear that participants are interacting in the same temporal context. For example, telling a friend you are "seconds away" is of no use if the message is read the next day. As noted above, many messages relate to impending plans, and would be expected to be read soon. It is clear from the following messages that they are considered more temporally immediate than e-mail or voice mail:

> your set. sorry it took so long. i ran into a guy i know
> [context explanation: I was waiting for an e-mail from this guy]

> Chk e-mail

> Made it-mom
> [context explanation: My parents were traveling back home to their house from my house and had tried to reach me via a phone call but I did not answer so my mom texted me to let me know they made it home safely.]

Interestingly, many messages also show that the physical context is shared between participants. A message such as the following, referring to "here," is traditionally more typical of conversation than any written register:

> R U here?

Text messaging is often done while on the move, and so one of the key purposes of sending a message is to identify the location of the sender.

Like e-mail and e-forum postings, text messages are in the electronic medium, and are written. They have the possibility of being planned and edited by the writer, and read at the recipient's leisure. As described in Chapter 5, time for planning and editing generally results in more complex grammatical structures, especially complex noun phrase structures and precise vocabulary. However, a number of situational factors constrain the size and complexity of text messages. First, some people still have phone plans that charge by the length of the text message (or for sending or receiving messages at all), so length can be constrained by the cost. Second, although text messages are sometimes sent by someone using a full-size computer keyboard, the vast majority are sent from a cell phone, where the size and set-up of the phone number pad is not convenient for typing a message in words. Some phones have pre-programmed expressions, but many texters mentioned that they were rarely useful. One texter summed up the disadvantage of texting: "It takes soo long to type on the cell phone!" The small screens on cell phones are not convenient for reading a long message either.

Clearly, then, there are limits on the amount of writing that is feasible in a text message. Still, the advantage of writing (as opposed to speaking) was mentioned by numerous participants as a strength of texting. Survey respondents noted that texting is a superior form of communication in places where you are expected to be quiet or do not want to disturb other people (e.g., a library, a doctor's office, a business meeting) and places that are too noisy for talking on the phone easily (such as a noisy bar). Other informants noted that texting is preferred when you just don't feel like participating in a longer telephone conversation.

There are a variety of communicative purposes for text messages. In the corpus for this case study, we found six general purposes. These categories are meant to give an overall sense of the purposes of texting; clearly more thorough studies with more specific sub-classifications are needed. (See Thurlow 2003 for a description of communicative purposes in a corpus of text messages in Wales, with results largely similar to those here.)

7.4.1.1   Purpose 1: Social organizing

This is an extremely common purpose for messages. Often, the sender is inquiring into a friend's location or activity, looking for someone to get together with:

> mike! what are you doing?

There are also many specific messages inviting a friend to do something:

> Vita cafe brunch at 11?

> Yo, u wanna see pirates tonight?

Messages also can explain the procedure for further social planning:

> i'll call u tomorrow when i get home from work & we'll figure out what time
> 2 do the pick-up.

7.4.1.2   Purpose 2: Staying connected while on the move

A large proportion of the messages are attempts to find someone/some place, or to inform someone about current whereabouts:

participant's context explanation	message
when driving to pick up a friend:	what's the intersection?
when expecting a friend to arrive:	R u on yer way?
mother trying to find her daughter in a store:	At the service desk
coming to meet friends at a restaurant:	On our way
how are you going to get home?:	I'm taking the bus.

7.4.1.3   Purpose 3: Information sharing

A few messages in this category ask for specific information, for example:

> Do u know where u saved that movie on my computer

Many of these messages continue a topic that has been under discussion previously (usually in face-to-face conversation, although it may have appeared in previous text messages as well). The following message was explained as being a suggestion related to an earlier discussion about playing at an open mic session:

> Taylor Swift..tear drops on my guitar! perfect song for open mic. check it
> out, its really acoustic sounding heh

Still other messages share new exciting or shocking news:

> OMG . . . my DAD's on MYSPACE!!!

> I'm a mother f-ing college graduate! [sent during the graduation ceremony]

> A new hawaiian bbq place opened up here called maui hawaiian bbq.
> According to da menu theres one whittier. [from a person in Fresno, California, to his girlfriend who lives near Whittier]

7.4.1.4   Purpose 4: Relationship maintenance

Many messages are simply a way of staying in touch or expressing emotion, rather than being focused on specific information. These messages ask how things are going or express caring for friends or intimate partners:

from a friend: Hey Shana how is your week going so far?

from a boyfriend after spending the morning with her family:
I love you so much sweetheart. You and your family mean everything to me.

from a co-worker upon moving to a new job: We all love you and will really miss you. Have a safe trip.

from a husband whose wife just hung up on him: Im so pissed @ U.

7.4.1.5   Purpose 5: Business reminders

Only a small number of the messages in the mini-corpus were business-related. They are similar to the informational and social organizing messages – for example, asking for information about a cost quote, explaining a delay for an appointment with a teaching assistant, or reminding a person of an appointment, for example:

> Massage on thurs!

Overall, text messages are highly focused on interpersonal relationships, as shown by the high interactiveness, level of shared knowledge, shared time (and sometimes place), and the most common purposes. At the same time, communication is distanced and somewhat impersonal in text messaging, a fact which was noted as both a disadvantage and advantage by survey respondents. On the one hand, texters commonly criticized the inability to express (or understand) the emotional content of a message clearly. Not hearing how something was "said" contributed to misunderstanding. Since the messages needed to be short, only the "gist" could be conveyed. On the other hand, texting was described as a quick, efficient way to communicate when a person did not have time (or was not in a place) for a longer conversation. Some respondents noted they had an easier time texting than talking when they had negative news (such as being late). Many found texting faster and easier than phoning, when they did not feel like having a longer conversation. Echoing the comments about e-mail, one participant noted that part of the efficiency and ease of texting specifically had to do with not following the norms for small talk: "Quick and efficient in many cases. Relief from the exhausting effort (I say only half-joking) of traditional ettiquette (Hi, how are you, what have you been up to, etc. etc.) when you just need a quick question answered." Another regular texter clearly explained how texting allows her to share quick thoughts when she doesn't want to have a full conversational interaction:

> It's great for inside jokes, sentimental memories, random thoughts, funny experiences, etc. I would never call someone up to say, "Oh, I was just thinking about . . ." or, "So, remember that one time . . ." or, "Oh my gosh, guess what just happened . . ." because I don't REALLY want to talk, I just want to share, or just to let someone know something reminded me of them or of us. Composing an e-mail would seem so formal . . . it seems to me to be so serious to sit down and set out to write out all that stuff, whereas it seems very casual or non-committal to do it by text-messaging . . . I don't want to open that dialog, I just want to say, "I was thinking of you."

7.4.2   Linguistic features of text messages

One of the distinctive characteristics of text messaging is its use of paralinguistic features. Two of the most salient features of text messages are their use of abbreviated forms and nonstandard punctuation and capitalization. There is a great deal of variation in the reliance on these features. At one extreme, a few of the 300 messages in our mini-corpus use standard English grammar, punctuation, and capitalization:

> I guess it will have to be next week. Have a great weekend.

> What is your address?

At the opposite extreme, a few messages have a very condensed form:

> pl pu cheese on ur way hm [please pick up cheese on your way home]

> Can u do lt dnr 9ish? [Can you do a late dinner at 9ish?]

However, the vast majority of text messages fall in between these two extremes, with varying use of punctuation, capitalization, and abbreviations:

> U Busy? Prolly workin. I'm sittin in traffic for the next 45 minutes . . .

> What aiports r good 4 houston?

> Weve 4 tickets, who should we take

In some cases (e.g., use of "your" rather than "you're") it is impossible to know if writers are using an abbreviated form or just making a mistake. However, repeated use of certain forms by multiple writers suggests that these are accepted condensed forms within this register, probably to make the typing task easier:

Abbreviations used by more than one person:

Abbreviation	Meaning
k	OK
R or r	are
U or u	you
ur	your
lol	laugh out loud
2	to
4	for
@	at
n	and

Emoticons are probably the most discussed feature of text-messaging; there are numerous books and websites that list dozens of these symbols. However, although emoticons are salient when they appear, only about 10 of the 300 messages in our mini-corpus use them. Emoticons were found in messages sent by both men and women. Generally, the meaning of the emotion has already been expressed (or at least suggested) in the message; the emoticon serves to emphasize this meaning:

> Then what do you want my sweetie:-∗ ? [a kiss]
> call me wen you land. I miss you :-([sad face]

With only about 3% of the messages including emoticons, they are not a common feature.

Section 7.2 above described some of the genre conventions of e-mail messages. Even the most informal e-mails often follow genre conventions for openings and closings. For example, Section 7.2.3 noted that about 30% of e-mails from friends and family identify the recipient in the salutation (*hi* plus first name, or first name only). In contrast, the short nature of text messages corresponds to an absence of formal openings and closings – that is, an absence of overt genre markers. Of the 300 text messages in our corpus, only one starts with a person's name:

> Max, sorry i missed ur cal yesterday. Cal me today.

Two start with a "hi" (one continuing the greeting with an endearment):

> Hi hope you guys had a great weekend with lots of progress with your yard. Bob

> Hi, Honey! Big kisses from Italy! I visited Venice, Ferrara, Bologna, Padova and Verona. It's a beautiful country! :D I'm going to Austria tomorrow. Take care!

Another twenty-one messages start with "hey" and one with "heya." But the large majority of text messages – over 90% – have no salutation at all. In this respect, text messaging is similar to face-to-face conversations among intimates, which often simply pick up where they left off, despite a period of absence.

Even fewer messages have a closing of any sort. One closes with "Take care!" Two messages are "signed" with the sender's name: one is from a friend (Bob) and the other from "mom." Interesting, both of these individuals are older than the majority of the message senders, and could perhaps be more used to e-mailing than texting.

To further describe the linguistic characteristic of text messages, we carried out quantitative investigations. In this analysis, we treated abbreviations as though they were the equivalent written word; for example, *R U* was analyzed as "are you" – a verb and a pronoun – not just as two letters of the alphabet.

The 300 messages in our corpus had a total of 3,049 words, or an average of about 10.2 words per message. Compared to the length of e-mails (208 words/message) and e-forum postings (46 words/message), text messaging clearly is a quick, short form of communication, whether because of the relatively inconvenient typing and reading, or the cost, or both.

Figure 7.8 (in the last section) displays the frequency of verbs, adverbs, pronouns, nouns, and adjectives in text messages relative to the other e-registers and conversation. Text messages have a very high frequency of verbs (higher even than the e-forum and conversation) and extremely high frequency of pronouns (even higher than conversation). The frequency of nouns is similar to the other e-registers, and the frequency of adverbs and adjectives is extremely low.

The high frequency of verbs in text messages is not surprising, given the reliance on clauses even in very short messages, for example:

> **Are** you **napping**???
> where *r* u???
> **swim** [in answer to a message asking about evening plans]

It is perhaps more surprising to see that both nouns and pronouns have high frequencies. Nouns tend to refer to events, places, and named activities:

> I want to be on a **porch** somewhere drinking a **beer** and doing **nothing**

> Im meeting some **dude** from the **internet** for happy **hour** ahh! **Wed** is a going away **dinner** for **renetta** call u soon!

A number of suggestions or answers to questions are also single word nouns:

> **food**?
> **gym**?
> **pinball** [in response to a message asking where the participant was in a crowded club]

First and second person pronouns are extremely common in text messages (see Figure 7.9), even more common than in conversation and e-mails. This reflects the primary focus on the sender and receiver. Because of the constraints on message length, texters tend to be utilitarian, focusing on the immediate interaction rather than other people, places, or things. Thus, there is an extremely frequent use of *I* and *you*, illustrated in most of the text messages given above. (In addition, senders sometimes omit *I*, as in *Will call you* ...)

The following messages show how verbs, nouns, and first and second person pronouns (and occasional indefinite pronouns) account for a great deal of the language in many messages:

> **nobody** *came* to the **park** yet, so **we'll meet u guys** at **starbucks**. **Dont forget** to **bring** *games*!

> **Landed. Will call you** once **i get** a **cab**.

> well **im** glad **i could bring** a **smile** 2 **your face**

Since text messages are short, adverbs and adjectives – which would modify verbs and nouns – are uncommon. The most common adverb is *just*, which is used to reduce the urgency of the message:

> Its ok babe. **Just** call me when ur done studying.
> hey .... **just** wondering whats up with you ... sorry i was driving earlier

Unlike e-forum postings, which used adverbs to show emphasis and emotion, text messages usually use extralinguistic devices like capital letters and exclamation points for emphasis:

> OMG . . . my DAD's on MYSPACE!!!
> Dude, give me a call it's my BIRTHDAYYY!

Emoticons and LOL (for "laugh out loud") are also used by a few writers, as discussed in the previous section. By and large, however, the messages are not overtly emotional. The exchange of information dominates, although it is information of a personal nature (having to do with the immediate participants). The one emotion repeatedly conveyed in the messages is with the word *love*, for example:

> Almost sent you a note on saturday, then realized it was only eight a.m!
> Love you!
>
> Just saying I love you
>
> aww . . . i love you
>
> Love you princess and miss you too

7.5   Chapter summary

The present chapter has illustrated how the set of registers in a culture is not static. Rather, as new types of communication arise, new registers are developed in response to the situational characteristics of those communication types. The onset of electronic communication has resulted in an unparalleled expansion in the set of new registers. We have described the situational and associated linguistic characteristics of three of those registers, but there are many others that could be investigated (see the chapter activities).

One of the recurring themes of this book has been that situational differences at any level correspond to systematic linguistic differences. The present chapter further illustrates this relationship. All three registers described here are similar in that they are instances of electronic communication. However, the chapter has shown how relatively subtle differences in the communicative purposes, production circumstances, and relations among participants correspond to systematic linguistic differences across the three registers. These electronic registers blend the situational characteristics of more traditional registers in interesting ways that systematically influence their associated linguistic characteristics.

In the following chapter, we turn to more comprehensive descriptions of register variation in a language, showing how more advanced analytical techniques are required for such analyses.

Chapter 7 activities

Reflection and review

1. Can you think of any other new situational characteristics that could be analyzed in an electronic register (like the status rating in e-forums)? What is the register, and what are the new situational characteristics? Do you have any hypotheses about linguistic features that might be associated with these situational characteristics?

2. Plan a comprehensive corpus for the study of electronic communication. Include every e-register that you can think of, noting how its situation of use differs from the other registers. Then propose methods for obtaining texts from these different registers. Discuss any issues that arise because of the nature of any of the electronic registers. For example, how will you deal with texts that are exactly the same as those that have written/published forms (e.g., information manuals that are printed and on-line)? In other words, what principles will you follow for defining an "e-register"?

3. List three concrete teaching applications for English-as-a-second-language students, based on any of the findings in this chapter.

Analysis practice

4. Instant messaging (IM) is another relatively new electronic register in which participants are online at the same time, typing messages sent directly to each other.
   The following data comes from a study of instant messaging by Nuckolls (2005), which compared three pairs of partners in conversation and instant messages. Using the data in Table 7.3 and Activity Text 16, answer the following questions.
   A. How does the use of minimal responses by participants compare in the two registers? How does the use of minimal responses in IM compare to e-mail and text messaging (as described in this chapter)? What situational characteristics likely account for the use of minimal responses in IM?
   B. Articles in the popular press often emphasize the use of emoticons and abbreviations in instant messaging and other electronic registers. Use the findings in Table 7.4 to determine the extent to which emoticons and other emotion-related features are used in IM interactions. How do these findings for IM compare to the information about e-mail and text messages in this chapter? What interpretations would you give, including both register factors and possible individual style factors?

Table 7.3 *Percentage of turns that are minimal responses in two registers*

Participant pair	Face-to-face Conversation	Instant Messaging
(1) Kristy & Lisa	8.0%	1.3%
(2) Jade & Marge	12.0%	0%
(3) Joe & Rudy	14.3%	1.1%

(Summarized from Nuckolls 2005 for 4–6 interactions/pair)

Table 7.4 *Frequency of emotion-related features in IM (normed per 500 words)*

Feature	Mean frequency	Range of frequency
Emoticons	5.3	0–16
Abbreviations	2.0	0–6
Capitalization	9.2	1–17
Words spelled out	5.5	<1–14

(Summarized from data in Nuckolls 2005.)

Definitions of features

Emoticon – a symbol used to express an emotion, e.g. :) [to show a smile]

Abbreviations – first letters used to describe emotional action or feeling, e.g., lol or LOL ("laugh out loud"), imho ("in my humble opinion")

Capitalization – word typed in capital letters to express emotion and emphasis, e.g. "WOW" (Note: One participant typed consistently in all capitals, which she said was for speed. Her frequency was not included in the counts.)

Words spelled out – emotion-related word written down, e.g. "smile" [to show the writer was smiling or teasing]

C. Are there other distinctive linguistic features that you notice in the IMs of Activity Text 16? If so, what situational characteristics are likely associated with the use of those features?

5. If you have personal e-mail stored in your mail inbox, or text messages saved on your phone, pick eight to ten messages from different people and analyze their communicative purposes, the use of at least three linguistic features, and any systematic genre conventions (including openings and closings). Compare your results to the findings presented in this chapter.

Project Ideas

6. Analyze the linguistic features in another e-forum community that includes ratings for its participants, comparing the patterns of language use to those in the iPhone e-forum described in this chapter. For example, determine whether the norm in this second e-forum is to use salutations and closing signatures or not. Do users with higher status (e.g., reflected by high ratings) in the community tend to use more openings and closings than lower-rated participants? Also examine the use of several lexico-grammatical features (including third person pronouns). Present your findings quantitatively (e.g., what percentage of the unrated users vs. high-rated users follow a particular pattern)?

7. Conduct a small-scale register analysis of electronic "chat." Gather samples from several chat rooms, and analyze the situational and linguistic characteristics. Compare and contrast this register with conversations and with other electronic registers.

8. Build and analyze your own mini-corpus of blogs, another relatively new e-register. First, identify the different types of blogs that you would like to include in your corpus. Second, choose a sample of blogs from each of the different types, collecting enough different blog texts to represent the variation across types. Finally, describe the situational and linguistic characteristics of blogs. Compare/contrast blogs to other registers, both traditional and electronic. (As an additional step, you can also carry out a more detailed analysis comparing the different subregisters of blogs.)

PART III

Larger theoretical issues

8   Multidimensional patterns of register variation

8.1   Comparing multiple registers

The preceding chapters have described the distinctive situational and linguistic characteristics of particular registers, including everyday conversation, newspaper writing, academic prose, e-mail messages, and text messaging. Through these descriptions, we have illustrated how register differences are pervasive in human communication: speakers of any language regularly encounter and use a range of registers, which all differ to some extent in their situational and linguistic characteristics.

Those chapters have also shown how register analyses are always comparative: register features are defined as linguistic characteristics that occur more frequently in the target register than in other comparison registers. Thus, in the preceding chapters, we have described the linguistic characteristics of a target register by comparison to other registers. In some cases, the situational differences between the registers being compared are large, as with the comparison of classroom teaching and textbooks in Chapter 3; in other cases, the situational differences between registers are more subtle, as with the comparison of e-mails, text messages, and conversation in Chapter 7. In all these cases, though, the comparison allows us to observe the linguistic differences associated with particular situational factors.

But what if an analyst wanted to compare the full range of registers used in a language? For example, the preceding chapters have shown how the language of conversation is dramatically different from academic writing. But what if the research goal was to compare both of these registers to other common registers, like e-mail messages and university classroom teaching? And more specifically, what if the goal was to describe the **extent** to which these registers were different linguistically, and the **particular ways** in which they were different from one another?

For example, based on the discussion in Chapter 7, you would probably conclude that e-mail messages and text messages are more similar to conversation than to textbooks. But what about university classroom teaching? Would you predict that it is more similar to conversation, e-registers, or textbooks? Or would you predict that classroom teaching is similar to conversation in some respects, but similar to e-registers and textbooks in other ways?

From a situational perspective, these registers are all shaped by different influences. University classroom teaching is complex, sharing some characteristics with both conversation and textbooks. Classroom teaching is similar to conversation in that it is spoken and interactive to some extent. At the same time, university classroom teaching is similar to textbook writing in its primary communicative purpose: to convey information. In fact, much classroom teaching has its roots in written textbooks, with students required to study textbooks before the class session, and the instructor then summarizing and explaining the information presented in those books. E-mail messages and text messages are similarly complex in their situational characteristics. And correspondingly, all of these registers have their own particular linguistic patterns.

The focus of the present chapter is on comprehensive descriptions of register variation: analyses that capture the patterns of variation among a large set of registers, with respect to a large set of linguistic characteristics. It would be possible to attempt such an analysis using only the techniques introduced in previous chapters, simply adding more registers to our comparisons, and carrying out those comparisons with respect to a larger set of linguistic features. We illustrate an analysis of this type in the following sub-sections, comparing five registers that have been described in previous chapters: conversation, e-mails, text messages, classroom teaching, and textbooks. We show in that section how such an analysis quickly becomes overwhelming, because there are so many points of comparison to consider. This discussion then leads into the introduction of an alternative methodological approach – ***multidimensional analysis*** – which permits comparisons of multiple registers along a relatively small number of underlying dimensions of variation.

One underlying goal of multidimensional analysis is to achieve a comprehensive description of linguistic variation and use in a language. Traditional linguistic descriptions treat a language as a homogeneous whole, describing the supposedly unified grammar of the entire language. The perspective in this book is dramatically different from this traditional approach, showing how each register has its own grammar of use. In the present chapter, we discuss how an entire language can be analyzed from a register perspective, considering the full range of registers and a comprehensive set of linguistic features. Such analyses complement structural descriptions of a language and enable comparisons of the patterns of register variation among different languages.

8.1.1   Generalizable descriptions of registers

At the end of Chapter 3, we noted that generalizable descriptions of a register must be based on a representative sample of texts from the register. In this regard, we have tried to walk a tightrope in this book. On the one hand, we have presented numerous case studies illustrated by analysis of a few individual texts from a register. It is at this level that the methods for doing register analysis are most accessible, and for that reason, most of the chapter activities also involve analysis of a few individual texts from a register. However, we have at the same time cautioned against basing generalizations on analyses of a few texts. There will always be variation among the texts within a register; if an analysis is based only on a single text from a register, there is no way to determine whether that text is typical. Thus, generalizable descriptions of a register must be based on a representative sample of texts. The present chapter illustrates analyses of this type.

In previous chapters, we have introduced corpus-based analysis as a research approach that can be used for large-scale register studies. That is, by empirically analyzing linguistic patterns in a large collection of texts from a register – a corpus – it is possible to document which linguistic features are in fact common or rare, including an assessment of the actual extent to which a linguistic feature is used. In many cases, corpus analyses produce surprising results, running counter to our prior expectations. In such cases, the corpus analysis confronts us with linguistic patterns that require a reassessment of the relative importance of different situational characteristics in the target register.

For the descriptions in previous chapters, we had previously carried out large-scale corpus-based register analyses, and thus we were able to select individual texts that were typical of the larger register category. Further, most of the quantitative findings presented in graphs in those chapters are based on large-scale corpus research (e.g., samples of around 1 million words for textbooks and around 5 million words for conversation). As a result, we can be confident that the quantitative linguistic descriptions based on those samples represent patterns of use that are typical of the target register. In the present chapter, the focus is entirely on the analysis of register patterns in large corpora of this type.

8.1.2   Which linguistic features to consider?

In addition to the sample of texts, a second major consideration for comprehensive descriptions of register variation is deciding on the linguistic features to analyze (see Section 3.4). In Chapter 3, we introduced the methodologies required for quantitative linguistic descriptions, and we further illustrated those methods in Chapters 4–6. However, there is one aspect of the linguistic analysis that we have not yet adequately addressed: that the comprehensive linguistic description of a register is multidimensional, with patterns of use that can be discovered only through comparative analysis of multiple registers with respect to a large set of linguistic features. Comparisons of a target register to several other registers are almost never simple. Rather, the target register is similar to register A with respect to some linguistic features, but similar to register B with respect to other features, and so on. It is only by considering the full set of linguistic features distributed across multiple registers that the researcher can uncover the multidimensional patterns of register variation.

To illustrate, consider Text Sample 8.1, from an upper division geology lecture. We introduced the linguistic characteristics of university classroom teaching in

Chapter 3, and we then provided detailed descriptions of several other registers in the following chapters, including conversation (Chapter 4), textbooks (Chapter 5), and e-mails and text-messages (Chapter 7). Based on those descriptions, try to identify ways in which this classroom teaching text is similar to and different from each of these other registers. Make a list of linguistic characteristics that strike you as being distinctive in Text Sample 8.1, noting for each feature whether the use here is similar to or different from the other registers.

Text Sample 8.1 Geology classroom teaching, upper division

Instructor: Right. So we've changed the amount of water that's stored. But we've also changed the amount of water that naturally came out of the system. so that's- this is – the concept you're mentioning is what's called – it is originally known as the principle of safe yield. $<\ldots>$ and actually in the state of Arizona we have a ground water management act that described how we manage water in a few major ground water extraction areas $<\ldots>$ now again this is from a new book I've been looking at. what this term does is it ignores how much water naturally comes out of the system. so if you're taking water out, you're taking that water away from where it naturally used to come out. So if you keep doing that long enough the eventual discharge point will dry up. The natural discharge point will eventually dry up if you pump as much water out as naturally comes in. so in the state of Arizona, we're managing those aquifers under a method that will eventually dry up the natural discharge places for those aquifer systems. So $<\ldots>$ eventually we're going to lose a lot of water that's stored in the system. Now, why is this an issue? well, some of you probably want to live in this state for a while. You want your kids to grow up here and your kids' kids. You might be concerned with does Arizona have a water supply which is sustainable? $<\ldots>$ Now I hope you see that these two terms are incompatible. The sustainability concept and safe yield concept, because sustainability means that it is sustainable for all systems dependent on the water.

[T2K-SWAL Corpus]

In the following section, we present corpus-based research findings that compare the general characteristics of classroom teaching to these other registers. Text Sample 8.1 is typical of classroom teaching in the multidimensional use of these features, and thus we return to it several times below.

8.1.3   Comparing the distribution of individual linguistic features across multiple registers

When the research goal is to compare the distribution of individual linguistic features across multiple registers, the analysis quickly becomes complex. For example, Figure 8.1 compares the use of six linguistic features across five registers, synthesizing research findings presented in the previous chapters. For the sake of discussion, we continue to focus here on classroom teaching in comparison to the other four registers, addressing the two basic issues identified

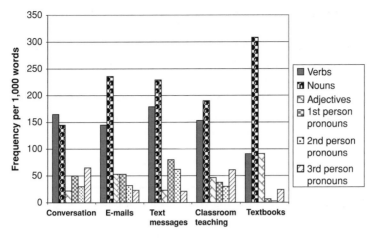

Figure 8.1 *Linguistic features across five registers*

above: **to what extent** does classroom teaching differ from these other registers, and **in what particular ways** does it differ?

A quick look at Figure 8.1 shows that there are not simple answers to these questions. For example, focusing on the use of verbs, Figure 8.1 shows that classroom teaching has a high frequency, similar to conversation and e-mail messages, but not quite as frequent as in text messages. All of these registers are strikingly different from textbooks, which use comparatively few verbs. In contrast, classroom teaching uses more nouns than conversation, but not nearly as many as textbooks. The two e-registers also both use more nouns than classroom teaching. The register distribution of adjectives is similar to nouns: more common in classroom teaching than conversation, but not nearly as common as in textbooks. But here text messages are similar to conversation in using few adjectives. Finally, each of the three pronoun classes has a distinct distribution. For example, first and second person pronouns are common in textbooks, similar to conversation and e-mails. But these two pronoun classes are even more frequent in text messages. At the other extreme, these pronoun classes are rare in textbooks.

Figure 8.1 provides an additional illustration of why the comparative approach is so important. If conversation was considered by itself, the researcher would conclude that nouns and verbs are equally important in that register, since they are equally frequent. However, comparing conversation to textbook writing shows that nouns are comparatively rare in conversation: only half as frequent as in textbooks. In contrast, verbs are extremely frequent in conversation: almost twice as frequent as in textbooks.

Further, a comparative approach shows that e-mails, text messages, and classroom teaching all have high frequencies of verbs but intermediate frequencies of nouns, despite the fact that nouns are more frequent than verbs in these registers. For example, verbs are more frequent in text messages than in any other of these four registers, so it is reasonable to conclude that this is a very high frequency for that feature. In contrast, nouns are considerably less frequent in text messages than in textbooks. Thus, even though nouns are more frequent than verbs in text messages, in comparative terms, verbs are extremely common in this register while nouns are only moderately common.

The example classroom text introduced above reflects these general patterns for classroom teaching in its dense use of verbs and pronouns, combined with its intermediate use of nouns. Text Sample 8.2 repeats this text with these target features highlighted:

Text Sample 8.2 Classroom teaching (repeated from Text Sample 8.1)

[Nouns are underlined; main verbs are in **bold**; pronouns are in ***bold italics***]

Instructor: Right. So ***we***'ve **changed** the amount of water that's **stored**. But ***we***'ve also **changed** the amount of water that naturally **came** out of the system. so ***that's*** - ***this*** **is** – the concept ***you***'re **mentioning is** what's **called** – ***it*** is originally **known** as the principle of safe yield. < . . . > and actually in the state of Arizona ***we*** **have** a ground water management act that **described** how ***we*** **manage** water in a few major ground water extraction areas < . . . > now again ***this*** **is** from a new book ***I***'ve been **looking** at. what this term **does is** ***it*** **ignores** how much water naturally **comes** out of the system. so if ***you***'re **taking** water out, ***you***'re **taking** that water away from where ***it*** naturally used to **come** out. So if ***you*** **keep doing** ***that*** long enough the eventual discharge point will **dry** up. The natural discharge point will eventually **dry** up if ***you*** **pump** as much water out as naturally comes in. so in the state of Arizona, ***we***'re **managing** those aquifers under a method that will eventually **dry** up the natural discharge places for those aquifer systems. So < . . . > eventually ***we***'re going to **lose** a lot of water that's **stored** in the system. Now, why **is** ***this*** an issue? well, some of ***you*** probably **want** to **live** in this state for a while. ***You*** **want** your kids to **grow** up here and your kids' kids. ***You*** might be **concerned** with does Arizona **have** a water supply which **is** sustainable? < . . . > Now ***I*** **hope** ***you*** **see** that these two terms **are** incompatible – the sustainability concept and safe yield concept, because sustainability **means** that ***it*** **is** sustainable for all systems dependent on the water.

[T2K-SWAL Corpus]

Figure 8.2 displays the patterns of use for additional linguistic features: two kinds of dependent clause – conditional and causative adverbial clauses, and *that* complement clauses – restricting the comparison to just three registers for the sake of simplicity. In Chapter 4, we described the use of these dependent clause types in conversation and office hours. Figure 8.2 shows that these structures are equally common in classroom teaching. In fact, similar to office hours, classroom teaching uses more of these adverbial clauses than in conversation. Both dependent-clause types are considerably less common in textbooks.

Finally, Figure 8.3 plots the frequency of relative clauses, showing a different pattern, with classroom teaching being more similar to textbook writing than

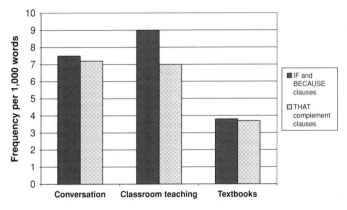

Figure 8.2 *Adverbial clauses and complement clauses across three registers*

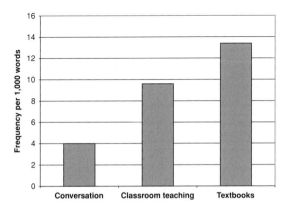

Figure 8.3 *Relative clauses across three registers*

conversation. The relatively frequent use of certain noun-modifying features in classroom teaching reflects its informational communicative purpose, similar to textbook writing.

The classroom teaching Text Sample 8.3 illustrates these additional patterns: the frequent use of adverbial (*if* and *because*) clauses and *that* complement clauses – similar to conversation – as well as the frequent use of relative clauses – similar to textbook writing:

Text Sample 8.3 Classroom teaching (repeated from Text Sample 8.1 above)

[Relative clauses are in **bold**; Adverbial clauses (*if* and *because*) and *that* complement clauses are underlined]

Instructor: Right. So we've changed the amount of water **that's stored**. But we've also changed the amount of water **that naturally came out of the system**. so that's-this is – the concept **you're mentioning** is what's called – it is originally known as the principle of safe yield. < . . . > and actually in the state of Arizona we have a ground water management act **that described how we manage water in a few major ground water extraction areas** < . . . > now again this is from a new book **I've been looking at**. what this term does is it ignores how much water naturally comes out of the system. so if you're taking water out, you're taking that water away from where it naturally used to come out. So if you keep doing that long enough the eventual discharge point will dry up. The natural discharge point will eventually dry up if you pump as much water out as naturally comes in. so in the state of Arizona, we're managing those aquifers under a method **that will eventually dry up the natural discharge places for those aquifer systems**. So < . . . > eventually we're going to lose a lot of water **that's stored in the system**. Now, why is this an issue? well, some of you probably want to live in this state for a while. You want your kids to grow up here and your kids' kids. You might be concerned with does Arizona have a water supply **which is sustainable**? < . . . > Now I hope you see that these two terms are incompatible. The sustainability concept and safe yield concept, because sustainability means that it is sustainable for all systems dependent on the water.

[T2K-SWAL Corpus]

Synthesizing the register patterns from all three of these figures illustrates the importance of a multidimensional perspective. If a researcher based an analysis on only one set of features – for example, verbs, pronouns, and adverbial/complement clauses – she might conclude that classroom teaching is very similar to conversation and interactive e-registers, and very different from textbooks. However, by considering a different set of features – for example, nouns, adjectives, and relative clauses – the researcher would conclude that classroom teaching and e-registers are intermediate between conversation and textbooks. More refined comparisons are possible, for example distinguishing among the particular register patterns for e-mails, text messages, and classroom teaching. The main point here, though, is that none of these perspectives is the single "correct" one; rather, all perspectives must be synthesized to fully capture the overall patterns of register variation.

Our primary goal in this chapter is to introduce comprehensive analyses of register variation: comparing many different registers with respect to their full range of linguistic characteristics. In relation to this goal, the small case study presented above is informative in three major ways.

1. The case study reinforces the importance of the comparative approach. That is, by comparing the patterns of use across registers, it is possible to document the truly distinctive linguistic characteristics of a target register.

2. The case study also shows how different sets of linguistic features reveal different relations among registers. No single parameter of linguistic variation is adequate by itself to capture the similarities and differences among registers. Rather, it is necessary to consider multiple "dimensions" of variation to adequately capture the patterns of register variation in a discourse domain.

3. Finally, the case study clearly illustrates the methodological difficulties in achieving a multidimensional description. That is, this study considered only

five registers and only ten different linguistic features. What if we expanded the comparison to an entire domain of use, like the full set of spoken and written registers used in universities? And what if we attempted to compare those registers with respect to a comprehensive set of linguistic features, including dozens of lexical and grammatical characteristics? Such an analysis is clearly beyond the scope of what a researcher could accomplish using the traditional methods introduced in the preceding chapters. Rather, we need additional analytical techniques that allow us to simultaneously compare the patterns of variation for numerous linguistic features across different registers. In the following sections, we introduce an analytical approach developed specifically for such analyses: multidimensional analysis.

8.2   Introduction to multidimensional analysis

Multidimensional (MD) analysis is a quantitative approach that allows the researcher to compare many different registers, with respect to several different linguistic parameters – the "dimensions." Two registers can be more or less different with respect to each dimension. By considering all linguistic dimensions, it is possible to describe both the ways and the extent to which registers differ from one another, and ultimately, the overall patterns of register variation in a language.

As shown in the last section, the relative distribution of common linguistic features, considered individually, cannot reliably distinguish among registers. There are simply too many different linguistic characteristics to consider. However, these features work together as distinct underlying dimensions. Each of these dimensions represents a group of features that co-occur: the features – as a group – are frequent in some registers and rare in other registers.

The importance of linguistic co-occurrence was recognized early on by linguists. For example, Brown and Fraser (1979: 38–39) observe that it can be "misleading to concentrate on specific, isolated [linguistic] markers without taking into account systematic variations which involve the co-occurrence of sets of markers." Ervin-Tripp (1972) and Hymes (1974) identify "speech styles" as varieties that are defined by a shared set of co-occurring linguistic features. Halliday (1988: 162) defines a register as "a cluster of associated features having a greater-than-random . . . tendency to co-occur."

The MD approach was developed to analyze the linguistic co-occurrence patterns associated with register variation in empirical/quantitative terms. The following section provides a brief conceptual overview of the approach. Then, in Section 8.3, we present a case study, showing how the patterns of variation among university registers can be analyzed from a multidimensional perspective.

8.2.1   Conceptual introduction to the multidimensional approach to register variation

MD analysis was developed as a methodological approach to (1) identify the underlying linguistic dimensions of variation in a language, in empirical/quantitative terms, and (2) compare spoken and written registers in the linguistic space defined by those dimensions.

The notion of linguistic co-occurrence is central to the MD approach, in that different co-occurrence patterns are analyzed as underlying *dimensions* of variation. The group of co-occurring linguistic features comprising each dimension is identified quantitatively. For example, the case study in the preceding section suggests that verbs and pronouns constitute a set of co-occurring linguistic features, while nouns, adjectives, and relative clauses constitute a second set of co-occurring linguistic features. In MD analysis, a statistical factor analysis is used to identify such groups of co-occurring features on a much larger scale, based on the distributions of numerous features in a large corpus of texts. (The methods used to identify these co-occurrence patterns are described in Section 8.3 below.)

It is not the case, though, that quantitative techniques are sufficient in themselves for MD analyses of register variation. Rather, like all register analyses, qualitative analysis is required to interpret the functional bases underlying each set of co-occurring linguistic features. The dimensions of variation have both linguistic and functional content. The linguistic content of a dimension comprises a group of linguistic features (e.g., nominalizations, prepositional phrases, attributive adjectives) that co-occur with a high frequency in texts. But the approach is also based on the assumption that linguistic features co-occur in texts because they reflect shared functions. A simple example is the way in which pronouns, direct questions, and imperatives co-occur because they are all related to interactiveness. Thus, the final step in an MD analysis is the same as the final step in register analyses generally (see Chapter 3): to explain the quantitative linguistic patterns in functional terms, by reference to situational differences among registers.

Multidimensional analysis uses the methodological tools of corpus linguistics, introduced in earlier chapters. By using computational techniques, it is possible to analyze the linguistic patterns found in a large corpus of texts. Such analyses include a comprehensive linguistic characterization of each text, based on a wide range of linguistic features.

The case study in the last section illustrates the concept of linguistic co-occurrence, and how registers can be more or less similar along different dimensions. But that case study also illustrated the difficulties in trying to identify the linguistic patterns of co-occurrence using traditional methods. In the MD approach, co-occurrence patterns are identified statistically: First, computer programs are used to analyze the distribution of linguistic features in a large corpus of texts, and then a statistical technique – *factor analysis* – is used to identify the sets of linguistic features that frequently co-occur in these texts. This is a bottom-up analysis. The researcher does not decide ahead of time which linguistic features co-occur, or which functions are going to be the most important ones. Rather, empirical corpus-based analysis is used to determine the actual patterns of linguistic co-occurrence and variation among registers, and subsequently the researcher interprets those patterns in functional terms.

8.2.2   Overview of methodology in the multidimensional approach

Multidimensional analysis follows six methodological steps:

1. An appropriate corpus is designed and collected based on previous research and analysis. The situational characteristics of each spoken and written register included in the study are documented.
2. Research is conducted to identify the set of linguistic features to be included in the analysis.
3. Computer programs are developed for automated grammatical analysis; the entire corpus of texts is analyzed to compute the frequency counts of each linguistic feature in each text.
4. The co-occurrence patterns among linguistic features are analyzed, using a factor analysis of the frequency counts.
5. Dimension scores for each text with respect to each dimension are computed; the mean dimension scores for each register are then compared to analyze the linguistic similarities and differences among registers.
6. The "factors" from the factor analysis are interpreted functionally as underlying dimensions of variation.

As noted above, the statistical technique used for identifying linguistic co-occurrence patterns is known as factor analysis, and each set of co-occurring features is referred to as a factor. In a factor analysis, a large number of original variables (in this case the linguistic features) are reduced to a small set of derived, underlying variables – the factors or "dimensions" of variation. Each factor represents a group of linguistic features that tend to co-occur in texts.

Once the dimensions have been identified, it is possible to compute a quantitative measure for each dimension in each text: the *dimension score*. These dimension scores then allow us to compare the similarities and differences among registers in a multidimensional space.

The MD approach is much easier to understand when illustrated through an actual case study. In the following section, we present the results from a large-scale MD analysis of spoken and written registers that occur in American universities, while at the same time explaining the analytical procedures in greater detail.

Table 8.1 *Composition of the T2K-SWAL Corpus*

Register	No. of texts	No. of words
Spoken:		
Class sessions	176	1,248,811
Classroom management	40	39,255
Labs/in-class groups	17	88,234
Office hours	11	50,412
Study groups	25	141,140
Service encounters	22	97,664
Total speech:	**251**	**1,665,516**
Written:		
Textbooks	87	760,619
Course packs	27	107,173
Course management	21	52,410
Other campus writing	37	151,450
Total writing:	**172**	**1,071,652**
TOTAL CORPUS:	**423**	**2,737,168**

8.3   MD analysis of university spoken and written registers

To illustrate the MD approach, we present here a multidimensional description of the spoken and written registers that students encounter during their university education. The TOEFL 2000 Spoken and Written Academic Language Corpus (T2K-SWAL Corpus) was used for this analysis (see Biber *et al.* 2002). The T2K-SWAL Corpus is relatively large (2.7 million words) and representative of the range of university registers that students must listen to or read. Table 8.1 shows the overall composition of the corpus by register category.

Once an appropriate corpus is identified, the next step in an MD analysis is to quantitatively analyze the distribution of all linguistic features that might be associated with register differences. This ends up being a much larger set of linguistic characteristics than what could be considered using traditional analytical techniques. For the present study, ninety linguistic features were included in the final analysis. These included:

1. vocabulary distributions (e.g., common vs. rare (technical) nouns);
2. part-of-speech classes (e.g., nouns, verbs, first and second person pronouns, prepositions);
3. semantic categories for the major word classes (e.g., activity verbs, mental verbs, existence verbs);
4. grammatical characteristics (e.g., nominalizations, past tense verbs, passive voice verbs);

5. syntactic structures (e.g., *that* relative clauses, *to* complement clauses);
6. lexico-grammatical combinations (e.g., *that*-complement clauses controlled by communication verbs vs. mental verbs).

A computer "tagging" program then identified and counted each of these features in each of the 423 texts of the T2K-SWAL Corpus.

The fourth major analytical step – the factor analysis – identifies the underlying factors (or dimensions) in the corpus. Each of these dimensions is a group of linguistic features that tend to co-occur in the texts of the corpus. Concretely, this means that the features as a group will all be common in some texts, and they will all be rare in other texts.

Four dimensions were identified in the study of university registers. Table 8.2 summarizes the important linguistic features that are grouped onto each dimension. (The MD analysis of university registers presented here is adapted from Biber 2006a, chapter 8).

One important point to keep in mind is that the researcher does not decide which features to group together; rather, the statistical analysis identifies the groupings that actually co-occur in texts. The approach here differs from previous chapters. In an MD analysis, the researcher does not attempt to decipher linguistic patterns through detailed inspection of individual texts: in fact, it is not feasible for an individual researcher to accurately identify co-occurrence patterns among dozens of linguistic features distributed across hundreds of texts. Rather, MD analysis is based on quantitative/computational analysis of linguistic features in all texts of the corpus, followed by statistical analysis to identify the most important linguistic co-occurrence patterns across all texts in the corpus.

All four of the dimensions summarized in Table 8.2 have both "positive" and "negative" features. These are actually two groupings of features: the positive features occur together frequently in texts, and the negative features occur together frequently in texts. The two groupings constitute a single dimension because they occur in complementary distribution: when the positive features occur with a high frequency in a text, that same text will have a low frequency of negative features, and vice versa. (Note that the positive and negative designations are mathematical, arising in the factor analysis; they are not evaluative.)

In the fifth major analytical step, the dimensions are used to analyze the linguistic characteristics of texts and registers by computing a "dimension score" for each text. Conceptually, a dimension score represents a simple sum of all linguistic features grouped on a dimension.[1] For example, the Dimension 1 score

---

[1] Feature counts are transformed in two ways to make them comparable. First, all feature counts are "normalized," converting them to their rate of occurrence per 1,000 words of text. This transformation makes the feature counts comparable across texts, even if some texts are longer than others.

Second, individual feature scores are standardized to a mean of 0.0 and a standard deviation of 1.0 (based on the overall mean and standard deviation of each feature in the corpus). This process translates the scores for all features to scales representing standard deviation units. Thus, regardless

Table 8.2 *Summary of the dimensions from the MD analysis of university registers*

	Positive features	Negative features
Dimension 1: Oral vs. literate discourse	**Contractions** **Pronouns:** demonstrative, *it*, 1st person, 2nd person, 3rd person, indefinite **Verbs:** present tense, past tense, progressive **Verbs:** mental, activity, communication **Adverbials:** time, place, certainty, likelihood, hedges, discourse particles **WH questions**, clause coordination, stranded prepositions **Adverbial clauses:** causative, conditional, other **Finite complement clauses:** WH clauses, *that*-clauses: controlled by certainty verbs, controlled by likelihood verbs, controlled by communication verbs, *that*-omission	**Nouns:** common nouns, nominalizations **Nouns:** abstract, group, human, mental **Word choice:** word length, type/token ratio **Prepositional phrases** **Adjectives:** attributive, relational **Passives:** agentless, *by*-phrase, postnominal modifiers **Relative clauses:** WH with prep fronting, WH with subject gaps *to*-**clauses:** controlled by stance nouns, controlled by adjectives phrasal coordination
Dimension 2: Procedural vs. content-focused discourse	**Modals:** necessity, future **Verbs:** causative, activity **Pronouns:** 2nd person **Common nouns:** group *to*-**clauses:** controlled by verbs of desire, controlled by "other" verbs **Adverbial clauses:** conditional	**Rare, technical words:** adjectives, nouns, adverbs, verbs **Verbs:** simple occurrence **Adjectives:** size *to*-**clauses:** controlled by probability verbs **Passives:** *by*-phrase
Dimension 3: Reconstructed account of events	**Pronouns:** 3rd person **Verbs:** past tense, communication, mental **Nouns:** human, mental *that*-**clauses:** controlled by communication verbs, controlled by likelihood verbs, controlled by stance nouns, *that*-omission	**Nouns:** concrete, technical+concrete, quantity
Dimension 4: Teacher-centered stance	*that* **relative clauses** **Stance adverbials:** certainty, likelihood, attitudinal **Adverbial clauses:** conditional, other *that*-**clauses:** controlled by stance nouns	WH questions stranded prepositions

Table 8.3 *Significance tests for the differences among*
registers with respect to Dimensions 1–4

	F score	p value	[df]	[r²]
Dimension 1	490.04	<.0001	(9,453)	90.7%
Dimension 2	53.78	<.0001	(9,453)	51.7%
Dimension 3	13.19	<.0001	(9,453)	20.8%
Dimension 4	41.47	<.0001	(9,453)	45.2%

is computed by adding together the frequencies of contractions, demonstrative pronouns, pronoun *it*, first person pronouns, present tense verbs, and so on – the features with positive loadings on Factor 1 (from Table 8.2) – and then subtracting the frequencies of nominalizations, word length, moderately common nouns, prepositions, and so on – the features with negative loadings. Once a dimension score is computed for each text, it is possible to compare the average dimension score for each register.

Inferential statistical techniques can be used to determine whether there are **significant** and **strong** differences among registers with respect to the dimension scores. Table 8.3 shows the results from an ANOVA, testing the significance of differences among the university registers with respect to the four dimensions.

The statistics given for F, p, and r^2 in Table 8.3 show that all four dimensions are significant and strong predictors of register differences. The F and p values give the results of an ANOVA, which tests whether there are statistically significant differences among the mean scores for the registers with respect to the dimension scores. A p-value smaller than .001 means that it is highly unlikely that the observed differences are due to chance (less than 1 chance in 1,000). The value for r^2 is a direct measure of strength or importance. The r^2 value measures the percentage of the variance among dimension scores that can be predicted by knowing the register categories.

In the present case, all four dimensions are statistically significant, and further, they are all strong or important predictors of register differences. For example, 90.7% of the variation in Dimension 1 scores can be accounted for by knowing the register category of each text. These statistics show that Dimension 1 is a significant as well as an extremely powerful predictor of register differences. Dimensions 2 and 4 are also both strong predictors of register differences (51.7% and 45.2% respectively). Dimension 3 is a less strong predictor (20.8%), although generally any predictor over 20% is considered noteworthy in social science research.

of whether a feature is extremely rare or extremely common in absolute terms, a standard score of +1 represents one standard deviation unit above the mean score for the feature in question. That is, standardized scores measure whether a feature is common or rare in a text relative to the overall average occurrence of that feature. The normalized frequencies are transformed to standard scores so that all features on a factor will have equivalent weights in the computation of dimension scores. The methodological steps followed to normalize and standardize frequency counts, and to compute dimension scores are described more fully in Biber 1988: 75–76, 93–97.

The final major step in an MD analysis is to interpret each dimension in functional terms. In the preceding chapters, we have shown how linguistic differences among registers are functional: A register makes frequent use of a linguistic feature because that feature is well suited to the communicative purposes and situational context of the register. Similarly, linguistic co-occurrence patterns are functional: linguistic features occur together in texts because they serve related communicative functions. The interpretation of a dimension is based on (1) analysis of the communicative function(s) most widely shared by the set of co-occurring features, and (2) analysis of the similarities and differences among registers with respect to the dimension. Table 8.2 (above) includes functional labels for each of the four dimensions in the present study, repeated here:

Dimension 1: Oral vs. literate discourse
Dimension 2: Procedural vs. content-focused discourse
Dimension 3: Reconstructed account of events
Dimension 4: Teacher-centered stance

In the following sections, we describe the patterns of register variation resulting from this particular MD analysis, including a discussion of the co-occurring linguistic features grouped on each dimension, the distribution of university registers along each dimension, and a detailed consideration of how these features function in particular texts.

8.3.1   Dimension 1: Oral vs. literate discourse

Dimension 1 is associated with a fundamental oral/literate opposition. (In Chapter 9, we discuss how a similar dimension has been found in nearly all MD analyses.) The positive features on Dimension 1 (see Table 8.2) are associated with several specific functions, but they all relate generally to "oral" discourse. These include: interactiveness and personal involvement (e.g., first and second person pronouns, WH questions), personal stance (e.g., mental verbs, *that*-clauses with likelihood verbs and factual verbs, factual adverbials, hedges), and structural reduction and formulaic language (e.g., contractions, *that*-omission, common vocabulary, lexical bundles). In contrast, the negative features are associated mostly with informational density and complex noun phrase structures (frequent nouns and nominalizations, prepositional phrases, adjectives, and relative clauses) together with passive constructions.

Figure 8.4 shows that all spoken registers in the university corpus have large positive scores on this dimension, reflecting a frequent use of the positive "oral" features. In contrast, all written registers have large negative scores on this dimension, reflecting a frequent use of the negative "literate" features. This distribution is surprising given that there are major differences in purpose and planning among the registers within each mode. For example, we noted previously how a researcher might expect that classroom teaching – an informational spoken register – would exploit the same styles of informational presentation as textbooks. However, with respect to Dimension 1 features, this is clearly not the case. Instead,

Oral discourse

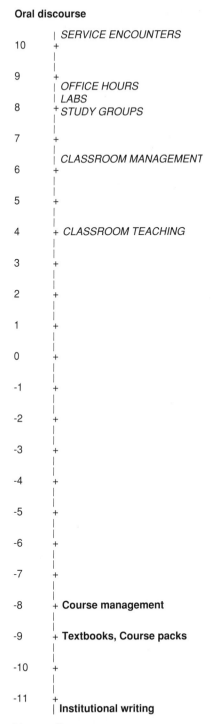

```
                | SERVICE ENCOUNTERS
    10          +
                |
                |
     9          +
                | OFFICE HOURS
                | LABS
     8          + STUDY GROUPS
                |
                |
     7          +
                |
                | CLASSROOM MANAGEMENT
     6          +
                |
                |
     5          +
                |
                |
     4          + CLASSROOM TEACHING
                |
                |
     3          +
                |
                |
     2          +
                |
                |
     1          +
                |
                |
     0          +
                |
                |
    -1          +
                |
                |
    -2          +
                |
                |
    -3          +
                |
                |
    -4          +
                |
                |
    -5          +
                |
                |
    -6          +
                |
                |
    -7          +
                |
    -8          + Course management
                |
                |
    -9          + Textbooks, Course packs
                |
                |
   -10          +
                |
                |
   -11          +
                | Institutional writing
```

Literate discourse

Figure 8.4 *Mean scores of university registers along Dimension 1 – "Oral vs. literate discourse"*

there is a fundamental opposition between the spoken and written modes here, regardless of purpose, interactiveness, or other pre-planning considerations.

Service encounters, office hours, and study groups – the registers with the largest positive Dimension 1 scores – are all directly interactive and "conversational." Many of the linguistic features associated with Dimension 1 have already been illustrated for office hours and service encounters in Chapter 4. Text Sample 8.4 further illustrates the use of positive Dimension 1 features in a service encounter. Notice the dense use of first and second person pronouns (*I, we, you*), contractions (e.g., *we're, don't, I'm, there's*), present tense verbs (e.g., *are, have, get*), time and place adverbials (e.g., *back, there, here, again*), indefinite pronouns (*something*), mental verbs (*think, want*), and causative clauses:

Text Sample 8.4 Service encounter: at the bookstore

Customer: Can I ask you something?
Clerk: Yeah.
Customer: We're at the previews and of course my book is back there with my husband. Do you have coupons?
Clerk: No we don't have any of them here. You guys only get them. Yeah.
Customer: OK.
Clerk: Did you want to come back? Cos I can hold onto your stuff.
Customer: Could you hold all this stuff? Cos I know if I'm getting a big sweatshirt there's one for a sweatshirt and one for a T-shirt.
Clerk: Yeah. I'll just hold onto them.
Customer: OK.
Clerk: I'll go ahead and just put them in a bag.

                                                          [T2K-SWAL Corpus]

At the other extreme, institutional writing (e.g., university catalogs) has the largest negative score on Dimension 1, making it even more "literate" than textbooks or course packs. The following program description for anthropology begins with a friendly, inviting sentence having an extremely simple syntactic clause structure. However, this short sentence is immediately followed by complex sentences with multiple levels of clausal and phrasal embedding. Note especially the dense use of noun phrase structures, often with adjectives and prepositional phrases as modifiers.

Text Sample 8.5 Institutional writing (web catalog academic program descriptions: anthropology)

Program description

Anthropology is the study of people. Its perspective is biological, social and comparative, encompassing all aspects of human existence, from the most ancient societies to those of the present day. Anthropology seeks to order and explain similarities and

> differences between peoples of the world from the combined vantage points of culture and biology.
>
> Cultural and Social Anthropology deal with the many aspects of the social lives of people around the world, including our own society: their economic systems, legal practices, kinship, religions, medical practices, folklore, arts and political systems, as well as the interrelationship of these systems in environmental adaptation and social change. Physical Anthropology describes and compares world human biology. Its focus is on humans and the primate order to which they belong as part of nature, and it seeks to document and understand the interplay of culture and biology in the course of human evolution and adaptation.
>
> [T2K-SWAL Corpus]

Many of the negative features on Dimension 1 reflect the dense use of nouns and noun modifiers in written informational texts. These features often occur together to build very complex noun phrase structures. For example, the second paragraph in Text Sample 8.5 begins with a very long sentence, which has only one main verb: *deal with*. Most of this sentence comprises a single noun phrase, functioning as the direct object of *deal with*. The sentence is marked up below to illustrate this extremely complex syntactic structure with multiple levels of embedding; head nouns of noun phrases are underlined; the main verb is in **bold**; and brackets are used to delimit postnominal modifiers.

> Cultural and Social Anthropology **deal with** the many aspects [of the social lives [of people [around the world]]], [including our own society: [their economic systems, legal practices, kinship, religions, medical practices, folklore, arts and political systems], as well as [the interrelationship [of these systems [in environmental adaptation and social change]]]].

Textbooks are similar to institutional writing in their reliance on these "literate" Dimension 1 features, although they are usually not as densely informational as the above excerpt from a course catalog (see the detailed discussion in Chapter 5).

You might expect that classroom teaching would have an intermediate score on Dimension 1, half way between the written informational registers (like textbooks) and spoken registers like office hours or study groups. As noted in Section 8.1 above, classroom teaching is similar to conversation in that it is spoken and interactive to some extent, but at the same time it is similar to textbook writing in its primary communicative purpose: to convey information. But it turns out that classroom teaching is not at all "literate" in its Dimension 1 score. Rather, it is much more similar to other spoken registers, including study groups and service encounters, than it is to written academic registers like textbooks. This score reflects an extremely dense use of pronouns, verbs and adverbs, questions, finite adverbial clauses, and *that* complement clauses. For example:

Text Sample 8.6 Classroom teaching (humanities; rhetoric; graduate)

Instructor: I think some of us feel sort of really caught in a bind between agency and acculturation. Sort of um, because you know I think a lot of us do want to use writing, use literacy to um, say what we want to say and to help other people say what they want to say but at the same time I think um, we're caught because we, I think we're questioning well, well you know, if, if we, if we teach X-genre are we promoting it? If we don't at the same time question it and dismantle it and kind of take it apart and look at it, and are there, are there other ways?

[T2K-SWAL Corpus]

Findings like this show how empirical register analyses can run directly counter to our prior expectations, requiring a rethinking of our initial situational analysis. In this case, the pattern along Dimension 1 shows that the real-time production circumstances of classroom teaching are apparently a much more important situational factor than the informational communicative purpose, resulting in a highly "oral" linguistic characterization.

8.3.2   Dimension 2: Procedural vs. content-focused discourse

In contrast to the spoken-written dichotomy identified by Dimension 1, Dimension 2 cuts directly across the spoken/written continuum. Figure 8.5 shows that the registers with large positive scores on this dimension all have communicative purposes related to the rules and procedures expected in university settings. These include both spoken registers (classroom management, service encounters, and office hours) and written registers (course management and institutional writing). In contrast, only written academic registers with an almost exclusive focus on informational content – course packs and textbooks – have the linguistic characteristics associated with the negative extreme of this dimension. Classroom teaching and study groups have intermediate scores on this dimension.

Table 8.2 above shows that the linguistic features associated with this dimension include necessity and prediction modal verbs (*must, should, have to, will, would, going to*), second person pronouns, causative verbs, *to*-clauses with verbs of desire (e.g., *want to, would like to*), and *if*-adverbial clauses. Considering these co-occurring linguistic features, together with the distribution of registers, the interpretive label "procedural vs. content-focused discourse" can be proposed for this dimension.

"Procedural" features are most common in spoken classroom management:

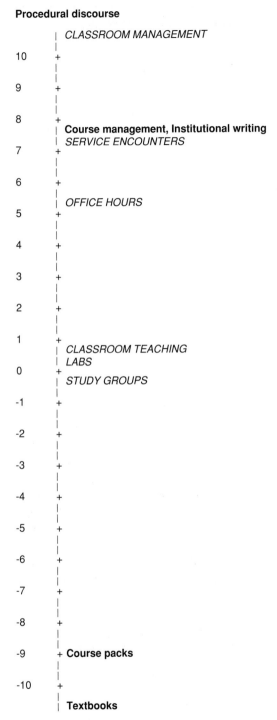

Figure 8.5 *Mean scores of registers along Dimension 2 – "Procedural vs. content-focused discourse"*

Text Sample 8.7 Classroom management (humanities; history; upper division)

[Positive Dimension 2 features are in **bold**]

um, let's see, **if** a student misses more than one week of classes **you** should talk to me immediately, **if** you know **you**'re **gonna** be gone. Let's say for example **you**'re **gonna** go to Montana for a couple of days this week or something like that **you** might **let** the instructor know **you**'re **gonna** be gone. Uh, **if you**'re, I had a woman who was pregnant one semester and she, said well I'm **gonna** be missing part of the class and I said yeah, I think you probably **will** be. OK, but **let** me know. Um, **you should let** me know **if you** miss more, **if you** miss a test, **you'd have to** bring me some type of written evidence as to why **you** were gone, just so that it's fair for everybody so that they don't **have to** deal with a whole lot of excuses.

[T2K-SWAL Corpus]

These same features are common in written course-management materials. Thus, compare the above spoken excerpt to the following examples from written course syllabi:

> At the end of each chapter, **you will** be assigned a series of problems to **help you** write a Chapter Summary. The purpose of the Chapter Summary problems is to **help you** pull together the main ideas of each chapter . . .
> **If you** miss class for two consecutive weeks, **you will** be dropped.
> **You will need to** access available resources to find answers to **your** questions and be willing to ask when **you** can't find them. **You will** find that many issues have answers which are complex or ambiguous.

The opposite end of Dimension 2 represents the dense use of technical vocabulary, including "rare" adjectives, nouns, adverbs, and verbs. These are words restricted to a particular discipline, like *adiabatic, arbuscules,* or *autodeliquescence.* Other negative Dimension 2 features include simple occurrence verbs (e.g., *become, happen, change, decrease, occur*), probability verb + *to*-clause constructions (e.g., *seem/appear to* . . .), and size adjectives (e.g., *high, large*). The dense use of these co-occurring features is restricted to the written academic registers; for example:

Text Sample 8.8 Textbook (natural science; chemistry; graduate)

Up to now we have been concerned with the magnetic resonance of a single nucleus and with explaining the physical basis of an nmr experiment. We will now turn our attention to the nuclear magnetic resonance spectra of organic molecules and in so doing will encounter two new phenomena: the chemical shift of the resonance frequency and the spin-spin coupling. These two phenomena form the foundation for the application of nuclear magnetic resonance spectroscopy in chemistry and related disciplines.

> The hypothetical spectrum of dimethyltrifluoroacetamide presented at the end of Chapter 1 may have suggested that nmr spectroscopy is employed for the detection of magnetically different nuclei in a compound.
>
> [T2K-SWAL Corpus]

8.3.3   Dimension 3: Reconstructed account of events

Dimension 3 is associated with a narrative orientation, reflected by features like third person pronouns, past tense, human nouns, and communication verb + *that*-clauses (see Table 8.2). However, these features also co-occur with several features that express epistemic stance, including:

- likelihood verb + *that*-clause (usually verbs expressing uncertainty, such as *assume, believe, doubt, gather, guess, imagine, seem, suppose, think*);
- epistemic stance noun + *that*-clause (e.g., *conclusion, fact, assumption, claim, feeling, idea, impression, opinion, possibility, suggestion, suspicion*).

That-omission co-occurs with these stance features, suggesting that they are usually used in colloquial rather than formal registers.

Figure 8.6 shows that the distribution of registers along Dimension 3 is strongly associated with the distinction between speech and writing (similar to Dimension 1): spoken university registers are consistently more "narrative" and "stanced" than written registers. But there are other patterns here as well: the management registers are the least "narrative" within each mode, while study groups and office hours are especially marked for the use of positive Dimension 3 features.

In study groups, students often negotiate with one another, trying to reconstruct course content. For example, Text Sample 8.9 illustrates narrative features being used to report past events and situations, while epistemic stance features are used by students to indicate varying degrees of (un)certainty about their knowledge:

Text Sample 8.9 Study group

[positive Dimension 3 features are marked in **bold**]

1: Uh in fact as far as, the three major religions, Muslim, Christian and Jew? The Islam are the most –

2: Tolerant.

1: Tolerant of all the three. So there **was** probably quite a few, in uh, in all the middle eastern countries for that matter. Because –

2: All for, the whole two thousand years?

1: Yeah because um, **they weren't they weren't** as discriminated against as **they were** in Europe and other countries so **they** –

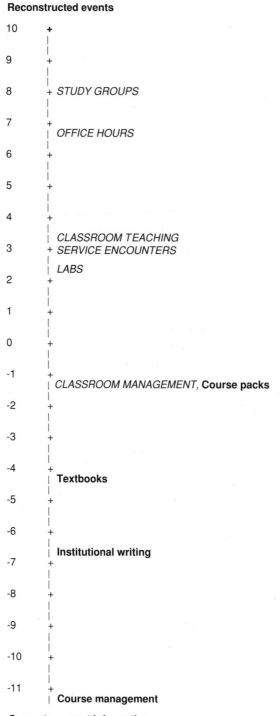

Figure 8.6 *Mean scores of registers along Dimension 3 – "Reconstructed account of events"*

2: OK.

1: All **they**, **everybody** had to pay tithes. See that's the other myth about Islam is **they** say, well it's the theocracy and **they** make you pay ten percent of your money.

2: Oh I **remember** – **they, they created** a um, what **did** – what **were they** called those uh, villages those districts with Jews and Christians? In the time of Mohammed? All the way through I can't **remember** what **they**'re called.

1: Mhm. But the point is **they**, **they** um, **did**n't tax. So, in this country if you come and you make money, you pay twenty percent tax.

2: Something like that.

1: In the middle east, in Islam countries you go and you make money and you pay a ten percent tithe, and that's wrong. But it's OK to pay a twenty percent tax. See what I **mean**?

2: Oh yeah I **remember** that.

1: It's like um.

2: I **forgot** about that . . . well I **was thinking** also um, that there might have been more Jews uh, during British occupation because they might have immigrated from uh, Great Britain?

1: Mhm I **suppose** it – you **know**, I don't **know**

[T2K-SWAL Corpus]

8.3.4   Dimension 4: Teacher-centered stance

Finally, the linguistic features on Dimension 4 are mostly associated with the expression of stance. These features include stance adverbials (certainty, likelihood, and attitudinal) and *that*-clauses controlled by stance nouns (e.g., *the fact that* . . .). Figure 8.7 shows that these features are used primarily in the instructor-controlled spoken registers: classroom management, classroom teaching, and office hours. In contrast, all written university registers are characterized by the relative absence of these features, as are the student-centered spoken registers (labs, study groups, and service encounters). Following are several examples of these academic stance features in classroom management:

Instructor: **actually** while I finish the outline, let me pass out the uh something I'd like you to uh look over here real quick and sign for me – that you acknowledge **the fact that** you've read and understand the syllabus.

Instructor: January eighteenth **of course** we don't have class. What day is that?

Student: [unclear]

Instructor: it's also my birthday, I always think that we're taking off on my birthday. uh, but if you link on the jazz home page, you can, there are, there's **actually** jazz music from the twenties

Instructor: all right for the remaining writings, when you take test one – **probably** the second week after spring break . . . you're going to have I think fifteen items . . . they won't be the exact wording of these but, **certainly** very comparable wording.

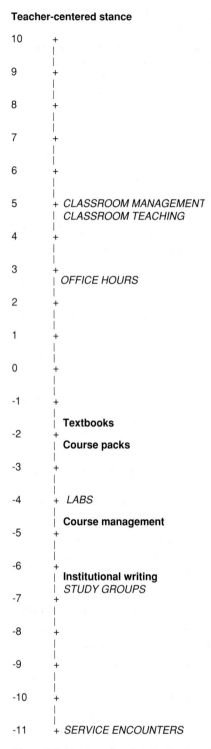

Teacher-centered stance

```
10      +
        |
        |
 9      +
        |
        |
 8      +
        |
        |
 7      +
        |
        |
 6      +
        |
        |
 5      + CLASSROOM MANAGEMENT
        | CLASSROOM TEACHING
        |
 4      +
        |
        |
 3      +
        | OFFICE HOURS
        |
 2      +
        |
        |
 1      +
        |
        |
 0      +
        |
        |
-1      +
        |
        | Textbooks
-2      +
        | Course packs
        |
-3      +
        |
        |
-4      + LABS
        |
        | Course management
-5      +
        |
        |
-6      +
        | Institutional writing
        | STUDY GROUPS
-7      +
        |
        |
-8      +
        |
        |
-9      +
        |
        |
-10     +
        |
        |
-11     + SERVICE ENCOUNTERS
```

Figure 8.7 *Mean scores of registers along Dimension 4 – "Teacher-centered stance"*

Instructor: Let's tabulate those tomorrow, too. Let's do this. Quite **possibly** none of these will be **entirely** satisfactory.

Instructor: quickly now – the department came down and I know, Mark's been working on those so, **hopefully**, first of next week, at the latest we ought to have it up and working. **kind of**, continuing the tradition that has gone on in the past, several semesters or at least the past semester.

8.3.5   Differences among academic disciplines

As described above, factor analysis is used in the MD approach to identify groups of co-occurring features, based on the distribution of linguistic features in texts. Register distinctions have no influence on the statistical identification of the factors. Rather, the factor analysis identifies the groupings of features that tend to co-occur in texts, regardless of the register of those texts. However, as shown in the last section, these dimensions are usually powerful predictors of register differences. This is because both linguistic co-occurrence patterns (the basis of factor analysis) and register differences have a functional basis.

The fact that dimensions are identified independently of register categories means that they can be used to explore the patterns of variation among any subregister categories that are represented in the target corpus. The present section illustrates this application by exploring differences among academic disciplines within classroom teaching and textbooks.

In the present analysis, there are interesting differences among academic disciplines with respect to Dimension 2 ("Procedural vs. content-focused discourse"), and Dimension 3 ("Reconstructed account of events"). Figure 8.8, which plots the academic disciplines along Dimension 2, identifies a surprising pattern. In most respects, engineering and natural-science texts are highly similar in their typical linguistic characteristics. However, along Dimension 2, these two technical disciplines are sharply distinguished: engineering is the most "procedural" discipline, within both teaching and textbooks, while natural science is by far the most "content-focused," again within both classroom teaching and textbooks. This distinction reflects the applied focus of engineering, in contrast to the more theoretical and descriptive focus of natural science.

In contrast to the pattern along Dimension 2, engineering and natural science are similar to each other in favoring non-narrative styles along Dimension 3 ("Reconstructed account of events"). Figure 8.9 shows that this preferred style is found in both classroom teaching and textbooks. In contrast, education, humanities, and social science are all much more likely to incorporate narrative "reconstructed accounts of past events." These features are most prominent in classroom teaching, but textbooks from these disciplines are also marked for the relatively frequent use of these narrative features. Text Sample 8.10 illustrates these characteristics from history classroom teaching, as the instructor tries to reconstruct historical settings and events in response to a student question:

Procedural discourse

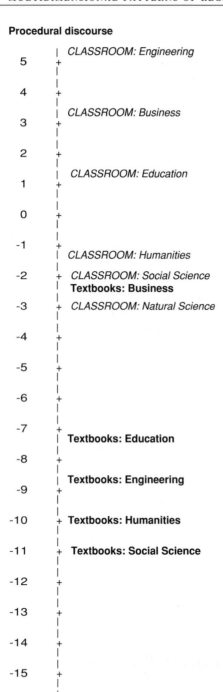

Content-focused discourse

Figure 8.8 *Mean scores of disciplines along Dimension 2 – "Procedural vs. content-focused discourse"*

Narrative orientation

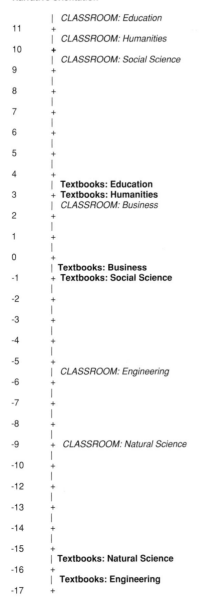

| CLASSROOM: Education
11   +
        | CLASSROOM: Humanities
10   **+**
        | CLASSROOM: Social Science
9   +
        |
8   +
        |
7   +
        |
6   +
        |
5   +
        |
4   +
        | **Textbooks: Education**
3   + **Textbooks: Humanities**
        | CLASSROOM: Business
2   +
        |
1   +
        |
0   +
        | **Textbooks: Business**
-1   + **Textbooks: Social Science**
        |
-2   +
        |
-3   +
        |
-4   +
        |
-5   +
        | CLASSROOM: Engineering
-6   +
        |
-7   +
        |
-8   +
        |
-9   + CLASSROOM: Natural Science
        |
-10   +
        |
-12   +
        |
-13   +
        |
-14   +
        |
-15   +
        | **Textbooks: Natural Science**
-16   +
        | **Textbooks: Engineering**
-17   +

Non-narrative orientation

Figure 8.9 *Mean scores of disciplines along Dimension 3 – "Reconstructed account of events"*

> **Text Sample 8.10 Classroom teaching (history; upper division)**
>
> [past tense verbs and third person pronouns are in **bold**; other positive Dimension 3 features are in ***bold italics***]
>
> Student: But why would, I ***mean***, why would, uh, China want to throw out Soviet technocrats . . .
>
> Instructor: And I ***think*** that's, you ***know***, that's like the key issue there in, is absolute [2 sylls] relationship as it develops that, that it's not one [2 sylls] process . . . Of course one can face Mao's dissatisfaction to some extent, the very very early roots of Mao's dissatisfaction with, uh, ideological dissatisfaction, I'm not ***talking*** just about personal dis-dissatisfaction, but from **his** ideological point of view from the way **he interpreted** history is toward the development, social development and the revolution particularly. From that view point, **his** earliest dissatisfactions with the, uh, leadership of the Soviet Union, with Stalin's leadership of the Soviet Union, will go all the way back to the nineteen thirties. I ***mean* he, believed**, even then, that there **was** not a clear understanding of China's situation, China's revolutionary situation, on the part of Stalin and the Soviet nation. Whereas Mao **was**, even back in the nineteen thirties **he was** already formulating that strategy.
>
> [T2K-SWAL Corpus]

Textbooks from disciplines with a focus on the past (e.g., history) also rely heavily on narrative discourse, including long prose sections written entirely in the past. Many lower-division history textbooks are written primarily in the past tense, since they primarily narrate past events and circumstances. These books sometimes also document the beliefs, expectations, and other attitudes of historical characters (using verb+*that*-clause constructions), but the majority of the text is simple narration; for example:

> **Text Sample 8.11 Textbook; humanities (history, lower division)**
>
> [past tense verbs and third person pronouns are in **bold**; other positive Dimension 3 features are in ***bold italics***]
>
> Much of the early history of the United States **was** written by New Englanders, who **were** not disposed to emphasize the larger exodus of Puritans to the southerly islands. When the mainland colonists **declared** independence in 1776, **they hoped** *that* these island outposts would join **them**, but the existence of the British navy **had** a chilling effect.
>
>   These common convictions deeply **shaped** the infant colony's life. Soon after arrival the franchise **was** extended to all "freemen". . .
>
> [T2K-SWAL Corpus]

As mentioned above, engineering and natural-science texts – from both classroom teaching and textbooks – have large negative scores on Dimension 3. These scores result from the absence of positive Dimension 3 features, coupled with frequent use of the negative features: especially quantity nouns (e.g., *length*, *amount*) and concrete nouns (including nouns referring to a specific entity but having a technical meaning, like *electron*). These negative dimension scores reflect an interesting combination of communicative purposes in these disciplines: highly technical discourse that discusses complex mathematical relationships among everyday concrete entities.

Text Sample 8.12 Textbooks; engineering (mechanical engineering; graduate)

[concrete nouns and quantity/mathematical nouns are in **bold**]

Although many ride problems are peculiar to a specific **road**, or **road** type, the notion of "**average**" **road** properties can often be helpful in understanding the response of a **vehicle** to **road** roughness. The general similarity in the spectral **content** of the **roads** seen in Figure 5.2 (that **elevation amplitude** diminishes systematically with increasing **wavenumber**) has long been recognized as true of most **roads**. Consequently, **road inputs** to a **vehicle** are often modeled with an **amplitude** that diminishes with **frequency** to the second or fourth **power** approximating the two linear segments of the **curve** shown in the figure. The **average properties** shown in the figure are derived from recent studies of a large **number** of **roads**.

[T2K-SWAL Corpus]

8.4   Summary and conclusion

The present chapter has illustrated how MD analysis can be used to capture the complex patterns of register variation in a discourse domain, including the co-occurrence patterns among a large set of linguistic features, and the relations among a large number of diverse registers and subregisters. We have illustrated this approach through a description of spoken and written registers in American universities.

By grouping together the linguistic features that work together in texts – the dimensions – it is possible to capture the most important similarities and differences among registers. Through this approach, it is possible to discover patterns of register variation that would go unnoticed otherwise.

Probably the most surprising finding of this MD analysis is the fundamental importance of the spoken versus written mode. The study was designed to include a wide range of the registers found in American universities, sampled to represent many different situational characteristics: different purposes and communicative goals, different settings, degrees of interactivity, and so on. However, it turns out that the distinction between speech and writing is by far the most important factor in determining the overall patterns of linguistic variation across university registers. Thus, one of the most striking patterns from the MD analysis is the extent to which linguistic characteristics are shared across all spoken university registers versus all written university registers, regardless of differences in audience, interactivity, or communicative purpose. It turns out that this fundamental distinction between spoken and written registers has been observed in many other studies as well, and so we return to this issue in Chapter 9.

However, there are additional unanticipated patterns that emerged from the MD analysis. For example, it would have been hard to predict the relations among spoken versus written student management registers: polar opposites in the use of Dimension 1 features, but essentially the same in their heavy reliance on the "procedural" features grouped on Dimension 2. It would also have been hard to predict the similarities and differences between teacher-centered spoken registers (e.g., classroom teaching and office hours) and student-centered spoken registers (e.g., study groups): essentially the same in their heavy reliance on "oral" Dimension 1 features, but polar opposites along Dimension 4, with the teacher-centered registers (whether interactive or not) being heavily "stanced," while these features are rare in the student-centered registers.

There have been numerous other MD analyses of register variation. The first MD analysis investigated the variation among general spoken and written registers in English (e.g., conversation, radio broadcasts, newspaper reportage, editorials, fiction); the chapter activities introduce you to that study. Later MD analyses have described the patterns of register variation in other languages, including Somali, Korean, and Spanish. There have also been more specialized MD analyses, for example, investigating job interviews, elementary-school registers, and historical patterns of change. In all these cases, the MD analysis identifies several parameters of linguistic variation that correspond to important functional/situational differences among the registers in that domain. As such, this has proven to be one of the most productive analytical approaches used to describe the overall patterns of register variation in a discourse domain.

Chapter 8 activities

Reflection and review

1. Explain in your own words why, in order to fully understand language use, it is necessary to conduct research that covers multiple registers and multiple linguistic features in the same study.

2. An MD study can focus on a general variety – such as a wide range of registers in American universities – or a more specialized domain, such as job interviews in a specific company. Choose a domain that interests you and design an MD study. What registers would you include, and why? (Or if you design a style study, how would you make sure to capture stylistic variation?) How would you get the texts? What applications might there be for the findings?

Analysis practice

3. Activity Text 17 is from the register of "course management" (specifically from a syllabus for an undergraduate business course). Analyze the extent to which this text

Table 8.4 *Summary of Dimensions 1 and 2 from the 1988 MD analysis of general English registers*

	Positive features	Negative features
Dimension 1: Involved vs. informational production	Mental verbs Present tense verbs Contractions Possibility modals 1st person pronouns 2nd person pronouns *it* Demonstrative pronouns Emphatics Hedges Discourse particles Causative subordination WH clauses *that*-clauses with the *that* omitted WH questions	Nouns Long words High type/token ratio Prepositional phrases Attributive adjectives Passive verbs
Dimension 2: Narrative vs. non-narrative discourse	Past tense verbs Perfect aspect verbs Communication verbs 3rd person pronouns	Present tense verbs Attributive adjectives

illustrates the general patterns of use for "course management" for Dimension 2 ("Procedural vs. content-focused discourse"). Refer to Table 8.2 for the features of Dimension 2 and Figure 8.5 for the mean score for course management on this dimension. (It will not be possible for you to produce quantitative findings to plot along the dimension, but you can discuss the extent to which the positive and negative linguistic features are used in the activity text.)

4. The original MD analysis of English (Biber 1988) investigated the patterns of variation among twenty-three general spoken and written registers (e.g., conversation, radio broadcasts, newspaper reportage, editorials, fiction, personal letters). Table 8.4 below lists the most important co-occurring linguistic features that are grouped on the first two dimensions from that analysis.

Following the same procedure illustrated in this chapter, these linguistic groupings were used to compute dimension scores and compare the typical characteristics of spoken and written registers. Figures 8.10 and 8.11 show the mean scores for these registers along Dimensions 1 and 2 from the 1988 study.

Propose functional interpretations for these two dimensions, based on the co-occurring linguistic features and the distribution of registers shown in Figures 8.10 and 8.11. Refer to the text samples in the appendix (or other sources that you have) to illustrate how the features are used. (Remember, any single text sample

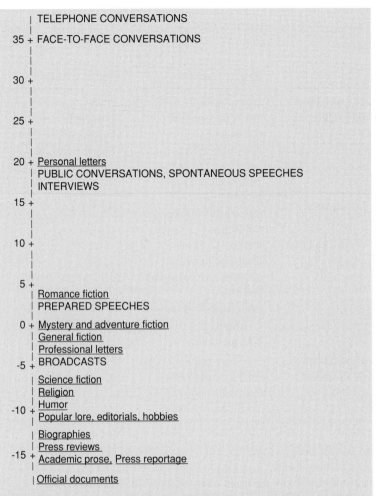

```
       | TELEPHONE CONVERSATIONS
       |
   35 + FACE-TO-FACE CONVERSATIONS
       |
       |
       |
       |
   30 +
       |
       |
       |
   25 +
       |
       |
       |
   20 + Personal letters
       | PUBLIC CONVERSATIONS, SPONTANEOUS SPEECHES
       | INTERVIEWS
       |
   15 +
       |
       |
       |
   10 +
       |
       |
       |
    5 +
       | Romance fiction
       | PREPARED SPEECHES
       |
    0 + Mystery and adventure fiction
       | General fiction
       | Professional letters
       | BROADCASTS
   -5 +
       | Science fiction
       | Religion
       | Humor
  -10 + Popular lore, editorials, hobbies
       |
       | Biographies
       | Press reviews
  -15 + Academic prose, Press reportage
       |
       | Official documents
```

Figure 8.10 *Mean scores of registers along 1988 Dimension 1*
[Written registers are underlined; SPOKEN REGISTERS ARE
CAPITALIZED]

may not be completely representative of the register. The MD analysis is based on the
typical patterns observed in a corpus of numerous texts.)

5. The 1988 MD analysis of general English registers has also been used as a
framework to study historical register change in English. For example, Figure 8.12
plots the historical patterns of change with respect to Dimension 1: "Involved versus
informational production" (see Table 8.4 above).

  Describe the historical patterns of register variation shown in Figure 8.12. How
different were "oral" and "literate" English registers in the seventeenth and
eighteenth centuries? How have these registers evolved to become more sharply
distinguished over the centuries? Review the linguistic features that comprise
Dimension 1. Specifically, describe the linguistic changes that are associated with the
increasingly large "negative" Dimension 1 scores for medical prose and science

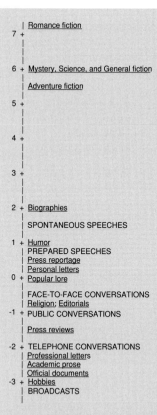

```
 7 +   | Romance fiction
       |
       |
       |
 6 +   | Mystery, Science, and General fiction
       |
       |   Adventure fiction
       |
 5 +   |
       |
       |
 4 +   |
       |
       |
 3 +   |
       |
       |
 2 +   | Biographies
       |
       |   SPONTANEOUS SPEECHES
       |
 1 +   | Humor
       |   PREPARED SPEECHES
       |   Press reportage
       |   Personal letters
 0 +   | Popular lore
       |
       |   FACE-TO-FACE CONVERSATIONS
       |   Religion; Editorials
-1 +   | PUBLIC CONVERSATIONS
       |
       |   Press reviews
       |
-2 +   | TELEPHONE CONVERSATIONS
       |   Professional letters
       |   Academic prose
       |   Official documents
-3 +   | Hobbies
       |   BROADCASTS
       |
```

Figure 8.11 *Mean scores for registers along 1988 Dimension 2 [Written registers are underlined; SPOKEN REGISTERS ARE CAPITALIZED]*

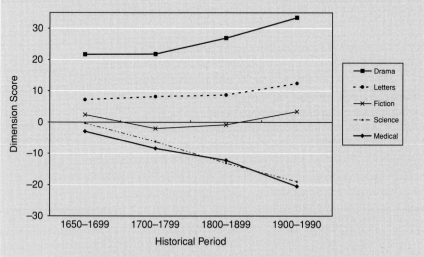

Figure 8.12 *Historical change along Dimension 1: "Involved vs. informational"*

Table 8.5 *Summary of Dimensions 1 and 2 from the MD analysis of fictional novels*

	Positive features	Negative features
Dimension 1	1st person pronouns,	Nouns
	2nd person pronouns	Prepositional phrases
	Mental verbs	Attributive adjectives
	Communication verbs	Long words
	Present tense verbs	High type/token ratio
	Modals (possibility, necessity, prediction)	
	that-clauses controlled by verbs (often with the *that* omitted)	
Dimension 2	3rd person pronouns	Present tense verbs,
	Past tense verbs	2nd person pronouns
	Perfect aspect verbs	Contractions

prose. Finally, illustrate these changes by reference to specific linguistic features, using examples from the activity texts in the appendix or text samples in Chapter 6.

Project ideas

6. Expand the analysis for activity 3 to a fuller description of course syllabi. First, describe the use of linguistic features from all four dimensions in the syllabus text sample (Activity Text 17). Then, collect syllabi of other types (e.g., from different academic disciplines or different academic levels) and explore the extent to which there is variation among those texts with respect to these linguistic dimensions.

7. An MD study of fictional styles was carried out, based on analysis of a corpus containing 185 novels. Because there are so many different kinds of fiction, the corpus was designed to include a wide spectrum of novels, such as prize-winners and obscure novels, older and contemporary novels, adult and adolescent literature, and so on. However, the primary goal of the study was to explore the style of individual novels, rather than to compare novels of different types.

Table 8.5 lists the most important co-occurring linguistic features that are grouped on two of the dimensions from this study. Figures 8.13 and 8.14 show the mean scores for selected individual novels along the dimensions, while activity texts 18–21 illustrate some of the different fictional styles.

Propose functional/stylistic interpretations for these two dimensions. Base your interpretations on the groupings of co-occurring linguistic features, the distribution of novels shown in Figures 8.13 and 8.14, and detailed analyses of these linguistic features in Activity Texts 18–21. (You can select other passages from any of the novels plotted in Figures 8.13 and 8.14 to determine whether they conform to the

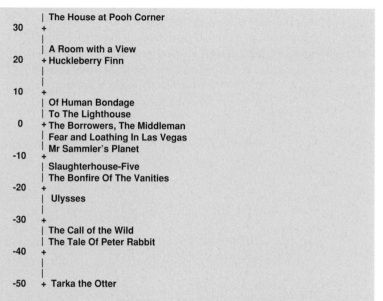

Figure 8.13 *Mean scores for selected novels along Fiction Dimension 1*

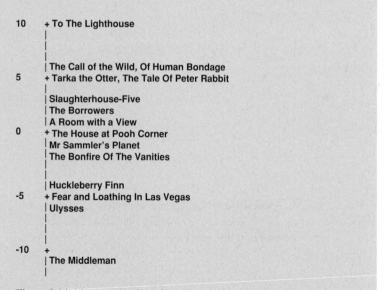

Figure 8.14 *Mean scores for selected novels along Fiction Dimension 2*

overall MD characteristics.) Discuss how the linguistic description resulting from this analysis corresponds to other stylistic descriptions of these novels that you are familiar with.

Finally, discuss the implications of these findings for the teaching of English Literature at primary- or secondary-school levels (for native speakers or second-language students). There are some surprising findings here: for example, some "elementary" or "adolescent" novels are highly "literate" in certain respects. Some classical "adult" novels are highly "oral" in some respects. Use these findings as the starting point for a discussion of the various kinds of complexities found in fictional prose, and the challenges of teaching these literary works at different educational levels.

9 Register studies in context

The preceding chapters have introduced the concept of *register* in relation to the related concepts of *genre* and *style*. These chapters have additionally described a framework for doing register analysis, presented several case studies that have applied this framework, and discussed research findings on the more general patterns of register variation and historical change. In the present chapter, we return to some of the themes introduced in Chapter 1, discussing the place of register studies in relation to other academic fields and in relation to real-world applications.

9.1 Register studies in the broader context of linguistics

It is possible to consider linguistics as comprising two major subfields: the study of language structure (e.g., phonology, morphology, grammar) and the study of language use, how people acquire language and what they actually do with the structural resources of a language. The study of language use is intimately connected to the study of linguistic variation. All human languages exhibit linguistic variation: related linguistic structures that express similar meanings. Variation exists at all linguistic levels, including: allophones (e.g., *t* vs. *t^h*), synonymous words (e.g., *dresser* vs. *chest of drawers*), morphemes (e.g., *-tion* vs. *-ment*), grammatical constructions (e.g., relative clauses with and without a relative pronoun, active voice vs. passive voice). In large part, the study of language use is the study of linguistic variation, investigating the question of why a speaker uses one set of linguistic forms rather than another at any given time and place.

Studying registers and genres – the focus of this book – is one of four major approaches that attempt to explain the patterns of linguistic variation. These approaches each focus on a different major non-structural factor: (1) information packaging, (2) historical time, (3) demographic characteristics of the speaker, and (4) the situational context and communicative purpose. In the first approach, often studied in the subfields of *pragmatics* or *functional linguistics*, the analyst investigates the informational properties of text elements, such as "given" or "new" informational status, "focus," "topic," and the preference to place "heavy" constituents at the end of a clause in English. These factors all can influence the choice of one linguistic variant over another. In the second approach – *historical linguistics* – scholars investigate variation across time periods: how one linguistic variant comes to be preferred over alternatives over time. In the third approach, *dialect studies* and *sociolinguistics*, the analyst studies how speakers from different places or from different demographic groups prefer one or another linguistic variant. And finally, the fourth approach has been the focus of the present book.

These four approaches also differ in the target of investigation; each approach assumes a different definition or understanding of *linguistic variation*. The strictest definition of linguistic variation is adopted by quantitative sociolinguists who study social dialect variation (e.g., represented by the work of Labov, Trudgill, Sankoff, and others; see Chapter 1, Section 5, and Section 9.4 below). In that subfield, the target of investigation includes only linguistic variation that is strictly meaning preserving. As a result, most studies within that framework focus on phonetic differences, for example pronouncing the word "car" as [kar] versus [ka]. (In contrast, variants like the choice between active and passive voice are excluded because they can sometimes express different truth-value meanings; see, e.g., Weiner and Labov 1983).

Pragmatic or functional studies of linguistic variation focus on equivalent structures that are not necessarily identical in their truth-value meanings. These are often grammatical features that would be excluded from sociolinguistic social dialect studies. For example, Prince (1978) studied the discourse contexts associated with the use of simple assertions versus *it*-clefts versus *WH*-clefts, as in:

    a. Today I want to talk about global warming.
    b. It is global warming that I want to talk about today.
    c. What I want to talk about today is global warming.

Such structures are roughly equivalent in meaning but have different presuppositions about what the speaker already knows or believes (e.g., in (c), the speaker already knows that there is something that the speaker wants to talk about). Other example studies in this tradition have investigated initial versus final adverbial clauses (Thompson 1985), omission of the complementizer *that* (Thompson and Mulac 1991), relative-clause types (Fox and Thompson 1990), causal sequences (Schiffrin 1985), VP preposing (Ward 1990), and dative alternation (Collins 1995).

The scope of linguistic variation investigated in register studies is considerably wider than in any of these other subfields. On the one hand, a register perspective can be used to study the use of variants that express roughly equivalent meanings, often incorporated as part of a sociolinguistic or pragmatic investigation. (Thus, for example, the Prince study cited above contrasted the patterns of use for *it*-clefts versus *WH*-clefts in speech versus writing.) However, register studies often go well beyond this focus by making the text the object of study rather than the linguistic token. This provides a fundamentally different perspective on linguistic variation. That is, in a traditional sociolinguistic or pragmatic study, the underlying assumption is that the speaker wants to express a particular meaning but chooses one or another linguistic variant to express that meaning. In contrast, register studies assume that speakers and writers in different circumstances will have different communicative goals, and thus need to express different kinds of meanings, and as a result will tend to rely on different sets of linguistic structures. As described in previous chapters, one underlying assumption here is that linguistic features are functional, being used to different extents in association with the communicative requirements of a register. As a result, texts from different registers vary in even the most fundamental ways in their typical linguistic characteristics, such as the extent of their reliance on nouns versus verbs.

The possibility of such linguistic variation is excluded in most quantitative studies of social dialects, because it is assumed (at least in practice) that all dialects are communicatively equivalent. However, there is no logical reason why dialects cannot be studied from this same perspective, contrasting the typical linguistic features used by speakers from different dialects (using the text as the unit of analysis, rather than focusing on an individual linguistic feature and its variants). In fact, such studies have been carried out under the umbrella of *conversational style* (e.g., Tannen 2005), an approach that focuses on the ways in which speakers of the same language construct conversation in different ways, in accordance with their norms of politeness, involvement, and so on. Thus, speakers from one cultural background might find it appropriate to discuss their own personal feelings and attitudes with a stranger whom they have just met, while a speaker from a different cultural or social background might not find it appropriate to talk much at all in this same situation. Differences of this type might be regarded as dialect distinctions, associated with different speaker groups of the same language. But unlike traditional dialect studies, the linguistic features that vary in this case are clearly not equivalent in meaning. Rather, each style has its own set of typical linguistic features that are preferred by speakers from a particular sub-culture.

These two approaches to linguistic variation can be applied in historical studies as well as synchronic studies. Thus, traditional studies in historical linguistics take a specific linguistic feature as the focus of analysis, describing how a word or structure changes over time to a variant word or structure that has an equivalent meaning (such as a shift in the pronunciation of a word, or a shift to a different word that has the same meaning). In contrast, historical register studies, which were introduced in Chapter 6, compare the typical linguistic characteristics of texts from different historical periods, adopting the wider perspective on linguistic variation that characterizes register studies generally.

The notion of *genre* is more difficult to characterize with respect to the study of linguistic variation. On the one hand, it is clearly an example of the fourth approach identified above, with a focus on the situational context and communicative purpose of texts. However, as described in Chapters 1 and 3, the linguistic focus of genre analyses is on the conventional features that are used to structure complete texts from a variety – linguistic features that typically occur only once, at a particular location in a text. Thus, quantitative analysis is much less relevant for the description of genres, and the notion of linguistic variation is realized as simple presence or absence of a feature in a text.

The textual perspective on linguistic variation, which forms the foundation of register analysis, has been largely disregarded in linguistics. For example, most introductory textbooks discuss only the linguistic variation that is realized as variants of equivalent words or structures. This equivalent-structure perspective on linguistic variation fits tidily into traditional structural descriptions of a language, which recognizes different linguistic levels (e.g., phonology, morphology, lexis, syntax) and variant realizations of words and structures at each level. In contrast, the textual perspective on linguistic variation does not fit into this traditional model, and thus variation in the typical linguistic features of texts from different registers is often overlooked in standard linguistic descriptions.

However, one of our primary goals in the present book has been to convince you that the textual perspective on linguistic variation is as important as the study of equivalent linguistic variants. Texts from different registers differ not only in their preference for one linguistic variant over another equivalent linguistic variant. Rather, texts from different registers are produced in fundamentally different circumstances, for fundamentally different communicative purposes; and as a result, these texts often use completely different sets of linguistic features that are functionally appropriate for those circumstances and purposes. Such patterns of variation are pervasive and extensive in all human language. Thus, although this approach to linguistic variation does not fit tidily into structural models of language, it cannot be ignored in any comprehensive description of language use.

9.2   Register variation in languages other than English

The case studies in this book have dealt with only English registers, so that the descriptions would be accessible to all students using this book. However, register variation is a universal of human language. Speakers of all languages communicate in different situations for different purposes, and linguistic features in those language vary accordingly.

In many respects, there are similar register patterns across languages. For example, multidimensional studies of register variation in Spanish, Korean, Somali, and English have all identified a first dimension with similar linguistic features and similar differences among registers. In all four languages, this dimension identifies a fundamental opposition between "oral" registers and "literate" registers. Table 9.1 summarizes these patterns.

The positive features on Dimension 1 for all four languages include frequent verbs, pronouns, adverbs, stance features, finite adverbial clauses and complement clauses, contractions, and questions; while the negative features include frequent nouns, adjectives, and noun modifiers. Conversational registers have large positive Dimension 1 scores in all four languages, while written expository

Table 9.1 *Co-occurring linguistic features and register patterns on Dimension 1, from the MD analyses of Spanish, Korean, and Somali*

| Language | Co-occurring linguistic features on Dimension 1 | | Register pattern along Dimension 1 | |
	Positive features	Negative features	Registers with large positive Dimension 1 scores	Registers with large negative Dimension 1 scores
English (Biber 1988)	Mental verbs, present tense verbs, possibility modals, 1st person pronouns, 2nd person pronouns, *it*, demonstrative pronouns, emphatics, hedges, discourse particles, causative subordination, WH clauses, *that*-clauses with the *that* omitted, WH questions, contractions	Nouns, attributive adjectives, prepositional phrases, long words, high type/token ratio, passive verbs	Face-to-face conversation, telephone conversation	Academic prose, press reportage, official documents
Spanish (Biber, Davies, Jones, & Tracy-Ventura 2006)	Indicative mood verbs, copula *SER*, copula *ESTAR*, present tense verbs, future *ir a*, perfect aspect, progressive aspect, mental verbs, communication verbs, 1st person pronouns, demonstrative pronouns, 1st person pro-drop, 3rd person pronouns, time adverbs, place adverbs, causal subordinate clauses, *que* verb complement clauses, yes–no questions	Singular nouns, plural nouns, derived nouns, postmodifying adjectives, premodifying attributive adjectives, definite articles, prepositions, postnominal past participles, type/token ratio, long words, *se* passives	Conversation (face-to-face and telephone)	academic prose, encyclopedia articles

(cont.)

Table 9.1. (cont.)

Language	Co-occurring linguistic features on Dimension 1		Register pattern along Dimension 1	
	Positive features	Negative features	Registers with large positive Dimension 1 scores	Registers with large negative Dimension 1 scores
Korean (Kim and Biber 1994, Biber 1995)	Fragmentary sentences, discourse verbal connectors, short negation, hedges, direct questions, contractions	Postposition/noun ratio, attributive adjectives, relative clauses, noun complementation, sentence length	Conversation, television drama	Editorials, textbooks, literary criticism
Somali (Biber 1995)	Independent verbs, main clauses, *waa* focus markers, *baa* focus markers, 2nd person focus markers, 1st person pronouns, time deictics, downtoners, conditional clauses, yes/no questions, "what if" questions, WH questions, stance adjectives, contractions	Nouns, derived adjectives, word length, dependent clauses, relative clauses, *waxaa* clefts, clause coordination, phrasal coordination	Conversation, family meetings	Press reportage, political pamphlets, editorials

registers have large negative Dimension 1 scores. Given that these languages are widely divergent in their linguistic/typological characteristics and in their socio-cultural contexts, there is no methodological bias in these analyses that would have resulted in a first dimension with these characteristics. Rather, it seems likely that this represents a universal pattern of register variation, at least for languages that have an established literacy tradition.

A second candidate for a universal register pattern is the distinction between narrative and non-narrative registers. All four of these languages have a dimension that distinguishes between written narrative registers (e.g., fiction, folk stories) and all other registers. And all four languages use similar linguistic features to define this dimension, including past tense, communication verbs, third person pronouns, and time adverbials.

At the same time, there are other register patterns that are distinctive to a particular language/culture. For example, personal letters in Somali are quite different from typical letters in English or Spanish, because they are almost always written to address a personal need (e.g., sending money, helping a relative, etc.) rather than focusing on social relationships. As a result, letters in Somali have very distinctive linguistic characteristics, with frequent optative clauses and directional pre-verbal particles combined with frequent first and second person pronouns (e.g., *let Xasan send the package to me*). This example illustrates two influences on register variation: the social requirements of a register in a given culture/language and the linguistic resources that can be exploited for those requirements. In this example, Somali exploits two grammatical devices not found in English: optative mood, which is marked on verb phrases to express polite directives, and directional pre-verbal particles, which indicate whether the action of the verb is occurring either towards or away from the speaker. Functionally, these features fit the social requirements of letters in Somali culture, resulting in this distinctive register pattern.

A second example of this type comes from Spanish, which has a series of highly productive "subjunctive" verb tenses. Subjunctive clauses in English are rare and very restricted in distribution, occurring mostly in *that*-clauses that express a mandate (e.g., *They insisted that he do the same*). In contrast, subjunctive verbs are much more prevalent in Spanish. The MD analysis of Spanish shows that these verbs co-occur frequently with obligation verbs, verbs of facilitation, conditional verbs, complement clauses (*que* clauses and infinitive clauses), future tense, and progressive aspect. This set of co-occurring linguistic features is especially common in political interviews and political debates, where speakers are expressing opinions and describing hypothetical situations. These features can all be used to describe personal feelings and attitudes, or possible events/states, but usually not to describe an actual event or state. Here again, we see the distinctive linguistic resources of a language being adapted to the functional requirements of registers in the given culture.

To date, there have been many more studies of register variation in English than in other languages. However, the research studies of other languages that have been conducted consistently show that they have systematic and often surprising patterns of register variation. Future studies of this type will greatly enhance our understanding of universal patterns of register variation and of the ways in which register differences can be realized through unique linguistic patterns.

9.3   Speech and writing

One of the major themes throughout this book has been the difference between speech and writing. At the same time, we have documented systematic differences within each mode, among spoken registers and among written registers. Many researchers over the past few decades have argued strongly for the importance of one or the other of these two perspectives: Some scholars have argued that speech and writing are fundamentally different from one or another; other scholars have argued that communicative purpose is most important for determining linguistic expression, and that it does not really matter whether those communicative purposes are realized in speech or writing.

The popular view held by many lay people is that writing is more real and valued than speech. "Talk is cheap," and it is difficult to hold someone accountable for what they said, because they can claim that what they **really** said was different. In contrast, written language is regarded as accurate and binding. "Literature" in Western societies is almost always written, and students are trained to become "good writers" with less attention to becoming "good speakers."

Linguists have traditionally taken the opposite view, arguing that speech is the basic mode of communication. All normal children grow up speaking a language without any special effort. In contrast, writing is a much more specialized mode of communication; children must deliberately learn to read and write, and not all children succeed at this task. All human languages are spoken, but there are many languages that have never been represented in writing. From a linguistic point of view, speech is inherent: it is part of what makes us human. In contrast, writing is a technology that humans have developed to represent language visually; writing is learned by many people but it is not a necessary part of the human experience.

There has been less agreement among linguists on how the language of speech compares to the language of writing. In many studies, conversation and academic writing are treated as the two stereotypical registers representing the spoken and written modes. And as previous chapters have shown, these two registers differ from each other in just about every conceivable way. Based on such differences, scholars like O'Donnell (1974), Olson (1977), and Chafe (1982) argued that written language is fundamentally different from speech in being more structurally complex, elaborated, and/or explicit.

Other scholars have focused on the ways in which written registers can be "oral." For example, as described in Chapters 6 and 7, registers like personal letters, e-mail messages, and text messaging are in many respects similar

linguistically to conversation, even though they are written. Because of the existence of such registers, some scholars have argued that there are essentially no
linguistic differences between speech and writing overall. For example:

> Literacy can be used (or not used) in so many different ways that the tech-
> nology it offers, taken on its own, probably has no implications at all (Bloch
> 1993: 87).

> In sum, orality and literacy share many common features and the features that
> have been identified with one or the other have more to do with the context in
> which language is used than with oral versus literate use (Hornberger 1994:
> 114).

The cumulative evidence of corpus-based register studies is highly relevant
to this debate, showing that there is a genuine difference between speech and
writing. Take a minute to think back on the register descriptions presented in
Chapters 4–8: In what ways are spoken registers all similar to one another (and
different from writing)? And what kinds of linguistic differences exist among
spoken registers? Ask the same questions about writing: In what ways are written
registers all similar to one another (and different from speech)? And what kinds
of linguistic differences exist among written registers?

The cumulative results of previous corpus-based studies are surprising, showing that neither extreme position about the speech/writing controversy is correct.
On the one hand, these studies consistently show that there are no absolute linguistic differences between speech and writing, because some written registers
are very similar to spoken registers in their typical linguistic characteristics (like
text messages and certain kinds of e-mail messages).

But at the same time, these studies have identified an important difference
between the two modes: speech and writing differ in their **potential** for linguistic
variation. That is, speech is highly constrained in its typical linguistic characteristics, while writing permits a wide range of linguistic expression, including some
discourse types not attested in speech. Thus, an author can create almost any kind
of text in writing, and so written texts can be highly similar to spoken texts, or
they can be dramatically different. In contrast, all spoken texts are surprisingly
similar linguistically, regardless of communicative purpose (excluding scripted
or memorized texts).

The major difference here is realized by highly informational written registers
produced for experts in a field – registers like academic research articles or
official documents. The descriptions in Chapters 5, 6, and 8 have shown how these
registers are highly distinctive in their typical linguistic features, with a frequent
use of nouns and technical vocabulary, and extremely complex noun phrase
constructions. Unlike all other registers – spoken or written – these specialist
written registers tend to rely on complex phrases, with relatively few verbs.

This type of discourse seems to be restricted to writing. Even a spoken register
like university classroom teaching, described in Chapter 8, does not employ the
linguistic features typical of academic writing. That is, even though classroom

teaching is informational in purpose, and the speaker has expert knowledge of the field, the typical linguistic characteristics of this register are surprisingly similar to conversation (and different from written academic prose): frequent verb phrases, modals, adverbial and complement clauses, pronouns, and so on. Thus, communicative purpose has a surprisingly small effect on the typical linguistic characteristics of spoken discourse. That is, whether a spoken register is interactive and interpersonal (as in normal conversation), or primarily monologic and informational (as in classroom teaching), it is characterized by the same set of typical linguistic features. And all of these spoken registers are characterized by the relative absence of complex noun phrase structures.

In summary, a synthesis of previous research on spoken and written registers shows three general distributional patterns: (1) linguistic features that are common in informational writing tend to be rare in the spoken registers, and vice versa; (2) spoken registers are surprisingly similar to one another in their typical linguistic characteristics, regardless of differences in communicative purpose, interactiveness, and pre-planning; but in contrast (3) written registers have a wide range of linguistic diversity. Thus, there is a genuine difference between speech and writing, but it is one-directional: speakers are highly constrained in the kinds of discourse that they are (normally) able to produce. That is, regardless of communicative purpose, speakers produce text that relies on frequent verbs and clauses. In contrast, writers have a much wider range of possibilities for the kinds of discourse that they can produce. As a result, written registers can have essentially the same linguistic characteristics as spoken registers. But written registers can also employ non-clausal discourse, characterized by extremely complex noun phrase constructions. This type of discourse is not attested in normal speech, regardless of communicative purpose, and thus seems to be a way in which the written mode is genuinely different from the spoken mode.

The linguistic uniformity among spoken registers can be attributed to their shared production circumstances. Spoken texts are normally produced in real time. As a result, spoken registers share a heavy reliance on finite clausal syntax, while it seems that the dense use of complex noun phrase structures is not normally feasible in speech, given the cognitive demands of these production circumstances. In contrast, there are large linguistic differences among written registers, corresponding to differences in purpose, interactiveness, author involvement, and so on. The production circumstances of writing give the author maximum flexibility, permitting types of linguistic expression very similar to those typical of speech, as well as types of expression that are apparently not feasible in speech. As a result, there is a fundamental difference between spoken and written registers: the written mode provides the **potential** for linguistic discourse types not found in the spoken mode.[1]

[1] Language that has its source in writing but performed in speech does not necessarily follow the generalizations here. That is, a person reading a written text aloud will produce speech that has the linguistic characteristics of the written text. Similarly, written texts can be memorized and then spoken.

Historical studies of register variation help us to further understand the nature of these differences between the spoken and written modes. For example, the description of noun phrase complexity in Chapter 6 (Section 6.4.1) shows that there was relatively little linguistic variation among registers in the seventeenth and eighteenth centuries. In fact, it is only in the twentieth century that the specialist informational registers in writing develop highly distinctive non-clausal discourse patterns, with extremely dense use of noun premodifiers and prepositional postmodifiers. Activity 5 in Chapter 8 shows similar historical patterns of change with respect to Dimension 1 from the MD analysis of English registers.

These historical findings suggest that it was not obvious to earlier authors that it was possible to produce the non-clausal discourse patterns found in modern specialist written registers. Thus, no register in the seventeenth or eighteenth century was characterized by the extremely dense use of complex noun phrase constructions. Rather, this type of discourse evolved gradually over the following centuries, with the most notable shift being in the twentieth century.

This historical change can be attributed to two influences: (1) an increasing need for written prose with dense informational content, associated with the "informational explosion" of recent centuries, and (2) an increasing awareness among writers of the production possibilities of the written mode, permitting extreme manipulation of the text.

In several chapters of this book, we have described the extremely dense use of complex noun phrase constructions in certain kinds of writing. As noted above, this discourse type is not normally feasible in speech, regardless of the communicative purpose. As a result, writers did not have models for discourse of this type in earlier centuries, and so even expository written registers did not incorporate these complex noun phrase structures in earlier centuries. It was only gradually that authors became aware that the production possibilities of the written mode allowed the creation of discourse with these linguistic characteristics. Here again, it is important to note that the written mode does not necessitate these distinctive linguistic styles. Rather, the written mode provides the potential

---

In addition, there have been a few gifted humans who can mentally compose extremely complex texts that are atypical of the spoken mode. For example, Maxamed Cabdille Xasan was a Somali poet who was able to compose dense, lexically elaborated texts, relying on memory without the aid of writing. Such texts go through multiple rounds of planning, revision, and editing, similar to the process of careful production described above for written registers. In this case, the process of careful production and revision requires an exceptional memory – the entire text is planned, revised, and edited over a period of weeks, relying on the powers of memory. The case of Somali oral poets show that such feats are humanly possible.

However, these are truly exceptional spoken registers. The vast majority of speech, in any language, is not memorized and has not been mentally revised and edited. Rather, speech is normally produced spontaneously in real time (even if it has been pre-planned, as in the case of university lectures). And the study of such spontaneous spoken registers, carried out from several perspectives, has shown repeatedly that spoken registers differ from written registers in that they do not provide the possibility of extreme lexical diversity, or the dense use of complex noun phrase constructions. Rather, such discourse types require extensive interaction with the text for planning, revision, and editing – processes that are normally possible only in writing.

for linguistic expression not normally possible in speech, and authors have only gradually come to exploit those possibilities over the past four centuries.

Thus, empirical studies of register variation indicate that there are genuine linguistic consequences of literacy. But these consequences relate to the linguistic potential of the two modes rather than the necessary linguistic characteristics of the two modes. In particular, the analyses summarized in the present section have shown that language production in the written mode enables types of linguistic expression not normally attested in speech, even though writers often choose not to exploit that linguistic potential.

9.4   Register variation and sociolinguistics

It would be easy to assume that the study of register variation is a major focus of sociolinguistics. This is because there are two main kinds of language varieties in any speech community: varieties associated with different speaker groups – *dialects* – and varieties associated with different situations of use – *registers*. The importance of both dialect and register variation in a speech community has been long recognized by functionally oriented linguists like Brown and Fraser, Crystal, Ferguson, Gumperz, Hymes, Halliday, and Pike. So it is natural to expect that the field of sociolinguistics would give equal attention to both kinds of variation.

Surprisingly, this is not the case: rather, quantitative sociolinguists (especially in the variationist tradition developed by Labov, Trudgill, and others) generally disregard register variation, instead focusing on dialect variation. Thus, textbooks and handbooks on sociolinguistics consistently include multiple chapters dealing with regional dialect variation and social dialect variation, but they provide only minimal discussion of register variation (see, e.g., Coulmas 1997, Wardhaugh 1992, Hudson 1980). This omission is especially surprising since nearly all of these treatments overtly discuss the notion of *speech community* as the locus of sociolinguistic investigation. However, in the variationist sociolinguistic tradition, the speech community has been studied almost exclusively by reference to variation across its speakers, not across the situations in which those speakers use language.

When situational variation is addressed within quantitative sociolinguistic studies, it has been approached under the rubric of *style*. But this term has a specialized and restricted meaning within variationist sociolinguistics, different from its use in the present book: variationist sociolinguists use the term *style* to refer only to the differences among the spoken tasks included as part of a *sociolinguistic interview* (e.g., telling a personal narrative, providing personal demographic information, and reading word lists). Most quantitative studies of social dialect variation have considered linguistic variation among sociolinguistic styles (e.g., Labov 1972, Trudgill 1974). However, as Coupland (2007: 9) points out, "in the sociolinguistics of variation, style has been a very limited concept and a peripheral concern." Coupland's (2007) book is one attempt to rectify that situation (see also the chapters in Eckert and Rickford 2002).

Within the framework of the present book, sociolinguistic "styles" would be regarded as different registers, but they represent an artificially restricted range of situational variation that has no obvious interpretation in the context of the larger speech community. First of all, sociolinguistic styles include only spoken varieties. Variationist studies of style do not acknowledge the role of written varieties in a speech community, and as a result they disregard what is probably the most important situational determinant of linguistic variation (see Section 9.2 above). But the operational definition of sociolinguistic style is even more restricted in that it includes only a very narrow range of the register variation found within speech in a normal community. Thus, spoken registers like classroom teaching, study groups, sermons, political debates, and even normal face-to-face conversation would all be excluded from consideration.

One major difference between variationist approaches and the methodological approach advocated in the present book has to do with the linguistic characteristics being analyzed (see Section 9.1 above). Analyses in variationist sociolinguistics are based on the *sociolinguistic variable*: a language characteristic that has several *variants* that, by definition, are meaning-preserving. A correlate of this requirement is that linguistic variation is regarded as strictly conventional and non-functional. For example, if Group A prefers the variant [kar], and Group B prefers the variant [ka], the variants are claimed to simply index different groups (and styles). It does not matter which group uses which variant and there is no functional difference between them.

In contrast, the approach developed in the present book is based on consideration of register features rather than linguistic variables. The concept of linguistic "choice" is realized in this approach as the set of linguistic features that are preferred in one register when compared to another. That is, speakers and writers choose from the entire inventory of lexico-grammatical characteristics of a language, selecting the linguistic features that are best suited functionally to their situations and communicative purposes. These choices are explicitly **not** meaning preserving, and they **are** explicitly functional, because different registers do not express the same kinds of meanings, and linguistic features clearly serve a range of communicative functions in different kinds of texts.

Given that the two approaches are so different in both the range of situational variation and the range of linguistic variation that they investigate, it is probably not surprising that they come to the opposite conclusions about the relative importance of dialect variation versus situational (register/style) variation. Variationist sociolinguistics has argued that dialect variation is basic, and that style variation is secondary; in studies of social dialects, the range of linguistic differences across dialects is consistently greater than the range of linguistic differences across sociolinguistic styles (see, e.g., Bell 1984, 2001). Register studies have come to the opposite conclusions: They have found that the range of linguistic differences

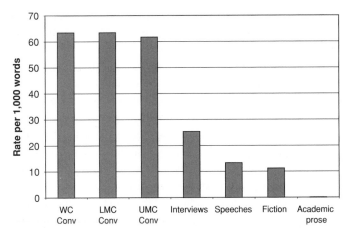

Figure 9.1 *Contractions across registers and social dialects (within conversation) [WC = Working Class, LMC = Lower Middle Class, UMC = Upper Middle Class]*

across registers is much greater than the range of linguistic differences across dialects, and in general, they conclude that register is more basic than dialect (see also Finegan and Biber 1994, 2001).

For example, Figure 9.1 plots the frequency of contractions across registers, illustrating the kind of patterns described throughout this book: large differences between spoken and written registers, as well as large differences within speech and writing associated with differences in purpose, interactiveness, and so on. However, Figure 9.1 further compares the patterns of use from three social dialects within conversation (based on analysis of the conversations in the British National Corpus), showing extremely small differences when compared to the scale of the register differences. Those social differences might be statistically significant (with upper-middle-class speakers using fewer contractions), but they are clearly not strong differences when compared to the full range of register differences.

This is not at all meant to suggest that the study of dialect differences is not important or interesting. One of the most important contributions to linguistics generally over the past fifty years has been the insight that linguistic variation is patterned and predictable, influenced by both structural and social factors. The variationist sociolinguistic approach has led the way in furthering our understanding of this relationship.

At the same time, there is clearly extensive variation within speech communities that is not accounted for by current variationist frameworks. And as a result, there are several fundamental research questions that have been disregarded to date. For example, to our knowledge there has never been a comprehensive linguistic description of a social dialect. Such an analysis would survey the full set of lexico-grammatical features, documenting the extent to which each dialect used each feature. National dialects of English have been described from this perspective (e.g., there have been relatively comprehensive grammatical descriptions of American versus British English), but social dialects have been described for only a small set of linguistic characteristics, within the framework of the sociolinguistic variable.

Of course, to make sense, such a description would need to compare the full set of registers across dialects. But the description would also need to describe the social distribution of registers across dialect groups: to what extent do different groups employ one or another register? That is, what is the register repertoire of each dialect group? There are obvious demographic differences here. For example, it seems obvious that younger people are more likely than older people to practice the register of text messages; professional occupations are more likely than manual labor occupations to produce the registers of e-mails and research reports. But these are just conjectures based on our own casual observations. To our knowledge, there has never been an empirical study to determine the distribution of registers across dialect groups.

A survey of this type would then lay the foundation for a comprehensive linguistic description of the patterns of variation within a speech community: across the full range of dialects and registers, with respect to the full set of lexico-grammatical linguistic features. Analyses of this type would not replace traditional variationist accounts of social dialect variation. Rather, they would be asking fundamentally different kinds of research questions: what are the comprehensive patterns of linguistic variation within a speech community, and specifically, how do the patterns of register variation interact with the patterns of dialect variation?

9.5   Register studies in the broader context of the world

Finally, we conclude the book with a discussion of how studies of register variation can be applied in the "real world." Essentially, register descriptions are relevant for any application of linguistics generally. In fact, in the 1960s and 70s, register studies (often referred to as *stylistics*) were carried out under the umbrella of "applied linguistics," because they were descriptive, in contrast to "theoretical linguistics," which focused more on formal analysis of specific theoretically relevant phenomena.

One applied domain where register studies have been influential is for the computational processing of language, for the purposes of *information retrieval* and *natural language processing* (e.g., the automated comprehension and production of texts). Machine translation is a related area of applied research that has been influenced by the awareness of register differences. In all of these applications, greater accuracy and naturalness can be achieved by incorporating knowledge of register differences into the computer applications that process language.

In a completely different arena, the tools of register analysis are useful for literary studies. We have illustrated how analyses of fictional style can be carried out using the techniques of register analysis. Such analyses can complement the more traditional approaches to literary criticism.

An awareness of register differences is useful in many other language-related occupations. For example, imagine that you are working as an editor for a publisher of academic books, or as a technical writing consultant for an engineering firm. In jobs such as these, it is essential to recognize and produce prose that is register-appropriate. It would be your job to advise others on the linguistic characteristics that are expected in professional texts for various audiences. For example, as a technical writing consultant, you might conduct seminars for engineers and technical writers to help them write more effective technical reports. Understanding the linguistic features that are typical of such reports, and the communicative functions that those features serve, should greatly improve your effectiveness as a consultant.

However, the most important application of register studies is in the area of language pedagogy (see, e.g., Biber and Reppen 2002; Conrad 1999, 2000, 2004, 2005; Reppen 1995). Language teaching at almost any level, for any target audience, can be informed by awareness of register differences. For example, many universities now have undergraduate courses that emphasize writing across the curriculum, focusing on the different kinds of writing tasks required by different academic disciplines for different communicative purposes. These are the same kinds of factors that we have discussed in the present book, considered in the situational analyses of different registers; the preceding chapters have illustrated many of the important linguistic differences that are systematically associated with these communicative factors.

A writing curriculum based on a comprehensive linguistic description of the written registers in a particular academic discipline will provide students with the tools that they need to progress to professional competence in that area. Even for instructors of a general composition course (designed to meet the needs of students in all disciplines), there is perhaps no more important task than helping students to develop an awareness of register differences, and specifically an awareness of the linguistic norms expected in academic written registers. Often university writing instructors have been trained as English literature scholars or as creative writers, and as a result, they sometimes focus on creative writing tasks or personal narratives in their teaching. The underlying belief of such an approach is that good style in creative writing will translate to success in other university courses. After working through the register analyses of the present book, you should be convinced that this assumption is ill-founded: the communicative goals and the associated linguistic features of research writing are dramatically different from those of creative writing or personal narratives. If you are a composition instructor, your background in register analysis will give you the tools required to effectively train your students for the actual writing tasks that they will encounter in their academic disciplines.

A related pedagogical application of register descriptions has been in the area of second-language teaching, associated with the subfields of English for Specific

Purposes (ESP), English for Academic Purposes (EAP), and more generally Language for Specific Purposes (LSP). ESP and EAP pedagogical approaches have been developed for learners of English, targeting the particular kinds of language use that are most relevant for a particular professional career. ESP focuses mostly on the specific kinds of language used for different occupations, such as the vocabulary and language structures that are most important for workers in hotel and restaurant jobs. ESP instruction can focus on either the spoken registers or the written registers required for these occupations. In contrast, EAP focuses primarily on the different kinds of written registers used in different academic disciplines, intended mostly to prepare students for university education in English. Careful register descriptions are important as the foundation for developing teaching materials for both ESP and EAP applications, and there are numerous books and even entire academic journals dedicated to these sub-disciplines. (The academic journals *English for Specific Purposes* and *Journal of English for Academic Purposes* are especially important outlets for research of this kind.) Similar pedagogical approaches have been applied to the instruction of languages other than English, under the rubric of LSP (see, e.g., Douglas 2000).

As a language instructor in whatever context, you will benefit from your awareness of how registers can differ from one another, helping your students to develop a similar awareness. Beyond that, though, you should benefit from the skills for doing your own register analyses, allowing you to prepare effective teaching materials and develop useful writing assignments that will help your students develop the register-specific writing and speaking skills needed for success in their chosen profession.

In sum, an awareness of register differences, and the ability to carry out your own register analyses, are foundational tools for any practicing language professional. Our goals for the present book have been to both provide you with the theoretical foundation needed to understand research in this sub-discipline, and to provide you with the analytical tools required to carry out your own register studies in your future studies and career.

Chapter 9 activities

Reflection and review

1. In your own words, explain the following for someone who is not a linguist:

a. What is a register and why is studying registers important?
b. Why is quantitative analysis an important component in register analyses?

2. Plan a multidimensional analysis study of a language other than English. What types of texts will you collect to cover the widest possible range of registers in this language, spoken and written (if the language has a written tradition)? What linguistic features that are different from those found in English will need to be identified in the computer analysis (like the optative clauses and directional pre-verbal participles in

Somali, described in Section 9.2)? Are there any register patterns that you predict will be distinctive for this language (functionally, linguistically, or both)?

3. Consider the case of text messages relative to the discussion of the basic dichotomy between speech and writing (Section 9.3). Do text messages have the linguistic potential that other written registers do? Is text messaging truly a written register? Does the fact that it was developed for use with telephones (an instrument for speech) have an impact? Does this electronic register, and perhaps other electronic registers, blur the distinction between speech and writing, or is text messaging just another example of a written register in which people choose not to use structures that are typical of the specialist written registers?

4. In your life today, or in the career you are planning to pursue, what are the most important applications of understanding registers and register variation?

Appendix A Annotation of major register/genre studies
By Federica Barbieri

I. *Spoken registers/genres*

Study	Genre/register	Features under investigation	Approach and methods	Major findings/issues
Bargiela-Chiappini and Harris 1997	Corporate meetings in Italy and the UK	Macro-structure; structural moves; coherence markers (pronouns, theme, metaphors, discourse markers); turn-taking behavior, etc.	(Cross-cultural) pragmatics, systemic functional linguistics, ethnographic, conversation analysis.	Cross-cultural differences are analyzed in corporate meetings. For example, the overall structure of Italian meetings is looser than British meetings. In British meetings, forms of address are rarely used as markers of power, status, or social distance, while they are in the Italian meetings. Important differences are found also in turn-taking behaviors, for example interruptions and overlaps.
Cazden 2001	K-12 classroom discourse	Various discourse practices	Ethnographic, qualitative	Examines various discourse features of classroom discourse and interaction, such as getting the floor, teacher questions, wait time between teacher's question and student responses.
Christie 2002	K-12 classroom discourse	Genres, macrogenres	Systemic functional linguistics; qualitative	Proposes that classroom discourse can be regarded as "curriculum genres," and "curriculum macrogenres," that is, larger units created by a text that include several "elemental" genres. Curriculum macrogenres can have a linear structure, with embedded genres at the beginning, middle, and end. They can be realized in a "regulative register," which has to do with the overall goals, directions, pacing and sequencing of classroom activity, and an "instructional register," which has to do with the particular content being taught. For example, in a linear macrogenre, the "curriculum initiation" (i.e., the beginning genre) establishes the activity and is realized in both the regulative and instructional registers.

Csomay 2005	University lectures	Various lexico-grammatical features	Quantitative, corpus-based analysis; multi-dimensional analysis.	University classroom talk is characterized by three dimensions of linguistic variation: (1) Contextual, directive orientation versus Conceptual, informative focus; (2) Personalized framing; (3) Interactive dialogue versus Teacher monologue.
Koester 2006	Workplace (office) conversations, in US and UK	Lexico-grammatical features of relational talk; interpersonal markers (e.g., modality, vague language)	Quantitative, corpus-based, genre-based; interactional sociolinguistics; conversation analysis, ethnographic	Different sub-genres (i.e., collaborative, unidirectional, non-transactional) of workplace talk are characterized by different uses of interpersonal markers. For example, modals and idioms are most frequent in collaborative genres (e.g., decision-making meetings). Vague language and hedges are most common in unidirectional genres (e.g., procedural conversations), where they perform face-saving politeness functions. Intensifiers are most common in non-transactional genres (e.g., gossip, small talk), where they function as solidarity and involvement markers.
Thompson 2003	University lectures	Text-structuring metadiscourse; intonation	Quantitative, comparison of "authentic" vs. EAP texts	Lectures are characterized by two main types of metadiscourse: markers of the global organization of the talk, and markers of new topics and sub-topics. Both types of markers can fulfill three major functions: making reference to the content or topic of the talk, making reference to (parts of) the talk itself, or including an interpersonal reference.

Other studies of spoken registers

Spoken academic registers

Bamford 2005; Barbieri 2005; Basturkmen 1999, 2002; Biber 2006a,b; Biber and Barbieri 2007; Csomay 2007; Fortanet 2004, 2005; Gardner 2004; Hood and Forey 2005; Jackson and Bilton 1994; Legg 2007; Lindermann and Mauranen 2001; Mauranen 2003, 2004; Mauranen and Bondi 2003; Nesi and Basturkmen 2006; Recski 2005; Reppen 2004; Reppen and Vásquez 2007; Shalom 1993; R. Simpson 2004; Simpson and Mendis 2003; Swales 2001; Tapper 1994; Thompson 1994, 2003; Webber 2005; Weissberg 1993.

Spoken professional/workplace registers

Bell 1984; Bülow-Møller 2005; Coupland 1980; Dubois 1980; Friginal 2008, 2009; Greatbatch 1988; Gunnarsson, Linell, and Nordberg (eds.) 1993; Halmari 2005; Jaworski and Galasinski 2000; Johansson 2006; Koester 2004; Kuiper and Haggo 1984; Kuiper and Tillis 1986; Kuo 2001, 2002, 2003; Lynch 1985; Marra and Holmes 2004; Merritt 1976; Nevile 2006; Pettinari 1988; Philips 1984, 1985; Raymond 2000; Ventola 1983; Ventola, Shalom, and Thompson (eds.) 2002.

Conversation

Adolphs 2008; Biber 1988, 2008; Biber, Johanson, Leech, Conrad, and Finegan 1999; Carter and McCarthy 1997, 2004; Conrad and Biber 2000; Laforest 2002; McCarthy 1998; McCarthy and Carter 2004; Quaglio 2004, 2009; Quaglio and Biber 2006; Tannen 1987, 1989, 2005; Tao 2007; Tracy-Ventura, Biber, Cortes 2007.

Other spoken registers

Ädel and Reppen 2008; Atifi and Marcoccia 2006; Bevitori 2005; Bolivar 1992; Cutting 1999, 2000; Dickerson 2001; Helt 2001; Inigo-Mora 2007; Jiang 2006; Lauerbach 2004; Milizia 2006; Placencia 2004; Schmidt and Kess 1985.

II. *General written registers and genres*

Study	Genre/register	Features under investigation	Approach and methods	Major findings/issues
Bednarek 2006	Media discourse; newspaper "hard news" in broadsheets and tabloids	Evaluation, stance features	Corpus-based analysis of intra-register variation	Both broadsheets and tabloids exhibit a distinct evaluative style: broadsheets are characterized by mitigation and negation, while tabloids are characterized by emotivity (e.g., writer's evaluations of aspects of events as good or bad; other references to emotions) and unexpectedness (i.e., use of evaluators such as *dramatic(ally)*, *strikingly*).
Biber, Connor, and Upton 2007	Academic research articles, fundraising letters, university lectures	Lexico-grammatical features and moves	Corpus-based analysis, from both genre and register perspectives	Explores how both genre analysis and register analysis can be applied to large corpora of written and spoken texts, with a focus on describing the internal discourse structure of texts.
Bunton 2005	PhD conclusion chapters	Moves	Genre analysis; cross-disciplinary comparison	Conclusion chapters in PhD theses present two typical structures: most conclusions restate purpose, consolidate research space, outline recommendations for future research and practical applications; a smaller number of theses adopt a problem-solution text structure or argument structure, focusing more on the disciplinary field than the thesis research itself.
Charles 2006a	PhD dissertations	Finite reporting clauses followed by *that*-clause	Quantitative; corpus-based analysis of cross-disciplinary comparison	In dissertations, writers employ reporting clauses to construct stance, to emphasize or hide responsibility for propositions in the text, and to report their own work. There is disciplinary variation in the type of stance constructed. For example, political science favors human subjects, while non-human and *it* subjects are common in materials science.

(*cont.*)

II. (cont.)

Study	Genre/register	Features under investigation	Approach and methods	Major findings/issues
Connor 1996	Writing in a second language	Lexico-grammatical and rhetorical	Contrastive rhetoric	This introduction to contrastive rhetoric reviews studies of academic and professional genres, such as the research article, the academic abstract, grant proposals and business letters.
Connor and Mauranen 1999	Grant proposals	Moves	Genre analysis, application of social constructionist theory	European Union grant proposals include ten moves (e.g., "territory," "gap," "goal," etc.) which reflect the affinity of grant proposals to both academic research articles and promotional registers, as well as moves specific to the grant proposal register (e.g., "compliance claim").
Conrad 1996	Research articles and textbooks in biology (compared with fiction and popular non-fiction)	Numerous lexico-grammatical features	Corpus-based, multidimensional analysis	Relative to other registers, academic texts in ecology tend to be highly informational, non-narrative, and characterized by an impersonal style. At the same time, textbooks and research articles within this register differ in important ways. Research articles have a more informational focus and more impersonal style. Textbooks have a more interactive, less impersonal style, reflecting more explanation and exemplification of concepts for students.
Flowerdew (ed.) 2002	Academic registers: abstracts, textbooks, PhD theses	Various: moves, reporting verbs, epistemic modality expressions, etc.	Various: quantitative, moves analysis, contrastive rhetoric, corpus-based analysis, ethnographic, systemic functional linguistics, etc.	The sixteen chapters in this collection illustrate the application of four major approaches (moves analysis, contrastive rhetoric, corpus analysis, ethnographic methods) to the study of various academic registers. For example, Love combines Hallidayan and moves analysis to explore lexico-grammatical features in a sociology textbook. McEnery and Kifle contrast the use of epistemic modality expressions in argumentative essays by Eritrean and British students, while Yakhonotova compares conference abstracts in Ukrainian and English.

Reference	Genre/text type	Linguistic features	Approach	Description
Flowerdew and Dudley-Evans 2002	(Summative) editorial letters	Moves, schematic structure, linguistic and politeness strategies	Genre analysis, pragmatic analysis	Summative editorial letters are characterized by four main moves: (1) preparing the reader for decision, (2) conveying the decision, (3) making recommendations for revision, (4) signing off. In these summative letters, editors also use a range of politeness and face-saving strategies that make letters more personal.
Ghadessy (ed.) 1993b	Various, mostly written	Various: evaluation markers, metaphor, etc.	Various: quantitative, systemic functional linguistics, pragmatic, etc.	This edited collection includes a mix of theoretical/methodological contributions (chapters by de Beaugrande; Leckie-Tarry; Webster; Cross; Matthiessen) and applied studies (chapters by Birch; Hunston; Eggings, Wignell, and Martin; Goatly; Ghadessy; Gunnarsson). Hunston looks at issues of persuasion, evaluation, and ideology in scientific discourse. The chapter by Eggins *et al.* focuses on grammatical metaphor in history; Goatly focuses on a variety of registers (conversation, news reporting, popular science, advertising, poetry). Gunnarson looks at pragmatic and macrothematic changes over time in science and popular-science articles in Swedish.
Halliday and Martin 1993	Science discourse, including professional books and high-school textbooks	Various (e.g., grammatical "texture," nouns, etc.)	Systemic functional linguistics	This book applies systemic functional linguistics to the analysis of the language of science, including both professional science discourse (e.g., science books and treaties) and science for novices (e.g., high-school textbooks). Chapters by Halliday take a historical perspective to the analysis of core lexico-grammatical, semantic, and socio-semiotic features in physical-science discourse. Halliday also analyzes the grammatical "texture" of Charles Darwin's *The Origin of Species*. Chapters by Martin focus on textbooks in the sciences and humanities used in secondary-school contexts.

(cont.)

II. (*cont.*)

Study	Genre/register	Features under investigation	Approach and methods	Major findings/issues
Hyland 1998	Research articles in biology	Hedges (hedging words or phrases)	Quantitative, pragmatic, corpus-based, ethnographic (interviews with professionals)	Scientific research articles (RAs) make extensive use of hedges to express uncertainty. Hedges in RAs are varied and extremely frequent (even more frequent than modals, a common marker of doubt and uncertainty). Hedges perform different functions in RAs versus textbooks. For example, in academic textbooks, hedges are used to represent matters which lack a consensus; in RAs, hedges are used primarily to express doubt.
Hyland 1999b	Textbooks and research articles in various disciplines (e.g., microbiology, marketing)	Textual and interpersonal metadiscourse (e.g., connectives, hedges, etc.)	Quantitative, corpus analysis of cross-register and cross-disciplinary comparisons	Textbooks and research articles both use metadiscourse, but differently. For example, textbooks use textual metadiscourse (e.g., logical connectives) more than interpersonal metadiscourse. Research articles instead favor interpersonal metadiscourse (e.g., hedges, personal and frame markers).
Hyland 2002a	Research articles, textbooks, L2 student essays	Directives (imperatives, modals of obligation, adjective + *to*-clause)	Quantitative, pragmatic, corpus analysis, ethnographic (interviews and focus groups)	(1) The functions of directives (e.g., guiding readers to some textual act, instructing readers to perform a physical act, steering readers to certain cognitive acts) vary across registers (e.g., textbooks and articles favor directives expressing cognitive actions). (2) The use of directives varies across disciplines (e.g., very common in the hard sciences; relatively uncommon in social sciences).

Hyland and Tse 2005	Abstracts from research articles, and theses and dissertations by L2 students	Evaluative *that*-clauses	Corpus-based, quantitative	Abstracts are characterized by *that*-clauses to convey writer's stance, with over 80% of evaluative *that*-constructions referring to the writer's own findings. Evaluative *that*-clauses allow writers to foreground an attitudinal or epistemic stance toward the proposition of the *that*-clause.
MacDonald 2005	Newspaper and magazine popular-science articles	Linguistic sources of sensationalism	Quantitative; systemic functional linguistics	In popular-science articles on healthcare research (in this case, hormone replacement), sensationalism is constructed through the use of non-epistemic sentence subjects (concrete nouns), concrete verbs of attribution and reporting, word order in attribution, and use of human narratives.
Samraj 2002a	Research article introductions	Moves	Genre analysis	Research article introductions in conservation biology and wildlife behavior differ in terms of organizational structure. Wildlife behavior introductions closely follow the CARS model. Conservation-biology introductions include more elements of persuasion and promotion. These differences are ascribed to the different characteristics of the fields: for example, conservation biology is an applied field and is interdisciplinary, while wildlife behavior is theoretical and disciplinary.
Stotesbury 2003	Research article abstracts	Rhetorical structure; evaluative stance expressions	Quantitative, cross-disciplinary comparison, analysis of rhetorical structure	Abstracts in different disciplines (humanities, social sciences, natural sciences) use different stance expressions. For example, abstracts in the humanities favor evaluative expressions (e.g., adjectives, nouns, adjuncts, etc.); abstracts in the natural sciences favor modal verbs. Cross-disciplinary differences also exist in the use of evaluative expression in relation to the rhetorical structure of abstracts. For example, in the natural sciences, expressions of epistemic modality are most common in the conclusion part of abstracts, while in the social sciences they are most frequent in the results section.

(cont.)

II. (*cont.*)

Study	Genre/register	Features under investigation	Approach and methods	Major findings/issues
Tognini-Bonelli and Camiciotti (eds.) 2005	Academic registers: book reviews, textbooks, research articles, PhD dissertations	Various: expressions of conflict, authorial stance, metadiscourse, etc.	Various: quantitative, corpus based, moves analysis; systemic functional linguistics; cross-language comparison, etc.	This collection includes nine chapters on written academic discourse, covering a range of different registers, and focusing on features for the expression of conflict (Hunston), stance (Thompson; Poudat and Loiseau; Okamura), argumentation (Freddi), evaluation (Römer; Suarez; Motta-Roht), and metadiscourse (Ädel). Some chapters compare the use of these features across languages, e.g., English vs. Spanish (Motta-Roht); English vs. Swedish (Ädel).
Upton and Connor 2001	Letters of application by American, Belgian, Finnish students	Moves, politeness strategies	Genre analysis, corpus-based analysis, contrastive rhetoric	There is great variation in the extent that American, Belgian, and Finnish students use key moves in application letters, such as indicating desire for an interview (Move 4) and expressing politeness and appreciation at the end of the letter (Move 5). Within these two moves, American, Belgian, and Finnish students all use both positive and negative politeness strategies, though in different degrees. For example, Americans are more patterned and formulaic than Belgians, who display a more individualistic style.
Vilha 1999	Newspaper, magazine articles, and guidebook samples in medical writing	Modality expressions	Corpus-based analysis of register variation	In popular medical articles and guidebooks, expressions of possibility are much more common than expressions of necessity, though guidebook samples also include high rates of deontic modals. Expressions indicating a higher commitment of the writer are more common in popular articles than in other medical subregisters.

Other studies of written registers

Research articles

Bamford 1997; Bazerman 1988; Bhatia 1993; Biber 2006a,b; Biber, Connor, and Upton 2007; Biber, Conrad, and Cortes 2004; Biber and Finegan 1994c; Biber, Johanson, Leech, Conrad, and Finegan 1999; Biber and Jones 2005; Bondi 1997, 1999; Brett 1994; Channel 1990; Conrad and Biber 2000; Cortes 2004; Dressen 2003; Ferguson 2001; Fortanet, Posteguillo, Palmer, and Kull 1998; Giltrow 2005; Gledhill 2000; Gosden 1992, 1993; Grabe and Kaplan 1996, 1997; Groom 2005; Gross, Harmon, and Reidy 2002; Harwood 2005, 2006; Hemais 2001; Hewings and Hewings 2002; Holmes 1997; Hunston 1993, 2005; Hyland 1996, 1998, 1999a, 2001a,b, 2002b,c, 2005; Kanoksilapatham 2005; Koutsantoni 2004; Kuo 1999; Lewin 1998; Luzon Marco 2000; Martinez 2001, 2003; Melander 1998; Moreno 1997; Myers 1989, 1990; Nwogu 1997; Oakey 2005; Okamura 2005; Ozturk 2007; Paltridge 1994, 1995, 1997; Pisanski Peterlin 2005; Posteguillo 1998; Poudat and Loiseau 2005; Ruiying and Allison 2003, 2004; Rundbald 2007; Salager-Meyer 1990, 1994; Salager-Meyer and Defives 1998; Samraj 2002a, 2005; Skelton 1997; Soler 2002, 2007; Swales *et al*. 1998; Tarone *et al*. 1981; Tarone *et al*. 1998; Thetela 1997; Thomas and Hawes 1994; Tucker 2003; Vihla 1999; Webber 1994; Williams 1996; Williams 1999.

Abstracts

Bhatia 1993; Bittencourt Dos Santos 1996; Bondi 1999; Kaplan *et al*. 1994; Lores 2004, 2006; Martín Martín 2003; Martín Martín and Burgess 2004; Meyer 1992; Salager-Meyer 1992; Samraj 2002b; Samraj 2005; Stotesbury 2003.

Textbooks

Biber 2006a,b; Biber and Barbieri 2007; Bondi 1997, 1999; Conrad 1996, 2001; Freddi 2005a, 2005b; Halliday and Martin 1993; Horesella and Sindermann 1992; Hyland 1999b; Love 1991, 1993, 2002; McCabe 2004; Moore 2002; Myers 1992; Shi and Kubota 2007; Vihla 1999; Young and Nguyen 2002.

PhD dissertations

Bunton 1999; Bunton 2002; Charles 2003, 2006a,b, 2007; Hopkins and Dudley-Evans 1988; Hyland and Tse 2004; Kwan 2006; Paltridge 2002; Thompson 2005a, 2005b.

Other written academic registers and genres e.g., book reviews, acknowledgments, etc.)

Abraham Varghese, Susheela, and Abraham 2004; Biber 2006a,b; Connor 2000; Connor and Upton 2004b; Crismore, Markannen, and Steffensen 1993; Evangelisti Allori (ed.) 1998; Feak, Reinhart, and Sinsheimer 2000; Flowerdew and Peacock 2001; Giannoni 2002; Groom 2005; Halleck and Connor 2006; Hewings (ed.) 2001; Horsella and Sindermann 1992; Hyland 2000; Hyland 2004; Lewin, Fine, and Young 2001; Maley 1987; Martin and Veel (eds.) 1998; McDonald 1994; McEnery and Amselom Kifle 2002; Nash 1990; Römer 2005; Thompson 2001; Ventola and Mauranen 1996.

Popular science

Gunnarson 1993; Luzon Marco 1999; Macdonald 2005; Master 1991; Nwogu 1991.

Letters

Besnier 1989; Bhatia 1993; Connor and Upton 2003; Crossley 2007; Ding 2007; Flowerdew and Wan 2006; Ghadessy 1993b; Henry and Roseberry 2001; Magnet and Carnet 2006; Okamura and Shaw 2000; Pinto dos Santos 2002; Precht 1998; Upton 2002; Vergaro 2004, 2005; Yeung 2007; Yunxia 2000; Zhu 2005.

Written media and professional registers

Adam Smith 1984; Badger 2003; Bargiela-Chiappini (ed.) 1999; Bazerman 1984; Bazerman and Paradis (eds.) 1991; Berkentotter and Huckin 1995; Bhatia 1997; Biber 2003; Bondi and Camiciotti 1995; Carolin and Selzer 1985; Carter 1988; Channell 1990; Connor-Linton 1988; Danet 1980; Donohue 2006; Eggins, Wignell, and Martin 1993; Fowler 1991; Fuertes-Olivera 2007; Ghadessy 1988a,b, 1993a; Gustafson 1984; Halliday 1988; Harris 1997; Harvey 1992, 1995; Henderson, Dudley-Evans, and Backhouse 1993; Hiltunen 1984, 1990; Hundt and Mair 1999; Kong 2006; Lemke 1990; Mann and Thompson (eds.) 1992; Mauranen 1993; McKenna 1997; Mellinkoff 1963; Mungra 2007; Myers 1991, 1992; Nelson 2006; O'Barr 1982; Porcelli 1999; Salager 1983; Samuels (ed.) 1990; Smith 1985; Thompson 1996; Van Dijk 1988; Yeung 2007; Zhu 2004.

Fiction and other written registers

Bhatia 2005; Biber 1987; Biber, Connor, and Upton 2007; Biber and Finegan 1989a,b, 1992; Biber, Johanson, Leech, Conrad, and Finegan 1999; Bondi 1997; Caballero 2003; Connor-Linton 2001; Coulthard 1994; del-Teso Craviotto 2006b; Henry and Roseberry 1997; Odell and Goswami (eds.) 1985; Reichman-Adar 1984; Semino and Short 2004; Thompson and Sealey 2007; Tony 1996; Webber 1994; Wells 1960.

III. *Spoken and written registers (see also Multidimensional analysis studies; VI below)*

Study	Genre/register	Features under investigation	Approach and methods	Major findings/issues
Bell 1991	Newspaper, radio, and other media registers	Phonological variables, advertisements, narratives, headlines	Quantitative, variationist, application of accommodation and audience-design theory	Newscasters shift their style according to the type of audience of the particular radio station. Similarly, news outlets (and copyeditors) apply rules of standardization (e.g., determiner deletion) to varying degrees depending on the audience of the media (audience design). Other media registers are often characterized by referee design, a rhetorical strategy by which speakers use resources typical of their speech community, such as jokes, anecdotes, narratives, etc.
Biber 2006a	Spoken and written university registers	Various lexical and syntactic features; lexical bundles; vocabulary patterns	Quantitative, multidimensional analysis; quantitative analyses of language use	This book presents comprehensive analyses of a wide range of linguistic features in university registers. The study is based on analysis of a large corpus that includes both spoken registers (e.g., university lectures, office hours, service encounters) and written registers (e.g., textbooks, course syllabi). Linguistic descriptions address: (1) variation in vocabulary patterns in textbooks and classroom teaching, (2) variation in the use of grammatical features, (3) variation in the use of lexical bundles (i.e., multi-word sequences), (4) the expression of stance, and (5) linguistic dimensions of variation.

(*cont.*)

III. (*cont.*)

Study	Genre/register	Features under investigation	Approach and methods	Major findings/issues
Biber, Conrad, and Cortes 2004	University lectures, textbooks, conversation, academic prose	Multi-word sequences (i.e., lexical bundles)	Quantitative, corpus-based analysis of cross-register comparison	University lectures use twice as many "lexical bundles" than conversation and four times as many bundles as textbooks. The discourse functions of lexical bundles in these registers also differ considerably. For example, lectures use more discourse-organizing bundles than conversation, but at the same time they use more referential bundles than academic prose. Lectures favor stance bundles, while textbooks favor referential bundles.
Biber and Finegan (eds.) 1994a	Various spoken and written registers from a variety of languages (English, Tok Pisin, Somali, Korean)	Various lexical, syntactic, and discourse features.	Quantitative, multidimensional analysis; qualitative	This introduction to the sociolinguistic study of register includes a wide range of registers in different languages, including coaching (Heath and Langman), personal ads (Bruthiaux), and sports commentary in Tok Pisin (Romaine). Other chapters adopt MD analysis to explore register variation in Somali (Biber and Hared) and Korean (Kim and Biber). The book also includes methodological chapters introducing an analytical framework for register analysis (Biber), theoretical chapters situating the register approach within sociolinguistic theory (Finegan and Biber) and a review of literature on register variation up to the year 1992 (Atkinson and Biber).
Biber, Johanson, Leech, Conrad, and Finegan 1999	Conversation, fiction, newspaper writing, academic prose	A comprehensive survey of grammatical and lexico-grammatical features of English	Quantitative, corpus-based analysis; cross-register comparisons	Based on a large, representative corpus of spoken and written British and American English, this reference grammar presents a comprehensive description of the grammatical and lexico-grammatical features of English. The use of each linguistic feature is compared across the four registers represented in the corpus (conversation, news, academic prose, and fiction), showing how language use varies

				dramatically according to register. The grammar also includes the most comprehensive grammatical description of naturally occurring conversation to date. The book includes a chapter devoted exclusively to conversation, which offers a thorough description of its situational characteristics, and then presents descriptions of the special lexical, syntactic, and discourse-pragmatic features found in conversation, such as discourse markers, ellipsis, tags, pauses, utterance-launchers, innovative quotative verbs, etc.
Swales 2004	Spoken and written academic genres	Moves, style, rhetorical and linguistic features	Genre analysis; critical discourse analysis, cross-disciplinary comparison	This book describes the structural and rhetorical characteristics of select written registers (i.e., research articles and PhD dissertations) as well as little-studied spoken academic research registers, such as the PhD defenses, research-group meetings, colloquia and paper conference presentations. For each, the book discusses the situational characteristics, communicative purpose(s), structure, and select rhetorical and linguistic features.

IV. *Historical registers/genres*

Study	Genre/register	Features under investigation	Approach and methods	Major findings/issues
Atkinson 1999	Scientific prose	Lexico-grammatical, rhetorical features	Rhetorical analysis; multidimensional analysis; diachronic comparison	Linguistic and rhetorical analyses of the *Philosophical Transactions of the Royal Society of London* over a period of 300 years (1675–1975) show a gradual decline of author-centered rhetoric in favor of a more object-centered rhetoric. A decline of narrative elements was matched by an increase in abstract/passivized language, contributing to the development of a more informational style.
Culpeper and Kytö (forthcoming)	Historical speech-based interactive registers	Various lexico-grammatical features and pragmatic features	Corpus-based analysis; pragmatic features	Investigates the linguistic nature of spoken interaction in the 17th and 18th centuries as represented by written records, such as court transcripts, depositions, drama, etc.
Fitzmaurice 2002a	Early-modern English familiar letter	Deixis, politeness, intersubjectivity	Pragmatic	Early-modern English epistolary writing shares many characteristics with face-to-face conversation: in both, meaning is produced interactively, thus generating meanings that are inter-subjective, rather than subjective. This characteristic can generate miscommunication and conflict.
Gross, Harmon, and Reidy 2002	Scientific article	Argumentative practices (style, presentation, argument)	Rhetorical, diachronic	Analysis of scientific prose over a period of 300 years (1665–1995) shows an evolution in the direction of representation of science as an "objective enterprise," and an increased use of stylistic and presentational devices designed to achieve more efficient communication and more effective arguments, including the use of visual representations.

Nevala 2004	Early-modern English personal letter	Forms of address and terms of reference	Quantitative, pragmatic, politeness theory; audience-design theory	In Early-Modern English (late 16th century) personal letters, the choice of positive or negative politeness forms is influenced mostly by the social status of the addressee or referent: when social status is high, it overrides social distance. Terms of reference are generally derived and selected from the repertoire of direct-address formulae used by writer or addressees to refer to the referent.
Salager-Meyer 1999	Research article	References (e.g., quotation)	Diachronic, social-constructionist theory	Analysis of medical research articles over almost two centuries (1810–1995) shows an evolutionary trend in referential behavior, with different reference patterns typical of the 19th century (e.g. verbatim quotation, general and specific reference) versus 20th century (e.g., footnotes, end-lists).
Taavitsainen and Pahta (eds.) 2004	Various: registers of medical writing (e.g., recipes, treatises)	Various, including vocabulary, intertextuality, vernacularization, scriptorial styles	Quantitative, descriptive, corpus-based	The chapters in this collection explore a wide range of key issues in late medieval medical writing, including the use of classical discourse conventions, the role of scriptorial styles, code-switching, and new vocabulary. The studies – many of which are based on the *Corpus of Middle English Medical Texts* – also explore various subregisters of medical writing, including learned treatises, surgical treatises, astrological treatises, and recipes.
Vande Kopple 1998	Physics research article	Relative clauses	Rhetorical, quantitative, systemic functional linguistics	The comparison of relative clauses in spectroscopic research articles from the *Physical Review* from two different historical periods (1893–1901 and 1980) reveals a decrease in clausal complexity matched by an increase in lexical complexity. This shift reflects a stylistic shift, from a "dynamic" style reflecting processes and actions, to a "synoptic" style, which reflects structures, categories, and hierarchies.

Other studies of historical registers

Archer 2002, 2006; Atkinson 1992, 1996; Bergs 2004; Biber 2004a, 2004b; Biber and Burges 2000; Biber and Clark 2002; Biber and Finegan 1989a, 1992; Biber, Finegan, and Atkinson 1994; Bugaj 2006; Claridge 2005; Collins 2006; Culpeper and Kytö 1999, 2000; Doty and Hiltunen 2002; Fitzmaurice 2002b,c, 2003; Fitzmaurice and Taavitsainen (eds.) 2007; Fludernik 2000; Fritz 2001; Geisler 2002; Gotti 1996; Gunnarsson 1993; Hundt and Mair 1999; Kahlas-Tarkka and Rissanen 2007; Kryk-Kastovsky 2000, 2006; Kytö 1991; Kytö and Walker 2003; Kytö, Rydén, and Smitterberg 2006; Leech, Hundt, Mair, and Smith (forthcoming); Leech and Smith 2006; Mair 2006; Mäkinen 2002; Salager-Meyer, Alcalaz Ariza, and Zambrano 2003; Salager-Meyer and Zambrano 2001; Studer 2003; Taavitsainen 2001; Taavitsainen and Pahta 2000.

V. *Special registers*

Study	Genre/register	Features under investigation	Approach and methods	Major findings/issues
Bruthiaux 1996	Newspaper classified advertising	Features of syntactic elaboration (e.g., definite articles, pronouns, modals, relativization, etc.), conventionalization (e.g., idioms, collocations), and functional variation	Quantitative; corpus-based	Different types of newspaper classified ads (e.g., auto ads, job ads) are characterized by different levels of syntactic elaboration. For example, auto and apartment ads lack a recognizable syntactic structure, consisting mostly of a series of content words. Job ads are more extensively elaborated than apartment and job ads. Personal ads are characterized by many abbreviations and a high level of creativity in lexical compounding. Different subregisters are also characterized by different levels of conventionalization. For example, auto ads are the most collocationally rigid, while apartment and job ads display a greater degree of variation; personal ads predominantly follow an active pattern of information sequencing.
Crystal 2001	Internet registers: e-mail, chatgroups, virtual worlds, and the WWW	Structural, lexical, grammatical, etc.	Descriptive	Describes common characteristics of internet registers (e.g., compounding, abbreviations, use of lower case, peculiar spelling conventions, minimal punctuation, use of symbols of programming languages), as well as situational, structural, and linguistic features of internet subregisters. For example, some distinctive features of e-mail are screen structure, message openings and closings, message length, dialogic features, and "framing" (i.e., cutting and pasting from an original message). Chatgroup messages tend to be short, are often introduced with an explicit reference to a previous posting, and in general are characterized by several features typical of face-to-face conversation.

(*cont.*)

V. (*cont.*)

Study	Genre/register	Features under investigation	Approach and methods	Major findings/issues
Ferguson 1983	Radio sports commentary ("Sports announcer talk")	Syntactic and lexical features (e.g., simplification, inversions, modifiers)	Descriptive	The language of radio sports commentary is characterized by several syntactic and lexical features which reflect the situational constraints of the register. These include: simplification through deletion of sentence-initial material, inversions, use of result expressions, use of heavy modifiers, tense usage, and routines (e.g., giving the count). These features are identified as markers of Sports Announcer Talk (SAT).
Fox, Butakto, Hallahan, and Crawford 2007	Computer-based Instant Messaging (IM)	Various lexico-grammatical, pragmatic, textual and thematic features	Descriptive	Examines sex-based differences in the use of a wide range of features associated with "expressive" (e.g., emoticons, textual representations of emphasis, compliments, expletives, tag questions) and "dominant" (e.g., insults, expletives) styles in the IM conversations of 35 undergraduate students. Factor analyses revealed that, like in face-to-face conversation and other on-line contexts, women are more "expressive" than men in IM.
Gains 1999	E-mail (academic and commercial)	Structural, stylistic, and textual features	Comparison of intra-register variation	Commercial e-mails do not significantly differ from commercial traditional letters in terms of structural and textual features, and thus they do not constitute a new genre. In contrast, academic e-mails present more variability in many respects, including expressions used in openings and closings, stylistic features (formality), and use of conversational features.

Reference	Register/variety	Features	Methodology	Description
Herring (ed.) 1996	Various internet-based and computer-mediated-communication (CMC) registers	Various linguistic, cultural, and social features	Various: descriptive, quantitative, MD analysis, corpus-based, systemic functional linguistics, genre analysis	This edited collection includes 14 chapters examining a range of internet-based and CMC registers, from linguistic, social, ethical and cross-cultural perspectives. For example, Collot and Belmore use MD analysis to identify distinctive characteristics of electronic bulletin board systems (BBSs). Yates examines variation in the use of textual (e.g., type/token ratio, lexical density), interpersonal (e.g., modal auxiliaries), and ideational features (e.g., personal pronouns) in a corpus of computer conferencing systems (CCSs). Chapters by Werry and Condon and Čech compare registers of synchronous communication with face-to-face conversation. Herring examines the relationship between gender of the writer, and frequency of posting and structure of electronic list serve messages.
Herring and Paolillo 2006	Weblogs (blogs)	Style, gender-linked features (e.g., pronouns, determiners, quantifiers, etc.)	Quantitative, intra-register variation	Two major types of weblogs are distinguished: diary (personal journals) and filter (reports of events external to the blogger's life). These differ in terms of their relative use of gender-linked features. Diaries use more female-linked features, such as first person pronouns; filters use more male-linked features, such as third-person pronouns, determiners, etc.
Janda 1985	Note-taking	Grammatical and lexical characteristics of notes	Descriptive, quantitative	University student notes on lectures are characterized by various features typical of simplified registers (e.g., omission of copula and most function words), as well as features unique to note-taking, such as omission of phrases, nominalizations, passivization, replacement of relative clauses with participials.

(*cont.*)

V. (*cont.*)

Study	Genre/register	Features under investigation	Approach and methods	Major findings/issues
Reaser 2003	Radio and TV sports commentary	Grammatical and lexical features of sports announcer talk (SAT)	Quantitative, corpus-based analysis of intra-register variation	Radio and TV basketball sports commentary differ in their relative use of various SAT features. For example, subject deletion occurs more than twice as often in radio as in TV broadcasts. The two subregisters are also characterized by functional differences which reflect different communication situations. For example, subject deletion is highly functional in radio broadcasts (reflecting different roles of the speakers) but symbolic in TV broadcasts.
del-Teso-Craviotto 2006a	Dating chats	Salient features of language of sexuality on chat	Conversation analysis, ethnographic (participant observation)	Dating chats are characterized by the use of playful discourse strategies, such as use of alter personae, laughter, emoticons, and humorous reproductions of pronunciations. Such practices play important interactional functions, such as allowing participants to flirt and manifest sexual desire while saving face.
Thurlow 2003	Mobile phone Instant/Text Messaging (IM)	Message length, themes (topics), innovative linguistic features (e.g., shortenings, contractions, non-conventional spellings)	Descriptive, quantitative, content analysis	Examines various textual and functional (thematic) characteristics of over 500 IMs written by 144 undergraduate students. IMs tend to be remarkably brief (c. 14 words) and make extensive use of a wide range of non-standard features, such as shortenings, contractions, "clippings" (i.e., dropping of g-endings, as in *goin* for *going*), acronyms, initialisms (e.g., LOL for "laughing out loud" or "lots of love"), letter/number homophones (i.e., U for "you"), misspellings, typos, non-conventional spellings (e.g., *nite* for "night"), and accent stylization (e.g., *da* or *de* for "the"). Youths use IMs mostly for friendship maintenance, salutory, informational-practical and practical arrangement functions.

Other studies of special registers

Adams and Winter 1997; Bowcher 2003; Bruthiaux 1994, 2005; de la Cruz Cabanillas *et al.* 2007; Edwards 2006; Fuertes-Olivera *et al.* 2001; Ghadessy 1988b; Gibbon 1981, 1985; Gimenez 2000; Hamilton 1998; Henzl 1974, 1979; Hoyle 1989; Hundt, Nesselhauf, and Biewer 2007; Johnson 1995; Karne and Winter 1997; Kline 2005; Koenraad and Haggo 1984; Koenraad and Tillis 1986; Kuo 2003; Lassen 2006; Leech 1966; Mardh 1980; Marley 2002; Montgomery 1988; Morrow 2006; Murray 1985; Myers 1999; Newman 2005; Oh 2001; Thornborrow 2001; Thornborrow and Morris 2004; van Mulken and van der Meer 2005; Zak and Dudley-Evans 1986; Zwicky and Zwicky 1980.

VI. *Multidimensional analysis studies*

Study	Genre/register	Features under investigation	Approach and methods	Major findings/issues
Biber 1988	23 spoken and written registers	67 different lexical and grammatical features	Quantitative, multidimensional analysis	Using a corpus of spoken and written English registers, this study identified six basic dimensions of linguistic variation. The analysis is also extended to subregisters, showing that they account for a considerable amount of the variation existing within the major register categories. For example, the seven subregisters of academic prose (e.g., mathematics, humanities, social science, etc.) are quite different from one another on all six dimensions.
Biber 1995	Various spoken and written registers in four languages	Numerous lexical and grammatical features	Quantitative, multidimensional analysis; cross-linguistic analysis	This book extends the model of multidimensional analysis presented in Biber 1988 to three additional, typologically different languages: Korean, Somali, and Nukulaelae Tuvuluan. The analyses revealed striking similarities in the patterns of register variation among these languages. These patterns hold at several different levels: for the co-occurrence of linguistic features which identify the underlying dimensions, for the synchronic and diachronic relations among registers, and for the linguistically defined text types. Such cross-linguistic similarities provide an empirically grounded basis for the hypothesis of the existence of cross-linguistic universals governing the patterns of discourse variation across registers and text-types.
Conrad and Biber (eds.) 2001	Various: historical and contemporary registers, e.g., scientific prose, TV series	Numerous lexical and grammatical features	Quantitative, multidimensional (MD) analysis	This edited collection presents an introduction to the methodology of MD analysis, as well as ten chapters illustrating the application of MD analysis to a wide variety of spoken and written registers, including diachronic variation (Atkinson; Biber and Finegan), specialized domains and subregisters (Connor-Linton; Conrad; Biber and Finegan), and dialect and social variation (Rey; Biber and Burges; Helt).

Other MD studies

Atkinson 1992, 1996; Besnier 1988; Biber 1986, 1987, 1991, 1992, 2006, 2008; Biber, Connor, and Upton 2007; Biber, Conrad, Reppen, Byrd, and Helt 2002; Biber and Finegan 1994b,c; Biber and Hared 1992, 1994; Biber and Jones 2005; Collot and Belmore 1996; Crossley and Louwerse 2007; Kim and Biber 1994; Lamb 2008; Parodi 2005, 2007; Reppen 2001; Rey 2001.

Appendix B Activity texts

Text 1. Novel 1, L. P. Hartley, *The Go-Between*, 1953

The last weeks of the Easter term were the happiest of my schooldays so far, and the holidays were irradiated by them. For the first time I felt that I was someone. But when I tried to explain my improved status to my mother she was puzzled. Success in work she would have understood (and happily I was able to report this also) or success in games (of this I could not boast, but I had hopes of the cricket season). But to be revered as a magician! She gave me a soft, indulgent smile and almost shook her head. In a way she was religious: she had brought me up to think about being good, and to say my prayers, which I always did, for our code permitted it as long as it was done in a perfunctory manner: soliciting divine aid did not count as sneaking. Perhaps she would have understood what it meant to me to be singled out among my fellows if I could have told her the whole story: but I had to edit and bowdlerize it to such a degree that very little of the original was left; and least of all the intoxicating transition from a trough of persecution to a pedestal of power. A few of the boys had been a little unkind, now they were all very kind. Because of something I had written in my diary which was rather like a prayer, the unkind boys had hurt themselves and of course I couldn't help being glad about it. "But ought you to have been glad?" she asked anxiously. "I think you ought to have been sorry, even if they were a little unkind. Did they hurt themselves badly?" "Rather badly," I said, "but you see they were my enemies." But she refused to share my triumph and said uneasily, "But you oughtn't to have enemies at your age." In those days a widow was still a figure of desolation; my mother felt the responsibility of bringing me up, and thought that firmness should come into it, but she never quite knew when or how to apply it. "Well, you must be nice to them when they come back," she sighed; "I expect they didn't mean to be unkind."

Text 2. Novel 2, Lynne Reid Banks, *The L-Shaped Room*, 1960

I felt cold shiver after cold shiver pass through me as I read this letter. It wasn't until it came that I realized how badly I had wanted him to try and make contact with me; and now he had, my disappointment was so acute at the cold formality of his manner that all my past dislike of him, my resentment of his patronage, returned full-force. "My responsibility." Yes, that was just what he would say. Not a word of warmth or welcome or affection, or even forgiveness. Anger would have been easier to bear than this stiffly-extended hand of duty, held out grudgingly under the banner of "Blood is Thicker than Water".

I screwed the letter up and shed hot, angry tears on it. Go back! I would see him in hell first. But my bitterly-phrased thoughts brought no relief, only renewed tears of guilt for which I refused to seek a cause. I threw the letter into the waste-paper basket. But that night when I came home from work I recovered it. I smoothed it out, and without re-reading, I put it into my suitcase with the Alsatians and told myself to forget it.

It hurt for a while, then stopped. I thought how quickly and easily all the ties of one life could be broken and those of a new one built up . . . It was sad to reflect that the new friends were probably just as transitory, and the links with them just as fragile. This thought was, at that time, the nearest I let myself get to the monstrous pit of insecurity which I could sense lurking just under the surface of the fool's paradise of respite I was letting myself bask in.

Text 3. Novel 3, Doris Lessing, *The Good Terrorist*, 1985

It was getting dark when Alice woke. She heard Bert's laugh, a deep ho, ho, ho, from the kitchen. That's not his own laugh, Alice thought. I wonder what that would be like? Tee hee hee more likely. No, he made that laugh up for himself. Reliable and comfortable. Manly. Voices and laughs, we make them up Roberta's made-up voice, comfortable. And that was Pat's quick light voice and her laugh. Her own laugh? Perhaps. So they were both back and that meant that Jasper was too. Alice was out of her sleeping bag, and tugging on a sweater, a smile on her face that went with her feelings for Jasper: admiration and wistful love.

But Jasper was not in the kitchen with the other two, who were glowing, happy, fulfilled, and eating fish and chips.

"It's all right, Alice," said Pat, pulling out a chair for her. "They arrested him, but it's not serious. He'll be in court tomorrow morning at Enfield. Back here by lunchtime."

"Unless he's bound over?" asked Bert.

"He was bound over for two years in Leeds, but that ended last month."

"Last month?" said Pat. Her eyes met Bert's, found no reflection there of what she was thinking – probably against her will, Alice believed; and, so as not to meet Alice's, lowered themselves to the business of eating one golden crisp fatty chip after another. This was not the first time Alice had caught suggestions that Jasper liked being bound over – needed the edge it put on life.

Text 4. Newspaper Report 1

The Court of Appeal allowed an appeal by the appellant, who was not named as a party to the action, against an order that he was liable to pay £861 with costs.

The plaintiff claimed damages of £2,000 for wrongful dismissal in 1983 from his employment as a community worker at the Islington Asian Centre.

The only defendant named was sued as "General Secretary of the Management Committee of the Islington Asian Centre, sued on his own behalf and on behalf of the members of the management committee". The centre was an unincorporated association run by its management committee.

In 1986 the plaintiff was awarded damages. The judge found that six members of the management committee, including the appellant and the defendant, resolved to dismiss the plaintiff.

In 1988 the plaintiff applied for a charging order on the defendant's house in respect of damages, interest and costs. The defendant applied for an order that the five other members of the management committee, including the appellant, be joined under Order 5, rule 5 as persons responsible to pay damages and costs to the plaintiff.

[LSWE Corpus]

Text 5. Newspaper Report 2

IN THE words of defence counsel James Hunt QC, the trial of Allitt at Nottingham Crown Court has been "unprecedented and without equal", not least due to the defendant's absence for much of the three-month hearing.

When arrested, Allitt weighed 13 stone, but in the following months she became anorexic, refusing to eat, and her weight plunged to around seven stone.

Three weeks after her trial began on February 15 this year, she collapsed, and from then the dock remained empty. The jury only heard her voice once when the prosecution played a tape-recorded interview with police, in which she protested her innocence.

The trial continued without her after the judge, Mr Justice Latham, was satisfied that was her wish and she was capable of instructing her lawyers.

Doctors at Rampton top security hospital said moving her could have a detrimental effect on her health.

But after Mr Hunt assured them Allitt did not want to give evidence, the trial continued. Mr Hunt went to Rampton each week to brief his client and receive further instructions.

Because Allitt opted not to go into the witness box, the defence case lasted just two-and-a-half days against the prosecution case of two-and-a-half months, at a likely cost of about £1.5 million.

[LSWE Corpus]

Text 6. Newspaper Report 3

THE new governor of the Bank of England will take a five-year pay freeze as a "personal statement" of his commitment to controlling inflation, it was announced yesterday.

Eddie George, known in the City as "Steady Eddie", who succeeds Robin Leigh-Pemberton in July, will receive more than £200,000 a year. The exact figure remains undisclosed, but will be the same as Mr Leigh-Pemberton's pay over the past year. The bank pointed out that it was "somewhat less" than £230,000 reported in yesterday's *The Independent* newspaper.

Full details of Mr George's salary are expected to be included in the bank's annual report published on May 26. The last published pay figure for a governor of the Bank of England was £198,546 to Mr Leigh-Pemberton for the year ending February 28, 1992.

The current governor ran into a storm when it was revealed he had received a 17% pay increase in 1991. It later emerged that he had waived about £34,000 of his £198,000 salary in response to the row.

The governor's pay is set by the bank's remuneration committee of external directors. A salary of between £200,000 and £230,000 would put Mr George at the top of the Civil Service pay tree and on a par with senior City bankers.

Mr George has a reputation as a hawk on inflation and his move yesterday will reinforce his credentials.

[LSWE Corpus]

Text 7. Conversation, A family in the car, on the way to school

Child 1:   Can I go in the front?

Mother: Fasten your belt up please. Fasten your belt up. – Okay, speedily – now

Child 2:   Oh crash, bang, wallop you're a –

Mother: can you er zip your zips up please? Keira. Can you zip your zip up?

Child 2:   I can't.

[pause]

Mother: What do you think you'll be doing at school today?

Child 2:   Recorder concert!

Mother: Oh! Have you got your recorder? In school?

Child 2:   No! Er, yes, yes

Mother: Yeah.

Child 2:   yes.

Mother: Now, what you gonna be playing?

Child 2:   Joe Joe stubbed his toe. Joe Joe stubbed his toe.

Mother: Oh!

Child 2:   And erm . . . the skateboard ride.

Mother:	<crunches gears> Ooh! That gear. Keeps changing with the
Child 2:	Mummy. You know what I've –
Mother:	Skateboard ride?
Child 2:	you know what, that I –
Mother:	What's that one?
Child 2:	ca= just can play that, I couldn't do recorders that well?
Mother:	Yes.
Child 2:	Well now erm, I'm really good at it.
Mother:	Can you do all the musical notes?
Child 2:	Yeah.

[LSWE Corpus]

Text 8. Conversation, Two friends talking in a café

Sally:	I've just explained that to him. And he said he didn't know that, that he would get hold of Sen and ring me first thing, thing in the morning – er, to tell me why Sen hasn't paid. He's got the invoice and everything. I said well you've sent us twenty thou= – I said there is no tax on it, which there should be! He says Has he got the invoice? I said yes. And I said, we've had the invoice since October for two and a half thousand dollars! I said, you actually owe me six thousand, one hundred and something! And I said, you have to realize I've got a small company, and that's – in one way I've had to set those conditions because you're failing to meet the thirty day payment!
Paul:	Yeah.
Sally:	And I said it's not on! I said we couldn't survive like that. And he said, well would you like to go on with the contract? I said we're too far committed now to, I say, to back out. I said, you know, we can't back out at this stage. And I said, but I said if there aren't payments of invoices when they are sent – then – you know, we've go= you've gotta look at it. So that invoice needs –
Paul:	Doing. Yeah.
Sally:	it needs doing and sending, and put in – I put twenty eight days on it.
Paul:	Yeah.

[LSWE Corpus]

Text 9. Conversation, Colleagues at work

| John: | I, I want to talk to you about er the conversation I had with Alec yesterday – he seems to be inundated with having to get details about his project on his er, all his paperwork and so on, and he seems to be inundated and he sounded a bit low, quite frankly, to |

me yesterday on the phone that he was getting inundated with all this

Sam: Mm, mm

John: work. I said I'm quite sure there must be something that could be done computer-wise

Sam: Right

John: but he sort of pooh-poohed it and sort of said well you know, we're getting a bit too old for all this modern sophistication of computers and so on, well I said well actually I am not totally in agreement with you, because as you probably know Clyde was looking into a program which will could alleviate a lot

Sam: Yes I know, I know

John: of the work, that I do, but I

Sam: yes it's on the –

John: would tell you right here and now, er I'm still retaining my bible – you know the book

Sam: Yeah, yes, yes

John: that I have downstairs, because it's, if it was to be computerized, it would be a massive great bloody great volume

Sam: Yes

John: and I would be carrying this around and it just wouldn't be feasible

Sam: yeah, right

John: so he said that apparently whenever he came back to B S H he was told by Neville roughly about eighteen hundred acres would be sort of his target

Sam: Target, right

John: and it's, it's multiplied by about three or four times that you see

Sam: Oh right, right, right

John: so consequently he's getting inundated, he really is apparently under pressure

Sam: Mm, mm, right

[LSWE Corpus]

Text 10. Classroom Teaching, American university first-year English composition class

Instructor: What I want you to do in your free writes is kind of reflect on what do you think he means here. Maybe, and what you could answer is would you want to live in that kind of place. Would you want to live there? And if you do, Why? and do not, Why? And how does Rymmer give you clues? I think Rymmer, especially in a poet like this, he talks about this hollowness at his core, sort of the absence of the bona fide, legitimate purpose to the whole thing. I think clues like this are embedded throughout that suggest that Rymmer's pretty negative, or skeptical about this whole project, right? And what I wanna know is, if you do want to live there, why is that, and if you don't, what is it about Rymmer's writing, or Rymmer's ideas that lead you to believe that you wouldn't want to live there. So freewrite this, I just want you to get words down on paper, practice writing, that's the whole idea of this. Nothing else. The idea is to write as much as you can and continue writing just get your ideas down on paper. It's not a perfect final paper, it's a free write.

[quiet, as students free write. noise of writing on the chalkboard]
[Later in the class period]

Instructor: And basically what we're gonna concentrate on doing today is peer review for most of the time someone should get a least two readers in of your paper. And I'm also gonna come around and talk to you a little bit about your papers in groups. But, before we get started on that, I got, Robin came up to me at the end of the class on Tuesday and she mentioned, you know, it's so hard to sit here and talk about these three articles, and how hard it is to kinda talk analytically about such a sensitive topic and such a really disturbing topic. I thought, yeah, you're absolutely right. But, it is really hard talking analytically about it, and part of the reason that I brought those articles in was that, tell a little story about to get to my point here, but, I was actually, when it happened a couple of weeks ago, I was talking on the phone with my friend, and he was, and I said, "did you hear what happened?" and he said, "yeah." So we talked about how horrible it was and he said, you know, but, he goes, I got really ticked off today because I was reading this article in a paper, which sounded a lot like the third article that we read, which was trying kinda to compare what happened to a larger societal problem in our in America. And he said, I read this article and it was talking, you know, about houses indicative of this huge problem in American culture and he said, I just don't think that's warranted. You know, one of them that's very horrific, to blow that up as a huge problem. And I said, Well, you know what, I disagree with you. I said, I think that it is indicative of the problem, because maybe those horrific type things aren't happening, but a lot of subtle things are happening everyday. Such as, with the third article, do you remember when he refers to what happened to him in his childhood where he remembers that derogatory term being used towards homosexuals, as a child, and not really knowing what the word meant? not knowing that it was what is was in reference to. But the fact that it was acceptable in his childhood. I remember that as well. Kids calling other kids, I don't like to say it but, that term, right? I mean, I remember that.

[T2K-SWAL Corpus]

Text 11. Academic Writing, university student research paper in applied linguistics

The results suggest that students are satisfied with having videos as part of the process of learning Spanish. Indeed having videos in the classroom for these students is helpful in learning about various aspects of the language such as: vocabulary in context, pronunciation, different accents, and different dialects of Spanish, phrases in Spanish as well as the use of grammar in context. They also pay attention to differences in culture. As Herron *et al.* (1999) suggest, culture plays a big role in learning another language and students in this study appreciate having videos to learn about a new culture.

Also, a variety of materials for learning Spanish is important for the students. They are gratified to hear other native speakers other than the instructor. Videos are a new type of authentic material that students think is fun, different from the traditional methods of teaching. As Bada & Okan (2000) state, it improves learning to incorporate various types of materials in the classroom that enhance students' interest in learning another language. The students of this study concur.

Although the majority of students like to watch videos, some expressed negative attitudes. These comments are relevant because before doing the study, as an instructor I did not realize these drawbacks until the students mentioned them. For example, they found the videos too fast, and not directly related to what they were learning. Another misconception I had before this study was the use of subtitles; I thought that having both English and Spanish subtitles was helpful. Contrarily, students reported they were distracted by English subtitles, they prefer only Spanish ones. As Bada & Okan (2000) suggests, it is necessary to incorporate what students want in order to make decisions about effective teaching.

In relation to learning through videos, most of the students corroborated that they learn vocabulary, phrases in real life contexts, and pronunciation. Also for visual learners, videos represent an appropriate material for learning Spanish, aspect that I did not consider beforehand. These results imply that students benefit from these videos because they learn from them about language itself and about the target culture. This finding is similar to what Xiao (2006) claims: videos are a powerful resource for students in learning vocabulary, pronunciation and culture.

Students also were asked whether they had expectations before they watched these videos: some of them said yes, and most of these related to having fun, seeing real life situations, and watching videos for lower levels. As the results suggest, I conclude that students do have fun watching videos. Therefore, these videos are pleasant for them to keep learning Spanish. Students expect to learn about culture, and since in these videos, culture plays an important role, they also learn about cultural aspects.

Finally, students were asked whether there were ways to improve the use of videos. Students made very useful suggestions, which I as teacher thought I was dealing with somehow. They suggested that subtitles definitely help them to comprehend better, although they were divided on this point. Some found the subtitles in English and Spanish helpful, but others found them distracting. I think this mixed response may be due to individual learning styles. I also learned that students prefer to watch the videos twice to better understand what is happening. This suggestion is definitely helpful because I could have done better in trying to focus on specific aspects of the videos and relate them to what we were studying. Finally, students asked for a summary of what happened in the videos after they watched them, in this way to corroborate what they saw. These general comments are significant for me as an instructor to make improvements in the way I teach. Also other teachers could benefit from this research too. They might evaluate whether they use videos effectively in their classroom and how students perceive them.

[Portland State University Corpus of Student Academic Writing]

Text 12. Historical drama, Samuel Beazley, *The Steward: or, Fashion and Feeling*, 1819

<Act II>
  <An Apartment at Mrs. Penfold's.>

LENNOX.	But my good Mrs. Penfold, do tell me who this divine creature is.
MRS. PENFOLD.	That's more, Mr. Lennox, than I can tell.
LENNOX.	But, how came she under your care?
MRS. PENFOLD.	That's more than I dare tell: And, I can assure you, I shall get into a pretty scrape, if it was known that you had even seen her.
LENNOX.	But that, you know, you could not help, since I caught a glimpse of her at the window; what is more, I have often seen, and often followed her, but could never before make out where she lived; little did I think she was a protégé of my good old nurse's.
MRS. PENFOLD.	Yes, yes, your good old nurse might have waited long enough for a visit, if you had not seen a young girl at her window.
LENNOX.	Well, well, I am sorry you won't let me see her; you are right, I dare say. But I am wrong to neglect one, to whom I owe so much as to my good nurse, Penfold; and I shall therefore redeem my character by visiting you much oftener than I have done. – <(Aside.)> Now to write to Mordent, that I have discovered my incognita, and make him assist me, in getting her into my power. He is under too many obligations to me to refuse – So farewell, Mrs. Penfold. <Exit.>

MRS. PENFOLD.   Ah, ah, master Lennox, you're a sly one tho' I nursed you myself, and I fear my cousin Item would stand little chance by your side. But, what can have come to my old avaricious relation, who, till now, has ever made money his god. Here he commissions me to praise him to her, and inspire her with favourable sentiments of him. There's some mystery in all this, which I cannot fathom. Ah! she comes.

<Enter Joanna.>

Well; my sweet Joanna – but why so melancholy? I left you, just now, all life and spirits.

JOANNA.   True, madam; nature has blest me with spirits to smile in the face of misfortune; yet, sometimes, the bitter remembrance, that I am disowned by my father, – that there is no hope that these lips will ever meet a parent's kiss, or this head receive a parent's blessing, will call a tear into my eye, and make my smiles appear traitors to the feelings of my heart.

MRS. PENFOLD.   Come, come; forget such unpleasant thoughts what should you care for one, who never cared for you?

[ARCHER Corpus]

Text 13. Contemporary drama, Simon Gray, *Otherwise Engaged*, 1975

<Stephen enters through the kitchen>

STEPHEN.   Si ... <Wood turns to look at him> Oh, sorry, I didn't real-ize ... <(He recognizes Wood and comes further into the room)> Good God, it is, isn't it? Old Strapley, from Wun-dale?

WOOD.   The name's Wood.

STEPHEN.   Oh, sorry. You look rather like a chap who used to be at school with us, or rather me, in my year, Strapley.

WOOD.   Really? What sort of chap was he?

STEPHEN.   Oh actually, a bit of what we used to call a plop, wasn't he, Simon? So you're quite lucky not to be Strapley who almost certainly had a pretty rotten future before him. <(He laughs)>

WOOD.   <(to Simon)> Thank you for the sherry.

<Wood turns quickly and goes out, closing the door and the front door>

SIMON.   Not at all.

STEPHEN.   I hope I haven't driven him off.

SIMON.   Mmmm. Oh no, it's not you that's driven him off. <(He picks up Wood's glass and puts it on the drinks table)>

STEPHEN.   What did he want?

SIMON.   He was looking for somebody I once resembled. A case of mistaken identity, that's all.

STEPHEN.   Well, if he had been Strapley, he'd hardly have changed at all, except that he's a quarter of a century older.

<(He sits in the swivel chair)>

[ARCHER Corpus]

Text 14. Historical letter, 1716, Lady Montagu to Alexander Pope

Vienna, Sept. 14, O.S.

Perhaps you'll laugh at me, for thanking you very gravely for all the obliging concern you express for me. 'Tis certain that I may, if I please, take the fine things you say to me for wit and raillery, and, it may be, it would be taking them right. But I never, in my life, was half so well disposed to take you in earnest, as I am at present, and that distance which makes the continuation of your friendship improbable, has very much encreased my faith in it. I find that I have (as well as the rest of my sex) whatever face I set on't, a strong disposition to believe in miracles. Don't fancy, however, that I am infected by the air of these popish countries; I have, indeed, so far wandered from the discipline of the church of England, as to have been last Sunday at the opera, which was performed in the garden of the Favorita, and I was so much pleased with it, I have not yet repented my seeing it. Nothing of that kind ever was more magnificent; and I can easily believe, what I am told, that the decorations and habits cost the Emperor thirty thousand pounds sterling. The stage was built over a very large canal, and at the beginning of the second act, divided into two parts, discovering the water, on which there immediately came, from different parts, two fleets of little gilded vessels, that gave the representation of a naval fight. It is not easy to imagine the beauty of this scene, which I took particular notice of. But all the rest were perfectly fine in their kind. The story of the Opera is the Enchantment of Alcina, which gives opportunities for great variety of machines and changes of the scenes, which are performed with a surprizing swiftness. [...]

But if their operas are thus delightful, their comedies are, in as high a degree, ridiculous. They have but one play-house, where I had the curiosity to go to a German comedy, and was very glad it happened to be the story of Amphitrion. [...] I thought the house very low and dark; but I confess the comedy admirably recompensed that defect. I never laughed so much in my life. It begun with Jupiter's falling in love out of a peep-hole in the clouds, and ended with the birth of Hercules. [...] But I could not easily pardon the liberty the poet has taken of larding his play with, not only indecent expressions, but such gross words as I don't think our mob would suffer from a mountebank. Besides, the two Sosia's very fairly let down their breeches in the direct view of the boxes, which were full of people of the first rank that seemed very well pleased with their entertainment, and assured me this was a celebrated piece. I shall conclude my letter with this remarkable relation, very well worthy the serious consideration of Mr. Collier. I won't trouble you with farewell compliments, which I think generally as impertinent, as curtisies at leaving the room when the visit has been too long already.

[ARCHER Corpus]

Text 15. Contemporary Letter, 1989, to a best friend

How you doing? I'm here at work waiting for my appointment to get here, it's Friday. Thank goodness, but I still have tomorrow, but this week has flown by, I guess because I've been staying busy, getting ready for Christmas and everything. Have you done your Christmas shopping yet? I'm pretty proud of myself. I'm almost finished. Me and L went shopping at Sharpstown last Monday and I got a lot done, I just have a few little things to get. Thanks for the poster, I loved it, I hung it in my room last night, sometimes I feel like that's about right. Miss ya lots – T.

Text 16. Instant Messages, excerpts from IM interactions between three participant pairs

Excerpts from Nuckolls (2005)
   [Note: Lines show how the IM was laid out on the screen. A single individual can have more than one line in a row, each line sent in sequence. Participant messages can also cross paths as they are transmitted, creating interwoven topics.]

Excerpts from Pair 1, Kristy and Lisa

Kristy:	hey do u know how the screw ur roomate thing works?
Lisa:	yeah
Kristy:	you set your roomate up with someone without telling her
Lisa:	ooh
Kristy:	and fill out the sheet
<...>	
Lisa:	and when u find each other u just do whatever?
Kristy:	just go out on a date
Lisa:	guess what?
Lisa:	harry barry's roomate is trying to set me up with him
Lisa:	:–P
Kristy:	oh really?
Kristy:	already?
Lisa:	lol
Lisa:	yea
Kristy:	how do you know?
Lisa:	my roomate got an email from his roomate
Kristy:	you're not supposed to know!!

<...>
Kristy: so you've never felt like this before
Kristy: it's crazy, huh!
Kristy: hello?
Lisa: yea...
Lisa: never felt like this b4
Lisa: he's still in the airport
Lisa: in AZ though
Kristy: have you.... ....:_*
Kristy: kissed
Lisa: he wont be home for another 2 hours
Lisa: hahaha
Lisa: lol
Lisa: yes we have
Lisa: that's how we started to go out
<...>
Lisa: it was sad to leave him today
Kristy: are you in loveeeeeee??
Kristy: did you almost cry?
Lisa: TOTALLY IN LOVEE WITH HARROLD
Kristy: :–)
Kristy: awwwwwwwwwwwwwww
Lisa: i did cry actually
Kristy: oh my goodness!
<...>
Kristy: well, i am happy for you lisa
Kristy: yay!
Kristy: just focus on your studies now!
Kristy: and don't do anything stupid!
Kristy: ;–)
Lisa: yea
<...>

Excerpts from Pair 2, Jade and Marge

[Note: Marge's use of CAPS was not included in the frequency counts because she often wrote all of her messages in caps, explaining that it saved time.]

Marge: Hi Hon, up to chatting???
Jade: hi mom
<...>
Marge: Did the gal call you, Private Investigator about the accident you witnessed?
Marge: Actually, told her you'd give me a time she could call you.
Jade: I was pretty mad at zip and Robby/////////Zip went to the garage and Robby to his house.
Marge: what did they do???

Jade:	yes, and she left a message but to tell you the truth I barely remember everything now.
Marge:	NOT TO WORRY I'LL TELL HER THAT.
Jade:	they were playing rough, knocked my vase on the floor and broke it in many piesces
Marge:	HOW ARE YOU FEELING TODAY?
Marge:	OH TOOO BAD . . .
<. . .>	
Jade:	she brought coffee and a treat SMILE.
<. . .>	
Marge:	MAKES ME LAUGH TOO BUT WITH A LITTLE BITTY TEAR AT HOW SENTIMENTAL YOU ARE . . .
Jade:	LOL OH MOM

Excerpts from Pair 3, Joe and Rudy

Rudy:	hey, you there?
Joe:	wassap
<. . .>	
Joe:	you background of your gallery is white.
Rudy:	cool
Rudy:	thanks
Rudy:	alot
Joe:	those pix are great
Joe:	the ones from the pix cam are best, they are already compressed you dig.
Rudy:	huh?
Joe:	from your picture camera, rather than dv.
Rudy:	oh, the still camera (
<. . .>	
Joe:	super, now flash crashes on me.
Joe:	hope I saved.
Rudy:	ooohh\
Joe:	here, tell me what I'm doing wrong.
<. . .>	
Joe:	just make a new album . . . yeah, exactly what you're saying.
Rudy:	right
Joe:	that's what I'd do (IM)
<. . .>	
Joe:	I would go 980–1000 at the longest size, IMHO
Rudy:	doesnt look like they need to be any bigger? you think?
Rudy:	imho?
Rudy:	i might have . . .
Rudy:	ok
Rudy:	IMHO????
<. . .>	
Joe:	so you can NEVER link to it if you choose.

Rudy: i under stand explicitly
Joe: or DO, either way.
Rudy: splendid.
<...>
Rudy: I'm just WAY too busy these days.

Text 17. University course syllabus, undergraduate business course

Each chapter lists Learning Objectives that indicate what you should be able to accomplish after completing the chapter. These Learning Objectives should guide your study and sharpen your focus.

Although assigned problems are not collected, it is essential that you complete all problems before I present and discuss them in class. This enables you to use my presentation and discussion of problems as feedback to gauge how well you are individually able to apply concepts to problem format. It is preferable for you to work problems yourself incorrectly and learn from your mistake than it is to merely copy problem solutions from the board. You should study the material and attend my office hours on a chapter by chapter basis, rather than "cramming" before exams.

Although class attendance is not an explicit component of the course evaluation, successful completion of the course requires your attendance at each and every class. I frequently distribute handouts and additional information at class. If you do not attend a class at which I distribute materials, it is your responsibility to obtain those materials.

[T2K-SWAL Corpus]

Text 18. Twentieth-century fiction, E. M. Forster, *A Room with a View*, 1908

"I want so to see the Arno. The rooms the Signora promised us in her letter would have looked over the Arno. The Signora had no business to do it at all. Oh, it is a shame!"

"Any nook does for me," Miss Bartlett continued; "but it does seem hard that you shouldn't have a view."

Lucy felt that she had been selfish. "Charlotte, you mustn't spoil me: of course, you must look over the Arno, too. I meant that. The first vacant room in the front–"

——"You must have it," said Miss Bartlett, part of whose travelling expenses were paid by Lucy's mother – a piece of generosity to which she made many a tactful allusion.

"No, no. You must have it."

"I insist on it. Your mother would never forgive me, Lucy."

"She would never forgive me."

Text 19. Twentieth-century fiction, Henry Williamson, *Tarka the Otter*, 1927

She ran over the bullock's drinking-place and passed through willows to the meadow, seeking old dry grasses and mosses under the hawthorns growing by the mill-leat, and gathering them in her mouth with wool pulled from the over-arching blackberry brambles whose prickles had caught in the fleeces of sheep. She returned to the river bank and swam with her webbed hind-feet to the oak tree, climbed to the barky lip of the holt, and crawled within. Two yards inside she strewed her burden on the wood-dust, and departed by water for the dry, sand-coloured reeds of the old summer's growth which she bit off, frequently pausing to listen. After several journeys she sought trout by cruising under water along the bank, and roach which she found by stirring up the sand and stones of the shallow wherein they lurked.

Text 20. Twentieth-century fiction, Virginia Woolf, *To the Lighthouse*, 1927

Nothing happened. Nothing! Nothing! as she leant her head against Mrs Ramsay's knee. And yet, she knew knowledge and wisdom were stored in Mrs Ramsay's heart. How then, she had asked herself, did one know one thing or another thing about people, sealed as they were? Only like a bee, drawn by some sweetness or sharpness in the air intangible to touch or taste, one haunted the dome-shaped hive, ranged the wastes of the air over the countries of the world alone, and then haunted the hives with their murmurs and their stirrings; the hives which were people. Mrs Ramsay rose. Lily rose. Mrs Ramsay went. For days there hung about her, as after a dream some subtle change is felt in the person one has dreamt of, more vividly than anything she said, the sound of murmuring and, as she sat in the wicker arm-chair in the drawingroom window she wore, to Lily's eyes, an august shape; the shape of a dome.

Text 21. Twentieth-century fiction, Bharati Mukherjee, *The Middleman*, 1988

All day I sit by the lime green swimming pool, sun-screened so I won't turn black, going through my routine of isometrics while Ransome's indios hack away the virgin forests. Their hate is intoxicating. They hate gringos – from which my darkness exempts me – even more than Gutierrez. They hate in order to keep up their intensity.

I hear a litany of presidents' names, Hollywood names, Detroit names – Carter, chop, Reagan, slash, Buick, thump – bounce off the vines as machetes clear the jungle greenness.

We spoke a form of Spanish in my old Baghdad home. I always understand more than I let on.

Text 22. Eighteenth-century newspaper story (1744, *The London Gazette*)

Naples, May 26. N.S. The Accounts from Sicily are at present very favourable. The Venetian Physician who has perfumed and purified the City of Messina, and the Villages that were infected with the Plague, has published a Declaration, whereby he asserts, that all Communication may with Safety be resumed with those Places. At Reggio in Calabria, and the adjacent Villages, the Sickness daily decreases.

Florence, June 2. N.S. On the 24th, Prince Lobkowitz went from his Camp at Monte Rotondo to Tome, attended by the Generals Brown and Linden, and about Fourscore Officers, and escorted by two Companeis of Grenadiers, who remained without the Gate of the Town. He went directly to Cardinal Albani's Palace, through the continual Accalations of infinite Crouds of People who were assembled to see him pass. In the Afternoon he had an Audience of the Pope, who received him very graviously, and gave him a Sett of Beads of Lapis Lazuli, and a Gold Medal, and Medals of Gold and Silver to all his Officers, according to their Ranks. Prince Lobkowitz returned in the Evening, in the same Manner in which he who gave the most publick Marks of their Attachment to the Qyeen of Hungary, and of their Aversion to the Spaniards. [. . .]

[ARCHER Corpus]

Text 23. Twentieth-century newspaper story (1990, Associated Press)

President Bush said Monday he would nominate former Tennessee Gov. Lamar Alexander as education secretary, choosing a teachers' son with a reputation as an education reformer to take over a department recently troubled by controversy.

Bush made no mention of last week's abrupt departure of his first education secretary, Lauro Cavazos, who was forced to resign by the White House. Praise for the choice of Alexander, currently president of the University of Tennessee, was quick and widespread, suggesting there would be no lingering ill effects from the firing of Cavazos. [. . .]

Alexander, 50, left the Tennessee governor's office in 1986 after two terms and moved to Australia for six months. In 1988, he was appointed to his university post.

He said his goals, in addition to improving schools for the nation's children, will include creating better training and adult education opportunities for American workers who need new skills for the changing workplace. [. . .]

While governor, Alexander unveiled an education reform package called Better Schools that included adding a career ladder of pay raises for teachers and principals, expanding basic education curriculum, putting computers in junior high schools and hiring more math and science teachers.

In early reaction to the choice:

- Richard F. Rosser, president of the National Association of Independent Colleges and Universities, called Alexander "one of the best people in the country" in terms of background and understanding of education. [...]
- Ernest Boyer, head of The Carnegie Foundation for the Advancement of Teaching, said, "Every signal suggests that not only does he have strong commitment but a realistic sense of what the priorities should be. It seems to me that he's looked at reform more broadly. There is nothing in his past record to suggest that he'd be narrow or ideological."

[ARCHER Corpus]

Text 24. Eighteenth-century advertisements; April 11, 1772, *The Censor* (an early American newspaper in Boston)

Ad No. 1:

Frazier & Geyer

Have received in the last Ships from LONDON,

A fresh Assortment of SPRING-GOODS,

Which are now ready for Sale,

At their Store the Corner of Wing's Lane, near the Market: – Where their Wholesale Customers, and all other Shopkeepers and Traders, in Town and Country, may at any Time be supplied with all Kinds, and any Quantity, of Staple Goods, usually imported from Great Britain, on as good Terms, in every Respect, as at any Store in America.

They Would also beg Leave to acquaint <SIC: acquant> those Gentlemen and Ladies <SIC: Laides> who are pleased to favour them with their Custom in the Retail Way, that they have a genteel Assortment of Fancy Goods; which, with all other Kind of Piece Goods, will be cut at said Store, and sold at such Price as will give full Satisfaction to the Purchaser, and the smallest Favours gratefully acknowledged.

Ad No. 2:

Imported in sundry Vessels lately arrived from ENGLAND, BY

Smith & Atkinson,

And now opening at their Store in King-Street.

A LARGE and very general Assortment of Piece-Goods, suitable for the Spring-Trade, which would be equally tedious and unnecessary to enumerate here; these Goods have been purchased on the best terms, and will be sold

(By wholesale only)

At such rates as may encourage all

Traders in Town and Country as well those who usually import their goods as others to apply for such articles as may be needful to compleat their assortments, there being at all seasons at the above store, a great variety of PIECE-GOODS. – Due encouragement will be given to those who pay ready money.

N. B. Gun-Powder, English Sail Duck, Connecticut BEEF, &c. &c.

POT-ASH KETTLES, cast at Salisbury from the best mountain ore.

[ARCHER Corpus]

References

Adams, Karen L., and Anne Winter. 1997. Gang graffiti as a discourse genre. *Journal of Sociolinguistics* 1 (3): 337–360.

Ädel, Annelie, and Randi Reppen (eds.). 2008. *Corpora and discourse: the challenges of different settings*. Amsterdam: John Benjamins.

Adolphs, Svenja. 2008. *Corpus and context: investigating pragmatic functions in spoken discourse*. Amsterdam: John Benjamins.

Archer, Dawn. 2002. "Can innocent people be guilty?": a sociopragmatic analysis of examination transcripts from the Salem witchcraft trials. *Journal of Historical Pragmatics* 3 (1): 1–30.

———. 2006. (Re)initiating strategies: judges and defendants in Early Modern English courtrooms. *Journal of Historical Pragmatics* 7 (2): 181–211.

Artemeva, Natasha. 2008. Toward a unified social theory of genre learning. *Journal of Business and Technical Communication* 22 (2): 160–185.

Atifi, Hassan, and Michel Marcoccia. 2006. Television genre as an object of negation: a semio-pragmatic analysis of French political "television forums". *Journal of Pragmatics* 38: 250–268.

Atkinson, Dwight. 1992. The evolution of medical research writing from 1735 to 1985: the case of the Edinburgh Medical Journal. *Applied Linguistics* 13: 337–374.

———. 1996. The Philosophical Transactions of the Royal Society of London, 1675–1975: a sociohistorical discourse analysis. *Language in Society* 25: 333–371.

———. 1999. *Scientific discourse in sociohistorical context: the Philosophical Transactions of the Royal Society of London, 1675–1975*. Hillsdale, NJ: Lawrence Erlbaum Associates.

Badger, Richard. 2003. Legal and general: towards a genre analysis of newspaper law reports. *English for Specific Purposes* 22: 249–263.

Bamford, Julia. 1997. The role of metaphor in argumentation in economic texts: the case of the research article on stock markets. In Bussi, Bondi, and Gatta 1997.

———. 2005. Subjective or objective evaluation? Prediction in academic lectures. In Tognini-Bonelli and Camiciotti 2005, 17–30.

Barbieri, Federica. 2005. Quotative use in American English: a corpus-based, cross-register comparison. *Journal of English Linguistics* 33 (3): 222–256.

Bargiela-Chiappini, Francesca, and Catherine Nickerson (eds.). 1999. *Writing business: genres, media, and discourses*. London: Longman.

Bargiela-Chiappini, Francesca, and Sandra Harris. 1997. *Managing language: the discourse of corporate meetings*. Amsterdam and Philadelphia: John Benjamins Publishing Company.

Basso, Keith H. 1974. The ethnography of writing. In *Explorations in the ethnography of speaking*, ed. by R. Bauman and J. Sherzer, 425–432. Cambridge: Cambridge University Press.

Basturkmen, Helen. 1999. Discourse in MBA seminars: towards a description for pedagogical purposes. *English for Specific Purposes* 18 (1): 63–80.

———. 2002. Negotiating meaning in seminar-type discussion and EAP. *English for Specific Purposes* 21: 233–242.

Baxter, Scott. 2004. *Imaginary summits*. Flagstaff, AZ: Vishnu Temple Press.

Bazerman, Charles. 1984. Modern evolution of the experimental report in physics: spectroscopic articles in physical review, 1893–1980. *Social Studies of Science* 14: 163–196.

———. 1988. *Shaping written knowledge: the genre and activity of the experimental article in science*. Madison: University of Wisconsin Press.

Bazerman, Charles, and James Paradis (eds.). 1991. *Textual dynamics of the professions: historical and contemporary studies of writing in professional communities*. Madison: University of Wisconsin Press.

Bednarek, Monika. 2006. *Evaluation in media discourse: analysis of a newspaper corpus*. London: Continuum.

Bell, Allan. 1984. Language style as audience design. *Language in Society* 13: 145–204.

———. 2001. Back in style: reworking audience design. In *Style and sociolinguistic variation*, ed. by P. Eckert and J. Rickford, 139–169. Cambridge: Cambridge University Press.

Bergs, Alexander T. 2004. Letters: a new approach to text typology. *Journal of Historical Pragmatics* 5 (2): 207–227.

Berkentotter, Carol, and Thomas N. Huckin. 1995. *Genre knowledge in disciplinary communication: cognition/culture/power*. Hillsdale, NJ: Lawrence Erlbaum Associates.

Besnier, Niko. 1988. The linguistic relationships of spoken and written Nukulaelae registers. *Language* 64: 707–736.

———. 1989. Literacy and feelings: the encoding of affect in Nukulaelae letters. *Text* 9: 69–92.

Bevitori, Cinzia. 2005. Attribution as evaluation: a corpus-based investigation of quotations in parliamentary discourse. *ESP across Cultures* 2: 7–20.

Bhatia, Vijay K. 1993. *Analysing genre: language use in professional settings*. London: Longman.

———. 1997. Genre-mixing in academic introductions. *English for Specific Purposes* 16 (3): 181–195.

———. 2002. A generic view of academic discourse. In Flowerdew 2002, 21–39.

———. 2005. Generic patterns in promotional discourse. In Halmari and Virtanen 2005, 213–225.

Biber, Douglas. 1986. Spoken and written textual dimensions in English: resolving the contradictory findings. *Language* 62: 384–414.

———. 1987. A textual comparison of British and American writing. *American Speech* 62: 99–119.

———. 1988. *Variation across speech and writing*. Cambridge: Cambridge University Press.

———. 1990. Methodological issues regarding corpus-based analyses of linguistic variation. *Literary and Linguistic Computing* 5: 257–269.

————. 1991. Oral and literate characteristics of selected primary school reading materials. *Text* 11: 73–96.

————. 1992. On the complexity of discourse complexity: a multidimensional analysis. *Discourse Processes* 15: 133–163.

————. 1993. Representativeness in corpus design. *Literary and Linguistic Computing* 8: 243–257.

————. 1994. An analytical framework for register studies. In *Sociolinguistic perspectives on register*, ed. by D. Biber and E. Finegan, 31–56. New York: Oxford University Press.

————. 1995. *Dimensions of register variation: a cross-linguistic comparison*. Cambridge: Cambridge University Press.

————. 1999. A register perspective on grammar and discourse: variability in the form and use of English complement clauses. *Discourse Studies* 1: 131–150.

————. 2003. Compressed noun phrase structures in newspaper discourse: the competing demands of popularization vs. economy. In *New media language*, ed. by J. Aitchison and D. Lewis, 169–181. London: Routledge.

————. 2004a. Historical patterns for the grammatical marking of stance: a cross-register comparison. *Journal of Historical Pragmatics* 5: 107–135.

————. 2004b. Modal use across registers and time. In *Studies in the history of the English language II: unfolding conversations*, ed. by A. Curzan and K. Emmons, 189–216. Berlin: Mouton de Gruyter.

————. 2006a. *University language: a corpus-based study of spoken and written registers*. Amsterdam: John Benjamins.

————. 2006b. Stance in spoken and written university registers. *Journal of English for Academic Purposes* 5: 97–116.

————. 2008. Corpus-based analyses of discourse: dimensions of variation in conversation. In *Advances in discourse studies*, ed. by V. Bhatia, J. Flowerdew, and R. Jones, 100–114. London: Routledge.

Biber, Douglas, and Federica Barbieri. 2007. Lexical bundles in university spoken and written registers. *English for Specific Purposes* 26: 263–286.

Biber, Douglas, and Jená Burges. 2000. Historical change in the language use of women and men: gender differences in dramatic dialogue. *Journal of English Linguistics* 28: 21–37.

Biber, Douglas, and Victoria Clark. 2002. Historical shifts in modification patterns with complex noun phrase structures: How long can you go without a verb? In *English historical syntax and morphology*, ed. by T. Fanego, M. J. López-Couso, and J. Pérez-Guerra, 43–66. Amsterdam: John Benjamins.

Biber, Douglas, Ulla Connor, and Thomas A. Upton. 2007. *Discourse on the move: using corpus analysis to describe discourse structure*. Amsterdam: John Benjamins.

Biber, Douglas, Susan Conrad, and Viviana Cortes. 2004. *If you look at . . .* : lexical bundles in university teaching and textbooks. *Applied Linguistics* 25: 371–405.

Biber, Douglas, Susan Conrad, and Randi Reppen. 1998. *Corpus linguistics: investigating language structure and use*. Cambridge: Cambridge University Press.

Biber, Douglas, Susan Conrad, Randi Reppen, Pat Byrd, and Marie Helt. 2002. Speaking and writing in the university: a multi-dimensional comparison. *TESOL Quarterly* 36: 9–48.

Biber, Douglas, Mark Davies, James K. Jones, and Nicole Tracy-Ventura. 2006. Spoken and written register variation in Spanish: a multi-dimensional analysis. *Corpora* 1: 7–38.

Biber, Douglas, and Edward Finegan. 1989a. Drift and the evolution of English style: a history of three genres. *Language* 65: 487–517.

———. 1989b. Styles of stance in English: lexical and grammatical marking of evidentiality and affect. *Text* 9: 93–124.

———. 1992. The linguistic evolution of five written and speech-based English genres from the 17th to the 20th centuries. In *History of Englishes: new methods and interpretations in historical linguistics*, ed. by M. Rissanen, O. Ihalainen, T. Nevalainen, and I. Taavitsainen, 688–704. Berlin: Mouton.

——— (eds.). 1994a. *Sociolinguistic perspectives on register*. New York: Oxford University Press.

———. 1994b. Multi-dimensional analyses of authors' styles: Some case studies from the eighteenth century. In *Research in humanities computing 3*, ed. by D. Ross and D. Brink, 3–17. Oxford: Oxford University Press.

———. 1994c. Intra-textual variation within medical research articles. In *Corpus-based research into language*, ed. by N. Oostdijk and P. de Haan, 201–222. Amsterdam: Rodopi.

———. 1997. Diachronic relations among speech-based and written registers in English. In *To explain the present: studies in the changing English language in honour of Matti Rissanen*, ed. by T. Nevalainen and L. Kahlas-Tarkka, 253–275. Helsinki: Société Néophilologique. (Reprinted in Conrad and Biber 2001, 66–83.)

Biber, Douglas, Edward Finegan, and Dwight Atkinson. 1994. ARCHER and its challenges: compiling and analyzing a representative corpus of historical English registers. In *Creating and using English language corpora*, ed. by U. Fries, G. Tottie, and P. Schneider, 1–14. Amsterdam: Rodopi.

Biber, Douglas, and Mohammed Hared. 1992. Dimensions of register variation in Somali. *Language Variation and Change* 4: 41–75.

———. 1994. Linguistic correlates of the transition to literacy in Somali: language adaptation in six press registers. In Biber and Finegan (eds.) 1994, 182–216.

Biber, Douglas, Stig Johansson, Geoffrey Leech, Susan Conrad, and Edward Finegan. 1999. *The Longman grammar of spoken and written English*. London: Longman.

Biber, Douglas, and James K. Jones. 2005. Merging corpus linguistic and discourse analytic research goals: discourse units in biology research articles. *Corpus Linguistics and Linguistic Theory* 1: 151–182.

Biber, D., and R. Reppen. 2002. What does frequency have to do with grammar teaching? *Studies in Second Language Acquisition* 24: 199–208.

Bloch, Maurice. 1993. The uses of schooling and literacy in a Zafimaniry village. In *Cross-cultural approaches to literacy*, ed. by Brian V. Street, 87–109. Cambridge: Cambridge University Press.

Bolívar, Adriana. 1992. The analysis of political discourse, with particular reference to the Venezuelan political dialogue. *English for Specific Purposes* 11: 159–175.

Bondi, Marina. 1999. *English across genres: language variation in the discourse of economics*. Modena: Edizioni Il Fiorino.

Bondi Paganelli, Marina. 1997. L'argomentazione analogica nel discorso economico: un esempio di analisi. In Bussi, Bondi, and Gatta (eds.) 1997, 105–121.

Bondi Paganelli, Marina, and Gabriella Del Lungo Camiciotti. 1995. *Analysing economics and news discourse*. Bologna: CLUEB.

Bowcher, Wendy L. 2003. Speaker contributions in radio sports commentary. *Text* 23 (4): 445–476.

Brett, Paul. 1994. A genre analysis of the results section of sociology articles. *English for Specific Purposes* 13 (1): 47–59.

Brown, Penelope, and Fraser Colin. 1979. Speech as a marker of situation. In *Social markers in speech*, ed. by K. R. Scherer and H. Giles, 33–62. Cambridge: Cambridge University Press.

Brown, R. W., and M. Ford. 1961. Address in American English. *Journal of Abnormal and Social Psychology* 62: 375–385.

Brown, R. W., and A. Gilman. 1960. The pronouns of power and solidarity. *American Anthropologist* 4: 24–39.

Bruthiaux, Paul. 1994. Me Tarzan, you Jane: linguistic simplification in "personal ads" register. In Biber and Finegan (eds.) 1994, 136–154.

––––––. 1996. *The discourse of classified advertising: exploring the nature of linguistic simplicity*. Oxford: Oxford University Press.

––––––. 2005. In a nutshell: persuasion in the spatially constrained language of advertising. In Halmari and Virtanen (eds.) 2005, 135–152.

Bugaj, Joanna. 2006. The language of legal writings in 16th century Scots and English: and etymological study of binomials. *ESP across Cultures* 3: 7–22.

Bülow-Møller, Anne Marie. 2005. Persuasion in business negotiations. In Halmari and Virtanen (eds.) 2005, 27–58.

Bunton, David. 1999. The use of higher level metatext in Ph.D. theses. *English for Specific Purposes* 18: 841–856.

––––––. 2002. Generic moves in Ph.D. thesis Introductions. In Flowerdew (ed.) 2002, 57–75.

––––––. 2005. The structure of PhD conclusion chapters. *Journal of English for Academic Purposes* 4: 207–224.

Bussi, Elisa, Marina Bondi, and F. Gatta (eds.). 1997. *Understanding argument: la logica informale del discorso: atti del convegno Forli, 5–6 Dicembre 1995*. Bologna: Cooperativa Libraria Universitaria Editrice Bologna.

Caballero, Rosario. 2003. Metaphor and genre: the presence and role of metaphor in the building review. *Applied Linguistics* 24 (2): 145–167.

Carter, Ronald. 1988. Front pages: lexis, style, and newspaper reports. In Ghadessy (ed.) 1988, 8–16.

Carter, Ronald, and Michael McCarthy. 1997. *Exploring spoken English*. Cambridge: Cambridge University Press.

––––––. 2004. Talking, creating: interactional language, creativity and context. *Applied Linguistics* 25 (1): 62–88.

Cazden, Courtney B. 2001. *Classroom discourse: the language of teaching and learning*. 2nd edn. Portsmouth, NH: Heinemann.

Chafe, Wallace. 1982. Integration and involvement in speaking, writing, and oral Literature. In *Spoken and written language: exploring orality and literacy*, ed. by D. Tannen, 35–53. Norwood, NJ: Ablex.

Channell, Joanna. 1990. Precise and vague quantifiers in writing on economics. In *The writing scholar: studies in academic discourse*, ed. by W. Nash, 95–117. Newbury Park: Sage Publications.

Charles, Maggie. 2003. "This mystery . . . ": a corpus-based study of the use of nouns to construct stance in theses from two contrasting disciplines. *Journal of English for Academic Purposes* 2: 313–326.

———. 2006a. The construction of stance in reporting clauses: a cross-disciplinary study of theses. *Applied Linguistics* 27 (3): 492–518.

———. 2006b. Phraseological patterns in reporting clauses used in citation: a corpus-based study of theses in two disciplines. *English for Specific Purposes* 25: 310–331.

———. 2007. Argument or evidence? Disciplinary variation in the use of the Noun *that* pattern. *English for Specific Purposes* 26: 203–218.

Christie, Frances. 2002. *Classroom discourse analysis*. London: Continuum.

Christie, Frances, and J. R. Martin (eds.). 1997. *Genre and institutions: social processes in the workplace and school*. London and New York: Continuum.

Claridge, Claudia. 2005. Questions in Early Modern English pamphlets. *Journal of Historical Pragmatics* 6 (1): 133–168.

Collins, Daniel E. 2006. Speech reporting and the suppression of orality in seventeenth-century Russian trial dossiers. *Journal of Historical Pragmatics* 7 (2): 265–292.

Collins, Peter. 1995. The indirect object construction in English: an informational approach. *Linguistics* 33: 35–49.

Collot, Milena, and Nancy Belmore. 1996. Electronic language: a new variety of English. In *Herring* (ed.) 1996, 13–28.

Connor, Ulla. 1996. *Contrastive rhetoric: cross-cultural aspects of second-language writing*. Cambridge: Cambridge University Press.

———. 2000. Variation in rhetorical moves in grant proposals of US humanists and scientists. *Text* 20: 1–28.

Connor, Ulla, and Anna Mauranen. 1999. Linguistic analysis of grant proposals: European Union research grants. *English for Specific Purposes* 18 (1): 47–62.

Connor, Ulla, Ed Nagelhout, and William V. Rozycki. 2008. *Contrastive rhetoric: reaching to intercultural rhetoric*. Amsterdam: John Benjamins.

Connor, Ulla, and Tomas A. Upton. 2003. Linguistic dimensions of direct mail letters. In *Corpus analysis: language structure and language use*, ed. by C. Meyer and P. Leistyna, 71–86. Amsterdam: Rodopi.

——— (eds.). 2004a. *Discourse in the professions*. Amsterdam: John Benjamins.

———. 2004b. The genre of grant proposals: a corpus linguistic analysis. In Connor and Upton (eds.) 2004a, 235–256.

Connor-Linton, Jeff. 1988. Author's style and world-view in nuclear discourse: a quantitative analysis. *Multilingua* 7: 95–132.

———. 2001. Author's style and world-view: a comparison of texts about nuclear arms policy. In Conrad and Biber (eds.) 2001, 84–93.

Conrad, Susan. 1996. Investigating academic texts with corpus-based techniques: an example from biology. *Linguistics and Education* 8: 299–326.

———. 1999. The importance of corpus-based research for language teachers. *System* 27: 1–18.

———. 2000. Will corpus linguistics revolutionize grammar teaching in the 21st century? *TESOL Quarterly* 34: 548–560.

_____. 2001. Variation among disciplinary texts: a comparison of textbooks and journal articles in biology and history. In Conrad and Biber (eds.) 2001, 94–107.

_____. 2004. Corpus linguistics, language variation, and language teaching. In *How to use corpora in language teaching*, ed. by J. Sinclair, 67–85. Amsterdam: John Benjamins.

_____. 2005. Corpus linguistics and L2 teaching. In *Handbook of research in second language teaching and learning*, ed. by E. Hinkel, 393–409. Mahwah, NJ: Lawrence Erlbaum.

Conrad, Susan, and Douglas Biber. 2000. Adverbial marking of stance in speech and writing. In Hunston and Thompson (eds.) 2000, 56–73.

_____ (eds.). 2001. *Variation in English: multi-dimensional studies*. London: Longman.

Cortes, Viviana. 2004. Lexical bundles in published and student disciplinary writing: examples from history and biology. *English for Specific Purposes* 23: 397–423.

Coulmas, Florian (ed.). 1997. *The handbook of sociolinguistics*. Oxford: Blackwell.

Coulthard, Malcolm (ed.). 1994. *Advances in written text analysis*. London: Routledge.

Coupland, Nikolas. 1980. Style-shifting at a Cardiff work-setting. *Language in Society* 9: 1–12.

_____. 2007. *Style: language variation and identity*. Cambridge: Cambridge University Press.

Crismore, Avon, Raija Markkanen, and Margaret Steffensen. 1993. Metadiscourse in persuasive writing: a study of texts written by American and Finnish university students. *Written Communication* 10 (1): 39–71.

Crossley, Scott. 2007. A chronotopic approach to genre analysis: an exploratory study. *English for Specific Purposes* 26: 4–24.

Crossley, Scott A., and Max M. Louwerse. 2007. Multi-dimensional register classification using bigrams. *International Journal of Corpus Linguistics* 12: 453–478.

Crystal, David. 2001. *Language and the internet*. Cambridge: Cambridge University Press.

Crystal, David, and Derek Davy. 1969. *Investigating English style*. London: Longman.

Csomay, Eniko. 2005. Linguistic variation within university classroom talk: a corpus-based perspective. *Linguistics and Education* 15: 243–74.

_____. 2007. Vocabulary-based discourse units in university class sessions. In Biber, Connor, and Upton 2007, 213–238.

Culpeper, Jonathan, and Merja Kytö. 1999. Modifying pragmatic force: hedges in Early Modern English dialogues. In *Historical dialogue analysis*, ed. by A. H. Jucker, G. Fritz, and F. Lebsanft, 293–312. Pragmatics and Beyond, new series 66; Amsterdam and Philadelphia: John Benjamins.

_____. 2000. Data in historical pragmatics: spoken interaction (re)cast as writing. *Journal of Historical Pragmatics* 1 (2): 175–199.

_____. Forthcoming. *Early modern English dialogues: spoken interaction as writing*. Cambridge: Cambridge University Press.

Culpeper, Jonathan, and Elena Semino. 2000. Constructing witches and spells: speech acts and activity types in Early Modern England. *Journal of Historical Pragmatics* 1(1): 97–116.

Cutting, Joan. 1999. The grammar of the in-group code. *Applied Linguistics* 20 (2): 179–202.

_____. 2000. *Analysing the language of discourse communities*. Amsterdam: Elsevier.

Danet, Brenda. 1980. Language in the legal process. *Law and Society Review* 14: 445–564.

de la Cruz Cabanillas, Isabel, Cristina Tejedor Martinez, Mercedes Diez Prados, and Esperanza Cerda Redondo. 2007. English loanwords in Spanish computer language. *English for Specific Purposes* 26: 52–78.

del-Teso-Craviotto, Marisol. 2006a. Language and sexuality in Spanish and English dating chats. *Journal of Sociolinguistics* 10 (4): 460–480.

_____. 2006b. Words that matter: lexical choice and gender ideologies in women's magazines. *Journal of Pragmatics* 38: 2003–2021.

Dickerson, Paul. 2001. Disputing with care: analysing interviewees' treatment of interviewers' prior turns in televised political interviews. *Discourse Studies* 3 (2): 203–222.

Ding, Huiling. 2007. Genre analysis of personal statements: analysis of moves in application essays to medical and dental schools. *English for Specific Purposes* 26: 368–392.

Donohue, James P. 2006. How to support a one-handed economist: the role of modalization in economic forecasting. *English for Specific Purposes* 25: 200–216.

Dos Santos, Mauro Bittencourt. 1996. The textual organization of research paper abstracts in applied linguistics. *Text* 16: 481–499.

Dos Santos, V. B. M. Pinto. 2002. Genre analysis of business letters of negotiation. *English for Specific Purposes* 21: 167–199.

Doty, Kathleen L., and Risto Hiltunen. 2002. "I will tell, I will tell": Confessional patterns in the Salem Witchcraft Trials, 1692. *Journal of Historical Pragmatics* 3 (2): 299–335.

Douglas, Dan. 2000. *Assessing languages for specific purposes*. Cambridge: Cambridge University Press.

Dressen, Dacia. 2003. Geologists' implicit persuasive strategies and the construction of evaluative evidence. *Journal of English for Academic Purposes* 2: 273–290.

Dubois, Betty Lou. 1980. Genre and structure of biomedical speeches. *Forum Linguisticum* 5: 140–166.

Duranti, A. 1981. *The Samoan fono: a Sociolinguistic study*. Canberra: The Australian National University.

_____. 1994. *From grammar to politics: linguistic anthropology in a western Samoan village*. Berkeley and Los Angeles: University of California Press.

Eckert, Penelope, and John R. Rickford (eds.). 2002. *Style and sociolinguistic variation*. Cambridge: Cambridge University Press.

Edwards, Derek. 2006. Facts, norms and dispositions: practical uses of the modal verb *would* in police interrogations. *Discourse Studies* 8 (4): 475–501.

Eggins, Suzanne, Peter Wignell, and J. R. Martin. 1993. The discourse of history: distancing the recoverable past. In Ghadessy (ed.) 1993a, 75–109.

Ervin-Tripp, Susan. 1972. On sociolinguistic rules: alternation and co-occurrence. In *Directions in sociolinguistics: the ethnography of communication*, ed. by J. Gumperz and D. Hymes, 213–250. New York: Holt.

Evangelisti Allori, Paola (ed.). 1998. *Academic discourse in Europe*. Rome: Bulzoni.

Feak, Christine, Susan Reinhart, and Ann Sinsheimer. 2000. A preliminary analysis of law review notes. *English for Specific Purposes* 19: 197–220.

Ferguson, Charles. 1983. Sports announcer talk: syntactic aspects of register variation. *Language in Society* 12: 153–72.

————. 1994. Dialect, register, and genre: working assumptions about conventionalization. In Biber and Finegan (eds.) 1994a, 15–30.

Ferguson, Gibson. 2001. If you pop over there: a corpus-based study of conditionals in medical discourse. *English for Specific Purposes* 20: 61–82.

Finegan, Edward, and Douglas Biber. 1994. Register and social dialect variation: an integrated approach. In Biber and Finegan (eds.) 1994, 315–347.

————. 2001. Register variation and social dialect variation: the register axiom. In *Style and sociolinguistic variation*, ed. by P. Eckert and J. Rickford, 235–267. Cambridge: Cambridge University Press.

Fitzmaurice, Susan M. 2002a. *The familiar letter in Early Modern English*. Amsterdam and Philadelphia: John Benjamins.

————. 2002b. "Plethoras of witty verbiage" and "heathen Greek": ways of reading meaning in English comic drama. *Journal of Historical Pragmatics* 3 (1): 31–60.

————. 2002c. Politeness and modal meaning in the construction of humiliative discourse in an early eighteenth-century network of patron–client relationships. *English Language and Linguistics* 6: 239–266.

————. 2003. The grammar of stance in early eighteenth-century English epistolary language. In *Corpus analysis: language structure and language use*, ed. by P. Leistyna and C. Meyer, 107–132. Amsterdam: Rodopi.

Fitzmaurice, Susan M., and Irma Taavitsainen (eds.). 2007. *Methods in historical pragmatics*. Berlin: Mouton de Gruyter.

Flowerdew, John (ed.). 2002. *Academic discourse*. Harlow: Longman.

Flowerdew, John, and Tony Dudley-Evans. 2002. Genre analysis of editorial letters to international journal contributors. *Applied Linguistics* 23 (4): 463–489.

Flowerdew, John, and Matthew Peacock (eds.). 2001. *Research perspectives on English for academic purposes*. Cambridge: Cambridge University Press.

Flowerdew, John, and Alina Wan. 2006. Genre analysis of tax computation letters: how and why tax accountants write the way they do. *English for Specific Purposes* 25: 133–153.

Fludernik, Monika. 2000. Narrative discourse markers in Malory's Morte D'Arthur. *Journal of Historical Pragmatics* 2 (1): 231–262.

Fortanet, Inmaculada. 2004. The use of "we" in university lectures: reference and function. *English for Specific Purposes* 23: 45–66.

————. 2005. Honoris Causa speeches: an approach to structure. *Discourse Studies* 7 (1): 31–51.

Fortanet, Inmaculada, Santiago Posteguillo, Juan Carlos Palmer, and Juan Franscisco Coll (eds.). 1998. *Genre studies in English for academic purposes*. Castellon: Universitat Jaume I.

Fowler, Roger. 1991. *Language in the news: discourse and ideology in the press*. London: Routledge.

Fox, Annie B., Danuta Butakto, Mark Hallahan, and Mary Crawford. 2007. The medium makes a difference: gender similarities and differences in instant messaging. *Journal of Language and Social Psychology* 26 (4): 389–397.

Fox, Barbara. A., and Sandra A. Thompson. 1990. A discourse explanation of the grammar of relative clauses in English conversation. *Language* 66: 297–316.

Freddi, Maria. 2005a. Arguing linguistics: corpus investigation of one functional variety of academic discourse. *Journal of English for Academic Purposes* 4: 5–26.

———. 2005b. From corpus to register: the construction of evaluation and argumentation in linguistics textbooks. In Tognini-Bonelli and Camiciotti 2005, 133–152.

Freeborn, Dennis. 1996. *Style: text analysis and linguistic criticism*. London: Palgrave.

Friginal, Eric. 2008. Linguistic variation in the discourse of outsourced call centers. *Discourse Studies* 10: 715–736.

———. 2009. *The language of outsourced call centers: a corpus-based study of cross-cultural interaction*. Amsterdam: John Benjamins.

Fritz, Gerd. 2001. Text types in a new medium: the first newspapers (1609). *Journal of Historical Pragmatics* 2 (1): 69–83.

Fuertes-Olivera, Pedro A. 2007. A corpus-based view of lexical gender in written business English. *English for Specific Purposes* 26: 219–234.

Fuertes-Olivera, Pedro A., Marisol Velasco-Sacristan, Ascension Arribas-Bano, and Eva Sarmaniego-Fernandez. 2001. Persuasion and advertising in English: metadiscourse in slogans and headlines. *Journal of Pragmatics* 33: 1291–1307.

Gains, Jonathan. 1999. Electronic mail – a new style of communication or just a new medium? An investigation into the text features of email. *English for Specific Purposes* 18 (1): 81–101.

Gardner, Sheena. 2004. Knock-on effects of mode change on academic discourse. *Journal of English for Academic Purposes* 3: 23–38.

Geisler, Christer. 2002. Investigating register variation in nineteenth-century English: a multi-dimensional comparison. In *Using corpora to explore linguistic variation*, ed. by R. Reppen, S. M. Fitzmaurice, and D. Biber, 249–271. Amsterdam: John Benjamins.

Ghadessy, Mohsen (ed.). 1988a. *Registers of written English: situational factors and linguistic features*. London: Pinter.

———. 1988b. The language of written sports commentary: soccer – a description. In Ghadessy (ed.) 1988a, 17–51.

———. (ed.). 1993a. *Register analysis: theory and practice*. London and New York: Pinter Publishers.

———. 1993b. On the nature of written business communication. In Ghadessy (ed.) 1993a, 149–164.

Giannoni, Davide Simone. 2002. Worlds of gratitude: a contrastive study of acknowledgement texts in English and Italian research articles. *Applied Linguistics* 23 (1): 1–31.

Gibbon, Dafydd. 1981. Idiomaticity and functional variation: a case study of international amateur radio talk. *Language in Society* 10: 21–42.

———. 1985. Context and variation in two-way radio discourse. *Discourse Processes* 8: 395–419.

Giltrow, Janet. 2005. Modern conscience: modalities of obligation in research genres. *Text* 25: 171–199.

Gimenez, Julio C. 2000. Business e-mail communication: some emerging tendencies in register. *English for Specific Purposes* 19: 237–251.

Gledhill, Chris. 2000. The discourse function of collocation in research article introductions. *English for Specific Purposes* 19: 115–135.

Gosden, Hugh. 1992. Discourse functions of marked theme in scientific research articles. *English for Specific Purposes* 11: 207–224.

———. 1993. Discourse functions of subjects in scientific research articles. *Applied Linguistics* 14 (1): 56–75.

Gotti, Maurizio. 1996. *Robert Boyle and the language of science*. Milan: Guerini.

Grabe, William, and Robert Kaplan. 1996. *Theory and practice of writing*. New York: Longman.

———. 1997. On the writing of science and the science of writing: hedging in science text and elsewhere. In *Hedging and discourse: approaches to the analysis of a pragmatic phenomenon in academic texts*, ed. by R. Markkanen, and H. Schroder, 151–167. Berlin: Walter de Gruyter & Co.

Greatbatch, David. 1988. A turn-taking system for British news interviews. *Language in Society* 17: 401–430.

Groom, Nicholas. 2005. Pattern and meaning across genres and disciplines: an exploratory study. *Journal of English for Academic Purposes* 4: 257–277.

Gross, Alan G., Joseph E. Harmon, and Michael S. Reidy. 2002. *Communicating science: the scientific article from the 17th century to present*. Oxford: Oxford University Press.

Gunnarsson, Britt-Louise. 1993. Pragmatic and macrothematic patterns in science and popular science: a diachronic study of articles from three fields. In Ghadessy (ed.) 1993a, 165–180.

Gunnarsson, Britt-Louise, Per Linell, and Bengt Nordberg (eds.). 1996. *Text and talk in professional contexts*. Uppsala: ASLA.

Gustafson, Marita. 1984. The syntactic features of binomial expressions in legal English. *Text* 4: 123–141.

Halleck, Gene B., and Ulla M. Connor. 2006. Rhetorical moves in TESOL conference proposals. *Journal of English for Academic Purposes* 5: 70–86.

Halliday, Michael Alexander Kirkwood. 1978. *Language as social semiotic: the social interpretation of language and meaning*. London: Edward Arnold.

———. 1988. On the language of physical science. In Ghadessy (ed.) 1988a, 162–178.

———. 1989. *Spoken and written language*. Oxford and New York: Oxford University Press.

Halliday, Michael Alexander Kirkwood, and J. R. Martin. 1993. *Writing science: literacy and discursive power*. Pittsburgh: University of Pittsburgh Press.

Halmari, Helena. 2005. In search of "successful" political persuasion: a comparison of the styles of Bill Clinton and Ronald Reagan. In Halmari and Virtanen (eds.) 2005, 105–134.

Halmari, Helena, and Tuija Virtanen (eds.). 2005. *Persuasion across genres: a linguistic approach*. Amsterdam and Philadelphia: John Benjamins.

Hamilton, Heidi E. 1998. Reported speech and survivor identity in on-line bone marrow transplantation narratives. *Journal of Sociolinguistics* 2 (1): 53–67.

Harris, Simon. 1997. Procedural vocabulary in law case reports. *English for Specific Purposes* 16 (4): 289–308.

Harvey, Annamaria. 1992. Science reports and indexicality. *English for Specific Purposes* 11: 115–128.

———. 1995. Interaction in public reports. *English for Specific Purposes* 14 (3): 189–200.

Harwood, Nigel. 2005. "We do not seem to have a theory . . . The theory I present here attempts to fill this gap": inclusive and exclusive pronouns in academic writing. *Applied Linguistics* 26 (3): 343–375.

————. 2006. (In)appropriate personal pronoun use in political science: a qualitative study and a proposed heuristic for future research. *Written Communication* 23 (4): 424–450.

Heath, Shirley Brice, and Juliet Langman. 1994. Shared thinking and the register of coaching. In Biber and Finegan (eds.) 1994a, 82–105.

Helt, Marie. 2001. A multi-dimensional comparison of British and American spoken English. In Conrad and Biber (eds.) 2001, 171–184.

Hemais, Barbara. 2001. The discourse of research and practice in marketing journals. *English for Specific Purposes* 20: 39–59.

Henderson, Willie, Tony Dudley-Evans, and Roger Backhouse (eds.). 1993. *Economics and language*. London and New York: Routledge.

Henry, Alex, and Robert L. Roseberry. 1997. An investigation of the functions, strategies, and linguistic features of the introductions and conclusions of essays. *System* 25 (4): 479–495.

————. 2001. A narrow-angled corpus analysis of moves and strategies of the genre: 'Letter of Application'. *English for Specific Purposes* 20: 153–167.

Henzl, Vera M. 1974. Linguistic register of foreign language instruction. *Language Learning* 23: 207–222.

————. 1979. Foreign talk in the classroom. *International Review of Applied Linguistics* 17: 159–167.

Herring, Susan C. (ed.). 1996. *Computer-mediated communication: linguistic, social and cross-cultural perspectives*. Amsterdam and Philadelphia: John Benjamins.

Herring, Susan C., and John C. Paolillo. 2006. Gender and genre variation in weblogs. *Journal of Sociolinguistics* 10 (4): 493–459.

Hewings, Martin (ed.). 2001. *Academic writing in context: implications and applications*. Birmingham: Birmingham University Press.

Hewings, Martin, and Ann Hewings. 2002. "It is interesting to note that . . . ": a comparative study of anticipatory "it" in student and published writing. *English for Specific Purposes* 21: 367–383.

Hiltunen, Risto. 1984. The type and structure of clausal embedding in legal English. *Text* 4: 107–121.

————. 1990. *Chapters on legal English: aspects past and present of the language of the law*. Annals of the Finnish Academy of Science ser. B 251; Helsinki: Finnish Academy of Science.

Holmes, Richard. 1997. Genre analysis, and the social sciences: an investigation of the structure of research article discussion sections in three disciplines. *English for Specific Purposes* 16 (4): 321–337.

Hood, Susan, and Gail Forey. 2005. Introducing a conference paper: getting interpersonal with your audience. *Journal of English for Academic Purposes* 4: 291–306.

Hopkins, Andy, and Tony Dudley-Evans. 1988. A genre-based investigation of the discussion sections in articles and dissertations. *English for Specific Purposes* 7 (2): 113–122.

Hornberger, Nancy H. 1994. Continua of biliteracy. In *Literacy across languages and cultures*, ed. by B. M. Ferdman, R.–M. Weber, and A. G. Ramirez, 103–139. Albany: State University of New York Press.

Horsella, Maria, and Gerda Sindermann. 1992. Aspects of scientific discourse: conditional argumentation. *English for Specific Purposes* 11: 129–139.

Hoyle, Susan M. 1989. Forms and footing in boys' sportscasting. *Text* 9: 153–173.

Hudson, Richard A. 1980. *Sociolinguistics*. Cambridge: Cambridge University Press.

Hundt, Marianne, and Christian Mair. 1999. "Agile" and "uptight" genres: the corpus-based approach to language change in progress. *International Journal of Corpus Linguistics* 4: 221–242.

Hundt, Marianne, Nadja Nesselhauf, and Carolin Biewer (eds.). 2007. *Corpus linguistics and the web*. Amsterdam: Rodopi.

Hunston, Susan. 1993. Evaluation and ideology in scientific writing. In Ghadess (ed.) 1993a, 57–74.

_____. 2005. Conflict and consensus: construing opposition in applied linguistics. In Tognini-Bonelli and Camiciotti 2005, 1–16.

Hunston, Susan, and Geoff Thompson (eds.). 2000. *Evaluation in text: authorial stance and the construction of discourse*. New York: Oxford University Press.

Hyland, Ken. 1996. Writing without conviction? Hedging in science research articles. *Applied Linguistics* 17 (4): 433–454.

_____. 1998. *Hedging in scientific research articles*. Amsterdam: John Benjamins.

_____. 1999a. Academic attribution: citation and the construction of disciplinary knowledge. *Applied Linguistics* 20 (3): 341–367.

_____. 1999b. Talking to students: metadiscourse in introductory coursebooks. *English for Specific Purposes* 18 (1): 3–26.

_____. 2000. *Disciplinary discourses: social interactions in academic writing*. Harlow: Longman.

_____. 2001a. Bringing in the reader: addressee features in academic articles. *Written Communication* 18 (4): 549–574.

_____. 2001b. Humble servants of the discipline? Self-mention in research articles. *English for Specific Purposes* 20: 207–226.

_____. 2002a. *Teaching and researching writing*. Harlow: Pearson Education.

_____. 2002b. Directives: argument and engagement in academic writing. *Applied Linguistics* 23 (2): 215–239.

_____. 2002c. What do they mean? Questions in academic writing. *Text* 22 (4): 529–557.

_____. 2004. Graduates' gratitude: the generic structure of dissertation acknowledgements. *English for Specific Purposes* 23: 303–324.

_____. 2005. Stance and engagement: a model of interaction in academic discourse. *Discourse Studies* 7 (2): 173–192.

Hyland, Ken, and Polly Tse. 2004. Metadiscourse in academic writing: a reappraisal. *Applied Linguistics* 25 (2): 156–177.

_____. 2005. Hooking the reader: a corpus study of evaluative *that* in abstracts. *English for Specific Purposes* 24: 123–139.

Hymes, Dell. 1974. *Foundations in sociolinguistics: an ethnographic approach*. Philadelphia: University of Pennsylvania Press.

_____. 1984. Sociolinguistics: stability and consolidation. *International Journal of the Sociology of Language* 45: 39–45.

Inigo-Mora, Isabel. 2007. Extreme case formulations in Spanish pre-electoral debates and English panel interviews. *Discourse Studies* 9 (3): 341–363.

Jackson, Jane, and Linda Bilton. 1994. Stylistic variation in science lectures: teaching vocabulary. *English for Specific Purposes* 13: 61–80.

Janda, Richard. 1985. Note-taking English as a simplified register. *Discourse Processes* 8: 437–54.

Jaworski, Adam, and Dariusz Galasinski. 2000. Vocative address forms and ideological legitimization in political debates. *Discourse Studies* 2 (1): 35–53.

Jiang, Xiangying. 2006. Cross-cultural pragmatic differences in US and Chinese press conferences: the case of the North Korea nuclear crisis. *Discourse and Society* 17 (2): 237–257.

Johansson, Marjut. 2006. Constructing objects of discourse in the broadcast political interview. *Journal of Pragmatics* 38: 216–229.

Johnson, Barry. 1995. Some features of maritime telex service communication. *English for Specific Purposes* 14 (2): 127–136.

Joos, Martin. 1961. *The five clocks*. New York: Harcourt.

Kahlas-Tarkka, Leena, and Matti Rissanen. 2007. The sullen and the talkative: discourse strategies in the Salem examinations. *Journal of Historical Pragmatics* 8 (1): 1–24.

Kanoksilapatham, Budsaba. 2005. Rhetorical structure of biochemistry research articles. *English for Specific Purposes* 24: 269–292.

Kaplan, Robert B., Serena Cantor, Cynthia Hagstrom, Lia D. Kahmi-Stein, Yumiko Shiotani, and Cheryl Boyd Zimmermann. 1994. On abstract writing. *Text* 14 (3): 401–426.

Kim, Young-Jin, and Douglas Biber. 1994. A corpus-based analysis of register variation in Korean. In Biber and Finegan (eds.) 1994a, 157–181.

Kline, Susan L. 2005. Interactive media systems: influence strategies in television home shopping. *Text* 25 (2): 201–231.

Koester, Almut Josepha. 2004. Relational sequences in workplace genres. *Journal of Pragmatics* 36: 1405–1428.

———. 2006. *Investigating workplace discourse*. London: Routledge.

Kong, Kenneth C. C. 2006. Property transaction report: news, advertisement or a new genre? *Discourse Studies* 8 (6): 771–796.

Koutsantoni, Dimitra. 2004. Attitude, certainty, and allusion to common knowledge in scientific research articles. *Journal of English for Academic Purposes* 18 (2): 163–182.

Kryk-Kastovsky, Barbara. 2000. Representations of orality in Early Modern English trial records. *Journal of Historical Pragmatics* 1 (2): 201–230.

———. 2006. Impoliteness in Early Modern English courtroom discourse. *Journal of Historical Pragmatics* 7 (2): 213–243.

Kuiper, Koenraad, and Douglas Haggo. 1984. Livestock auctions, oral poetry and ordinary language. *Language in Society* 13: 205–234.

Kuiper, Koenraad, and Frederick Tillis. 1986. The chant of the tobacco auctioneer. *American Speech* 60: 141–149.

Kuo, Chih-Hua. 1999. The use of personal pronouns: role relationships in scientific journal articles. *English for Specific Purposes* 18 (2): 121–138.

Kuo, Sai-Hua. 2001. Reported speech in Chinese political discourse. *Discourse Studies* 3 (2): 181–202.

———. 2002. From solidarity to antagonism: the uses of the second-person singular pronoun in Chinese political discourse. *Text* 22 (1): 29–55.

———. 2003. Involvement vs detachment: gender differences in the use of personal pronouns in televised sports in Taiwan. *Discourse Studies* 5 (4): 479–494.

Kwan, Becky S. C. 2006. The schematic structure of literature reviews in doctoral theses of applied linguistics. *English for Specific Purposes* 25: 30–55.

Kytö, Merja. 1991. *Variation and diachrony, with Early American English in focus*. Frankfurt: Peter Lang.

Kytö, Merja, Mats Rydén, and Erik Smitterberg (eds.). 2006. *Nineteenth-century English: stability and change*. Cambridge: Cambridge University Press.

Kytö, Merja, and Terry Walker. 2003. The linguistic study of Early Modern English speech-related texts: how "bad" can "bad" data be? *Journal of English Linguistics* 31 (3): 221–248.

Labov, William. 1966. *The Social Stratification of English in New York City*. Washington DC: Center for Applied Linguistics.

———. 1972. *Sociolinguistic patterns*. Philadelphia: University of Pennsylvania Press.

Laforest, Martry. 2002. Scenes of family life: complaining in everyday conversation. *Journal of Pragmatics* 34: 1595–1620.

Lamb, William. 2008. *Scottish Gaelic speech and writing: register variation in an endangered language*. Belfast: Queen's University Belfast.

Lassen, Inger. 2006. Is the press release a genre? A study of form and content. *Discourse Studies* 8 (4): 503–530.

Latour, B., and S. Woolgar. 1986. *Laboratory life: the construction of scientific facts*. Princeton: Princeton University Press.

Lauerbach, Gerda. 2004. Political interviews as hybrid genre. *Text* 24 (3): 353–397.

Lee, David. 2001. Genres, registers, text types, domains, and styles: clarifying the concepts and navigating a path through the BNC jungle. *Language Learning and Technology* 5: 37–72.

Leech, Geoffrey N. 1966. *English in advertising*. London: Longman.

Leech, Geoffrey N., and Nicholas Smith. 2006. Recent grammatical change in written English 1961–1992. In *The changing face of corpus linguistics*, ed. by A. Renouf and A. Kehoe, 185–204. Amsterdam: Rodopi.

Leech, Geoffrey N., Marianne Hundt, Christian Mair, and Nicholas Smith. forthcoming. *Contemporary change in English: a grammatical study*. Cambridge: Cambridge University Press.

Leech, Geoffrey N., and Michael H. Short. 1981. *Style in fiction*. London: Longman.

Legg, Miranda. 2007. From question to answer: the genre of the problem-based tutorial at the University of Hong Kong. *English for Specific Purposes* 26: 344–367.

Lemke, Jay L. 1990. *Talking science: language, learning and values*. Norwood, NJ: Ablex.

Lewin, Beverly, A. 1998. Hedging: form and function in scientific research articles. In Fortanet *et al.* (eds.) 1998, 89–104.

Lewin, Beverly A, Jonathan Fine, and Lynne Young. 2001. *Expository discourse: a genre-based approach to social science research texts*. London: Continuum.

Lindermann, Stephanie, and Anna Mauranen. 2001. "It's just really messy": the occurrence and function of *just* in a corpus of academic speech. *English for Specific Purposes* 20: 459–475.

Lorés, Rosa. 2004. On RA abstracts: from rhetorical structure to thematic organisation. *English for Specific Purposes* 23: 280–302.

———. 2006. "I will argue that": first person pronouns as metadiscoursal devices in research articles in English and Spanish. *ESP across Cultures* 3: 23–40.

Love, Alison M. 1991. Process and product in geology: investigation of some discourse features of two introductory textbooks. *English for Specific Purposes* 10: 89–109.

————. 1993. Lexico-grammatical features in geology textbooks: process and product revisited. *English for Specific Purposes* 12: 197–218.

————. 2002. Introductory concepts and "cutting edge" theories: can the genre of the textbook accommodate both? In Flowerdew (ed.) 2002, 76–91.

Luzon Marco, Maria Jose. 1999. Procedural vocabulary: lexical signaling of conceptual relations in discourse. *Applied Linguistics* 20 (1): 1–21.

————. 2000. Collocational frameworks in medical research papers: a genre-based study. *English for Specific Purposes* 19: 63–86.

Lynch, Michael. 1985. *Art and artifact in laboratory science: a study of shop work and shop talk in a research laboratory*. London: Routledge.

MacDonald, Susan Peck. 2005. The language of journalism in treatments of hormone replacement news. *Written Communication* 22 (3): 275–297.

Magnet, Anne, and Didier Carnet. 2006. Letters to the editor: still vigorous after all these years? A presentation of the discursive and linguistic features of the genre. *English for Specific Purposes* 25: 173–199.

Mair, Christian. 2006. *Twentieth century English: history, variation and standardization*. Cambridge: Cambridge University Press.

Mäkinen, Martti. 2002. On interaction in herbals from Middle English to Early Modern English. *Journal of Historical Pragmatics* 3 (2): 229–251.

Maley, Yon. 1987. The language of legislation. *Language in Society* 16: 25–48.

Mann, William C., and Sandra A. Thompson (eds.). 1992. *Discourse description: diverse linguistic analyses of a fund-raising text*. Amsterdam: John Benjamins.

Marley, Carol. 2002. Popping the question: questions and modality in written dating advertisements. *Discourse Studies* 4 (1): 75–98.

Marra, Meredith, and Janet Holmes. 2004. Workplace narratives and business reports: issues of definition. *Text* 24 (1): 59–78.

Martin, J. R. 1985. Factual writing: exploring and challenging social reality. Geelong: Deakin University Press.

————. 1997. Analysing genre: functional parameters. In Christie and Martin (eds.) 1997, 3–39.

————. 2001. Language, register and genre. In *Analysing English in a global context*, ed. by A. Burns and C. Coffin, 149–166. London: Routledge.

Martin, J. R., and Robert Veel (eds.). 1998. *Reading science: critical and functional perspectives on discourses of science*. London: Routledge.

Martín, Pedro Martín. 2003. A genre analysis of English and Spanish research paper abstracts in experimental social sciences. *English for Specific Purposes* 22: 25–43.

Martín, Pedro Martín, and Sally Burgess. 2004. The rhetorical management of academic criticism in research article abstracts. *Text* 24 (2): 171–195.

Martinez, Iliana A. 2001. Impersonality in the research article as revealed by analysis of the transitivity structure. *English for Specific Purposes* 20: 227–247.

————. 2003. Aspects of theme in the method and discussion sections of biology journal articles in English. *Journal of English for Academic Purposes* 2: 103–123.

Master, Peter. 1991. Active verbs with inanimate subjects in scientific prose. *English for Specific Purposes* 10: 15–33.

Matthiessen, Christian M. I. M. 1993. Register in the round: diversity in a unified theory of register analysis. In Ghadessy (ed.) 1993a, 221–292.

Mauranen, Anna. 2003. "A good question." Expressing evaluation in academic speech. In *Domain-specific English: textual practices across communities and classrooms*, ed. by G. Cortese and P. Riley, 115–140. New York: Peter Lang.

———. 2004. "They're a little bit different": Variation in hedging in academic speech. In *Discourse patterns in spoken and written corpora*, ed. by K. Aijmer and A. B. Stenström, 173–197. Amsterdam: John Benjamins.

Mauranen, Anna, and Marina Bondi. 2003. Evaluative language use in academic discourse. *Journal of English for Academic Purposes* 2: 269–271.

McCabe, Anne. 2004. Mood and modality in Spanish and English textbooks: the construction of authority. *Text* 24 (1): 1–29.

McCarthy, Michael. 1998. *Spoken language and applied linguistics*. Cambridge: Cambridge University Press.

McCarthy, Michael, and Ronald Carter. 2004. There's millions of them: hyperbole in everyday conversation. *Journal of Pragmatics* 36: 149–184.

McEnery, Tony, and Nazareth Amselom Kifle. 2002. Epistemic modality in argumentative essays of second-language writers. In Flowerdew (ed.) 2002, 182–195.

McEnery Anthony, Richard Xiao, and Yukio Tono. 2006. *Corpus-based language studies*. London: Routledge.

McKenna, Bernard. 1997. How engineers write: an empirical study of engineering report writing. *Applied Linguistics* 18 (2): 189–211.

Melander, Björn. 1998. Culture or genre? Issues in the interpretation of cross-cultural differences in scientific articles. In Fortanet *et al.* (eds.) 1998, 211–226.

Mellinkoff, David. 1963. *The language of the law*. Boston: Little, Brown and Co.

Merritt, Marilyn. 1976. On questions following questions in service encounters. *Language in Society* 5: 315–357.

Milizia, Denise. 2006. Classifying phraseology in a spoken corpus of political discourse. *ESP across Cultures* 3: 41–65.

Montgomery, Martin. 1988. D-J talk. In *Styles of discourse*, ed. by N. Coupland, 85–104. London: Croom Helm.

Moore, Tim. 2002. Knowledge and agency: a study of "metaphenomenal discourse" in textbooks from three disciplines. *English for Specific Purposes* 21: 347–366.

Moreno, Ana I. 1997. Genre constraints across languages: causal metatext in Spanish and English RAs. *English for Specific Purposes* 16 (3): 161–179.

Morrow, Phillip R. 2006. Telling about problems and giving advice in an Internet discussion forum: some discourse features. *Discourse Studies* 8 (4): 531–548.

Mungra, Philippa. 2007. A research and discussion note: the macrostructure of consensus statements. *English for Specific Purposes* 26: 79–89.

Murray, Thomas. 1985. The language of singles bars. *American Speech* 60: 17–30.

Myers, Gregory. 1989. The pragmatics of politeness in scientific articles. *Applied Linguistics* 10: 1–35.

———. 1990. *Writing biology: texts in the social construction of scientific knowledge*. Madison: University of Wisconsin Press.

———. 1991. Lexical cohesion and specialized knowledge in science and popular science texts. *Discourse Processes* 14 (1): 1–26.

———. 1992. "In this paper we report . . .": Speech acts and scientific facts. *Journal of Pragmatics* 16: 295–313.

———. 1999. Functions of reported speech in group discussions. *Applied Linguistics* 20 (3): 376–401.

Nash, Walter (ed.). 1990. *The writing scholar: studies in academic discourse*. Newbury Park: Sage Publications.

Nelson, Mike. 2006. Semantic associations in Business English: a corpus-based analysis. *English for Specific Purposes* 25: 217–234.

Nesi, Hilary, and Helen Basturkmen. 2006. Lexical bundles and discourse signaling in academic lectures. *International Journal of Corpus Linguistics* 11: 283–304.

Nevala, Minna. 2004. Accessing politeness axes: forms of address and terms of reference in early English correspondence. *Journal of Pragmatics* 36 (12): 2125–2160.

Nevile, Maurice. 2006. Making sequentiality salient: and-prefacing in the talk of airline pilots. *Discourse Studies* 8 (2): 279–302.

Newman, Michael. 2005. Rap as literacy: a genre analysis of Hip-Hop ciphers. *Text* 25 (3): 399–436.

Nuckolls, Kandace. 2005. IM communicating: a conversational analysis of instant message conversations. Unpublished master's thesis. Portland, OR: Portland State University.

Nunan, David. 2008. Exploring genre and register in contemporary English. *English Today* 24 (2): 56–61.

Nwogu, Kevin Ngozi. 1991. Structure of science popularizations: a genre-analysis approach to the schema of popularized medical texts. *English for Specific Purposes* 10 (2): 111–123.

———. 1997. The medical research paper: structure and functions. *English for Specific Purposes*, 16 (2): 119–138.

Oakey, David. 2005. Academic vocabulary in academic discourse: the phraseological behaviour of EVALUATION in economics research articles. In Tognini-Bonelli and Camiciotti 2005, 169–184.

O'Barr, William M. 1982. *Linguistic evidence: language, power, and strategy in the courtroom*. New York: Academic Press.

Odell, Lee, and Dixie Goswami (eds.). 1985. *Writing in nonacademic settings*. New York: Guilford.

O'Donnell, Roy C. 1974. Syntactic differences between speech and writing. *American Speech* 49: 102–110.

Oh, Sun-Young. 2001. A focus-based study of English demonstrative reference: with special reference to the genre of written advertisements. *Journal of English Linguistics* 29: 124–148.

Okamura, Akiko, and Philip Shaw. 2000. Lexical phrases, culture, and subculture in transactional letter writing. *English for Specific Purposes* 19: 1–15.

Olson, D. 1977. From utterance to text: the bias of language in speech and writing. *Harvard Educational Review* 47 (3): 257–281.

Ozturk, Ismet. 2007. The textual organization of research article introductions in applied linguistics: variability in a single discipline. *English for Specific Purposes* 26: 25–38.

Paltridge, Brian. 1994. Genre analysis and the identification of textual boundaries. *Applied Linguistics* 15: 288–299.

_____. 1995. Working with genre: a pragmatic perspective. *Journal of Pragmatics* 24: 393–406.

_____. 1997. *Genres, frames and writing in research settings*. Amsterdam: John Benjamins.

_____. 2002. Thesis and dissertation writing: an examination of published advice and actual practice. *English for Specific Purposes* 21: 125–143.

Parodi, Giovanni (ed.). 2005. *Discurso especializado e instituciones formadoras*. Valparaíso: Universitarias de Valparaíso.

_____. (ed.). 2007. *Working with Spanish corpora*. London: Continuum.

Pettinari, Catherine Johnson. 1988. *Task, talk and text in the operating room: a study in medical discourse*. Norwood, NJ: Ablex.

Philips, Susan. 1984. The social organization of questions and answers in courtroom discourse: a study of changes of plea in an Arizona court. *Text* 4: 225–248.

_____. 1985. Strategies of clarification in judges' use of language: from the written to the spoken. *Discourse Processes* 8: 421–436.

Pisanski Peterlin, Agnes. 2005. Text-organising metatext in research articles: an English-Slovene contrastive analysis. *English for Specific Purposes* 24 (3): 307–319.

Placencia, Maria E. 2004. Rapport-building activities in corner shop interactions. *Journal of Sociolinguistics* 8 (2): 215–245.

Porcelli, Gianfranco. 1999. *The language of communication and information sciences: analysis and examples*. Milan: Sugarco.

Posteguillo, Santiago. 1998. The schematic structure of computer science research articles. *English for Specific Purposes* 18 (2): 139–160.

Precht, Kristen. 1998. A cross-cultural comparison of letters of recommendation. *English for Specific Purposes* 17 (3): 241–265.

Prince, Ellen F. 1978. A comparison of *Wh*-clefts and *It*-clefts in discourse. *Language* 54: 883–906.

Quaglio, Paulo. 2004. The language of NBC's Friends: a comparison with face-to-face conversation. Unpublished Ph.D. Dissertation, Northern Arizona University.

_____. 2009. *Television dialogue: the sitcom Friends vs. natural conversation*. Amsterdam: John Benjamins.

Quaglio, Paulo, and Douglas Biber. 2006. The grammar of conversation. In *The handbook of English linguistics*, ed. by B. Aarts and A. McMahon, 692–723. Oxford: Blackwell.

Raymond, Geoffrey. 2000. The voice of authority: the local accomplishment of authoritative discourse in live news broadcasts. *Discourse Studies* 2 (3): 354–379.

Reaser, Jeffrey. 2003. A quantitative approach to (sub) registers: the case of "sports announcer talk." *Discourse Studies* 5 (3): 303–321.

Recski, Leonardo. 2005. Interpersonal engagement in academic spoken discourse: a functional account of dissertation defenses. *English for Specific Purposes* 24: 5–23.

Reichman-Adar, Rachel. 1984. Technical discourse: the present progressive tense, the deictic "that," and pronominalization. *Discourse Processes* 7: 337–369.

Reppen. Randi. 1995. A genre-based approach to content writing instruction. *TESOL Journal* 4: 32–35.

_____. 2001. Register variation in student and adult speech and writing. In Conrad and Biber (eds.) 2001, 187–199.

_____. 2004. Academic language: an exploration of university classroom and textbook language. In Connor and Upton (eds.) 2004a, 65–86.

Reppen, Randi, and Camilla Vásquez. 2007. Using corpus linguistics to investigate the language of teacher training. In *Corpora and ICT in language studies*, ed. by J. Walinski, K. Kredens, and S. Gozdz-Roszkowski, 13–29. Frankfurt: Peter Lang.

Rey, Jennifer M. 2001. Historical shifts in the language of women and men: gender differences in dramatic dialogue. In Conrad and Biber (eds.) 2001a, 138–156.

Römer, Ute. 2005. "This seems counterintuitive, though . . .": negative evaluation in linguistic book reviews by male and female authors. In Tognini-Bonelli and Camiciotti 2005, 97–116.

Ruiying, Yang, and Desmond Allison. 2003. Research articles in applied linguistics: moving from results to conclusions. *English for Specific Purposes* 22: 365–385.

———. 2004. Research articles in applied linguistics: structures from a functional perspective. *English for Specific Purposes* 23: 264–279.

Rundbald, Gabriella. 2007. Impersonal, general, and social. The use of metonymy versus passive voice in medical discourse. *Written Communication* 24 (3): 250–277.

Salager, Françoise. 1983. The lexis of fundamental medical English: classificatory framework and rhetorical function (a statistical approach). *Reading in a Foreign Language* 1: 54–64.

Salager-Meyer, Françoise. 1990. Metaphors in medical English prose: a comparative study with French and Spanish. *English for Specific Purposes* 9 (2): 145–159.

———. 1992. A text-type and move analysis study of verb tense and modality distribution in medical English abstracts. *English for Specific Purposes* 11: 93–113.

———. 1994. Hedges and textual communicative function in medical English written discourse. *English for Specific Purposes* 13 (2): 149–170.

———. 1999. Referential behavior in scientific writing: a diachronic study (1810–1995). *English for Specific Purposes* 18 (3): 279–305.

Salager-Meyer, Françoise, Maria Angeles Alcalaz Ariza, and Nahirana Zambrano. 2003. The scimitar, the dagger and the glove: intercultural differences in the rhetoric of criticism in Spanish, French and English Medical Discourse (1930–1995). *English for Specific Purposes* 22: 223–247.

Salager-Meyer, Françoise, and Gérard Defives. 1998. From the gentleman's courtesy to the scientist's caution: a diachronic study of hedges in academic writing (1810–1995). In Fortanet *et al.* (eds.) 1998, 133–172.

Salager-Meyer, Françoise, and Nahirana Zambrano. 2001. The bittersweet rhetoric of controversiality in nineteenth- and twentieth-century French and English medical literature. *Journal of Historical Pragmatics* 2 (1): 141–174.

Samraj, Betty. 2002a. Introductions in research articles: variations across disciplines. *English for Specific Purposes* 21: 1–17.

———. 2002b. Disciplinary variation in abstracts: the case of wildlife behavior and conservation biology. In Flowerdew (ed.) 2002, 40–56.

———. 2005. An exploration of a genre set: research article abstracts and introductions in two disciplines. *English for Specific Purposes* 24: 141–156.

Samuels, Warren J. (ed.). 1990. *Economics as discourse: an analysis of the language of economics*. Boston, Dodrecht and London: Kluwer Academic Publishers.

Schiffrin, Deborah. 1985. Multiple constraints on discourse options: a quantitative analysis of causal sequences, *Discourse Processes* 8: 281–303.

Schmidt, Rosemarie, and Joseph F. Kess. 1985. Persuasive language in the television medium. *Journal of Pragmatics* 9: 287–308.

Semino, Elena, and Mick Short. 2004. *Corpus stylistics: speech, writing and thought presentation in a corpus of English writing*. London: Routledge.

Shalom, Celia. 1993. Established and evolving spoken research process genres: plenary lecture and poster session discussions at academic conferences. *English for Specific Purposes* 12: 37–50.

Shi, Ling, and Ryuko Kubota. 2007. Patterns of rhetorical organization in Canadian and American language arts textbooks: an exploratory study. *English for Specific Purposes* 26: 180–202.

Simpson, Paul. 2004. *Stylistics: a resource book for students*. London: Routledge.

Simpson, Rita. 2004. Stylistic features of spoken academic discourse: the role of formulaic expressions. In Connor and Upton (eds.) 2004a, 37–64.

Simpson, Rita, and Dushyanthi Mendis. 2003. A corpus-based study of idioms in academic speech. *TESOL Quarterly* 37: 419–441.

Skelton, John. 1997. The representation of truth in academic medical writing. *Applied Linguistics* 18 (2): 122–140.

Smith, E. L., Jr. 1985. Functional types of scientific prose. In *Systemic perspectives on discourse*, ed. by W. S. Greaves and J. D. Benson, 241–257. Norwood, NJ: Ablex.

Soler, Viviana. 2002. Analysing adjectives in scientific discourse: an exploratory study with educational applications for Spanish speakers at advanced university level. *English for Specific Purposes* 21: 145–165.

_____. 2007. Writing titles in science: an exploratory study. *English for Specific Purposes* 26: 90–102.

Stotesbury, Hikka. 2003. Evaluation in research article abstracts in the narrative and hard sciences. *Journal of English for Academic Purposes* 2: 327–241.

Studer, Patrick. 2003. Textual structures in eighteenth-century newspapers: a corpus-based study of headlines. *Journal of Historical Pragmatics* 4 (1): 19–44.

Swales, John. 1981. *Aspects of article introductions*. Birmingham, AL: University of Aston.

_____. 1990. *Genre analysis: English for academic and research settings*. Cambridge: Cambridge University Press.

_____. 2004. *Research genres: explorations and applications*. New York: Cambridge University Press.

Swales, John M. 2001. Metatalk in American academic talk: the cases of *point* and *thing*. *Journal of English Linguistics* 29: 34–54.

Swales, John M., Ummul K. Ahmad, Yu-Ying Chang, Daniel Chavez, Dacia F. Dressen, and Ruth Seymour. 1998. Consider this: the role of imperatives in scholarly writing. *Applied Linguistics* 19 (1): 97–121.

Taavitsainen, Irma. 2001. Middle English recipes: genre characteristics, text type features and underlying traditions of writing. *Journal of Historical Pragmatics* 2 (1): 85–113.

Taavitsainen, Irma, and Päivi Pahta. 2000. Conventions of professional writing: the medical case report in a historical perspective. *Journal of English Linguistics* 28 (1): 60–76.

_____ (eds.). 2004. *Medical and scientific writing in late Medieval English*. Cambridge: Cambridge University Press.

Tannen, Deborah. 1987. Repetition in conversation: toward a poetic of talk. *Language* 63: 574–605.

————. 1989. *Talking voices: repetition, dialogue, and imagery in conversational discourse*. Cambridge: Cambridge University Press.

————. 2005. *Conversational style: analyzing talk among friends*. Rev. edn. Oxford: Oxford University Press.

Tao, Hongyin. 2007. A corpus-based investigation of *absolutely* and related phenomena in spoken American English. *Journal of English Linguistics* 35 (1): 5–29.

Tapper, Joanna. 1994. Directives used in college laboratory oral discourse. *English for Specific Purposes* 13 (3): 205–222.

Tarone, Elaine, Sharon Dwyer, Susan Gillette, and Vincent Icke. 1981. On the use of the passive in two astrophysics journal papers. *ESP Journal* 1: 123–140.

————. 1998. On the use of the passive and active in astrophysics journal papers: with extensions to other languages and fields. *English for Specific Purposes* 17: 113–132.

Thetela, Puleng. 1997. Evaluated entities and parameters of value in academic research articles. *English for Specific Purposes* 16 (2): 101–118.

Thomas, Sarah, and Thomas P. Hawes. 1994. Reporting verbs in medical journal articles. *English for Specific Purposes* 13 (2): 129–148.

Thompson, Geoff. 1996. Voices in the text: discourse perspectives on language reports. *Applied Linguistics* 17 (4): 502–530.

————. 2001. Interaction in academic writing: learning to argue with the reader. *Applied Linguistics* 22 (1): 58–78.

Thompson, Paul. 2005a. Points of focus and position: intertextual reference in PhD theses. *Journal of English for Academic Purposes* 4: 307–323.

————. 2005b. Aspects of identification and position in intertextual reference in PhD theses. In Tognini-Bonelli and Camiciotti 2005, 31–50.

Thompson, Paul, and Alison Sealey. 2007. Through children's eyes? Corpus evidence of the features of children's literature. *International Journal of Corpus Linguistics* 12 (1): 1–23.

Thompson, Sandra A. 1985. Grammar and written discourse: initial vs. final purpose clauses in English. *Text* 5: 55–84.

Thompson, Susan. 1994. Frameworks and contexts: a genre-based approach to analyzing lecture introductions. *English for Specific Purposes* 13 (2): 171–186.

————. 2003. Text-structuring metadiscourse, intonation and the signalling of organisation in academic lectures. *Journal of English for Academic Purposes* 2: 5–20.

Thompson, S. A., and A. Mulac. 1991. The discourse conditions for the use of the complementizer *that* in conversational English. *Journal of Pragmatics* 15: 237–251.

Thornborrow, Joanna. 2001. Questions, control and the organization of talk in calls to a radio phone-in. *Discourse Studies* 3 (1): 119–143.

Thornborrow, Joanna, and Deborah Morris. 2004. Gossip as strategy: the management of talk about others on reality TV show 'Big Brother'. *Journal of Sociolinguistics* 8 (2): 246–271.

Thurlow, Crispin. 2003. Generation Txt? The sociolinguistics of young people's text-messaging. *Discourse Analysis Online* (1). Available at: http://extra.shu.ac.uk/daol/articles/v1/n1/a3/thurlow2002003.html.

Tognini-Bonelli, Elena, and Gabriella Del Lungo Camiciotti. 2005. *Strategies in academic discourse*. Amsterdam and Philadelphia: John Benjamins.

Tracy-Ventura, Nicole, Douglas Biber, and Viviana Cortes. 2007. Lexical bundles in Spanish speech and writing. In *Working with Spanish corpora*, ed. by G. Parodi, 217–231. London: Continuum.

Trudgill, Peter. 1974. *The social differentiation of English in Norwich.* Cambridge: Cambridge University Press.

Tucker, Paul. 2003. Evaluation in the art-historical research article. *Journal of English for Academic Purposes* 2: 291–312.

Upton, Thomas A. 2002. Understanding direct mail letters as a genre. *International Journal of Corpus Linguistics* 7 (1): 65–85.

Upton, Thomas A., and Ulla Connor. 2001. Using computerized corpus-analysis to investigate the textlinguistic discourse moves of a genre. *English for Specific Purposes* 20: 313–329.

Ure, Jean. 1982. Introduction: approaches to the study of register range. *International Journal of the Sociology of Language* 35: 5–23.

Van Dijk, Teun A. 1988. *News as discourse.* Hillsdale, NJ: Lawrence Erlbaum.

van Mulken, Margot, and Wouter van der Meer. 2005. Are you being served? A genre analysis of American and Dutch company replies to customer inquiries. *English for Specific Purposes* 24: 93–109.

Vande Kopple, William J. 1998. Relative clauses in spectroscopic articles in the Physical Review, beginnings and 1980. *Written Communication* 15 (2): 170–202.

Varghese, Susheela Abraham, and Sunita Anne Abraham. 2004. Book-length scholarly essays as a hybrid genre in science. *Written Communication* 21 (2): 201–231.

Ventola, Eija. 1983. Contrasting schematic structures in service encounters. *Applied Linguistics* 4: 423–448.

Ventola, Eija, and Anna Mauranen. 1996. *Academic writing: intercultural and textual issues.* Amsterdam: John Benjamins.

Ventola, Eija, Celia Shalom, and Susan Thompson (eds.). 2002. *The language of conferencing.* Frankfurt am Main: Peter Lang.

Vergaro, Carla. 2004. Discourse strategies of Italian and English sales promotion letters. *English for Specific Purposes* 23: 181–207.

———. 2005. "Dear Sirs, I hope you will find this information useful": discourse strategies in Italian and English "For Your Information" (FYI) letters. *Discourse Studies* 7 (1): 109–135.

Vilha, Minna. 1999. *Medical writing: modality in focus.* Amsterdam: Rodopi.

Ward, Gregory L. 1990. The discourse functions of VP preposing. *Language* 66: 742–763.

Wardhaugh, Ronald. 1992. *An introduction to sociolinguistics.* Oxford: Blackwell.

Webber, Pauline. 1994. The functions of questions in different medical journal genres. *English for Specific Purposes* 13 (3): 257–268.

———. 2005. Interactive features in medical conference monologue. *English for Specific Purposes* 24: 157–181.

Weiner, E. Judith, and William Labov. 1983. Constraints on the agentless passive. *Journal of Linguistics* 19: 29–58.

Weissberg, Bob. 1993. The graduate seminar: another research process genre. *English for Specific Purposes* 12: 23–35.

Wells, Rulon. 1960. Nominal and verbal style. In *Style in language*, ed. by T. A. Sebeok, 213–220. Cambridge, MA: MIT Press.

Williams, Ian A. 1996. A contextual study of lexical verbs in two types of medical research report: clinical and experimental. *English for Specific Purposes* 15 (3): 175–197.

———. 1999. Results sections of medical research articles: an analysis of rhetorical categories for pedagogical purposes. *English for Specific Purposes* 18: 347–366.

Yeung, Lorrita. 2007. In search of commonalities: some linguistic and rhetorical features of business reports as a genre. *English for Specific Purposes* 26: 156–179.

Young, Richard F., and Hahn Thi Nguyen. 2002. Modes of meaning in high school science. *Applied Linguistics* 23 (3): 348–372.

Yunxia, Zhu. 2000. Structural moves reflected in English and Chinese sales letters. *Discourse Studies* 2 (4): 473–496.

Zak, Helena, and Tony Dudley-Evans. 1986. Features of word omission and abbreviation in telexes. *ESP Journal* 5: 59–71.

Zhu, Wei. 2004. Writing in business courses: an analysis of assignments types, their characteristics, and required skills. *English for Specific Purposes* 23: 111–135.

Zhu, Yunxia. 2005. *Written communication across cultures*. Amsterdam and Philadelphia: John Benjamins.

Zwicky, Ann D., and Arnold M. Zwicky. 1980. America's national dish: the style of restaurant menus. *American Speech* 55: 83–92.

Index